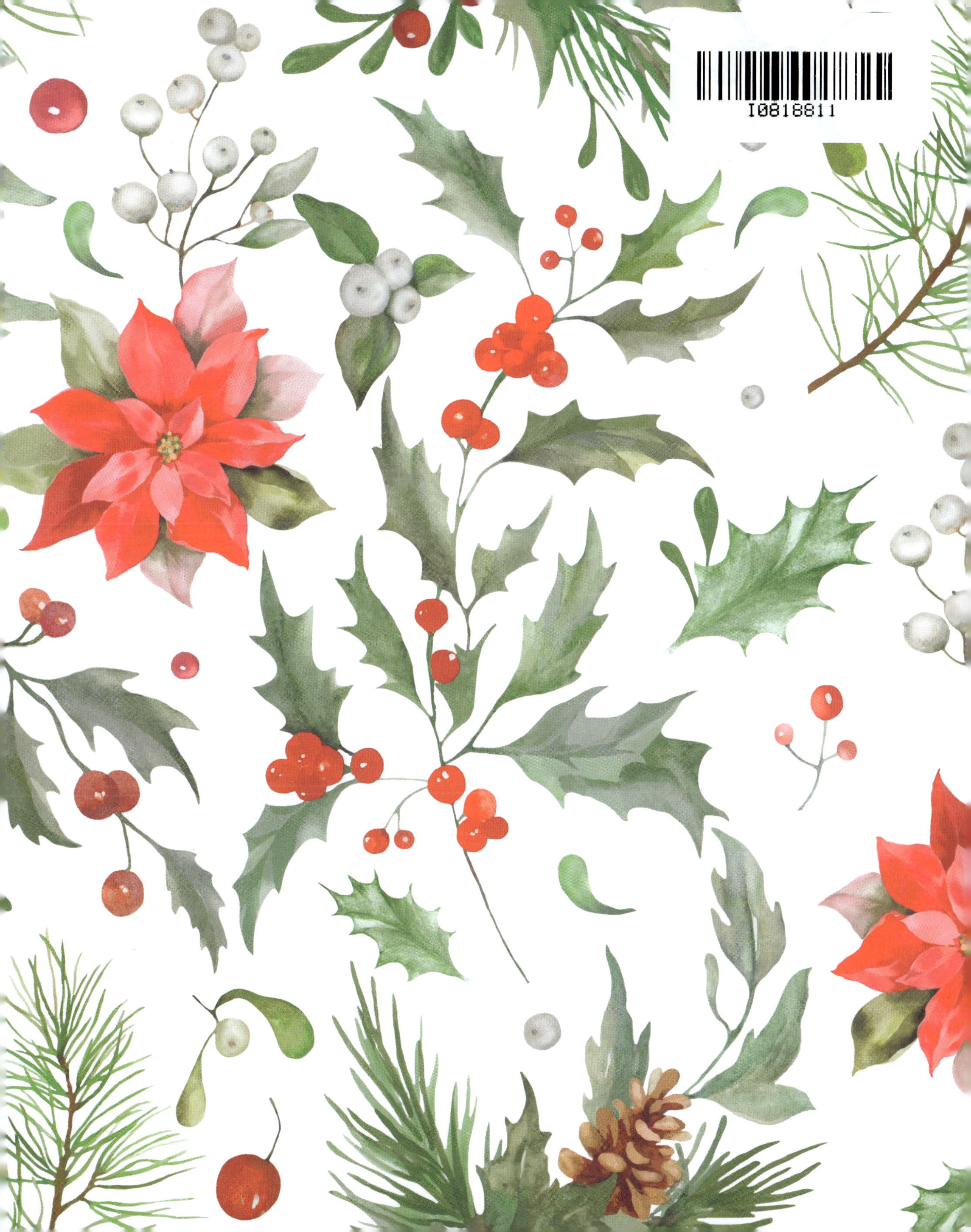
I0818811

HOME FOR CHRISTMAS

Around the World

teNeues

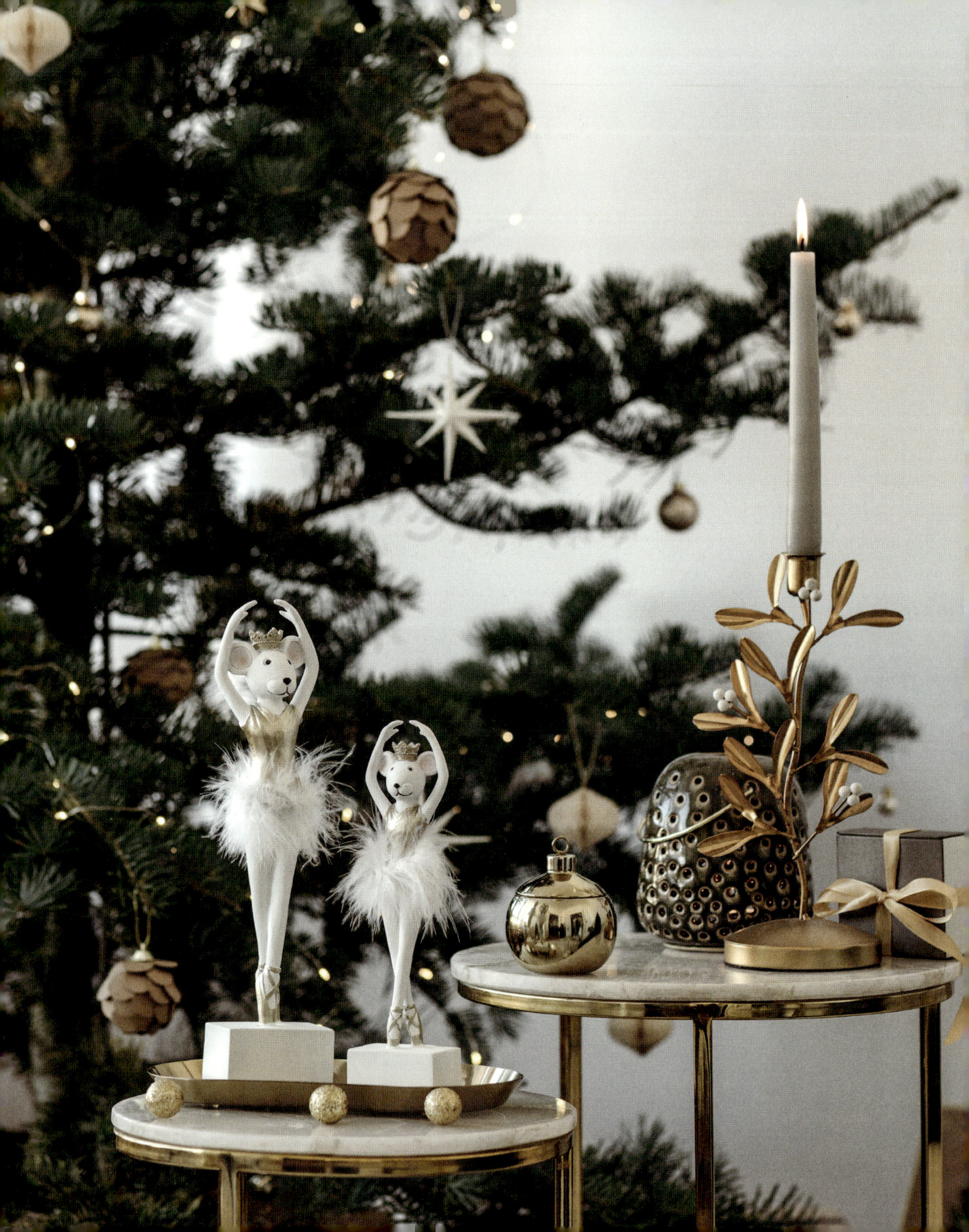

Contents

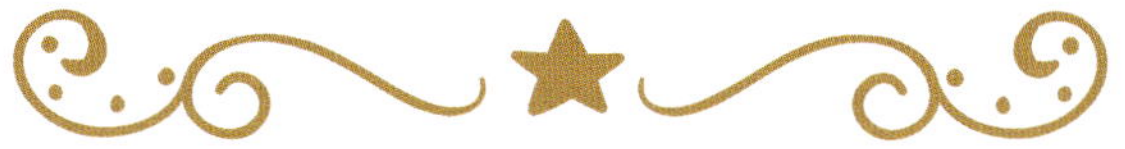

THE ENCHANTING WORLD OF CHRISTMAS TRADITIONS

As the festive season draws near, we are once again reminded of the warmth and joy that Christmas traditions bring to our lives. Celebrated across diverse cultures and regions, Christmas is a joyful festival characterized by generosity, love, and community spirit. But how do different countries around the world commemorate this special occasion? How do people adorn their homes, and what delightful treats grace their tables during the holiday season?

With the arrival of winter, the world transforms into a captivating wonderland. Sparkling fairy lights twinkle in the darkness like stars scattered across the night sky while the aroma of freshly baked cookies wafts through neighborhoods. Many homes are decorated with care and creativity. At the heart of countless celebrations is the Christmas tree, a vibrant centerpiece laden with decorations, garlands, and shimmering glass ornaments that tell stories of tradition and personal memories. Yet, not all Christmas trees follow the same narrative! In parts of the United States, the beloved custom of the "Christmas pickle" stands out. A glass pickle ornament is hidden within the branches, and the first to find it is rewarded with a special gift or a year of good luck—adding a playful twist to the festive spirit.

Another charming American tradition is the "Elf on the Shelf," inspired by a whimsical book authored by Carol Aebersold and her daughter Chanda Bell in 2005. This mischievous elf is said to watch over children during the Advent season, getting into humorous predicaments to ensure they're on their best behavior. It echoes the Scandinavian folklore surrounding the Christmas gnome—known as *tomte* in Swedish and *nisse* in Danish and Norwegian. This sprightly creature resides with a family during this time, aiming to assist them in various ways, even if sometimes his help leads to mischief!

In Norway, a delightful and somewhat quirky tradition unfolds on Christmas Eve as many Norwegians secure their brooms. This practice dates back to ancient beliefs that witches and dark spirits would roam on the night before Christmas. To thwart any nighttime mischief, brooms were hidden safely away. Though most modern Norwegians regard such tales with skepticism, this charming custom persists as a nostalgic nod to the past.

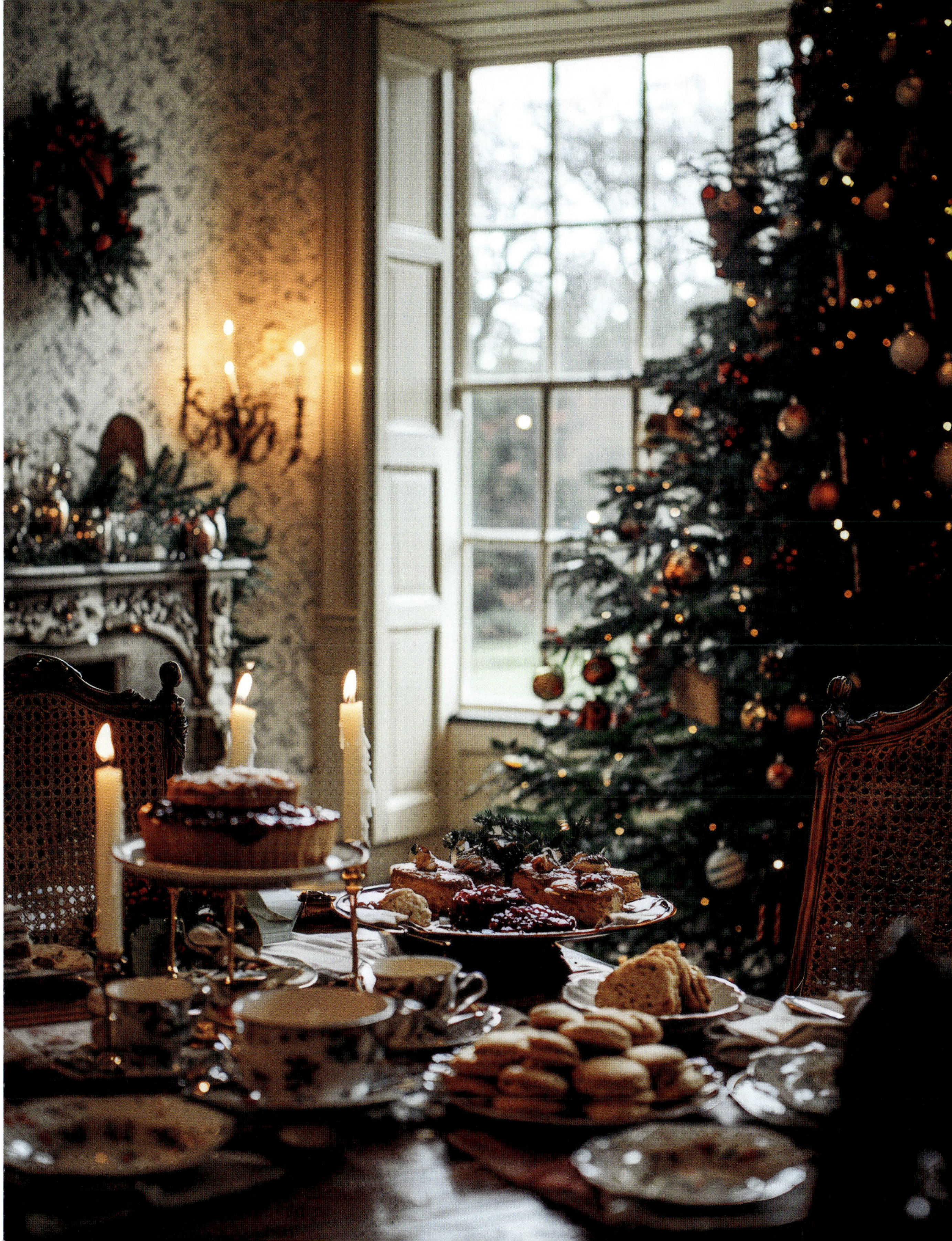

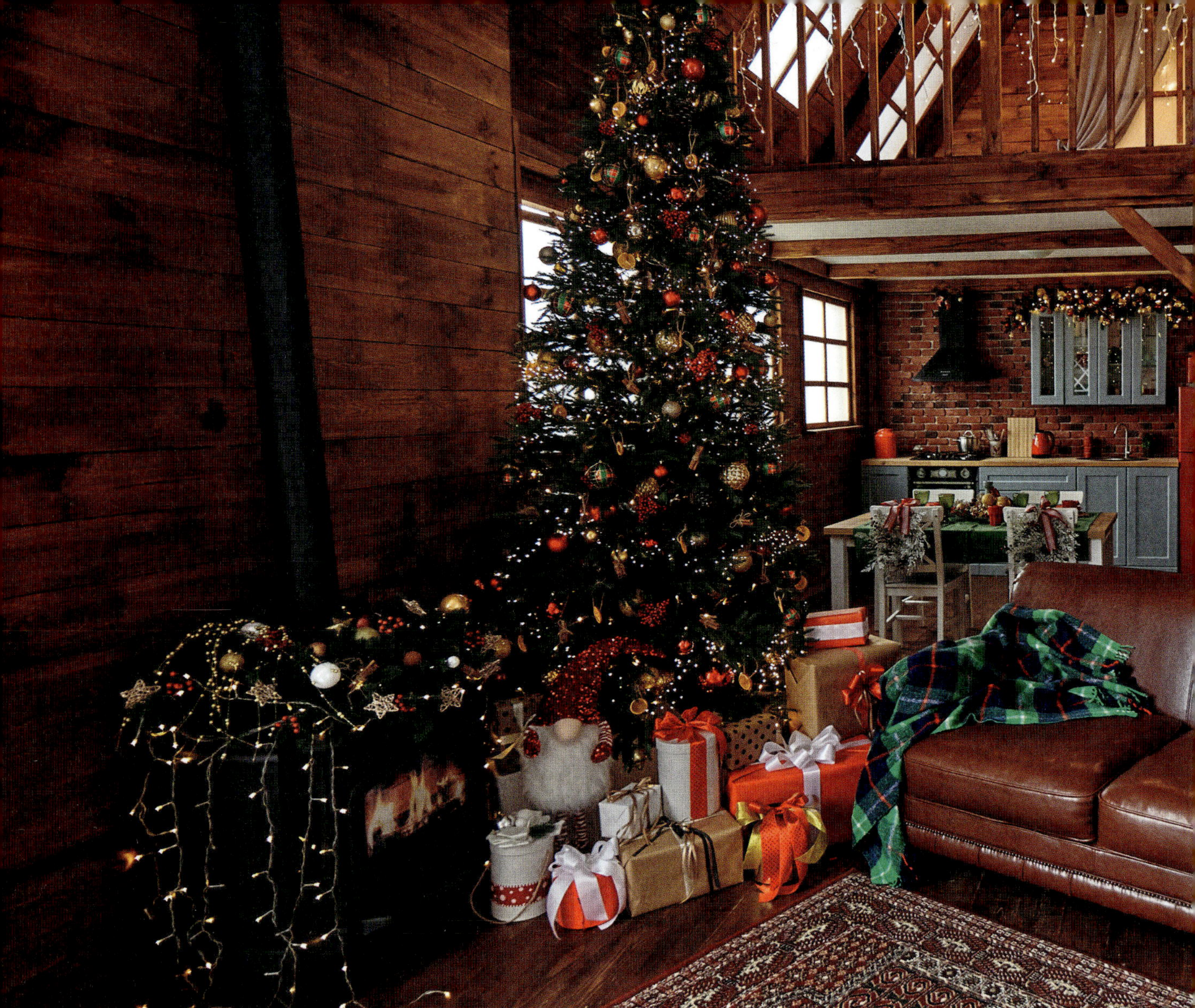

Icelandic Christmas celebrations are often colored by eerie yet fascinating folklore. The legendary *Jólakötturinn*, or Christmas cat, serves as a chilling reminder of the importance of new clothes. This enormous creature is said to prowl the night of Christmas, devouring children who do not have new garments to wear. While originally a cautionary tale encouraging children to complete their chores, it has transformed into an intriguing story shared to amplify the excitement of the holiday season.

The culinary traditions of the Nordic countries make the festive season even more enjoyable. In Sweden, the *julbord* comes alive—a lavish Christmas buffet boasting an array of traditional dishes like pickled herring, smoked salmon, and *köttbullar* (meatballs). Mistletoe plays a significant role in the celebrations here as well, symbolizing peace and connection. Anyone found beneath the mistletoe is expected to share a kiss, adding an extra layer of warmth and joy to the festivities!

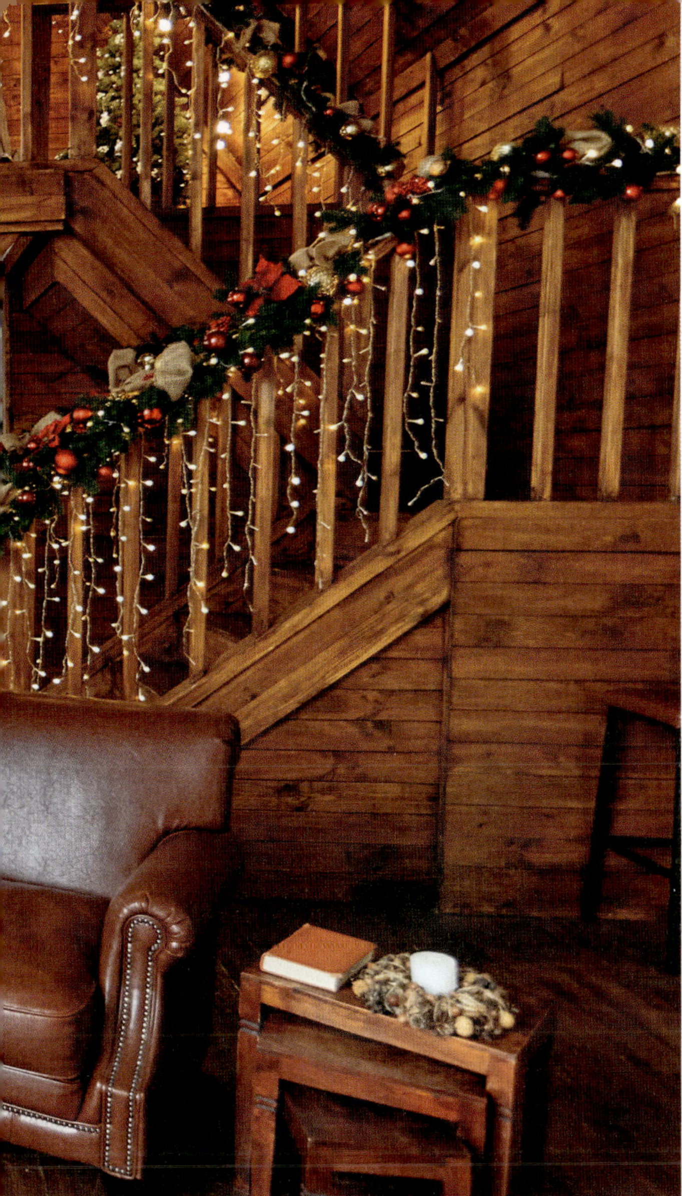

Speaking of festive delicacies, we can't overlook Italy's panettone, a beloved sweet bread filled with a medley of dried fruits and nuts. This airy treat is a staple at many holiday gatherings, often served as a sweet finale to Christmas dinner. With its delightful citrus flavors, panettone embodies the essence of family togetherness as loved ones gather around the table to enjoy it.

In Mexico, the Christmas season is enriched by the story of Las Posadas, symbolizing Mary and Joseph's journey in search of hospitality. This lively tradition sees people participate in processions from house to house, culminating in joyous celebrations filled with traditional dishes such as tamales and *ponche*—a warm spiced punch that brings comfort during the colder nights.

Conversely, in warmer regions like Australia and South America, Christmas traditions adapt to their sunny climates. Celebrating in the height of summer, Australians often embrace beach outings and barbecues called "barbies," replacing heavy roasts with fresh seafood and salads. Families may participate in delightful Christmas swims, splashing in the ocean on Christmas Day to cool off and enjoy summer's embrace.

These customs and tales reveal a rich tapestry of traditions that vary dramatically from one region to another, cherished and handed down through generations. They serve as a poignant reminder that this season's beauty lies in its diversity, with each custom holding its own unique charm. May this book inspire you to learn about new traditions and perhaps even spark the creation of your own delightful rituals to enhance your Christmas experience.

In the chapters that follow, we will embark on an itinerary across different continents, immersing ourselves in the enchanting aspects of Christmas celebrations worldwide. From the festive flavors that grace our tables to the unforgettable decorations that light up our lives, this book welcomes you to explore the multitude of Christmas traditions, hoping to inspire your own festive cheer within your home.

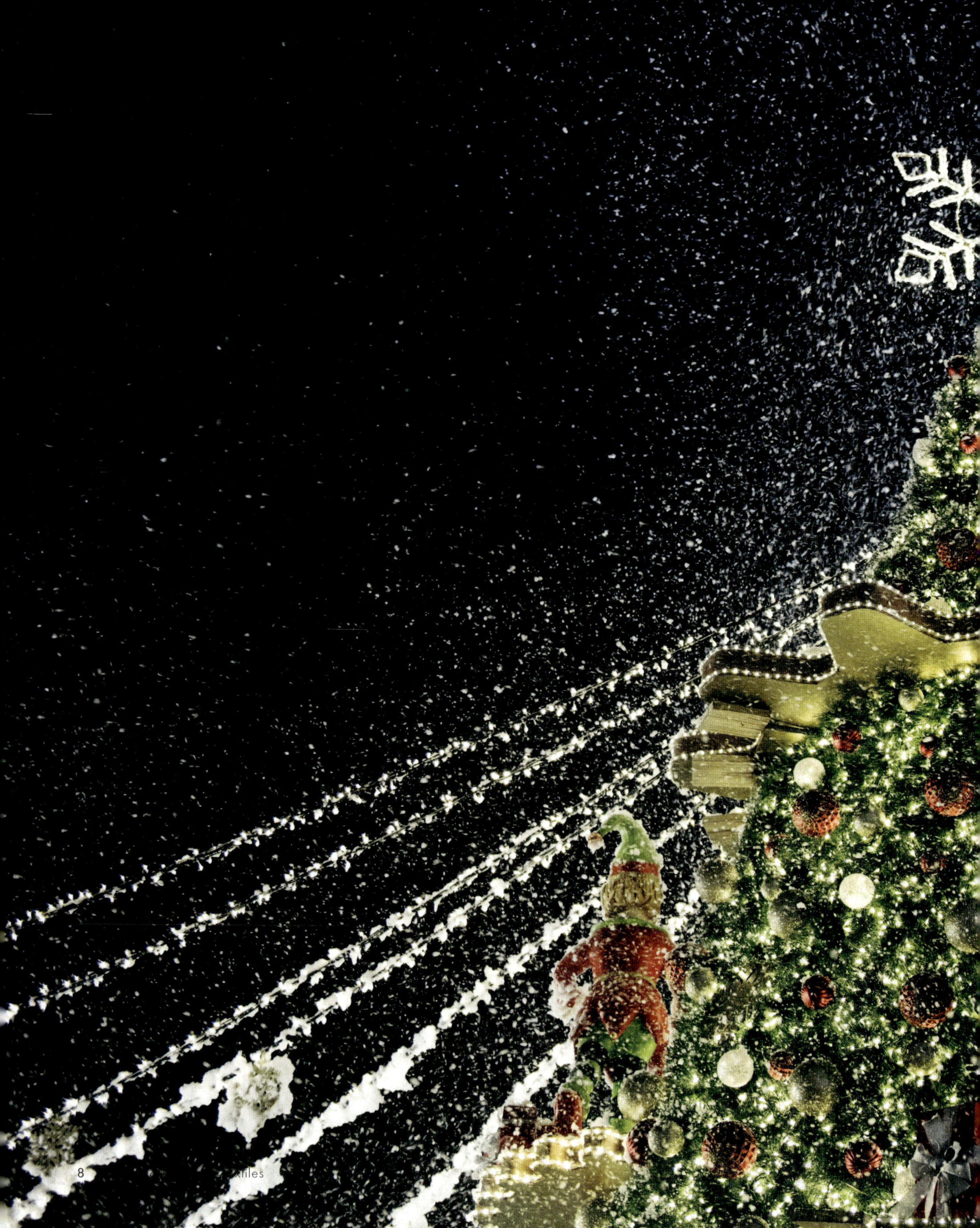

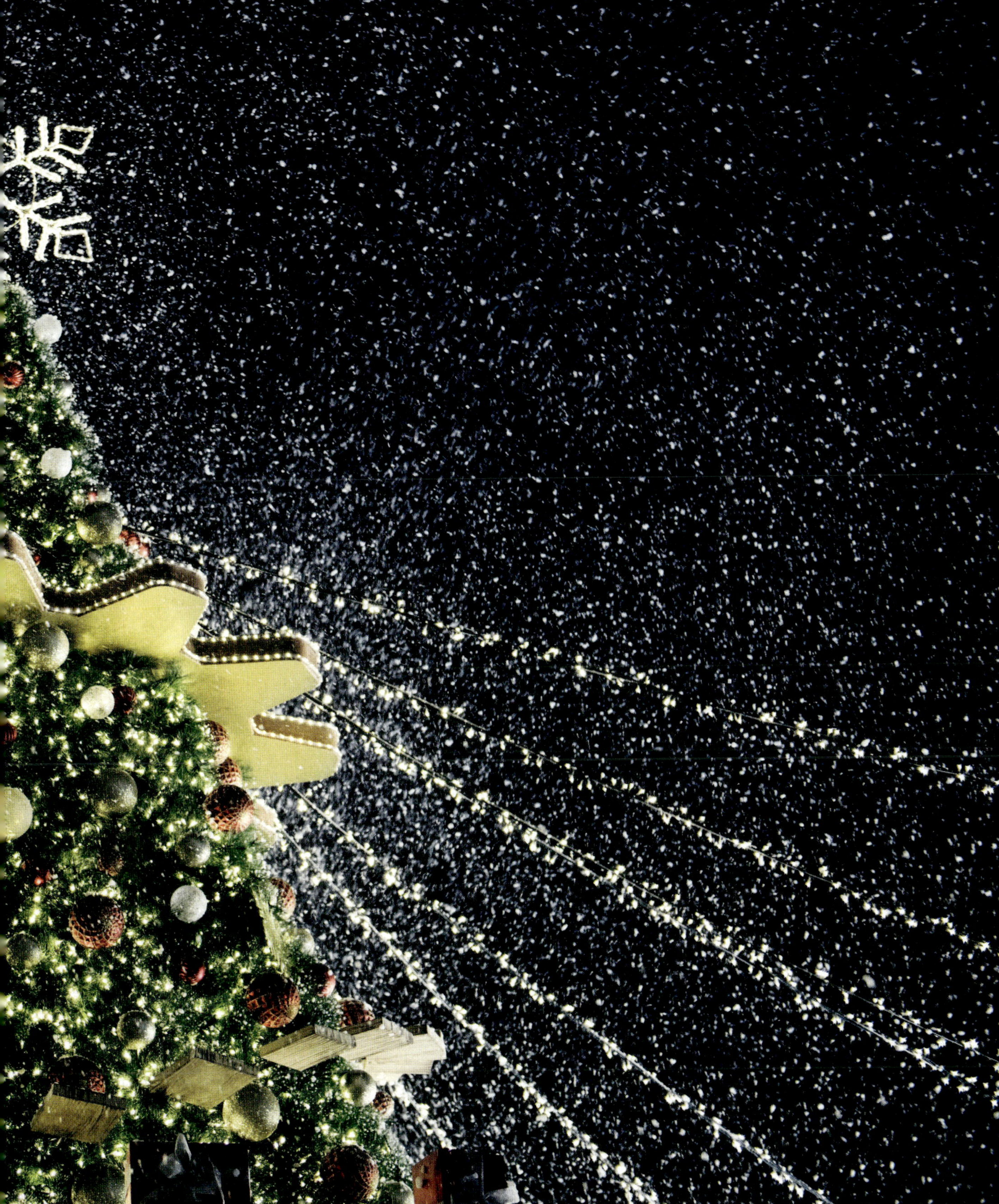

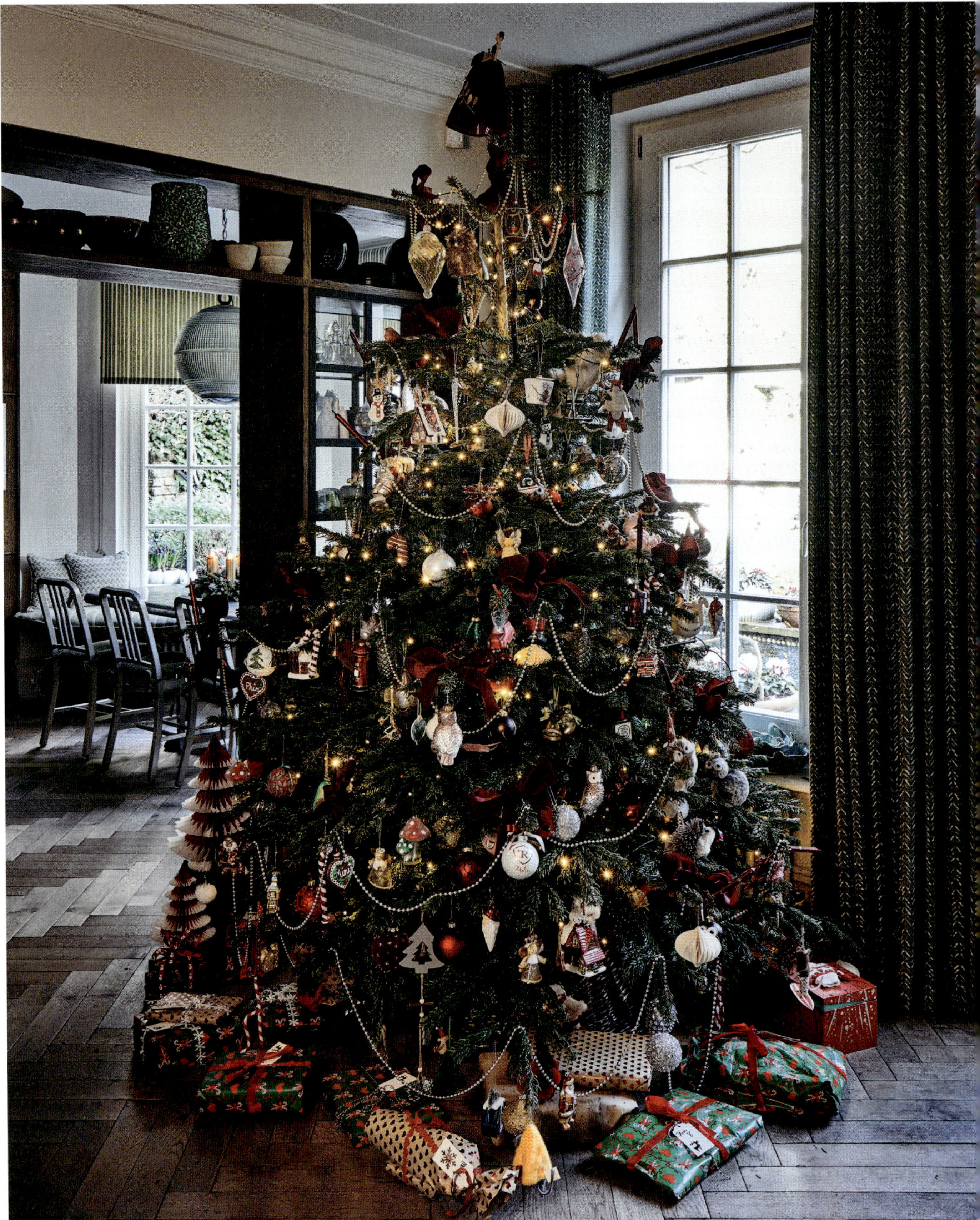

FEATURE
FESTIVE FLAIR IN LONDON

Opposite page: A bright red wreath adorns the front door of the home that Deborah Brett shares with her husband and three children in London.

Combining Traditions Perfectly

Deborah Brett, Fashion Editor-at-Large for Wardrobe Icons and a founding member of the British Fashion Council's Fashion Trust, is a multifaceted London-based creative. Her talents span fashion, ceramics, and baking, garnering her a significant following on Instagram. Additionally, her intuition for homemaking infuses her London and Ibiza homes with inspiration. As a wife to film director Tom Edmunds and mother of three, Deborah cherishes family time and strives to recreate the traditions of her childhood Christmases in Germany.

She merges these German customs with her Jewish upbringing in London and Tom's British family rituals and creates an atmosphere that is rich in sights and scents. "Tom and I feel fortunate to have positive childhood memories of Christmas," Deborah shares. "We decided early on to blend our family traditions." Until a few years ago, this meant flying to Remscheid, Germany—Deborah's mother's hometown—ten days before Christmas. After her mother's passing, Deborah would travel with the children while Tom joined them later. They would enjoy her family's traditional Christmas Eve dinner before embarking on a nighttime journey to catch the Eurostar to Kent, allowing their kids to wake up with Tom's family on Christmas morning. Now, with Deborah's grandmother having passed, they celebrate Christmas dinner earlier in Germany and return to the UK in time for the holiday.

Deborah reflects on her childhood experiences of celebrating an extravagant German Christmas, filled with roasted goose, knödel, and red cabbage, alongside Hanukkah in London with latkes. "In Germany, the Christmas tree went up on the 23rd, adorned by adults while we slept, revealed in all its glory on Christmas Eve." When they began their life together, Deborah and Tom bought a large tree and cherished glass ornaments, decorating it with their children at the beginning of December. "It's wonderful to have that Christmas spirit in our home for a month, especially against the cold, gray backdrop outside."

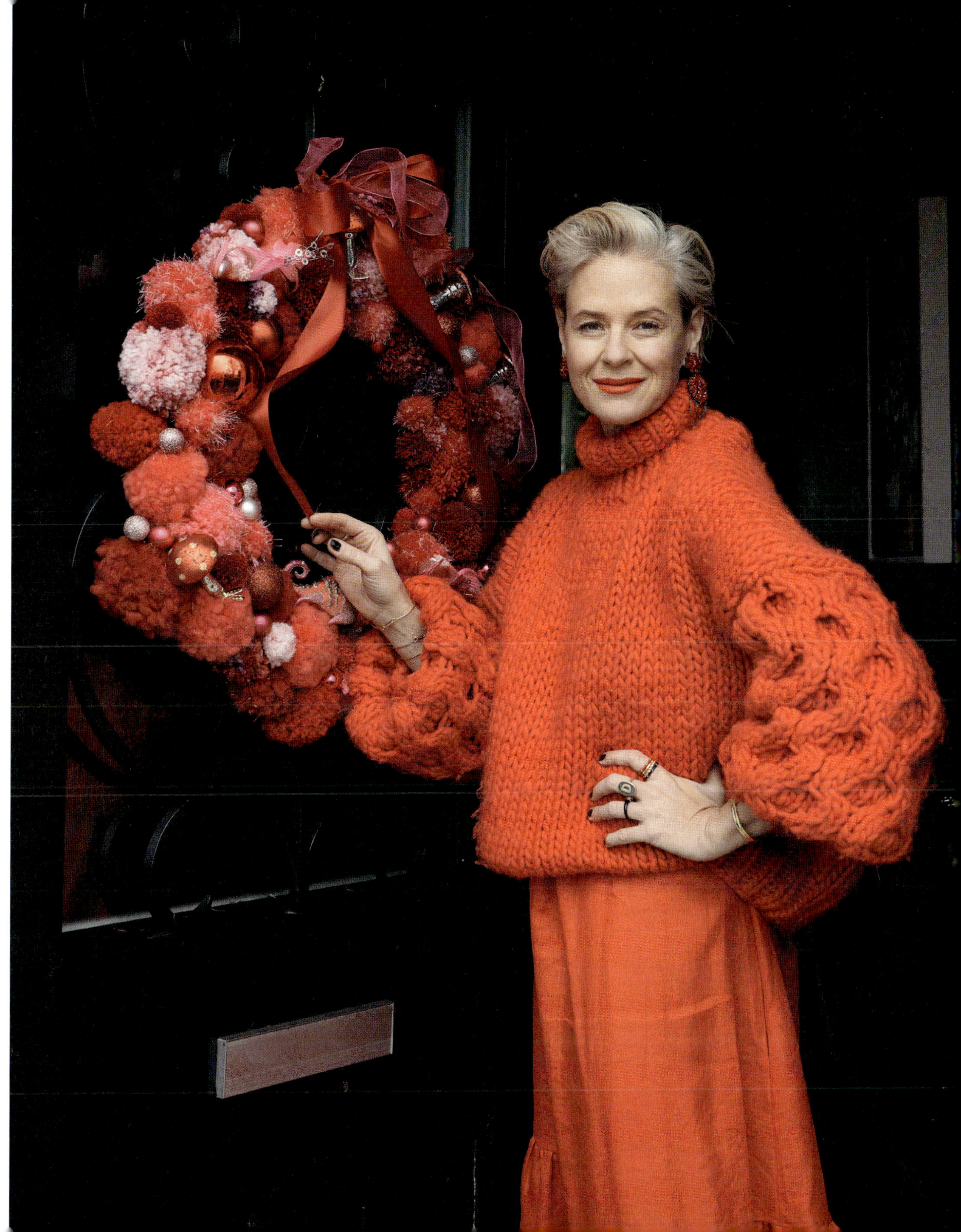

With Deborah's predilection for beauty, everything from the tables to the mantelpiece have some kind of festive trim or flash of color to tempt the eye. Not to mention her incredible Christmas tree that almost touches the ceiling of their living room. "In this world of ours and at this time, we have to amplify the magic wherever we can," she says with a smile. "It's a lot of hard work, but I wouldn't have it any other way."

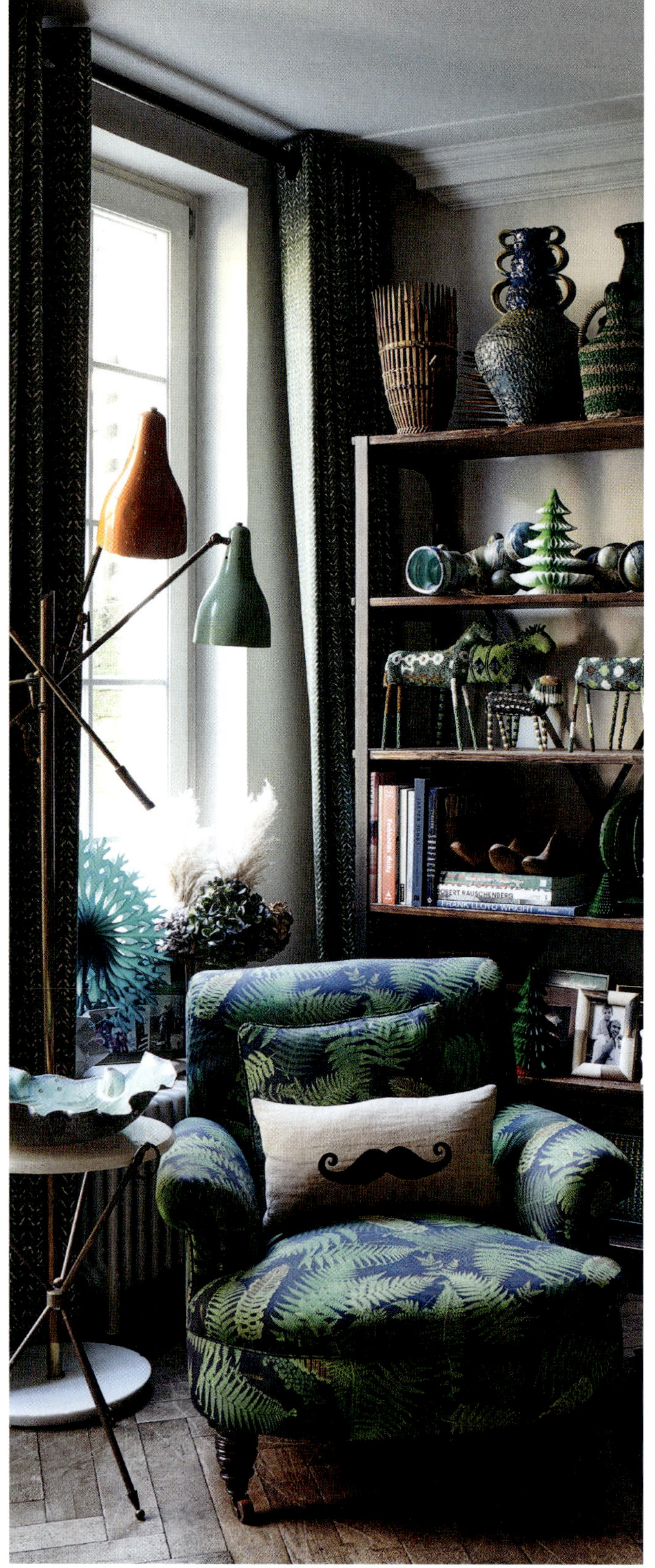

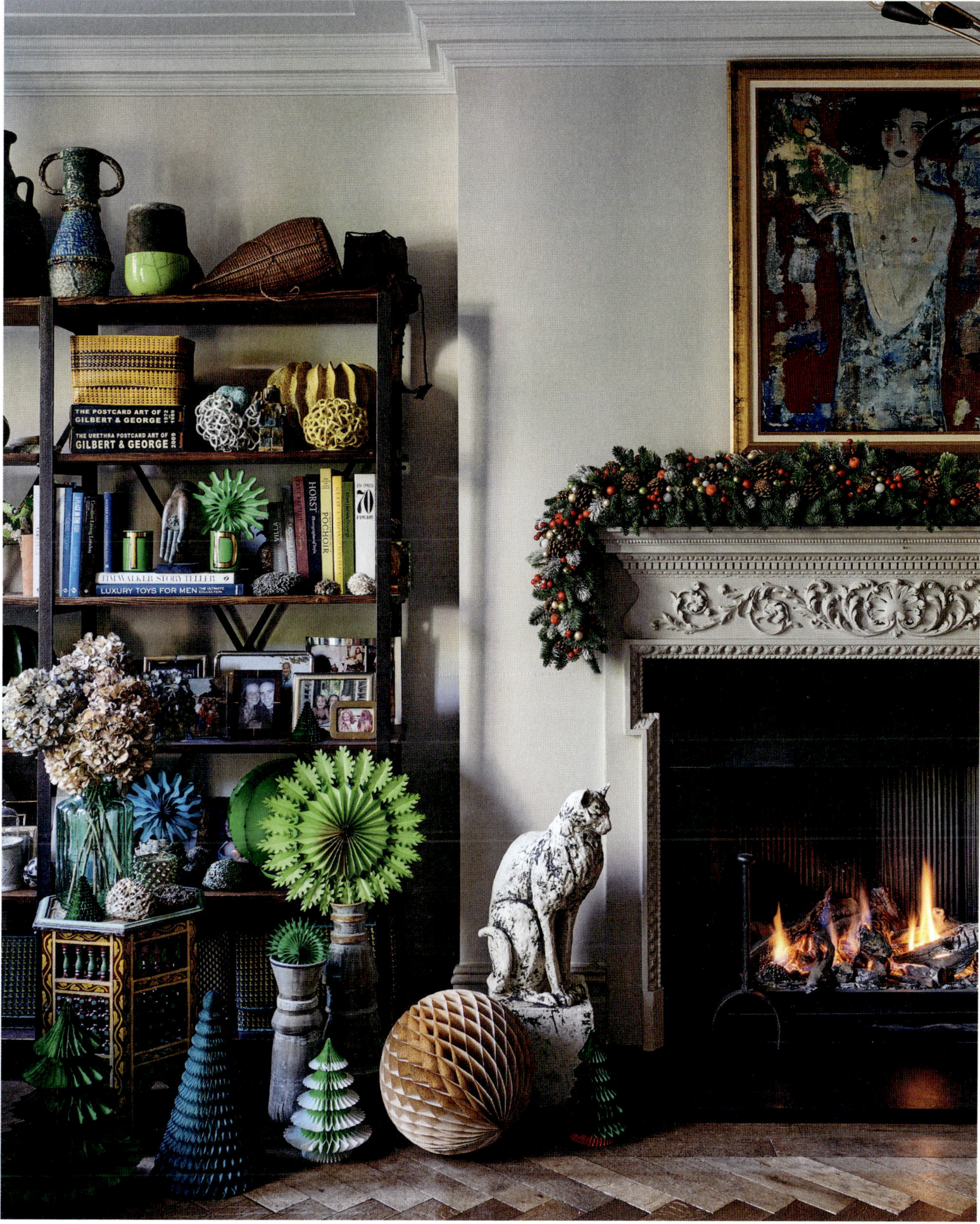
THE POSTCARD ART OF GILBERT & GEORGE
THE URETHRA POSTCARD ART OF GILBERT & GEORGE
HORST
POCHOIR
TIM WALKER STORY TELLER
LUXURY TOYS FOR MEN

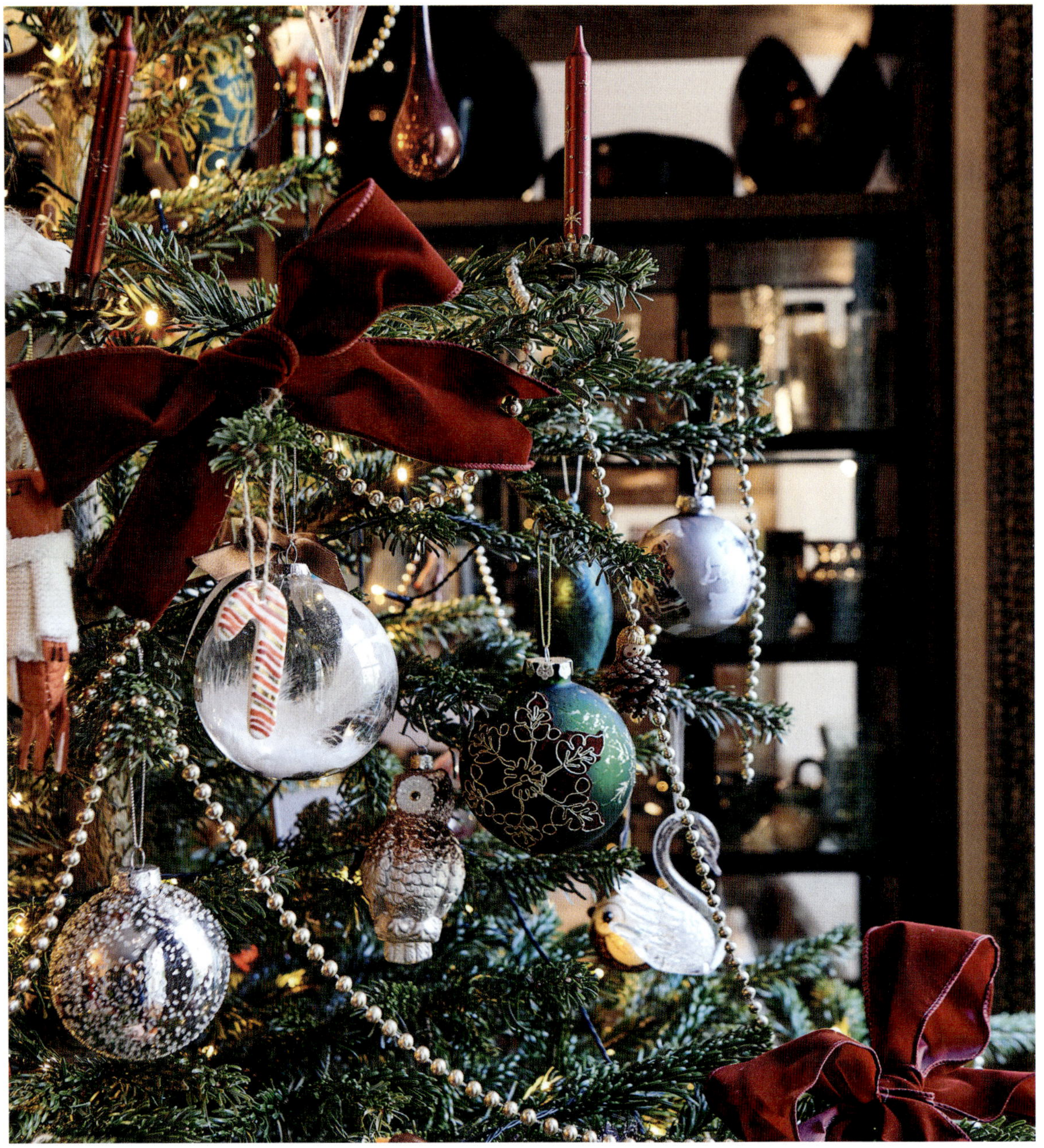

The Christmas tree features beloved glass ornaments collected through the years. Even the staircase gets the festive treatment with floral arrangements and presents lining the stairs. "I can't help myself," laughs Deborah. "And it certainly stops the children in their tracks."

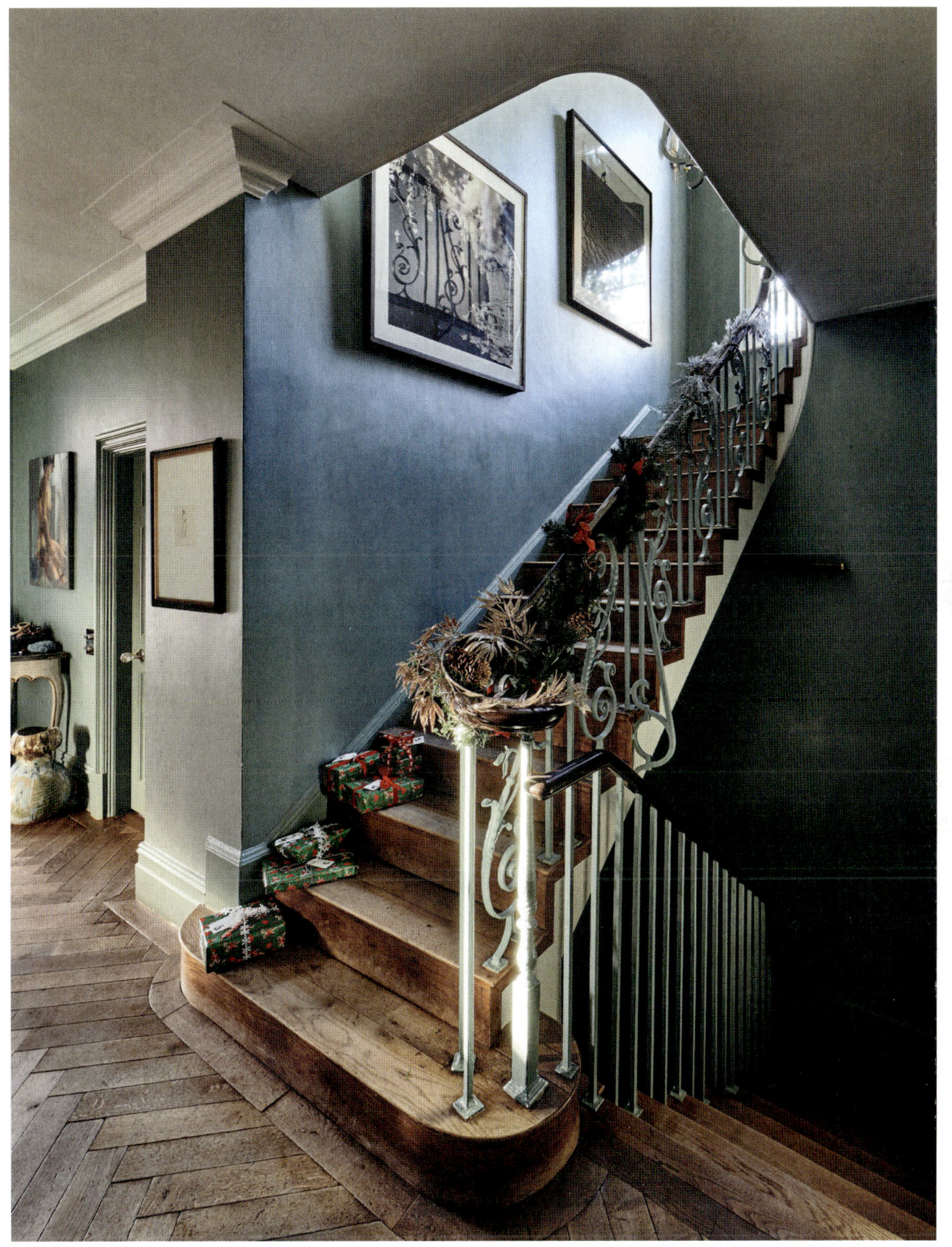

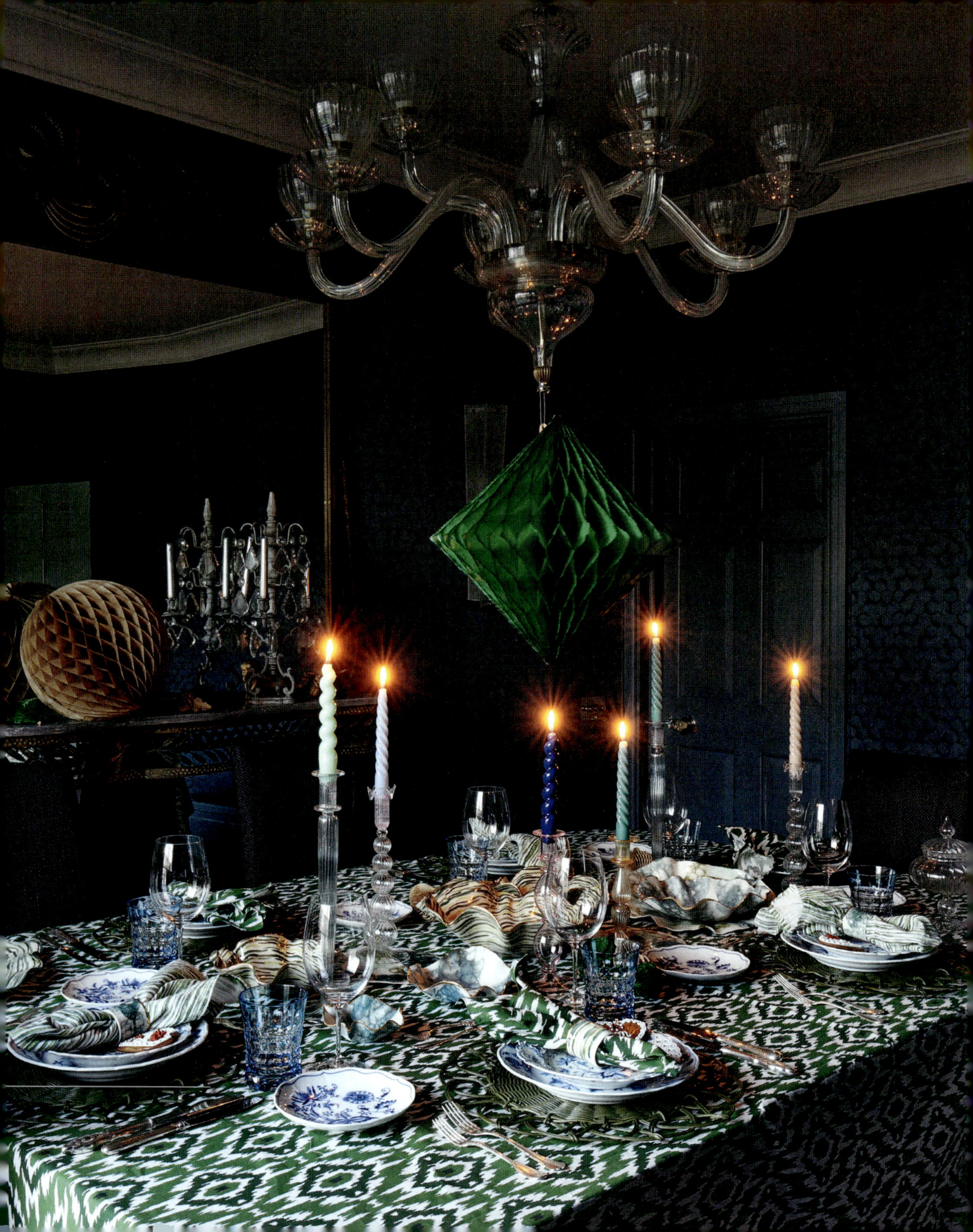

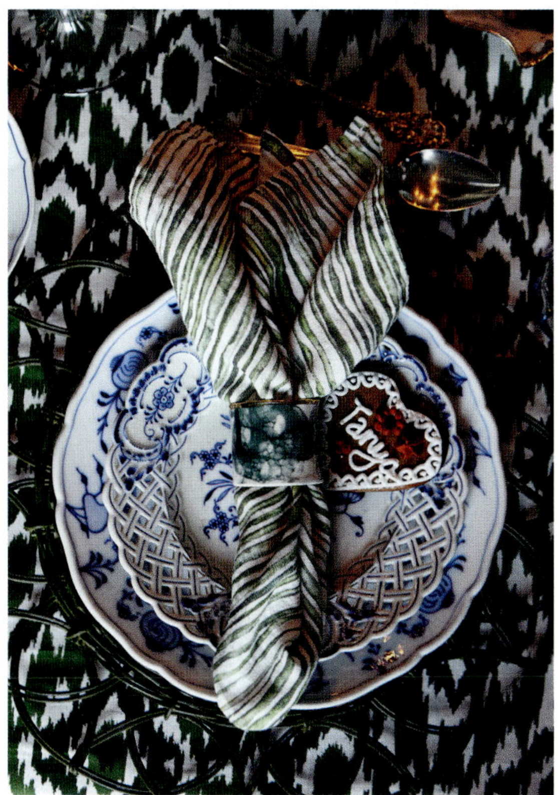

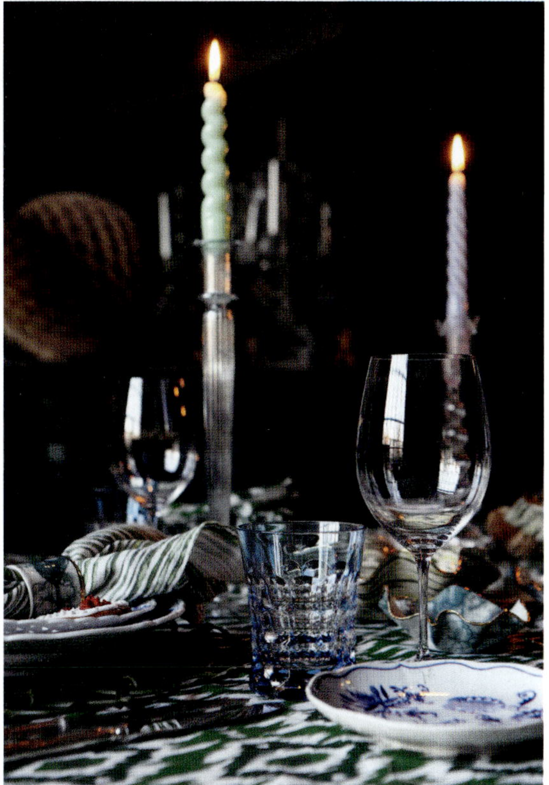

DEBORAH ON TRADITIONS, TABLE-SETTING, AND GINGERBREAD HOUSES

The family's festive celebrations now feature a pre-Christmas Eve dinner in Germany, Christmas Day lunch with Tom's family—complete with turkey and all the trimmings—and eight nights of Hanukkah in London. "Tom and I had to make a decision on just how to incorporate all these traditions for our kids, as it was beginning to feel like a lesson in instant gratification with sweets and gifts 24/7," Deborah explains. While they give gifts during Hanukkah, the children receive Christmas presents from their grandparents and (of course) Santa.

One cherished German tradition Deborah has integrated is the creation of the *Knusperhaus* (gingerbread house), which they begin in early December and only eat on Christmas Eve. This tradition evolved a few years ago when local shops in Germany sold out, forcing Deborah to make her own. "We all find joy in planning the design, baking the gingerbread, and selecting the sweets," she says, noting that this detailed activity requires patience. "I realized early on that if I wanted to include my children in the baking and retain my sanity, I'd need to spread the making of this over a couple of days," laughs Deborah.

As for Hanukkah, Deborah delights in setting beautiful tables for every meal throughout the eight-day holiday. "I love a beautifully laid table, especially now, when I try to make it extra special," she shares. According to Deborah, table settings should be fun, reflecting your unique style while incorporating basic elements.

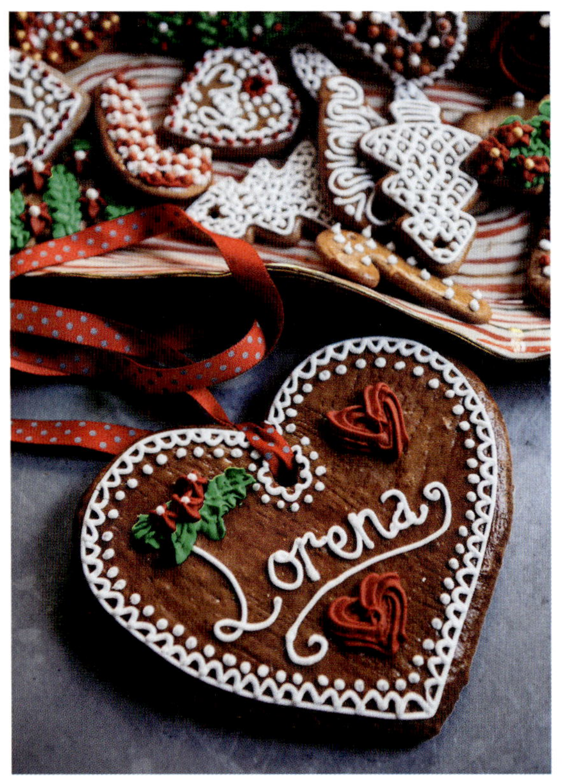

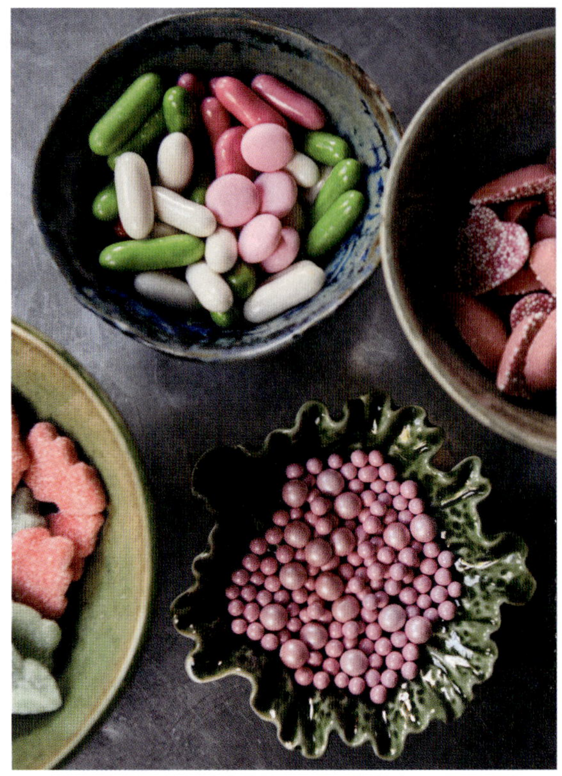

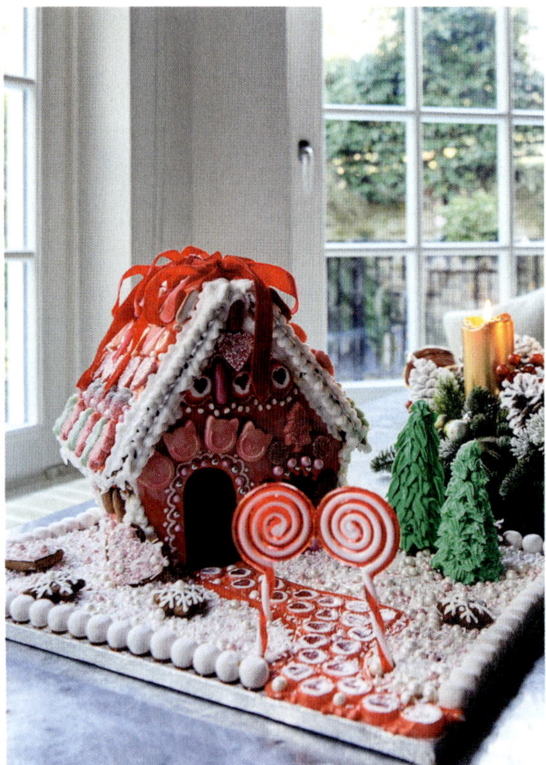

BAKING WITH DEBORAH

"I pre-measure all the ingredients, especially if I'm doubling up on recipes." Deborah also suggests decorating the *Knusperhaus* flat, that is, before you connect the walls and roof together, as then you won't have the problem of candy sliding off a vertical surface. It's an epic undertaking but one that never fails to disappoint, with stained glass windows, elaborate gardens, and even a forest worthy of Hansel and Gretel. Another tradition that Deborah does every year is to make lebkuchen cookies that she gives to the children's teachers as a gift and that they use to decorate the tree.

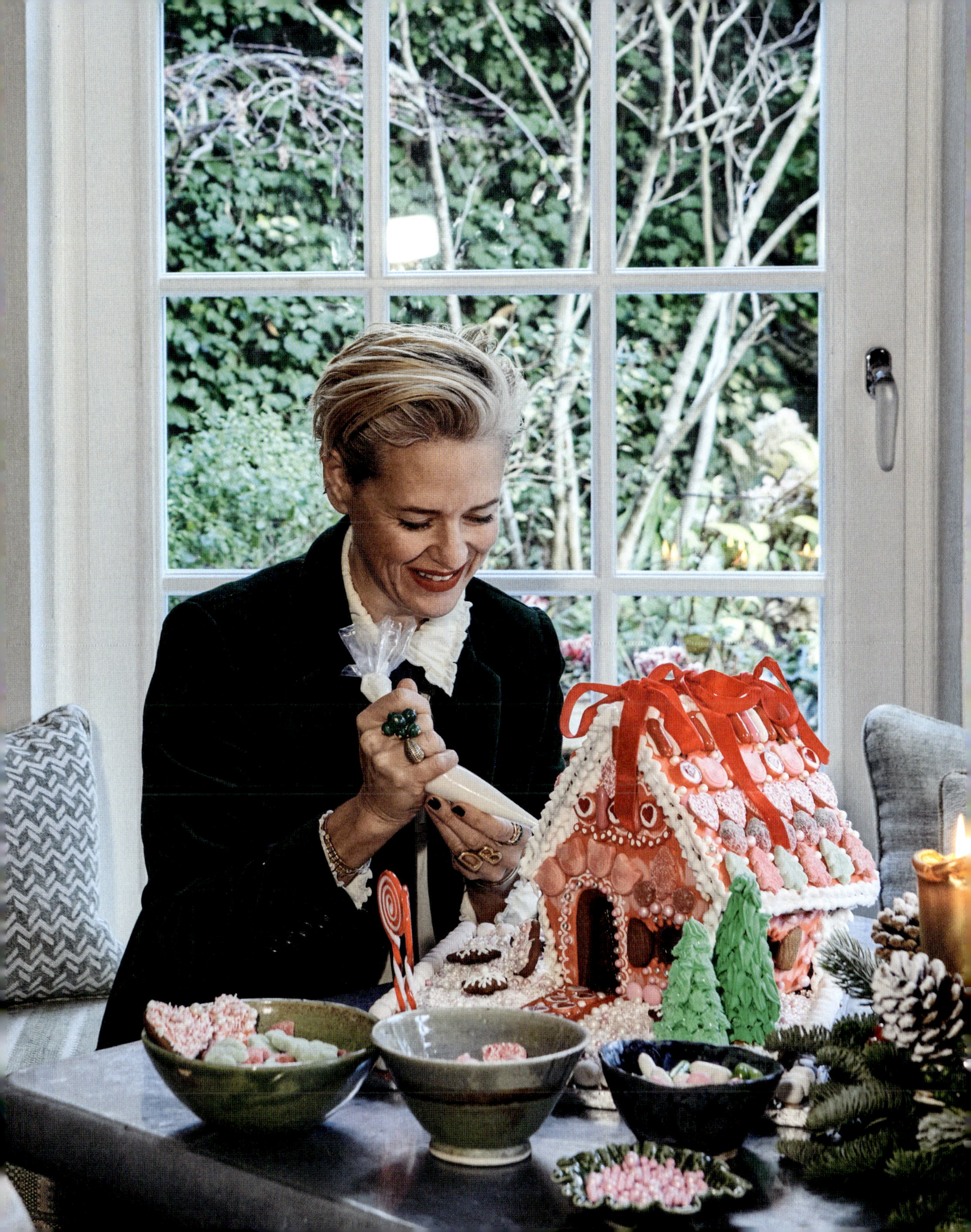

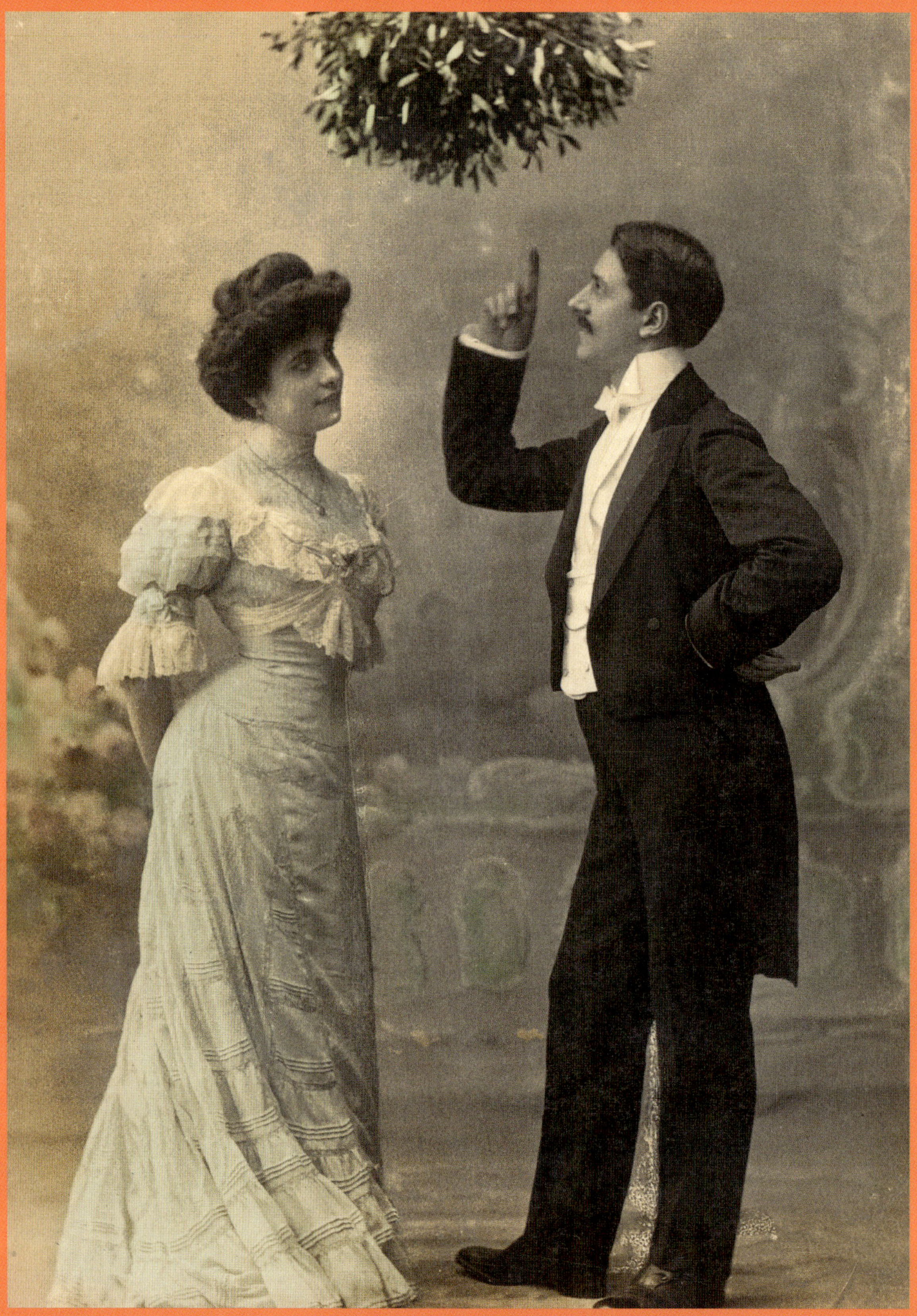

Traditions

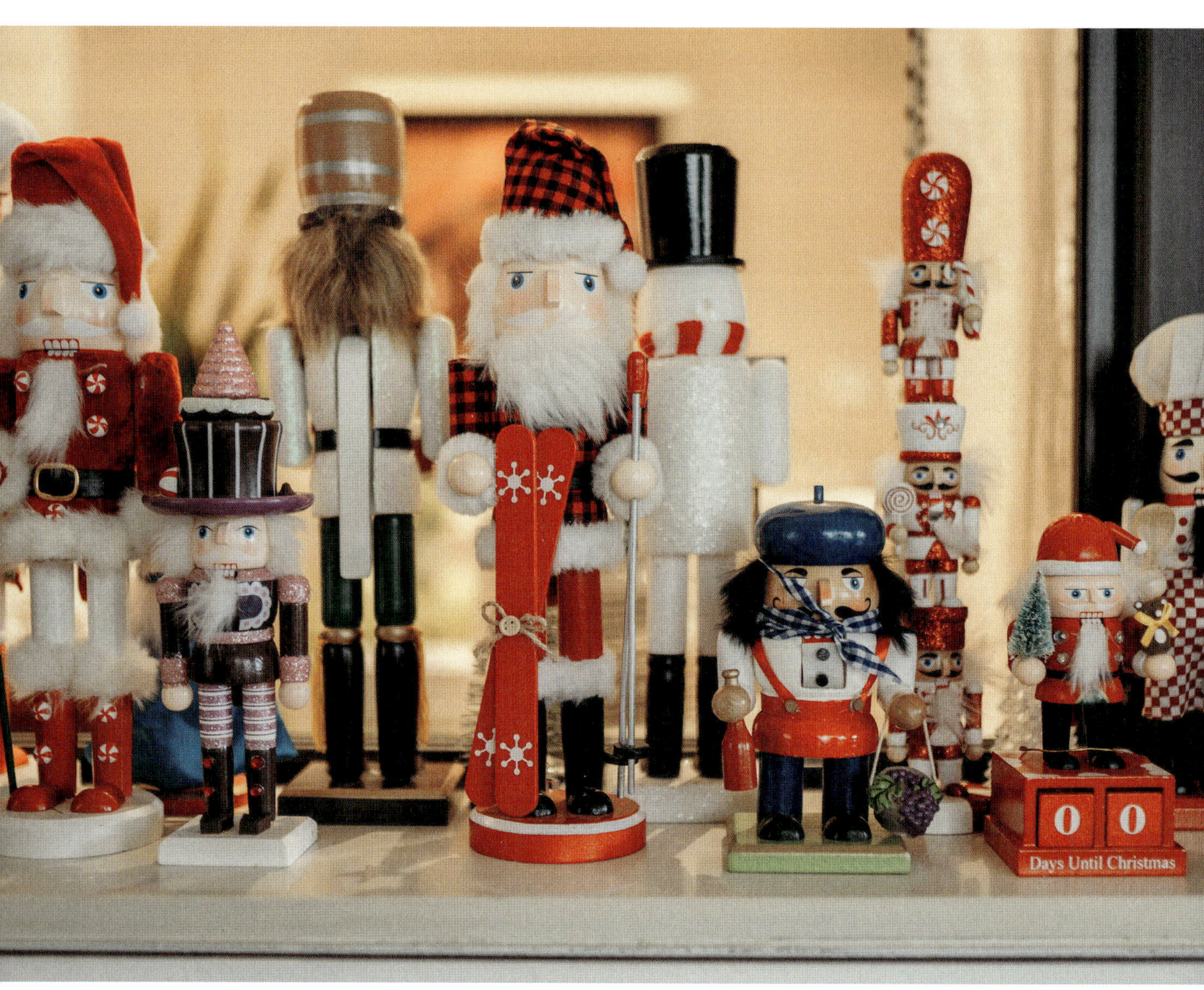

Traditional craftsmanship from the Ore Mountains. The nutcracker, a beloved Christmas decorative item, can be found on shelves worldwide in various designs and colors. Some even grace beach promenades in places like Florida as larger-than-life figures.

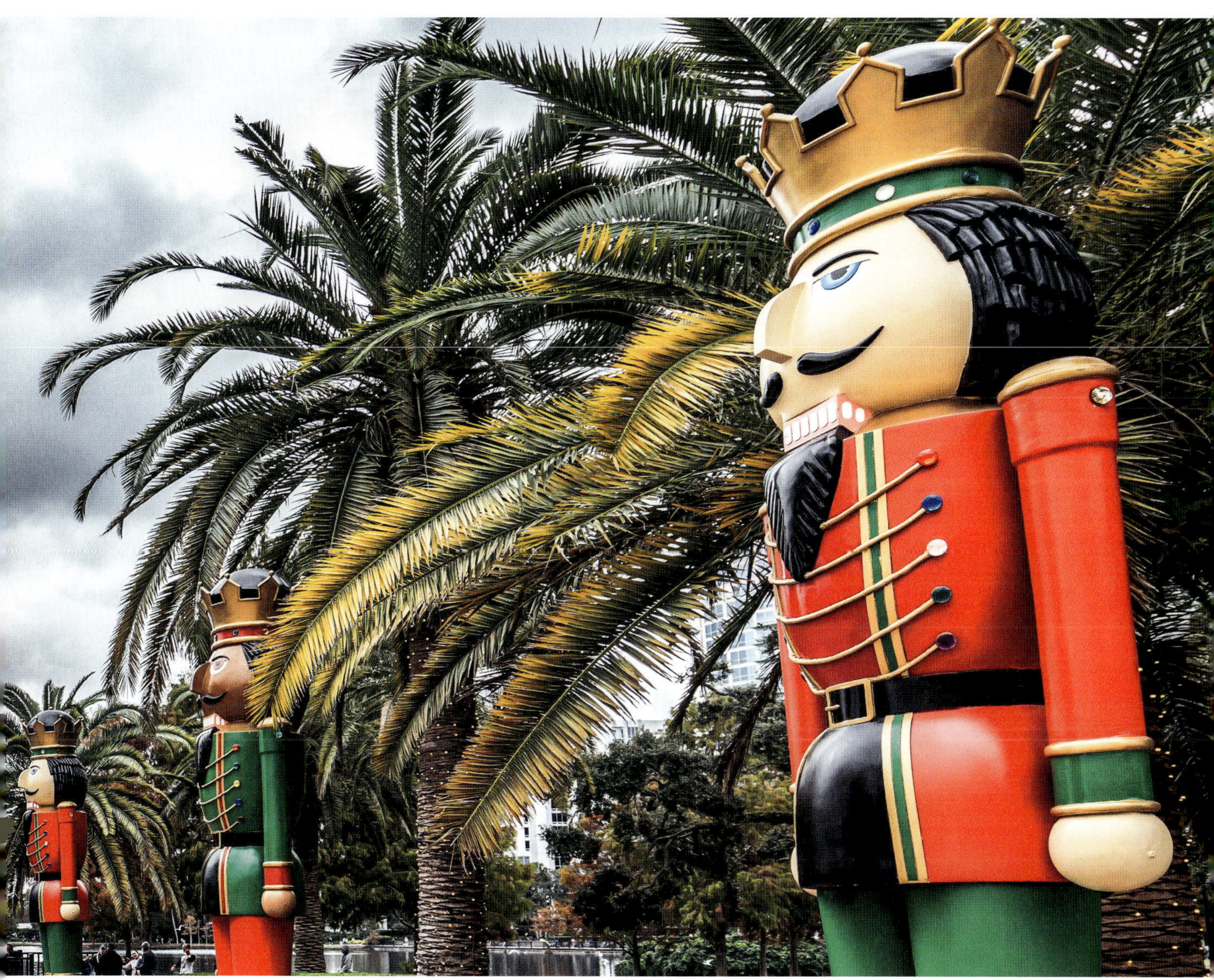

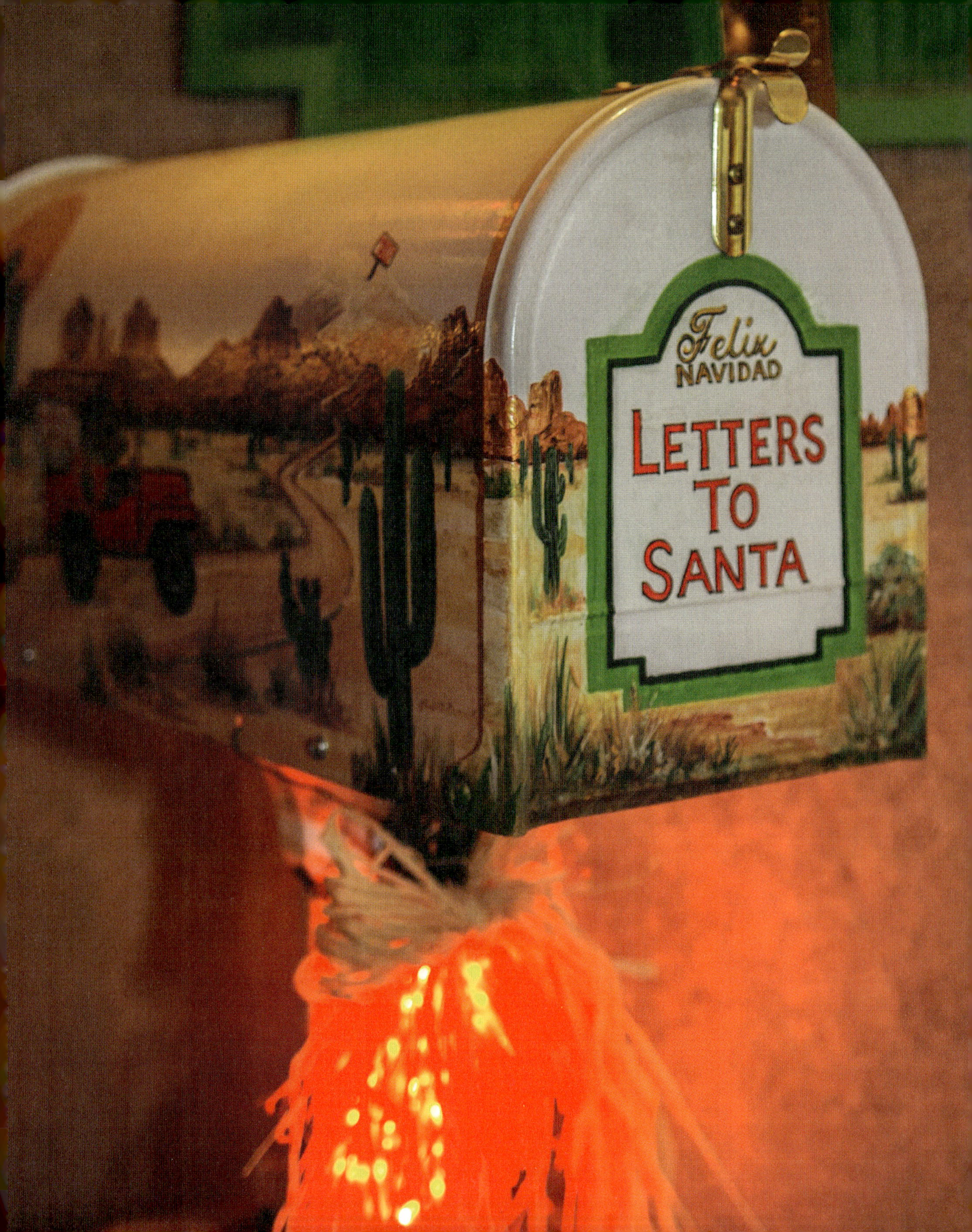
Felix
NAVIDAD
LETTERS
TO
SANTA

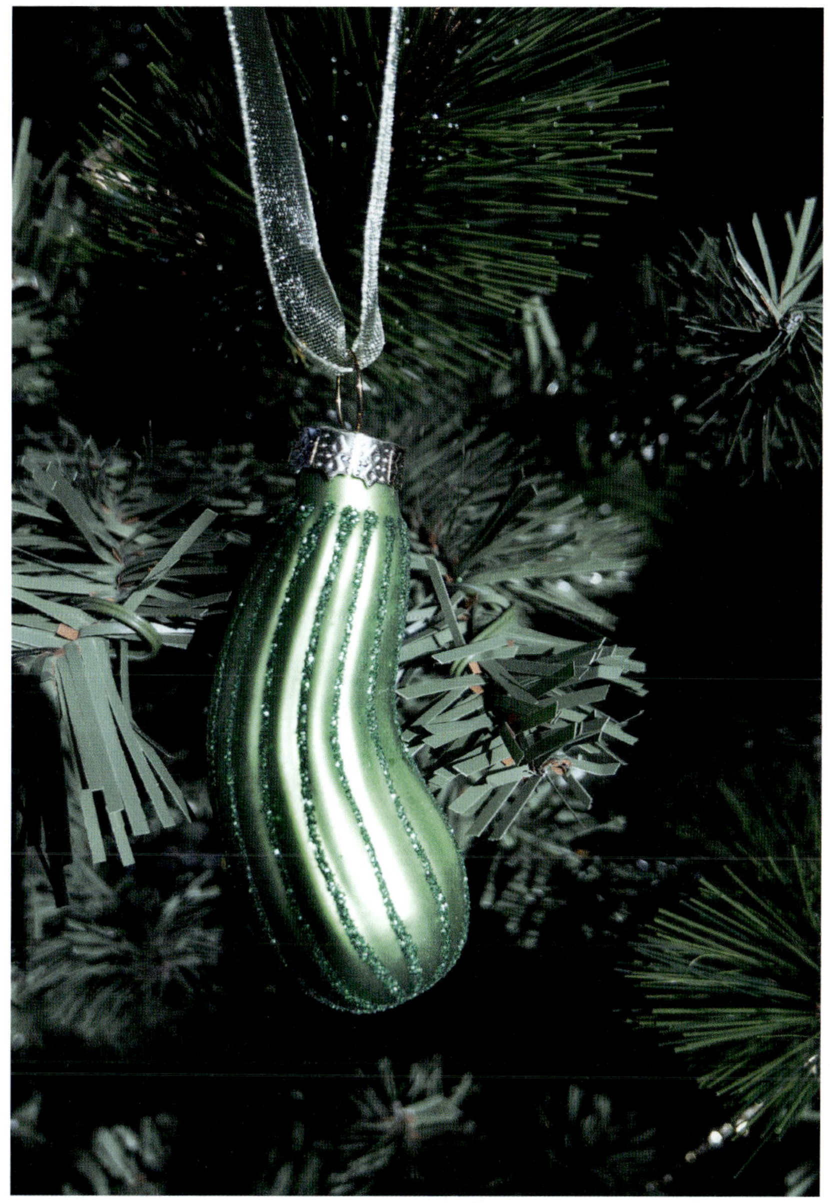

The Christmas pickle is a quirky tradition in America believed to have originated in the 19th century, often linked to German immigrants. Interestingly, this custom is virtually unknown in Germany itself.

The custom of sending letters to Santa Claus is a cherished holiday tradition in many countries, allowing children to share their Christmas wishes and dreams. Several post offices around the world embrace this tradition by actively responding to these letters. One of the most famous is the Santa Claus Mail Trail in Canada, where letters addressed to Santa are sent to the North Pole, and volunteers help to ensure children receive a reply. Similarly, the Himmelpfort post office in Germany has become well known for its Santa letters, celebrating its 40th anniversary in 2024 and handling around 2,000 letters each day during the Advent season.

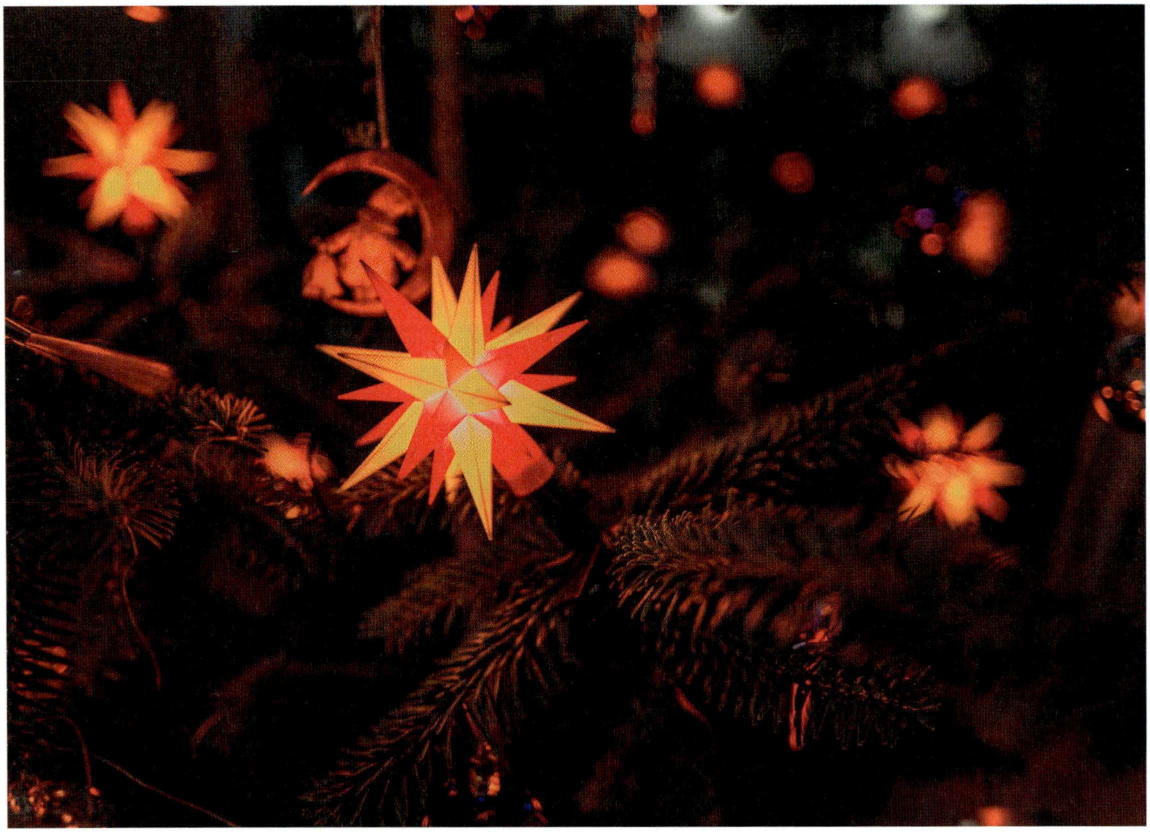

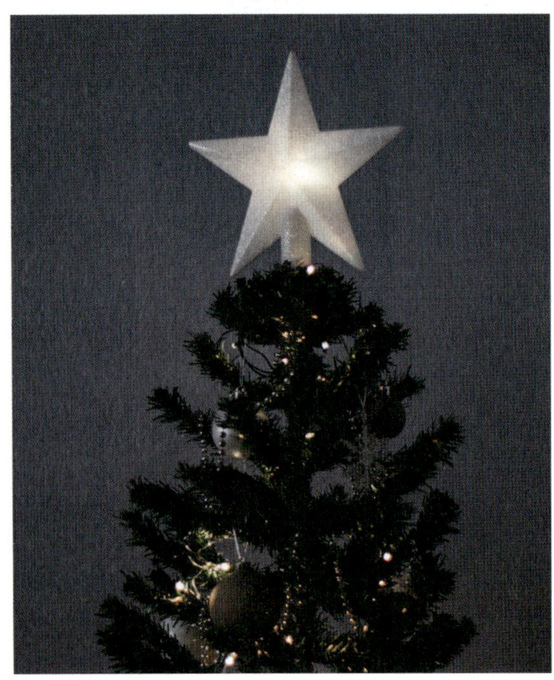

Stars hold significant meaning during the Christmas season, symbolizing light, hope, and the birth of Jesus. The tree topper star represents the Star of Bethlehem, while Moravian stars, known for their distinctive geometric shape, serve as popular decorations. In Mexico, Las Posadas celebrations feature brightly colored star-shaped piñatas, with the pointed cones representing earthly temptations.

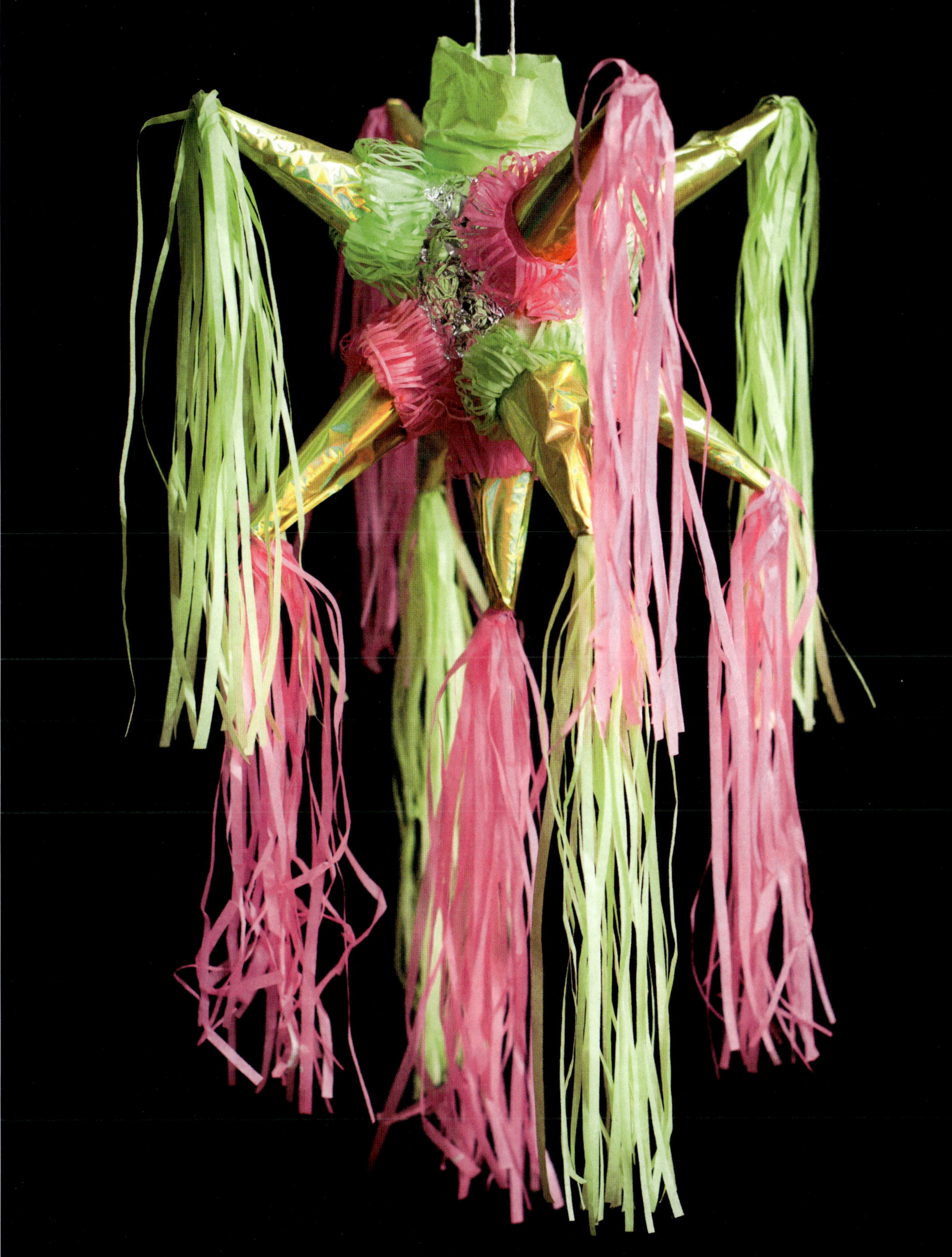

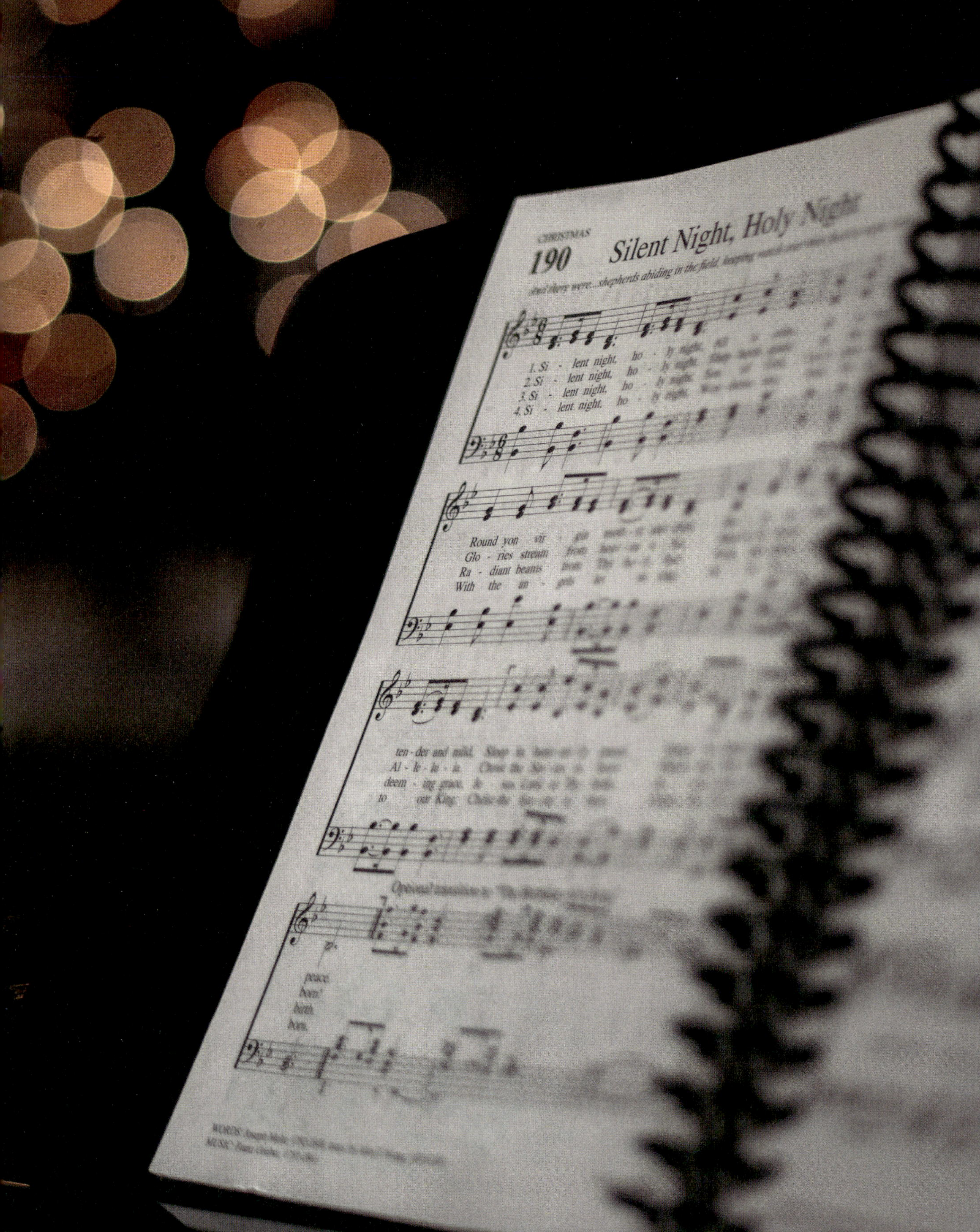

CHRISTMAS
190
Silent Night, Holy Night
1. Si - lent night, ho -
2. Si - lent night, ho -
3. Si - lent night, ho -
4. Si - lent night, ho -
Round yon vir -
Glo - ries stream
Ra - diant beams
With the an -
ten - der and mild,
Al - le - lu - ia.
deem - ing grace,
to our King;
peace.
born!
birth.
born.

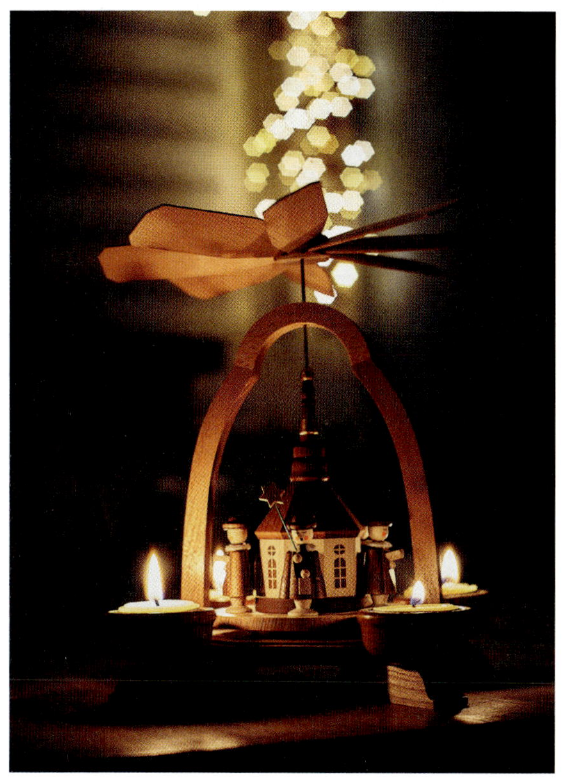

Beyond gnomes, Christmas caroling and assembling Christmas pyramids are cherished traditions. These wooden pyramids, beautifully crafted in both traditional and modern styles, depict the Christmas story and are adorned with candles representing light and hope.

"Silent Night," first performed in Austria in 1818, remains the most recognized Christmas carol, translated into over 300 languages.

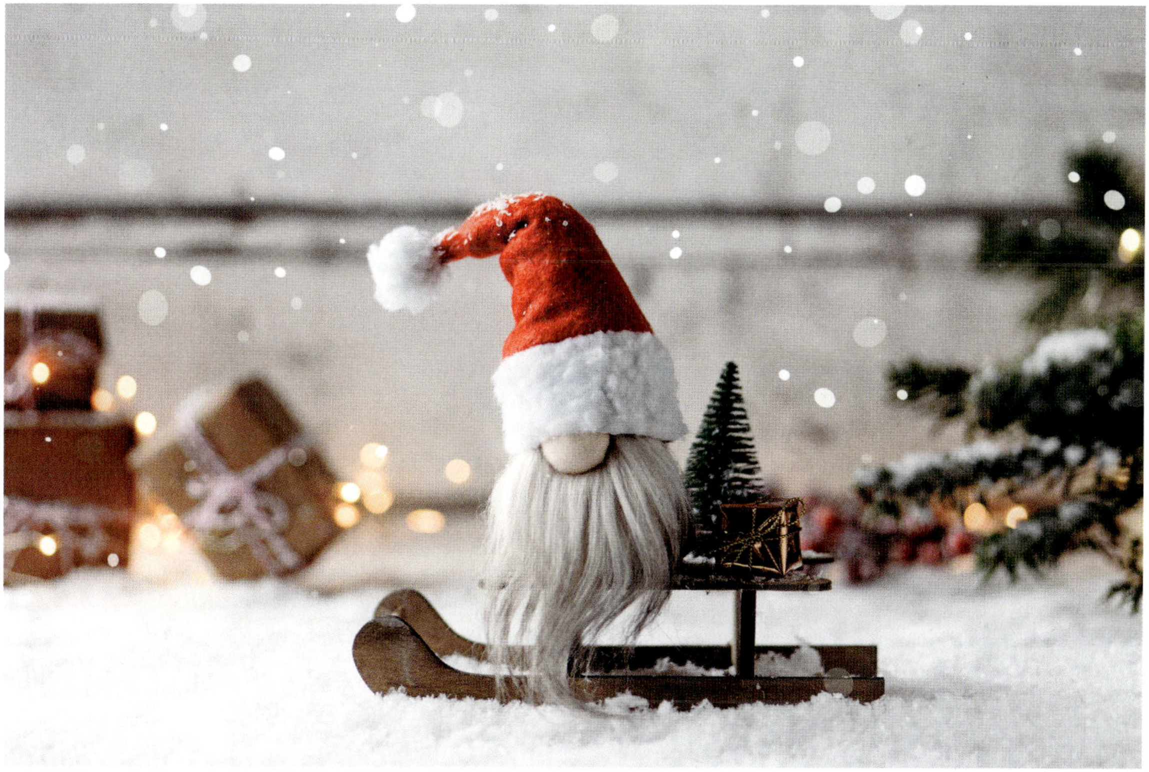

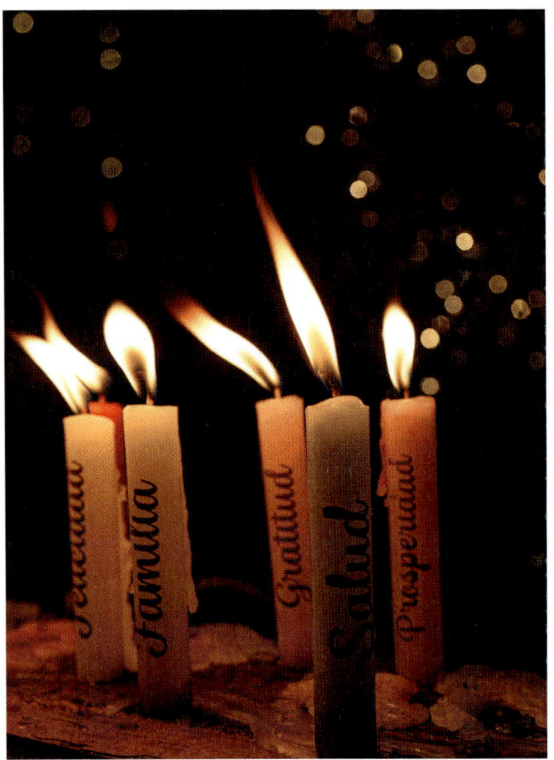

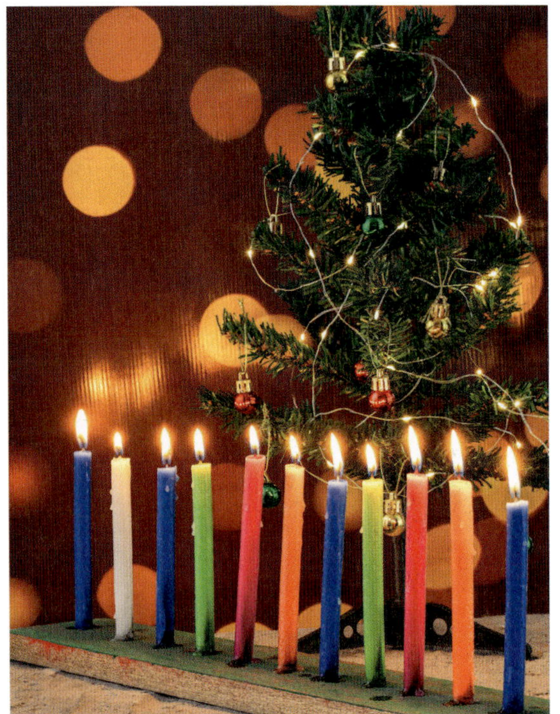

Candles and light are essential to the spirit of Christmas. In Colombia, the Noche de las Velitas, celebrated on the night of December 7th, honors colorful candles. On this special night, small candles and lanterns illuminate streets and homes as a warm welcome to the Advent season.

In San Fernando, Philippines, December brings the Giant Lantern Festival (Ligligan Parul), a dazzling display of enormous lanterns crafted from vibrant paper that attract visitors from across the globe.

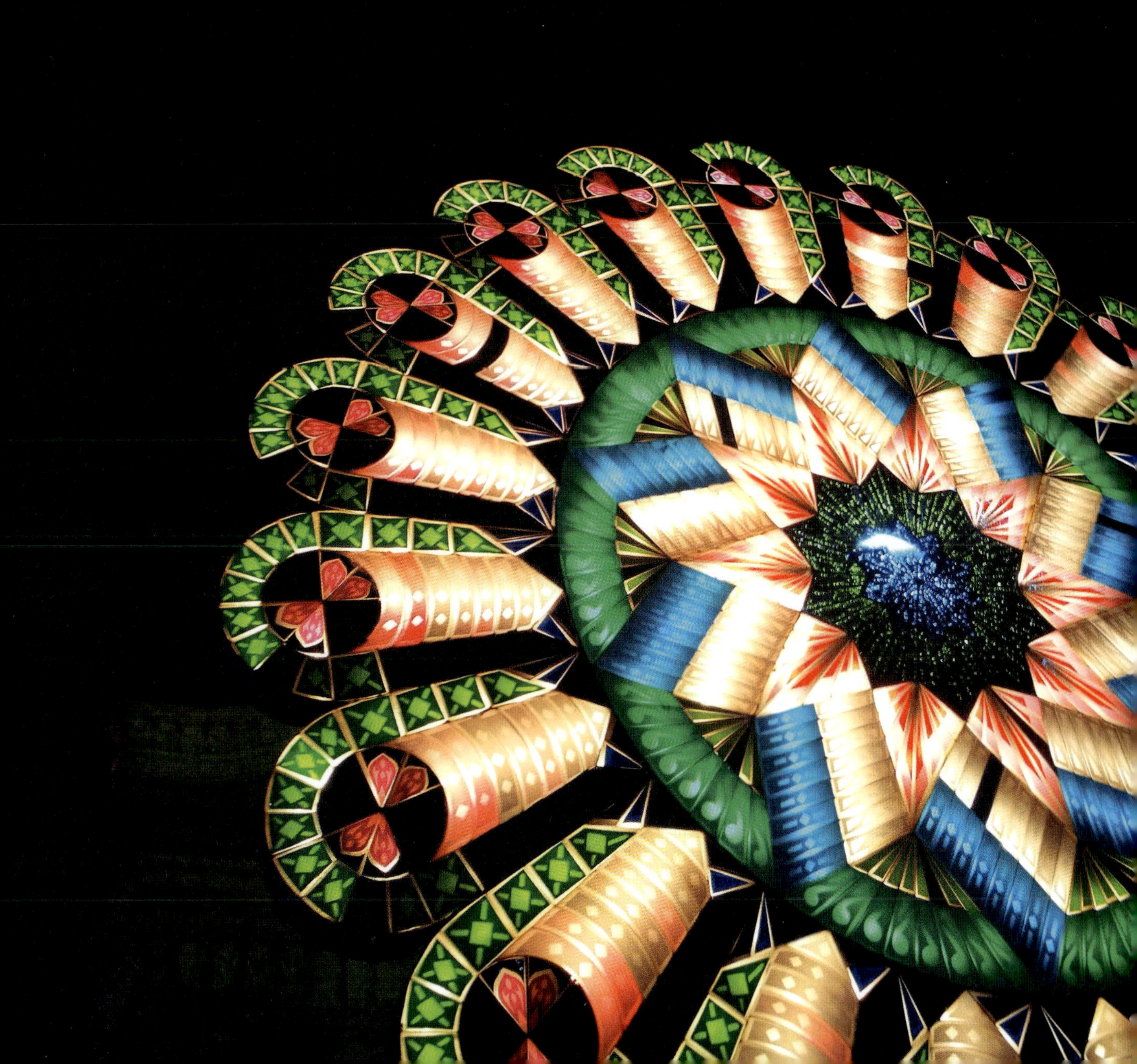

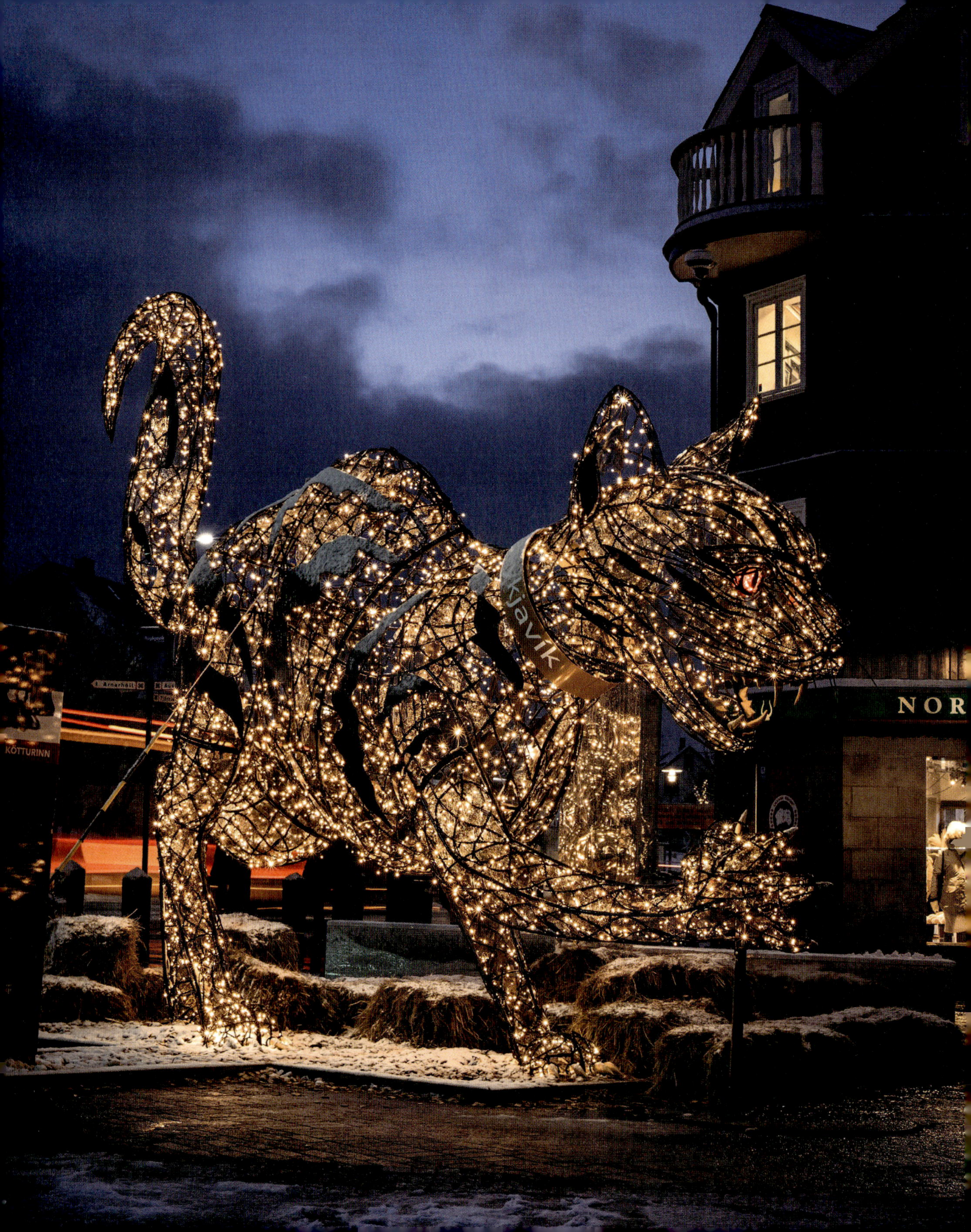
kjavík
KÖTTURINN
NOR

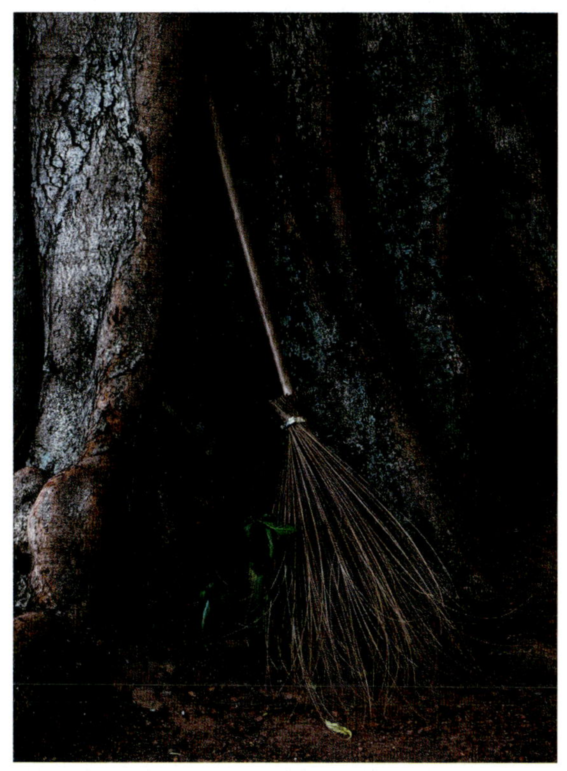

Nordic countries embrace their unique Christmas traditions, such as Iceland's eerie Christmas cat, *Jólakötturinn*, who supposedly devours people, who don't wear new clothes for Christmas Eve, or Norway's custom of concealing brooms. Other countries have spooky legends too, like the artificial cobwebs and spider used for decorating Ukrainian Christmas trees, said to bring good fortune.

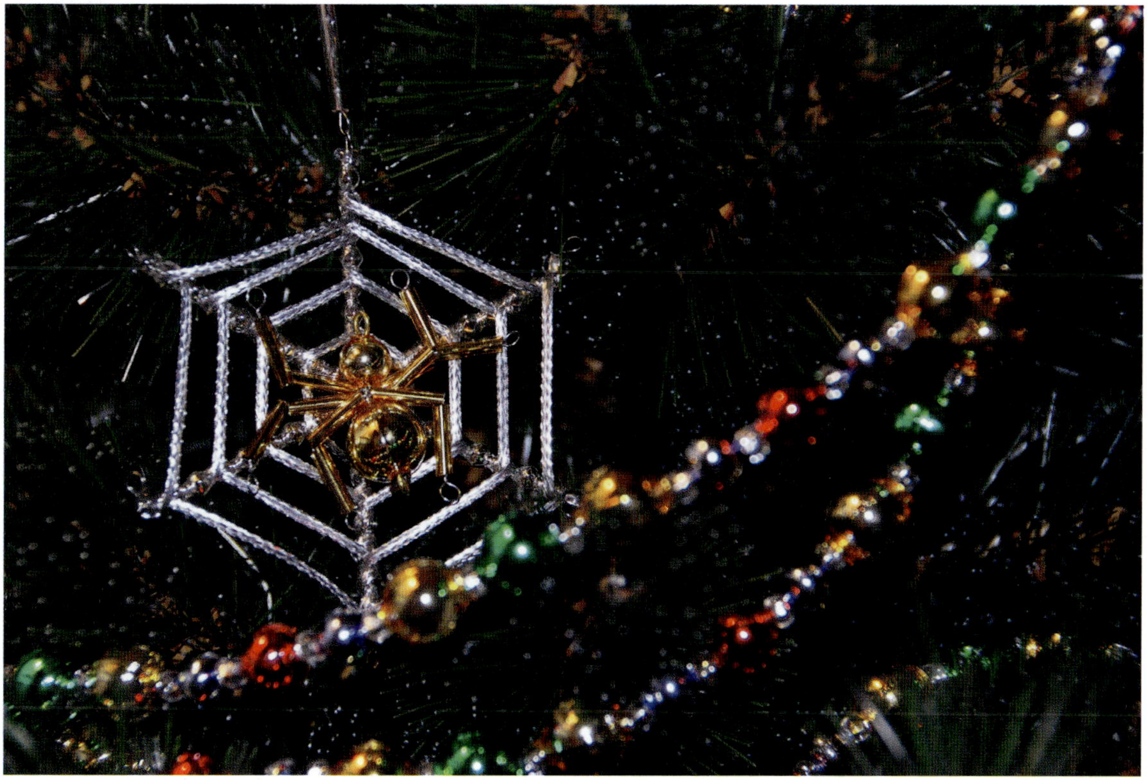

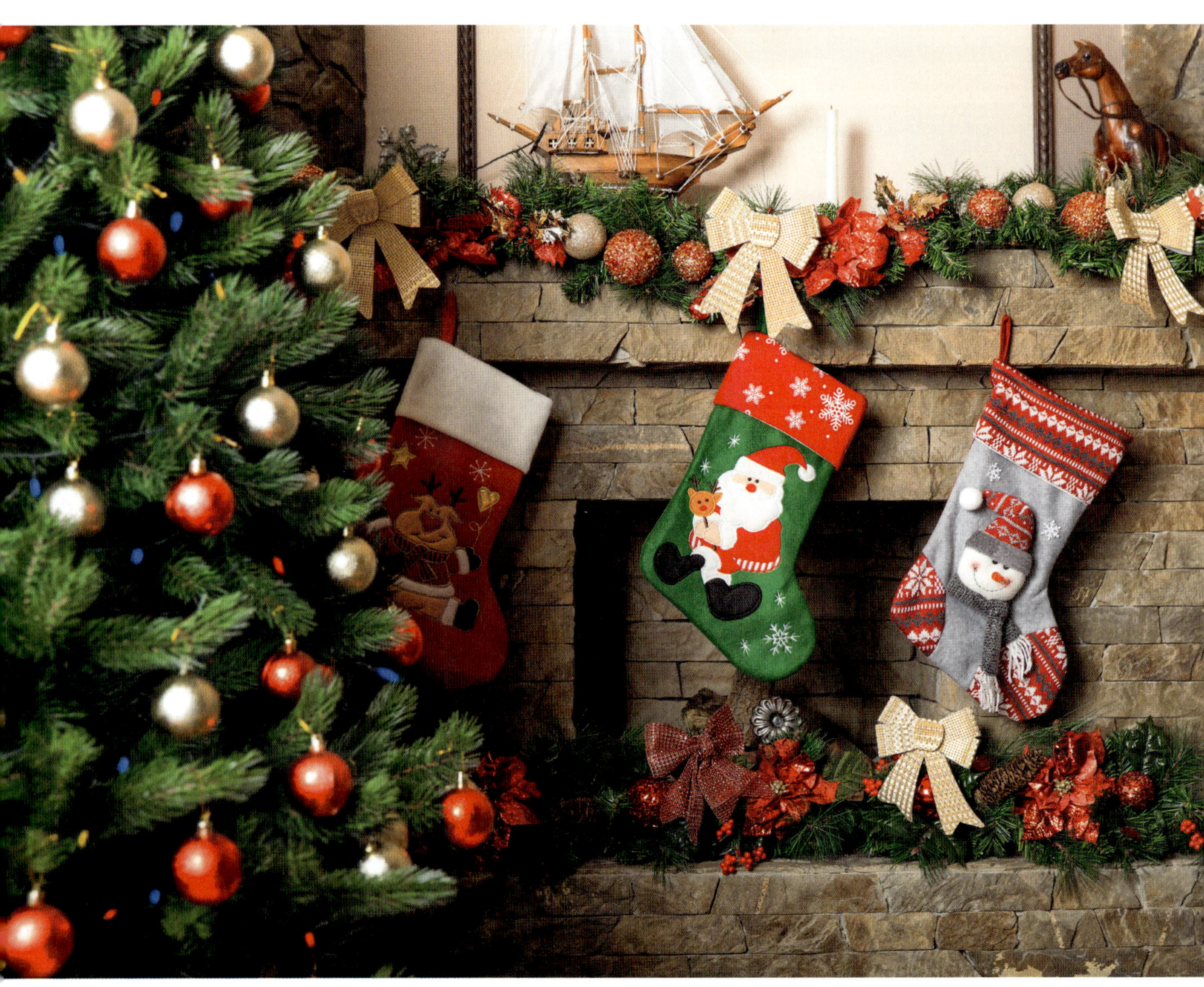

Hanging Christmas stockings on fireplaces, banisters, or beds is a widespread tradition, especially in the USA and Europe, where they are filled with treats and gifts.

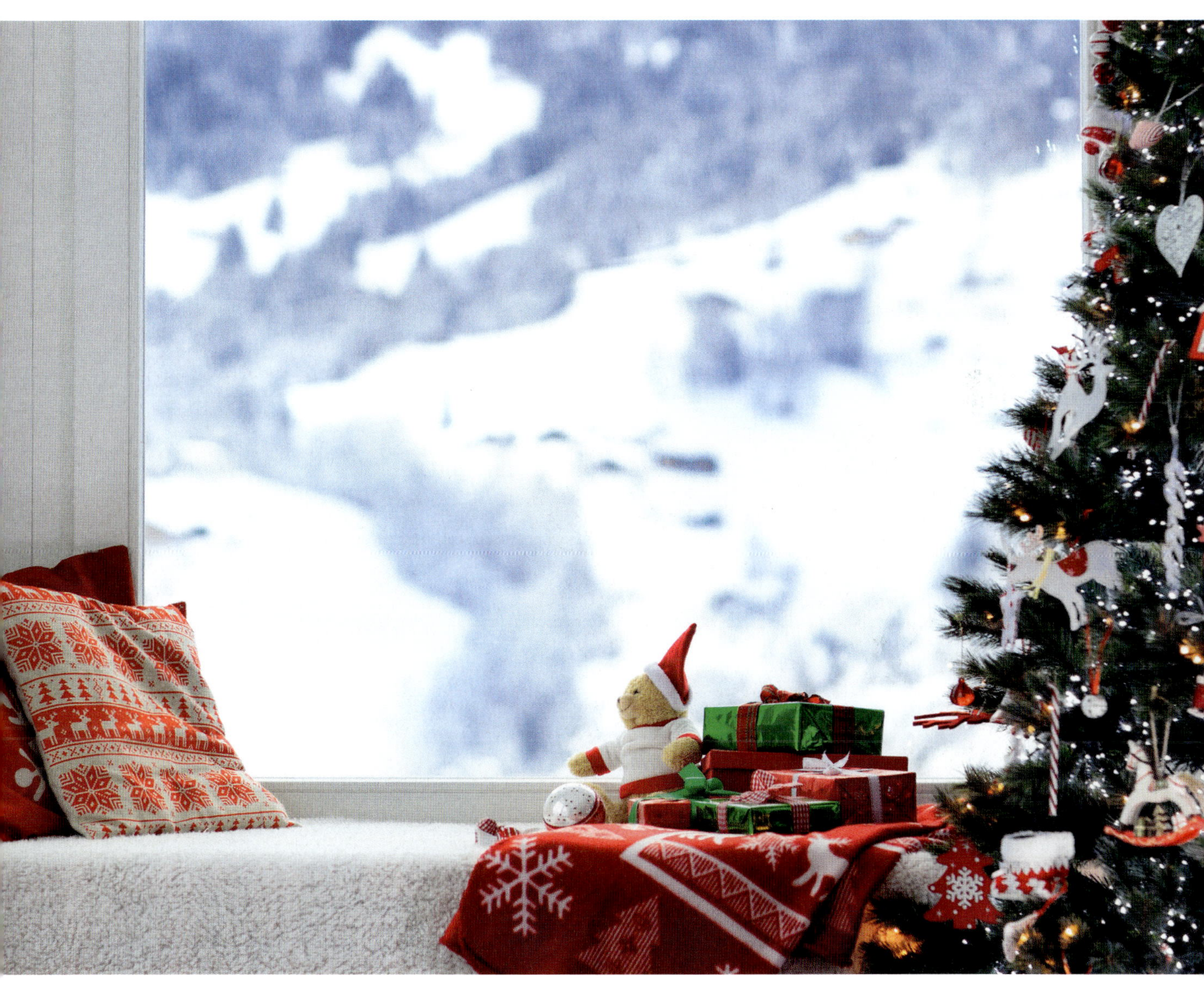

Christmas cushions, often adorned with festive designs, bring warmth and comfort to homes. These decorative cushions are popular in many countries during the holiday season and foster a cozy atmosphere. In England, it's also customary to hide presents in cushion covers or to make a wish while seated on them.

FEATURE

CHRISTMAS IN THE MOUNTAINS

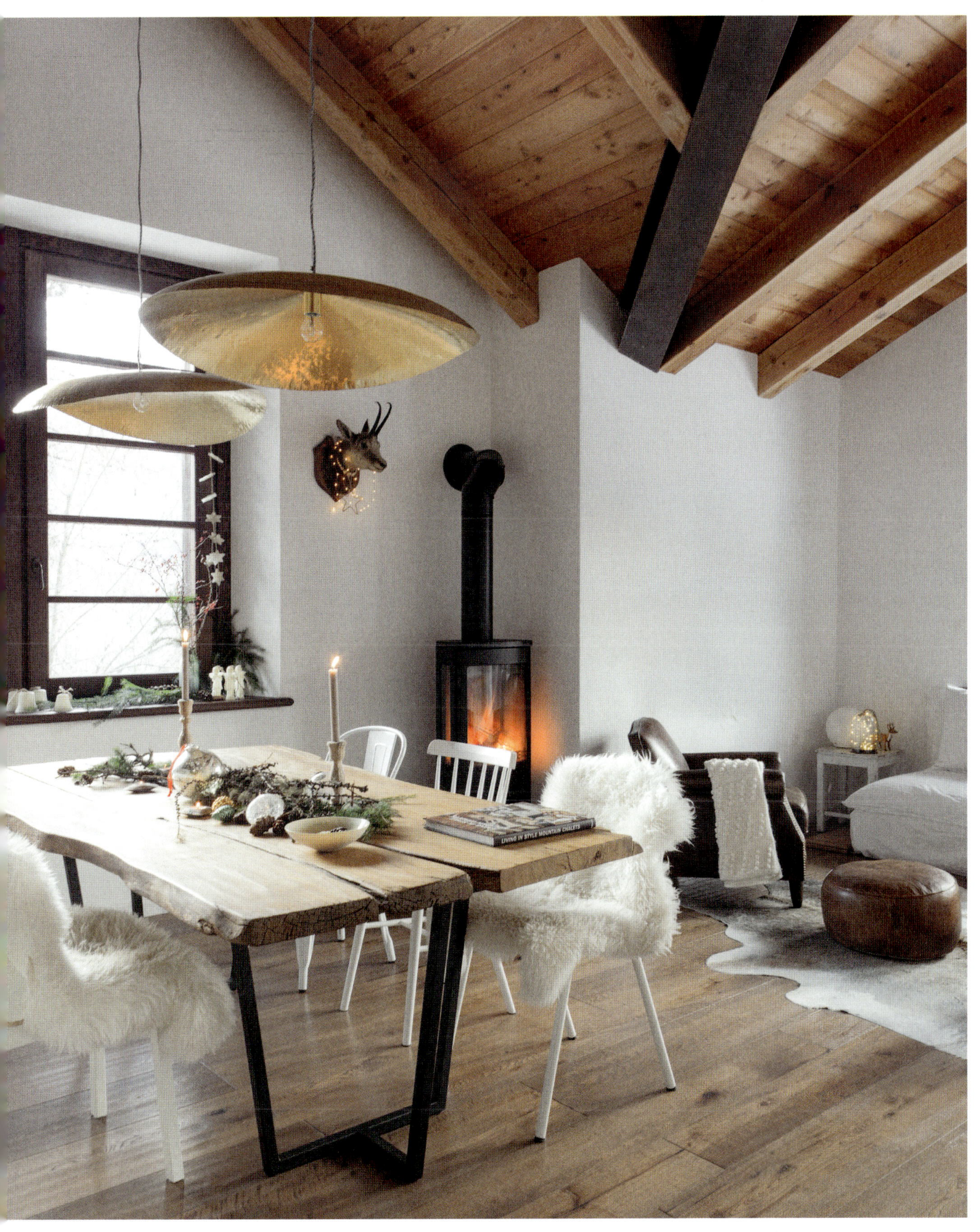
LIVING IN STYLE MOUNTAIN CHALETS

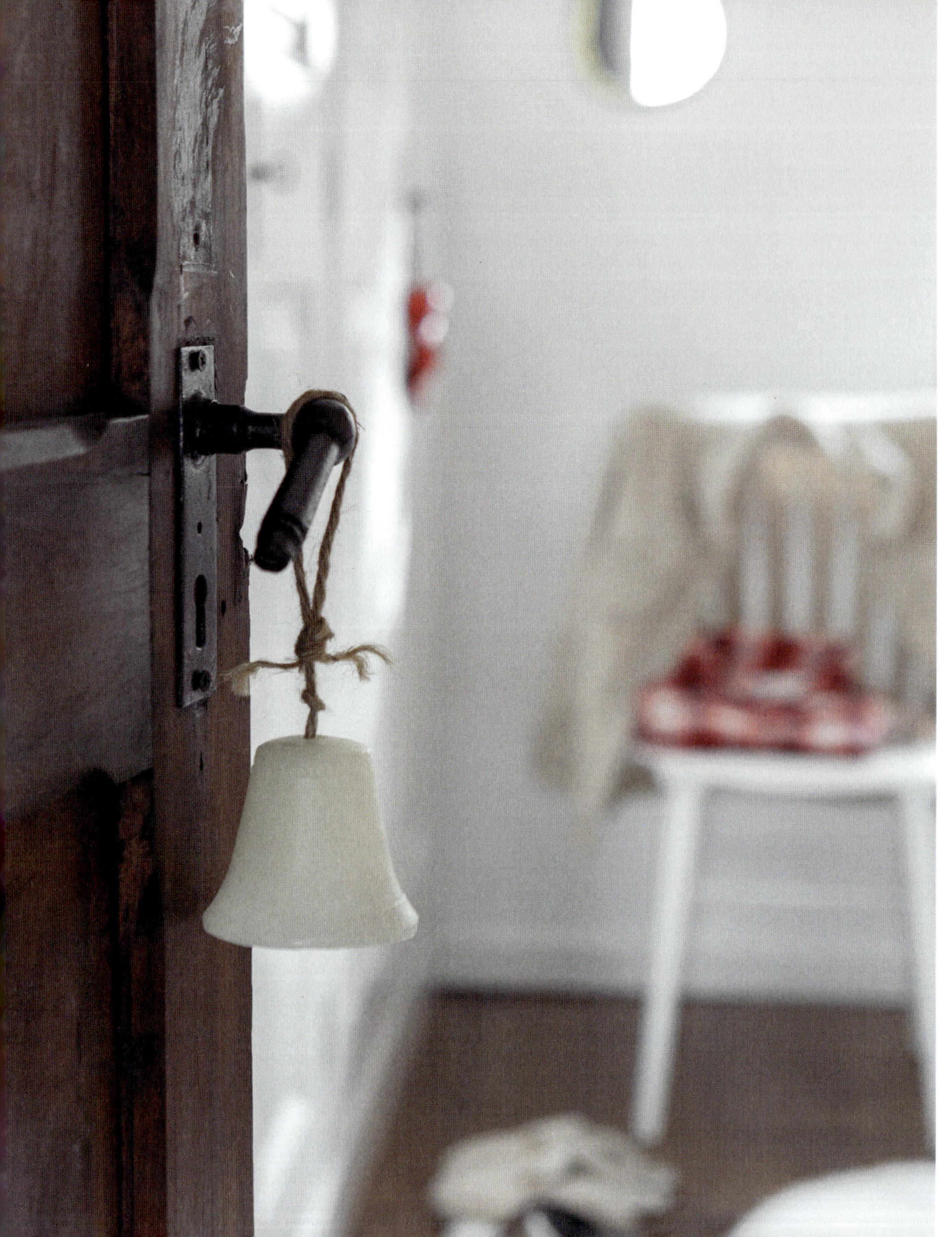

A Retreat for the Holidays

Cristina Colombini's holiday home at the foot of Mont Blanc offers a serene retreat for her family. Nestled in a grove of pine trees, the house features expansive windows that invite nature inside, complemented by warm wood tones, soft hues, and cozy mountain-inspired furnishings.

Located in Courmayeur, a prestigious ski destination in the Valle d'Aosta just a couple of hours from Milan, Cristina spends her holidays here with her husband Thomas and their three daughters. After running her own shop for 15 years, Cristina is now focused on her family and renovating their home, alongside her work with a notable hotel and restaurant and setting up and decorating their interior spaces.

Built in the early 20th century as a boarding school, the historic residence is adorned with a private chapel nestled within its grounds. The architecture is robust and traditional, reflecting Alpine building methods, while inside, a warm atmosphere embraces visitors. Cristina's choice of white for furnishings creates a light, airy feel, further enhanced by exposed wooden beams, honey-colored parquet, and scattered candles that amplify the cozy ambiance.

The home is designed for both comfort and practicality, accommodating the needs of a lively family. Cristina has cleverly reconfigured spaces, such as the primary bedroom, by replacing walls with a white iron-and-glass structure for a more open feel. The open-plan living area includes a kitchenette and dining space that overlooks Mont Blanc, featuring a long wooden table perfect for gatherings with friends.

Cristina describes her home as a cherished place that fosters togetherness and joy. The intimate sleeping quarters, adorned in neutral tones with soft lighting and decorative pine branches, invite relaxation. For sports enthusiasts, skiing is easily accessible, but the true allure also lies in the comfort and warmth of the house itself.

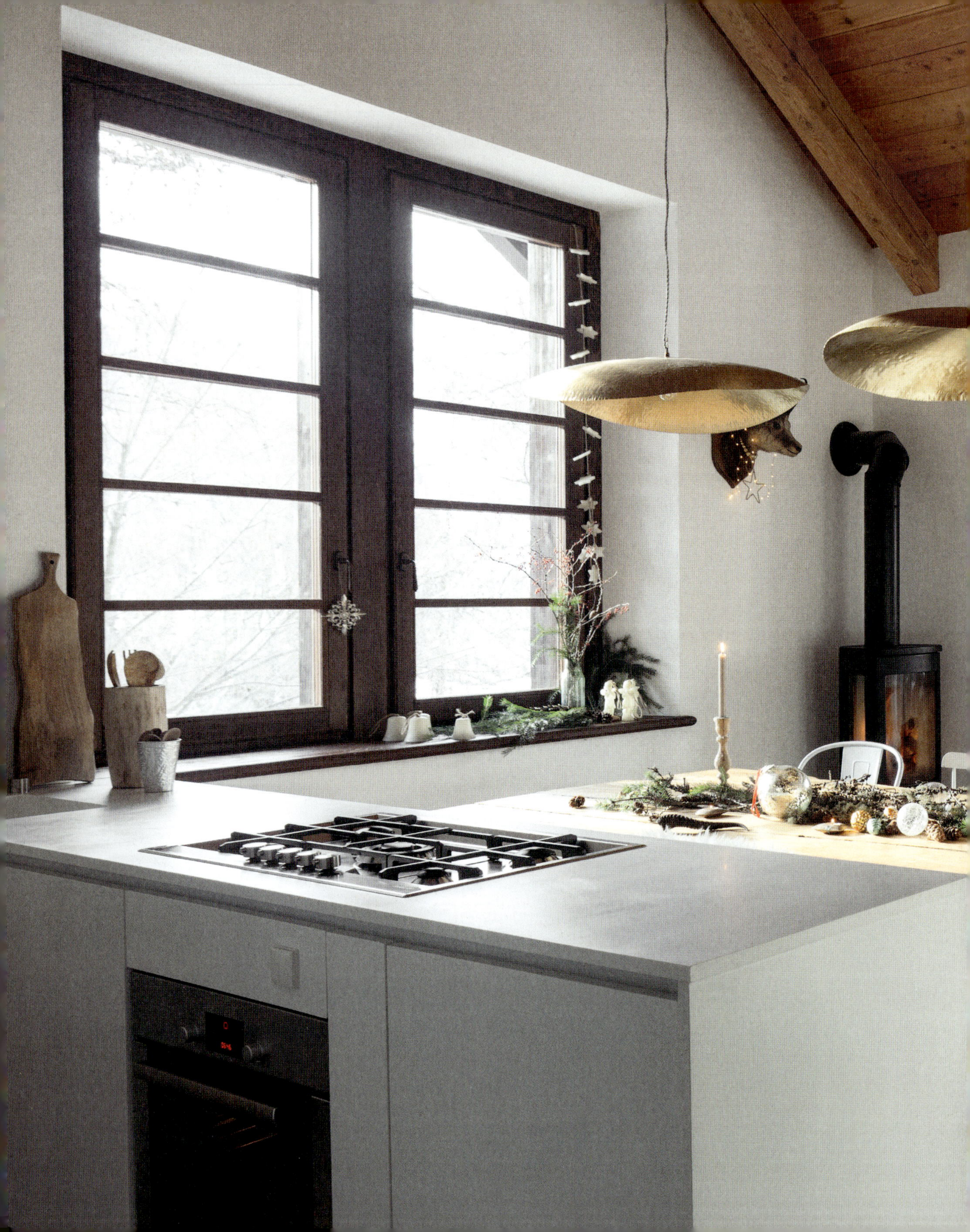

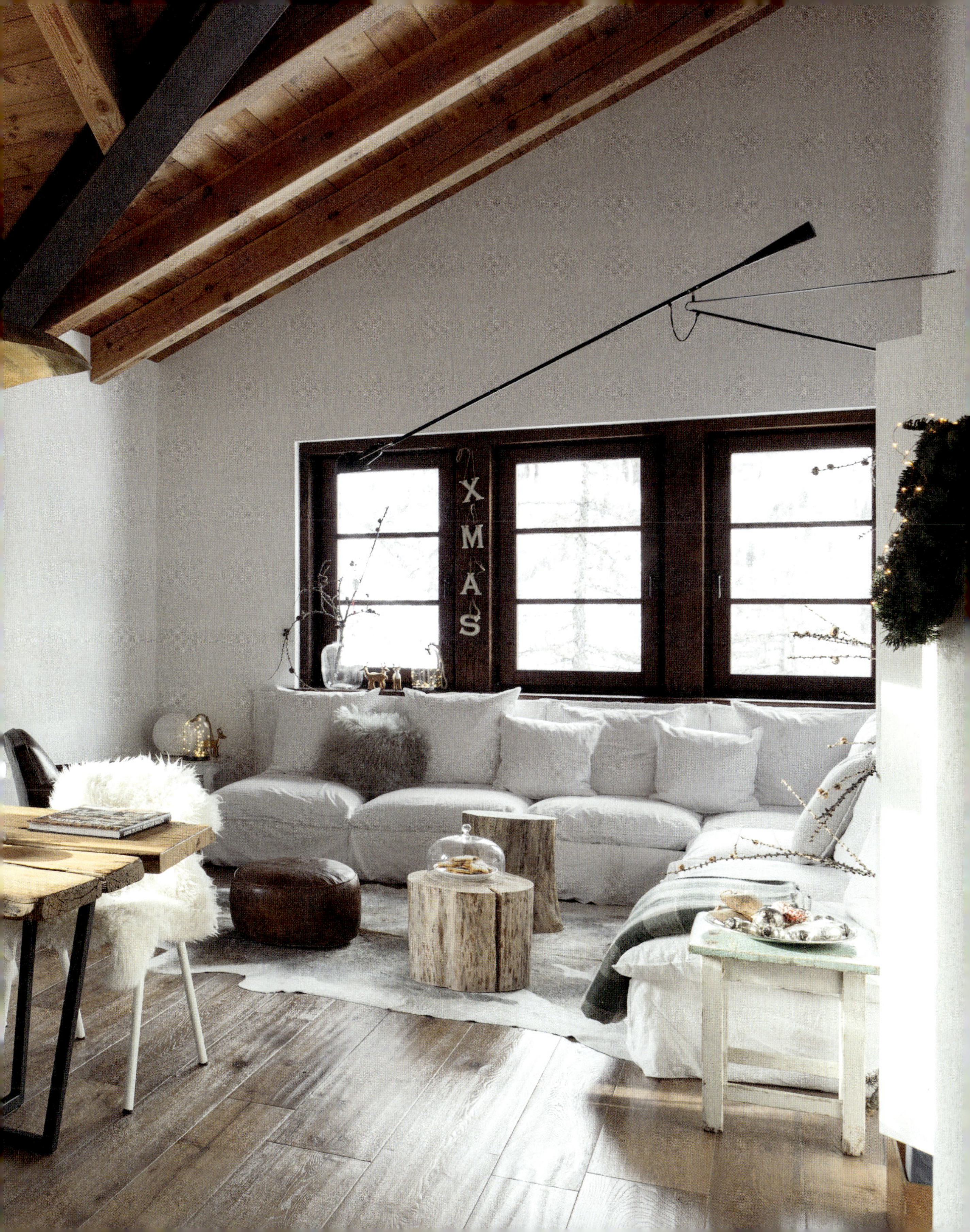
XMAS

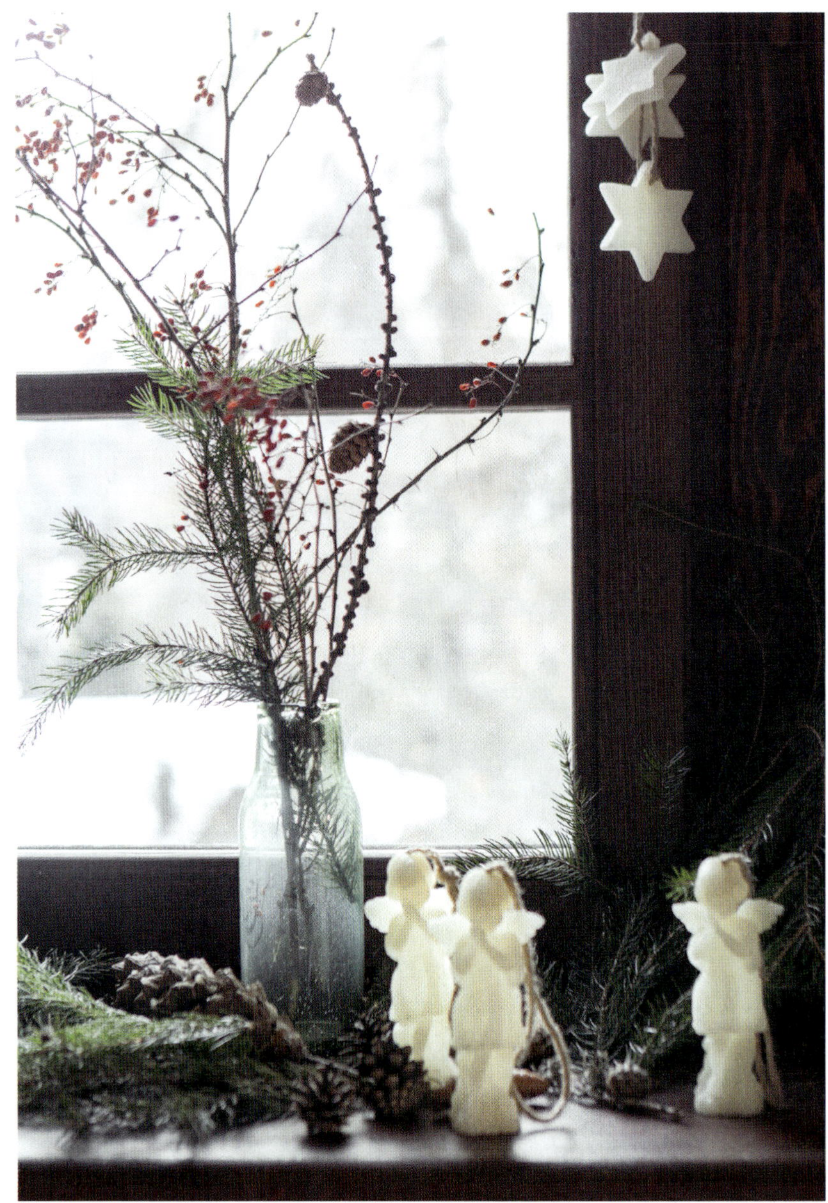

SETTING ACCENTS

Cristina embraces a minimalist Christmas spirit with simple touches: a few pine boughs and pine cones in the bathroom, a single ornament atop neatly stacked towels, a charming wreath hanging from the kitchen shelf, and delicate wax angels gracing the windowsill—subtle yet festive details that create a cozy, holiday ambiance.

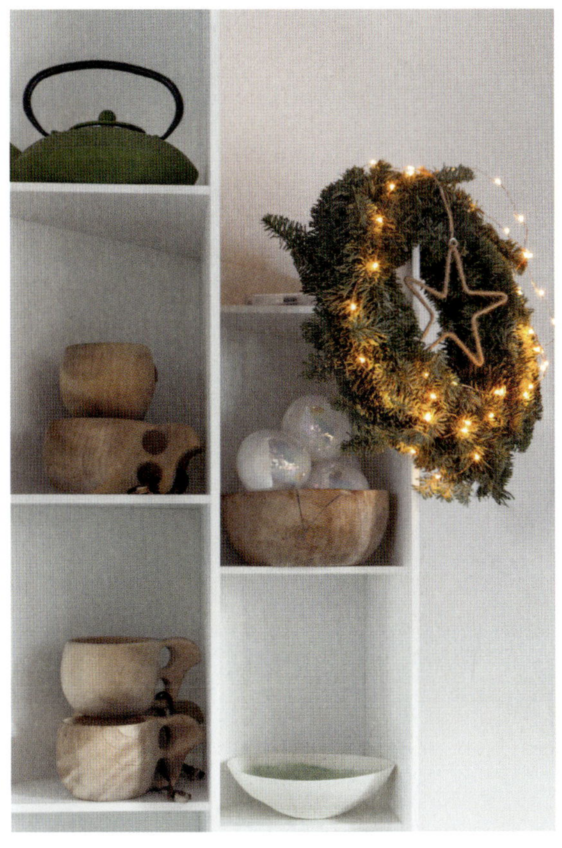
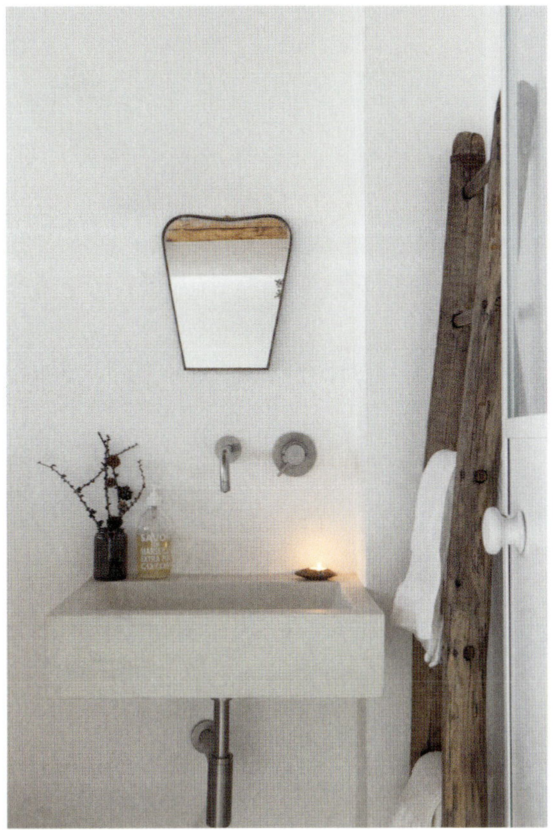
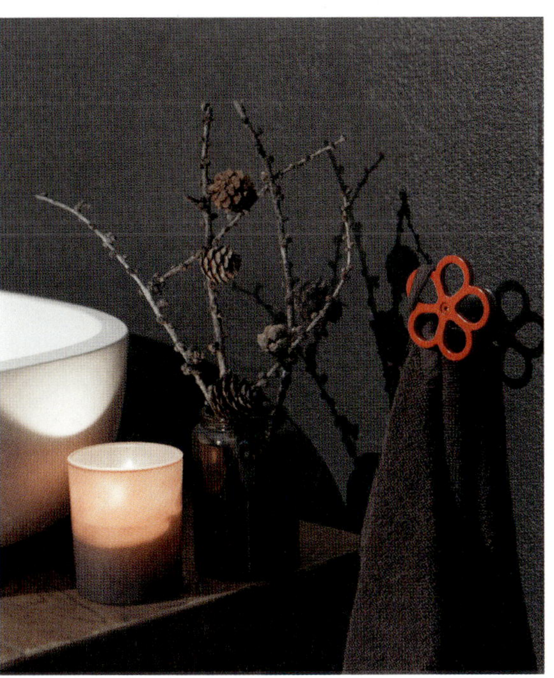
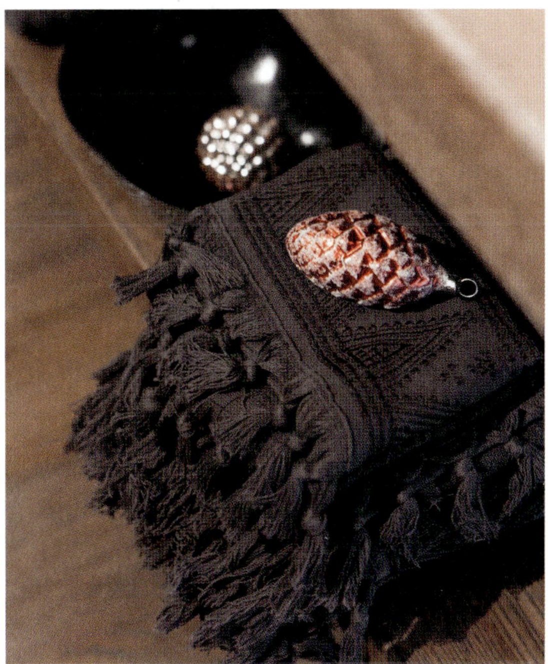

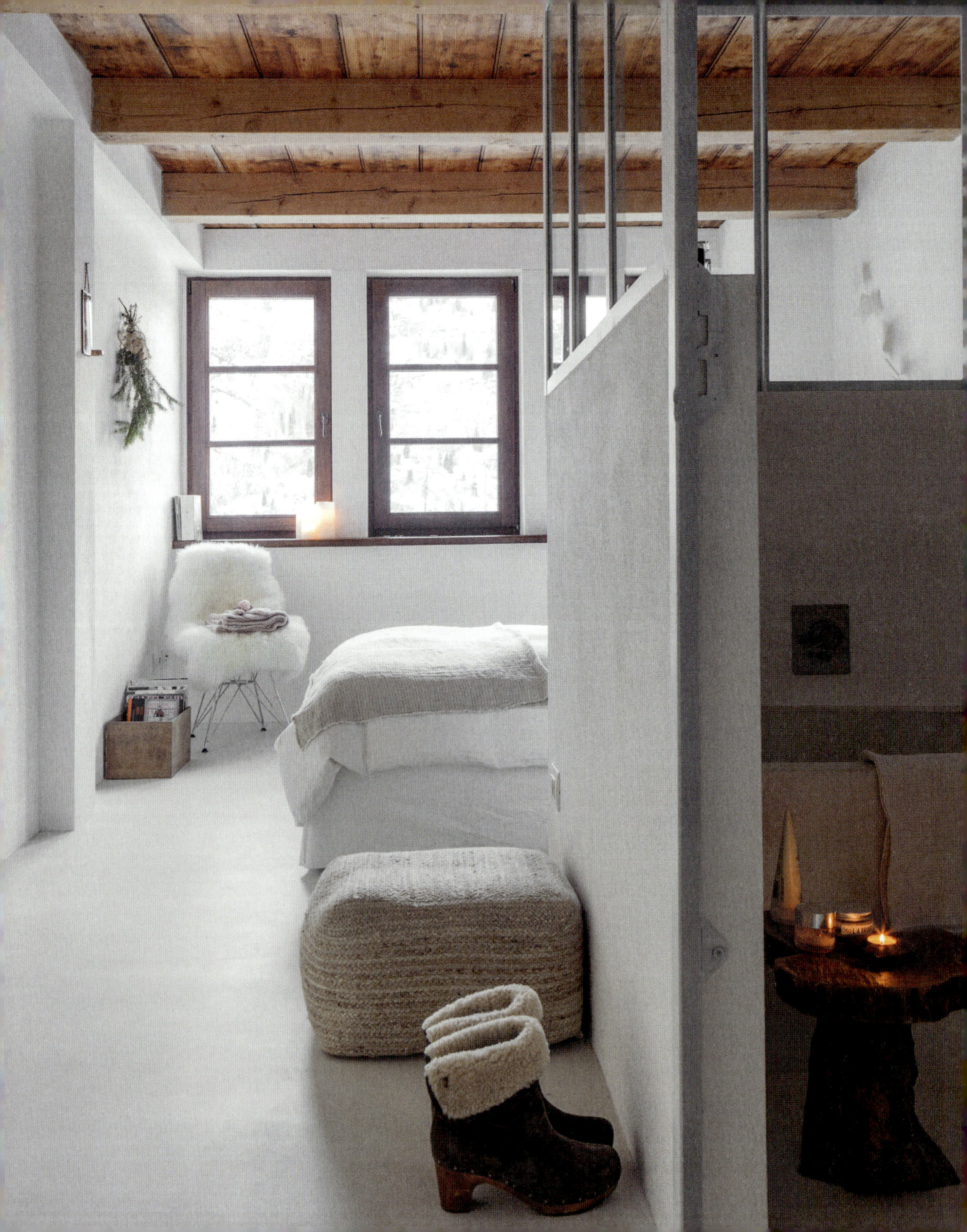

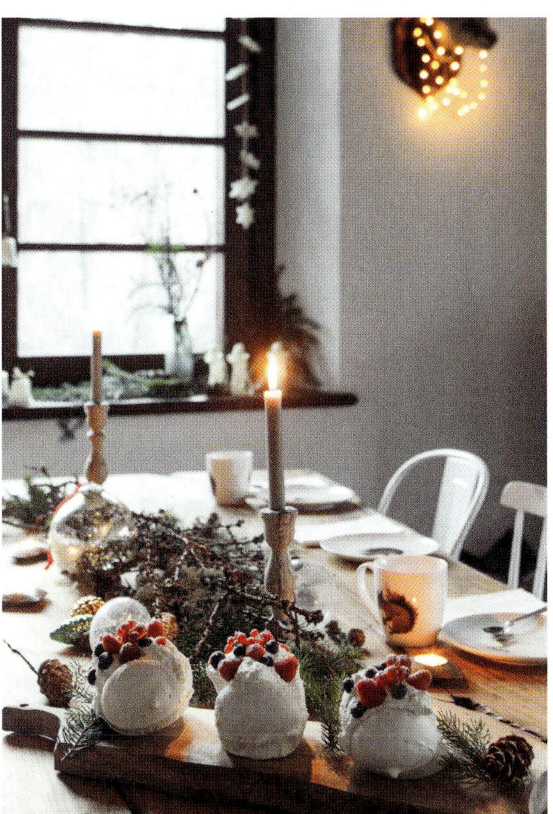

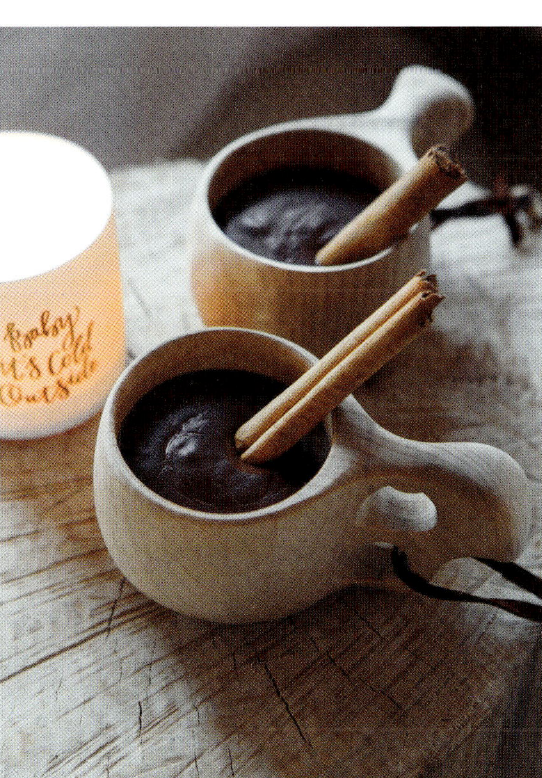

"This is my favorite part of the house," says Cristina, referring to the primary bedroom. "We have removed the walls of the bathroom to make the bedroom look more airy, replacing them with a structure made of white iron and glass."

In the living room, the chairs are all different, but all strictly white. The space is always heated by the stove, while the wooden table is decorated with pine branches picked up in the woods. There are handmade decorations on display everywhere in the living area. "We love to create the perfect place to welcome our friends," Cristina says. And what is more welcoming than a good hot chocolate and berry meringue treats?

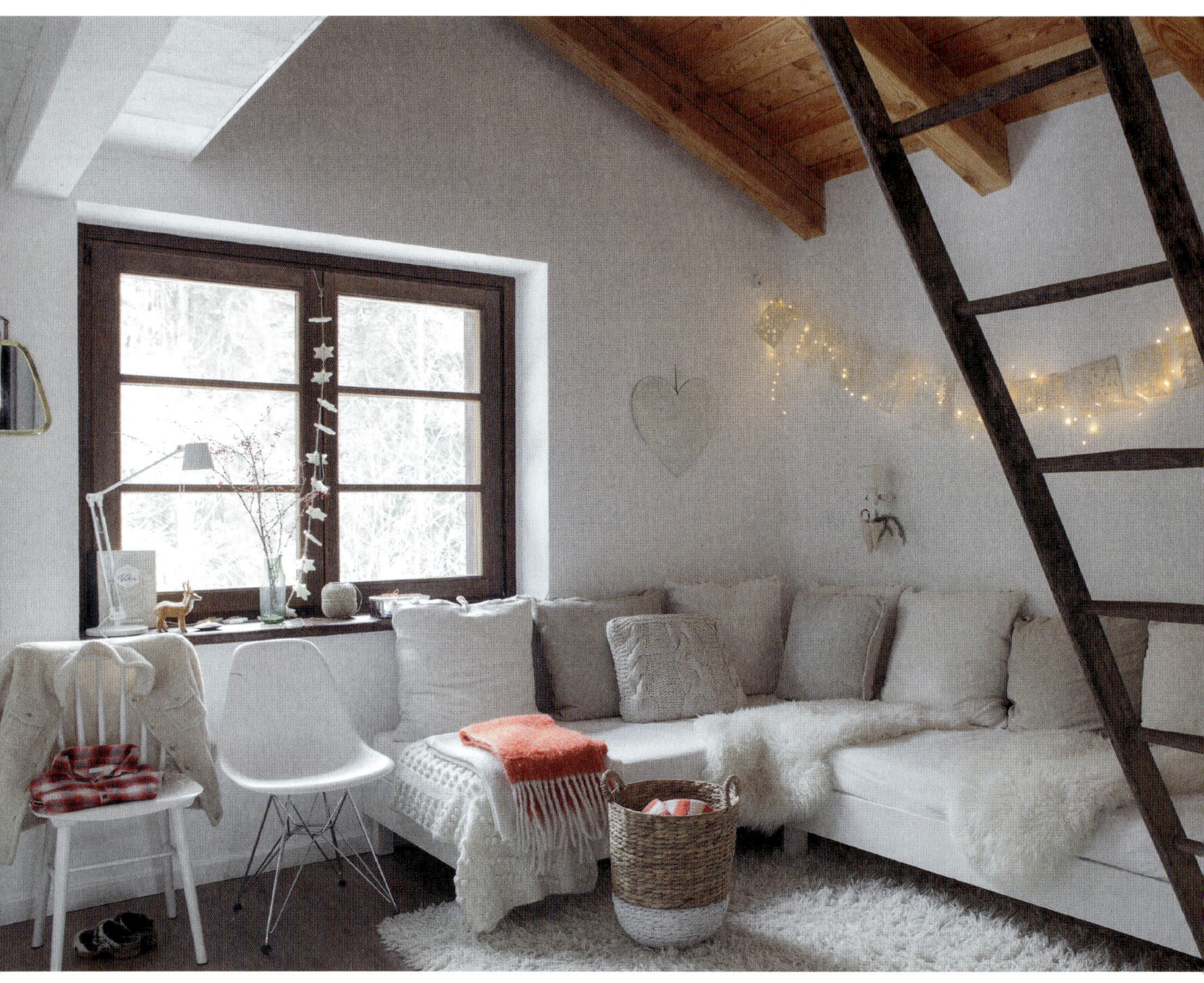

Rugs, carpets, wool blankets and lots of soft cushions—the color palette predominantly consists of beige, gray, and above all, white tones. Even the festive garlands in the main bedroom and the girls' room are in light shades.

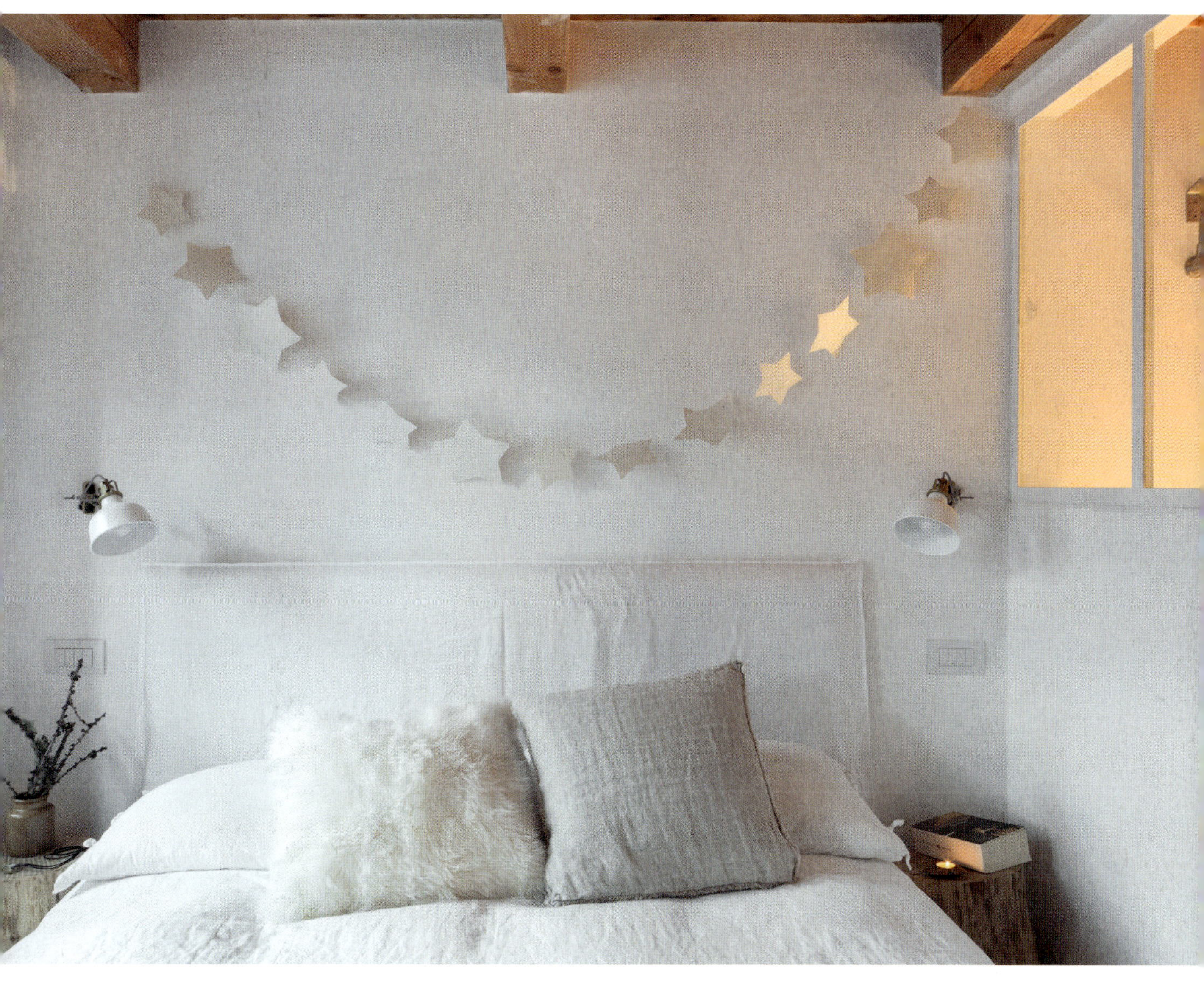

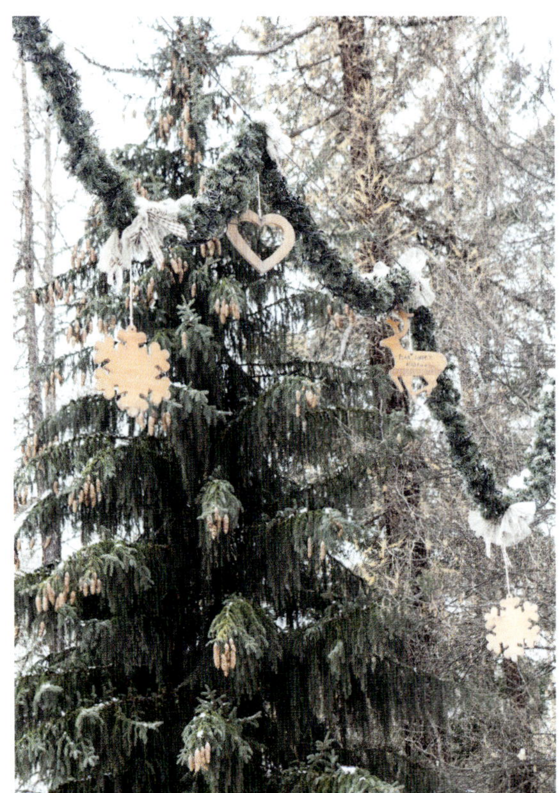

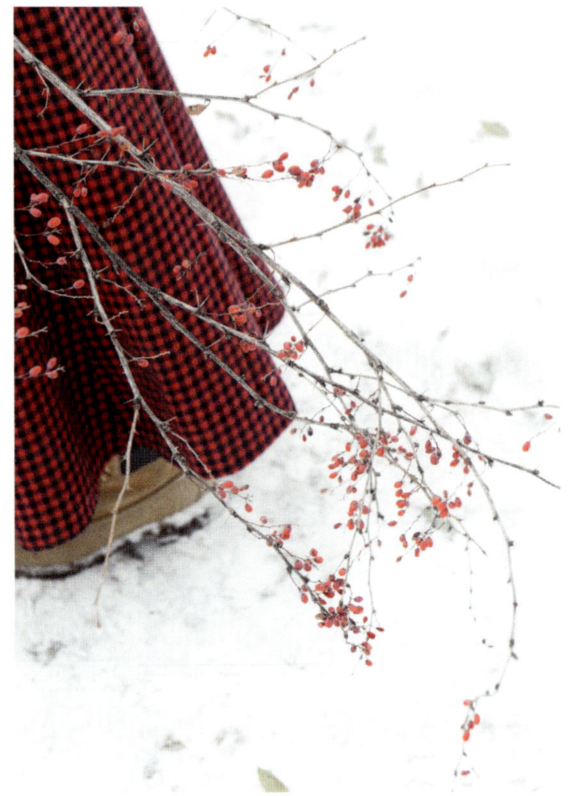

Cristina with one of her daughters in front of their historic holiday home, which was once a boarding school. With a stunning view of Mont Blanc, the solid stone facade exudes charm and tradition.

The lady of the house uses branches and red berries from her own garden to decorate the interior of her home. But the outdoors are decorated as well: the pine pictured above has been adorned beautifully by the whole family.

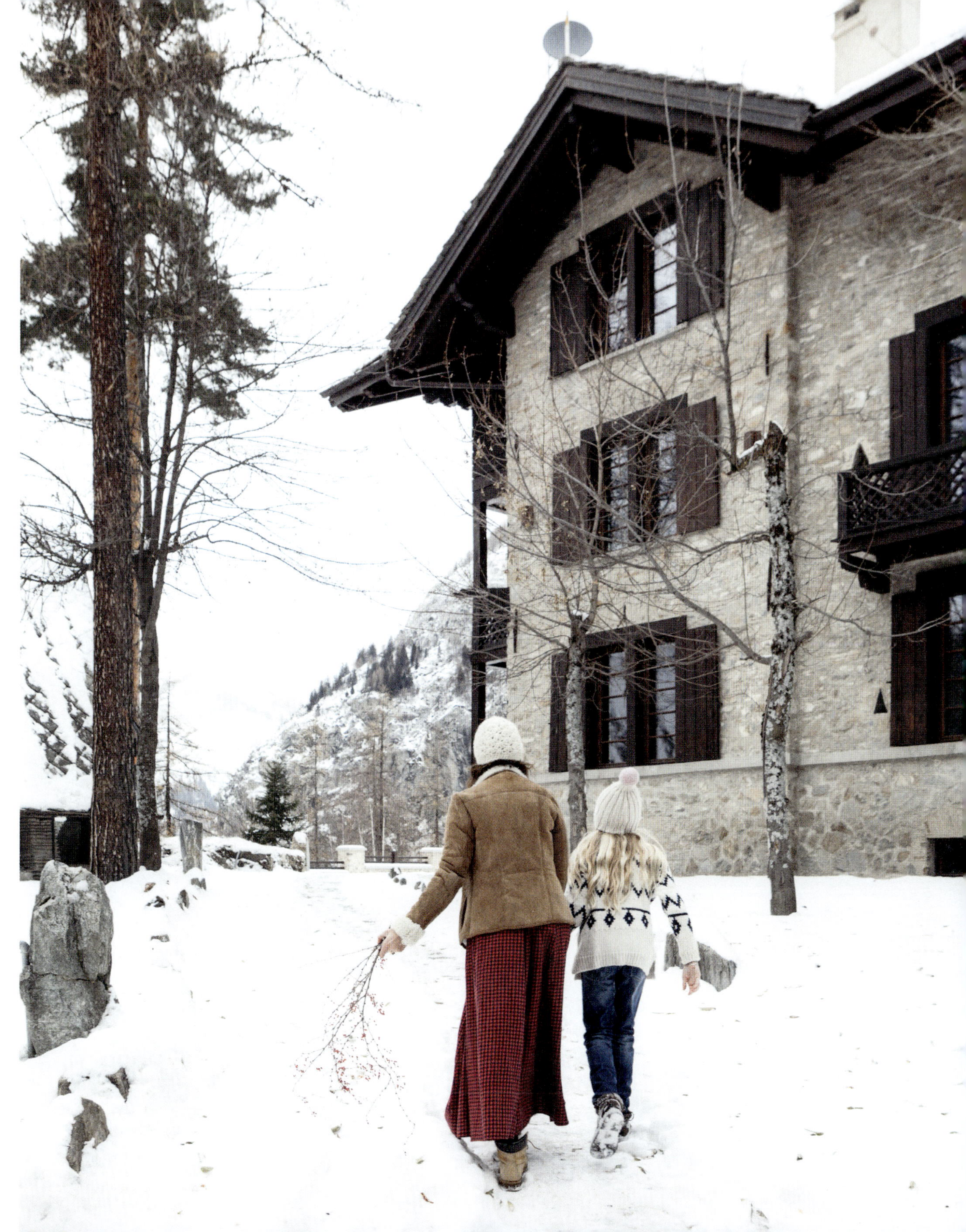

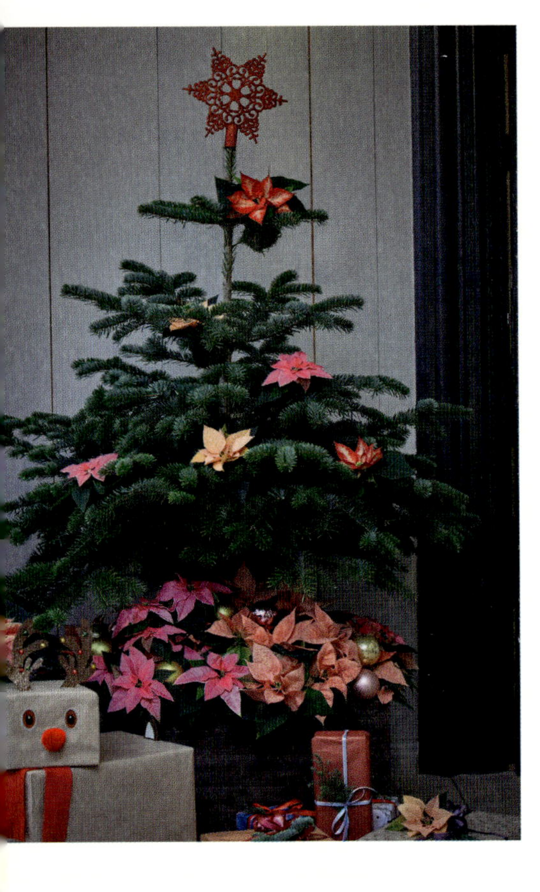

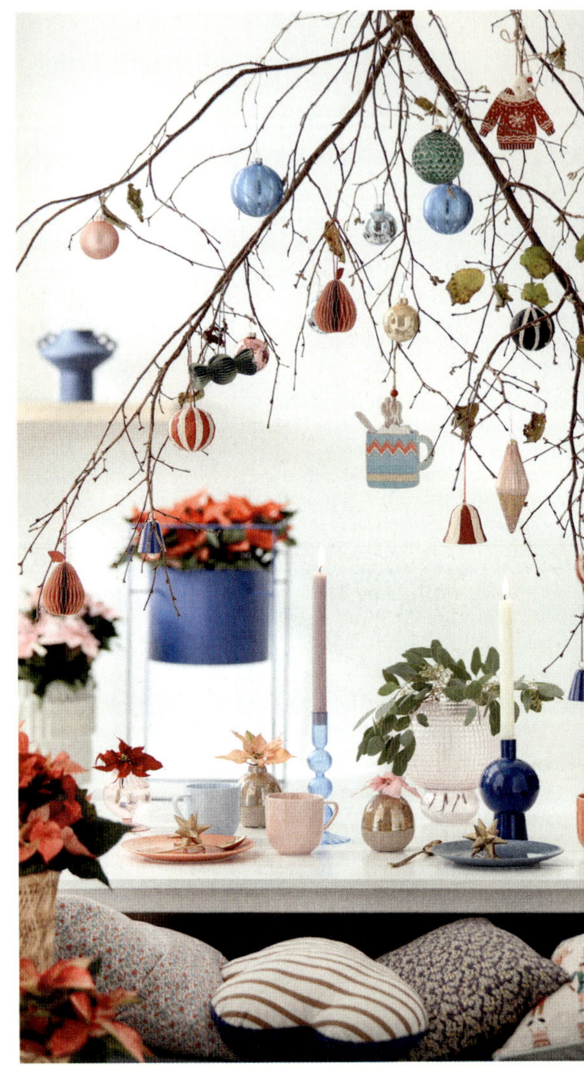

Poinsettia Power

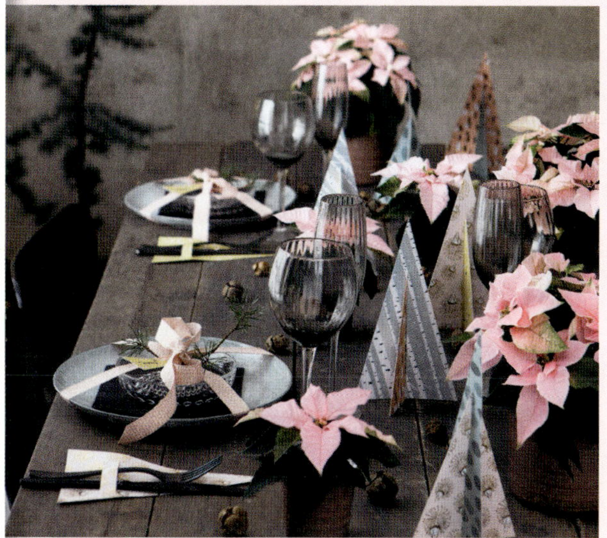

A standout star in the realm of Christmas decorations is the poinsettia, celebrated for its vibrant red leaves. Native to Mexico, this striking plant graces many homes around the world during the Advent season, bringing festive cheer.

According to a Mexican legend, a young girl named Pepita wished to present the Virgin Mary with a humble gift crafted from gathered weeds. When she laid the weeds before the manger, they miraculously transformed into beautiful poinsettias.

This stunning plant actually comes in a range of varieties, colors, and sizes. Its versatility allows it to enhance various decorative themes, from elegant table arrangements to festive tree accents or gift embellishments.

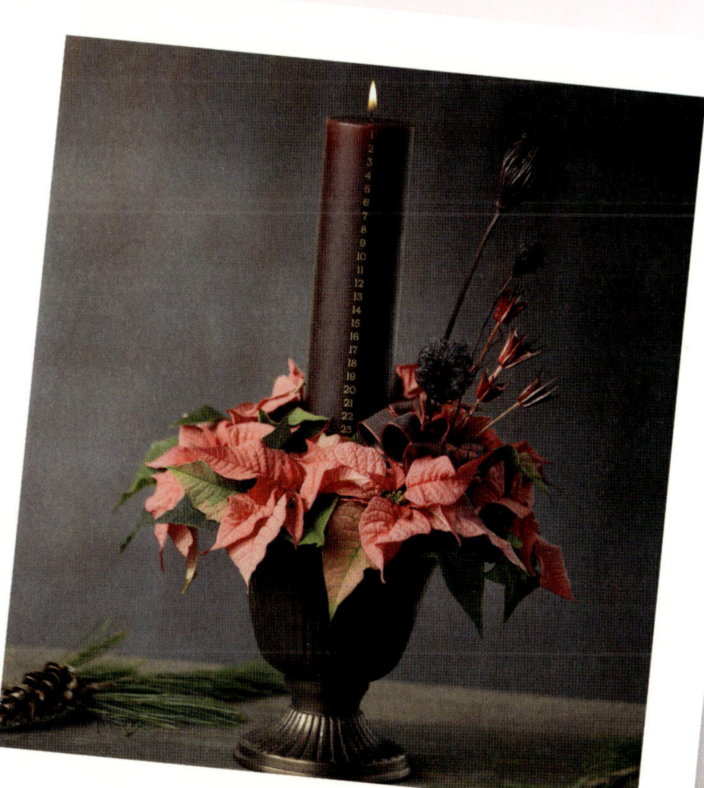

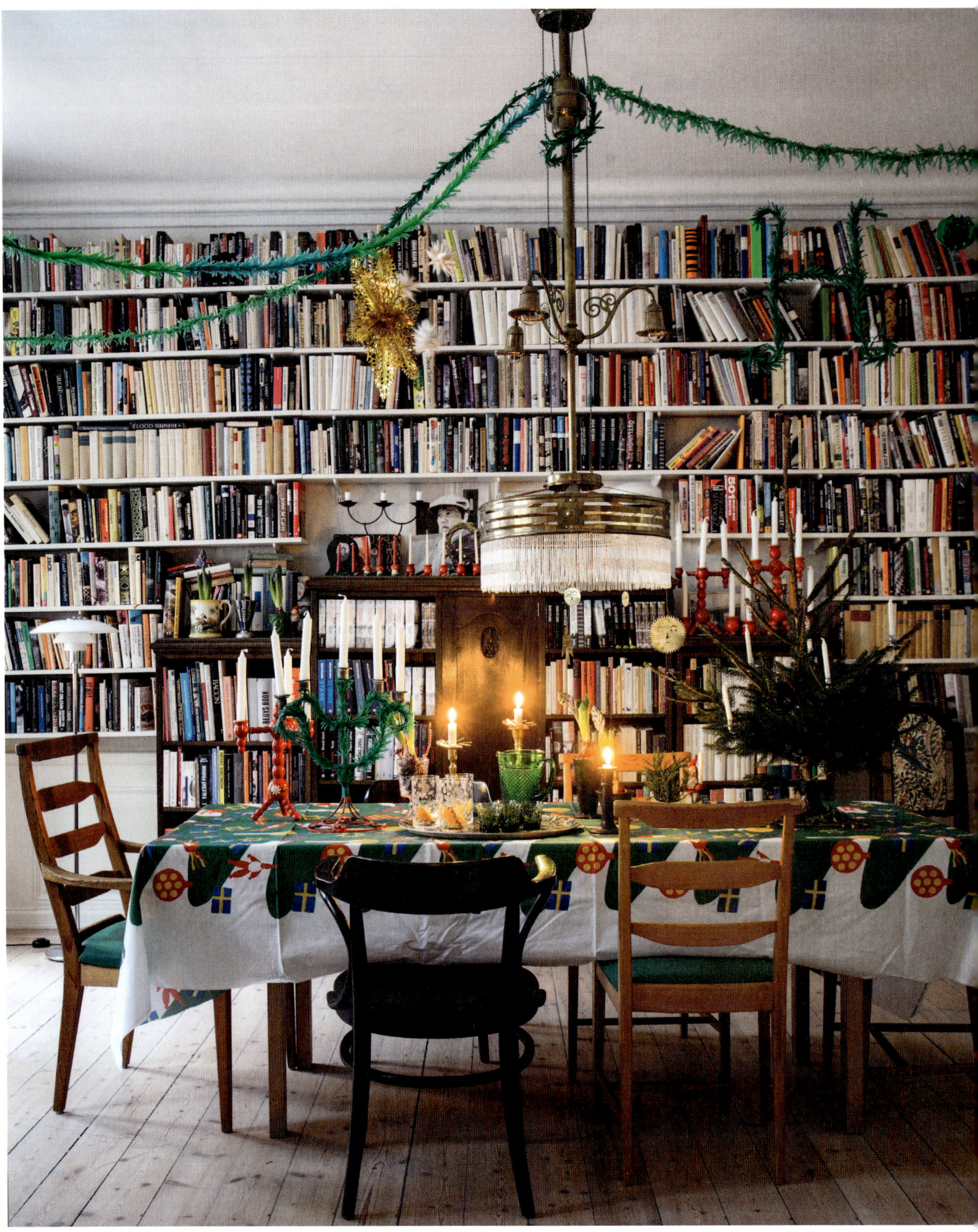

FEATURE

COLORFUL CHRISTMAS IN SWEDEN

Lotta's Holiday Magic

Lotta Kühlhorn, a graphic designer, illustrator, pattern designer, and author has lived in her charming 18th-century apartment in Södermalm, Stockholm, with her husband, author Håkan Östlundh, since the year 2000. The 1,227-square-foot (114-square-meter) home features four rooms and a kitchen, providing a cozy retreat now that their three children have moved out.

Lotta has a deep attachment to Christmas, describing it as "magical" and almost believing in Santa Claus. Her childhood celebrations, rich with fairy tales, advent calendars, and Viktor Rydberg's poem "Tomten," significantly shaped her holiday spirit. "I become full of energy before Christmas, but after Christmas Day, I finally collapse," she admits, fascinated by how much can be accomplished during the season. "I think it wouldn't feel like Christmas otherwise, but it usually turns out well."

Traditions play a significant role in their festivities. On Christmas Eve, the family hangs stockings by their beds and sneaks around to fill one another's stockings. The Christmas tree is decorated a few days prior, a time-consuming task, as Lotta has collected many ornaments over the years. This year, she plans to finish decorating by December 22nd, allowing for a relaxing day on the 23rd filled with Christmas drinks and holiday movies.

Christmas Eve morning starts with breakfast, followed by the arrival of her children at one o'clock. Together they eat rice pudding, complete with a hidden almond—a symbol of luck. Some family members wrap gifts while others rest before having a gathering with about 12 relatives for afternoon tea and the traditional Disney special on TV.

As evening arrives, Lotta lays out their holiday dishes, and once the grandchildren are present, it's time to hand out gifts. "If it snows, we try to go outside to play in the snow with the kids," she shares, capturing the joy and warmth of the season.

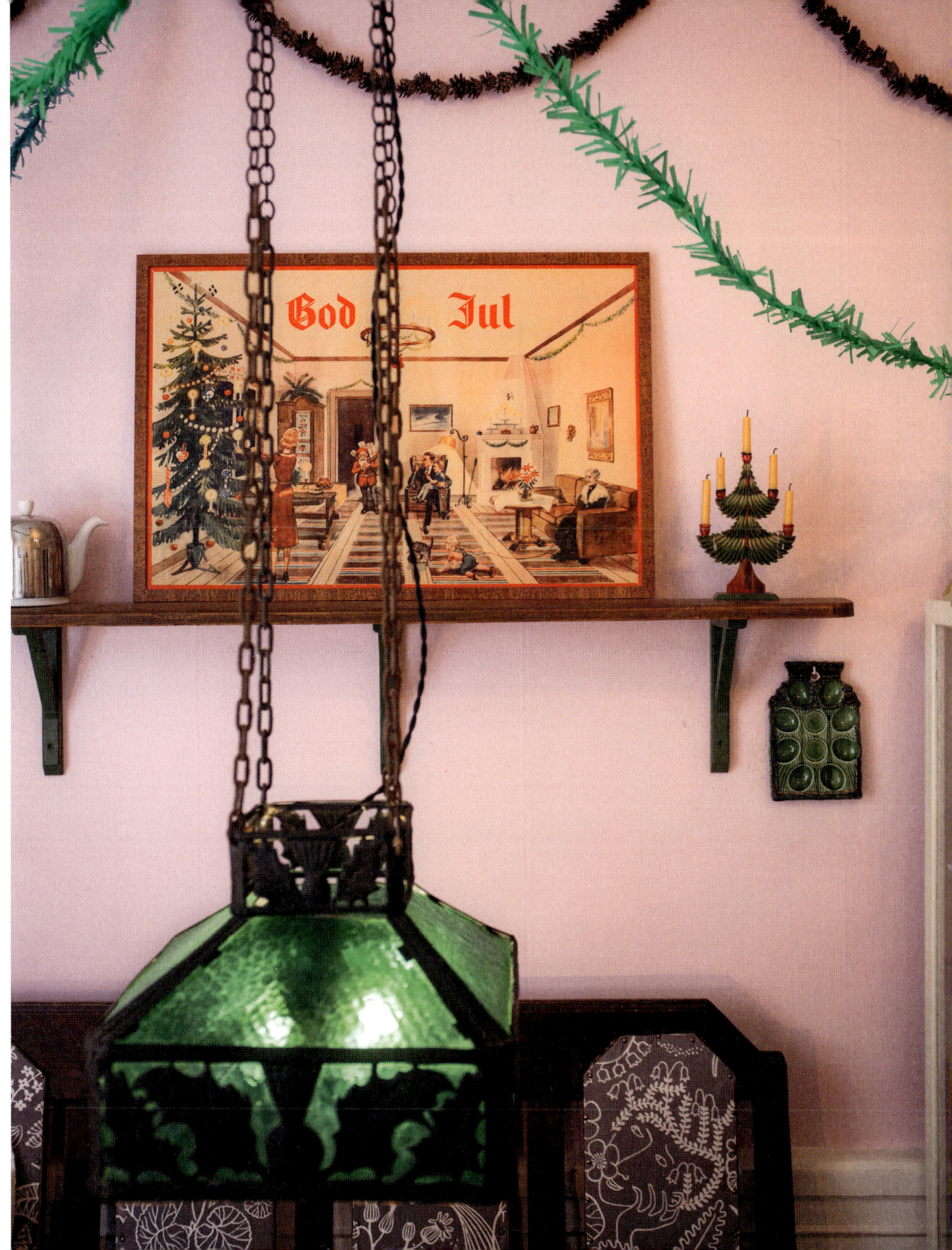
God Jul

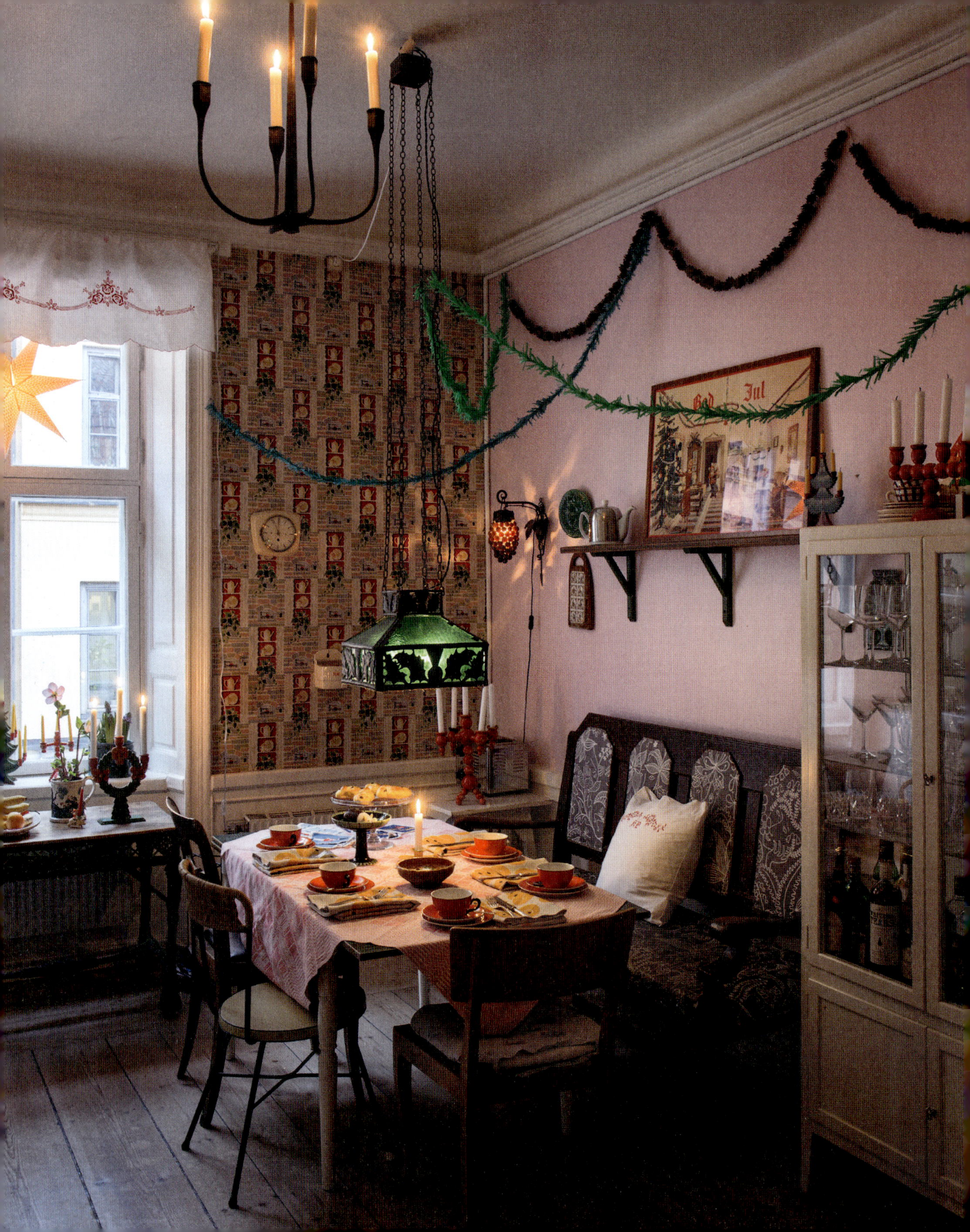
Jul

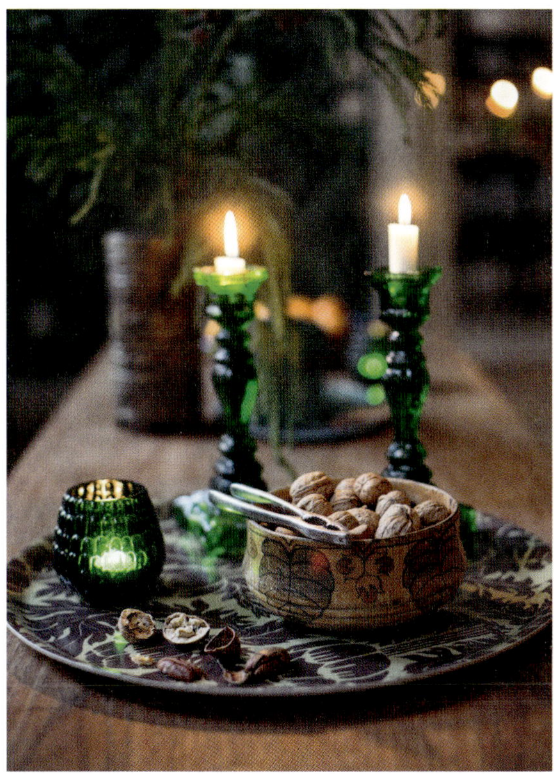

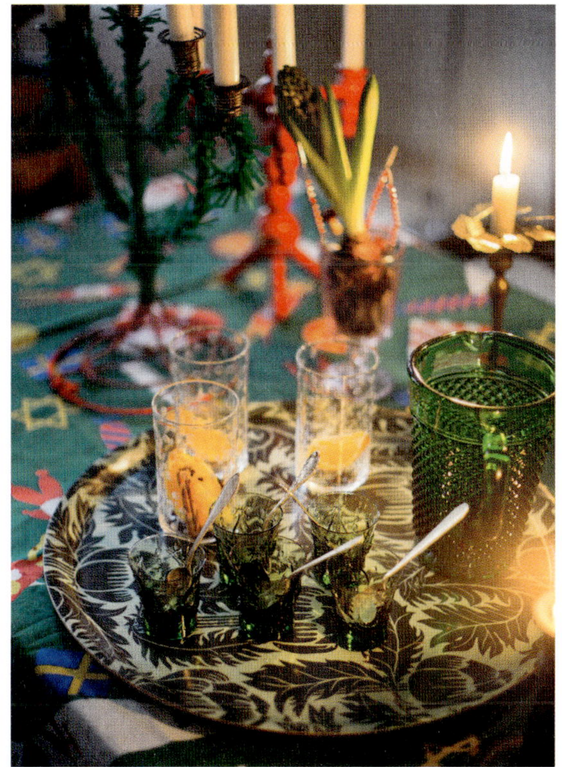

LOTTA'S CHRISTMAS MUST-HAVES

- ◊ Homemade decorations
- ◊ Bright-blue pine cone candles
- ◊ Rhymes on all the Christmas gifts
- ◊ All linens should be ironed, and the laundry basket empty
- ◊ There should be special jars of assorted candies in the cabinet
- ◊ Candles in old cookie jars
- ◊ A wooden butter dish
- ◊ Grandmother's bread and her friend's special cheese
- ◊ Eight boxes of decorations of which most are used
- ◊ Christmas shopping with a friend, preferably visiting Skansen, the outdoor museum in Stockholm, or the Museum of Nordic History

Lotta's family is very interested in cooking, and it usually shows, with plenty of vegetarian dishes, all homemade. The table setting is also important, and may vary from year to year but lots of time is spent on it.

As for flowers, "I like typical Christmas flowers but often I prefer the ones planted in pots. I don't really have time to arrange fresh-cut flowers—except for amaryllis. By all beds I want hyacinths. And I also buy twigs of various unusual conifers. One year I had seven Christmas trees," Lotta laughs.

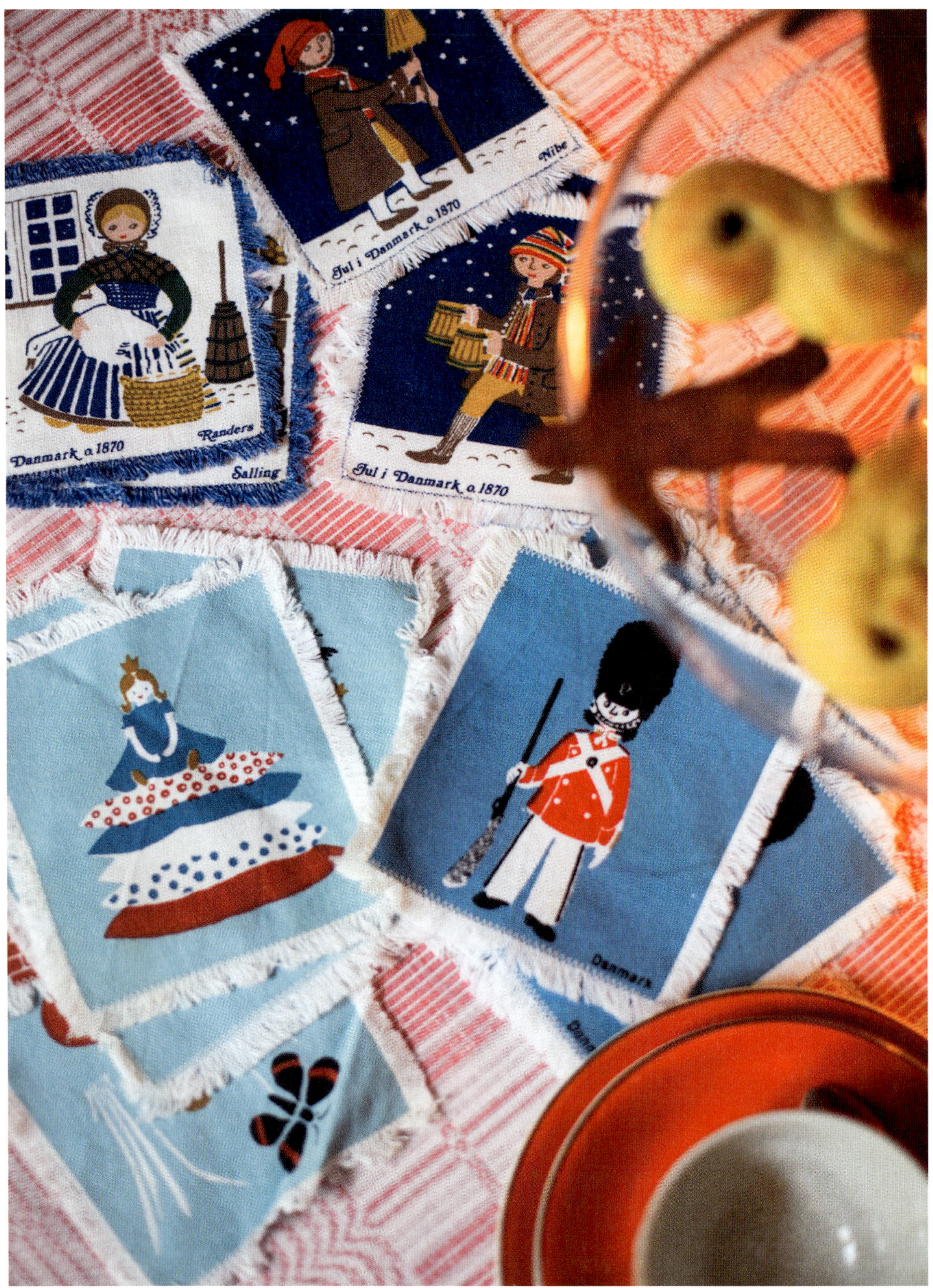
Nibe
Randers
Salling
Danmark

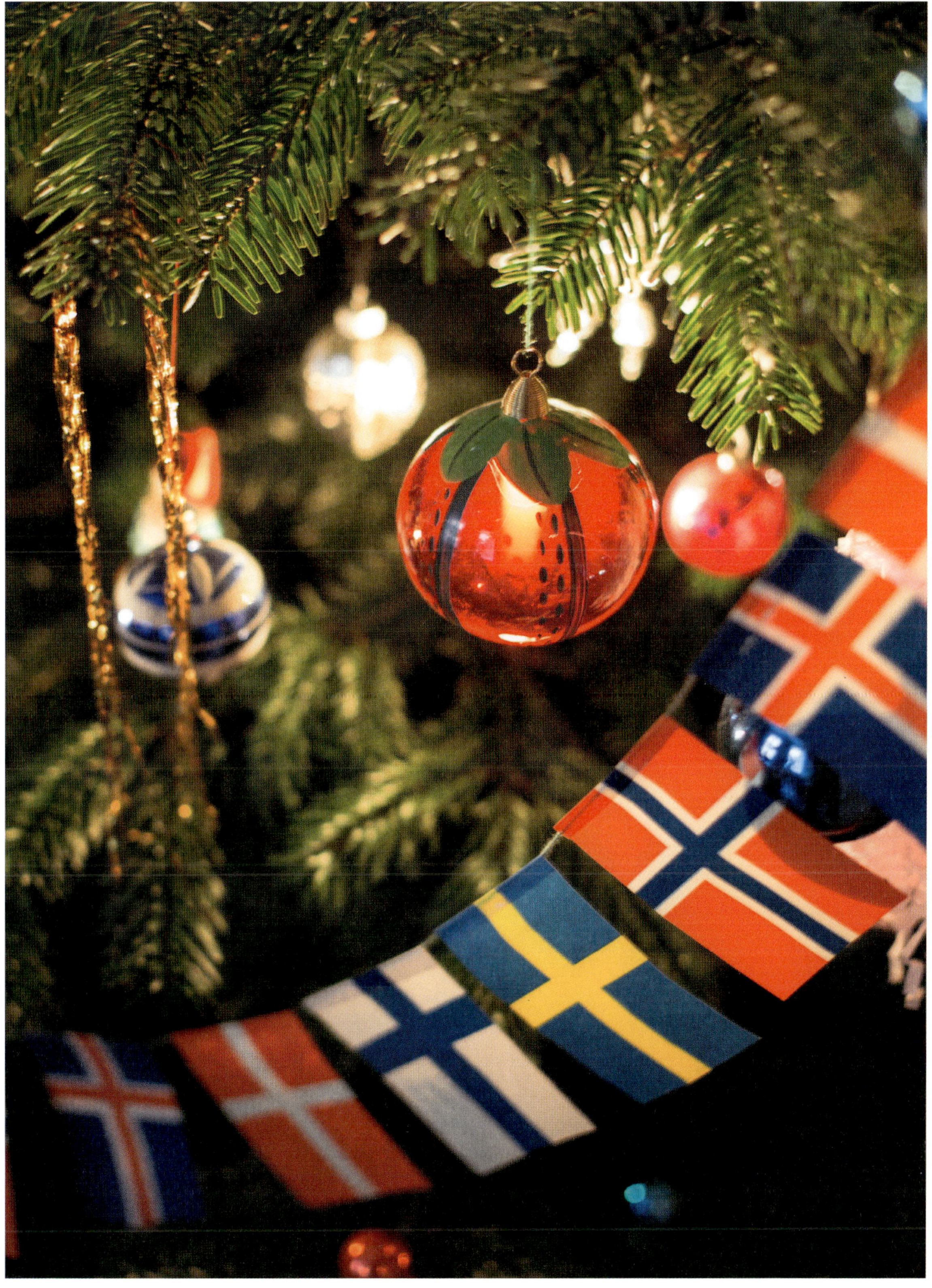

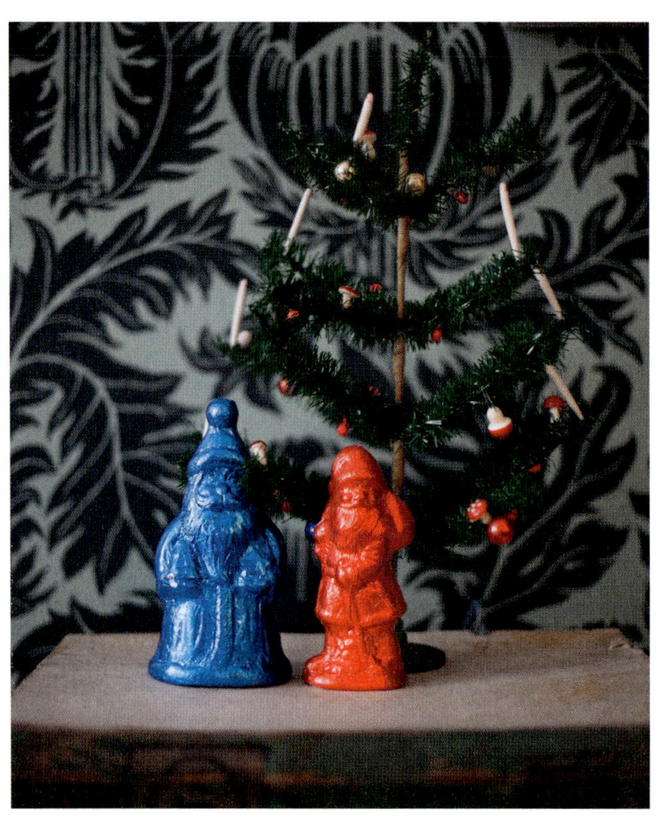

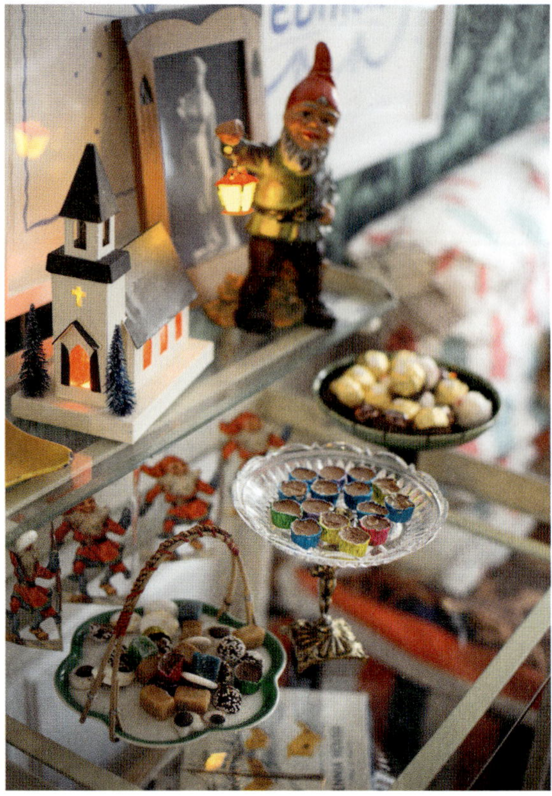

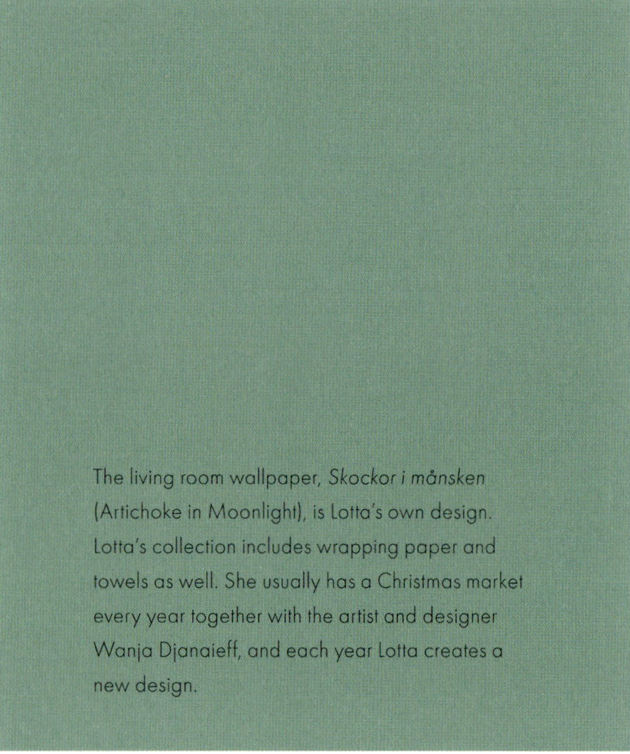

The living room wallpaper, *Skockor i månsken* (Artichoke in Moonlight), is Lotta's own design. Lotta's collection includes wrapping paper and towels as well. She usually has a Christmas market every year together with the artist and designer Wanja Djanaieff, and each year Lotta creates a new design.

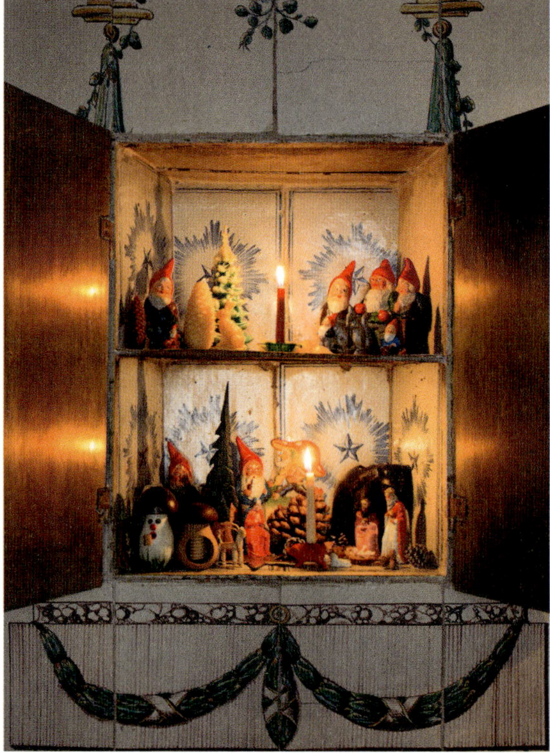

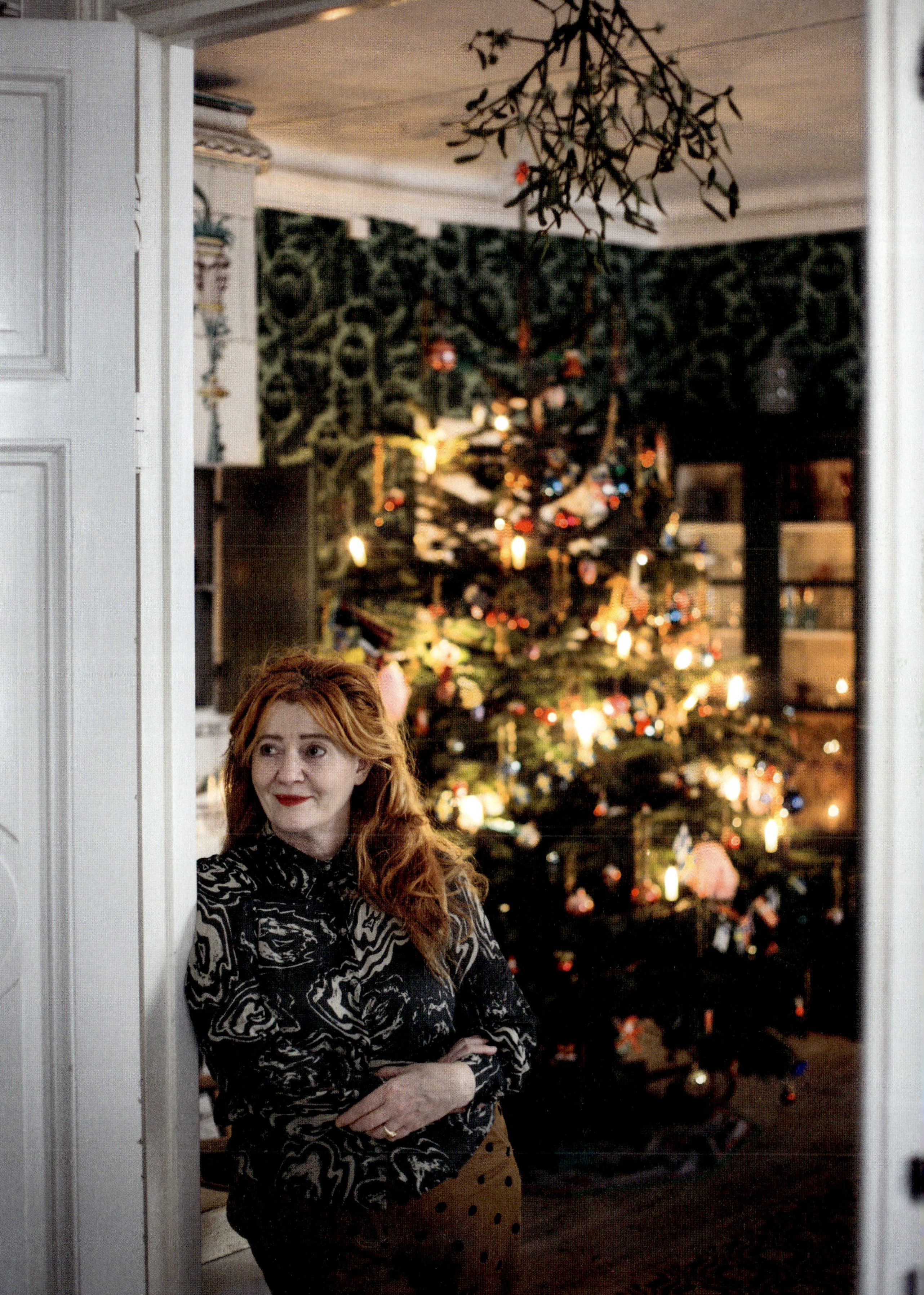

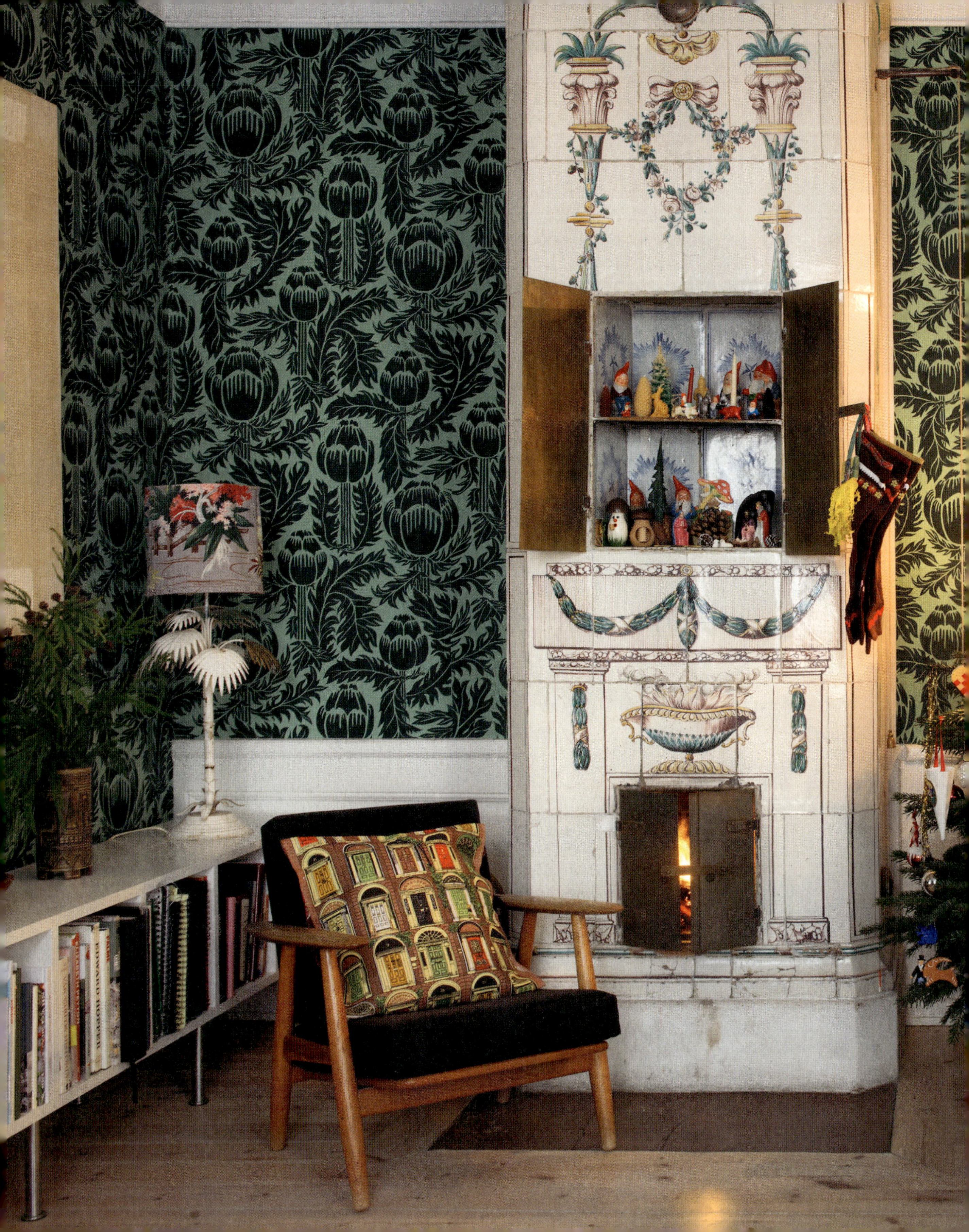
EDWARD HOPPER

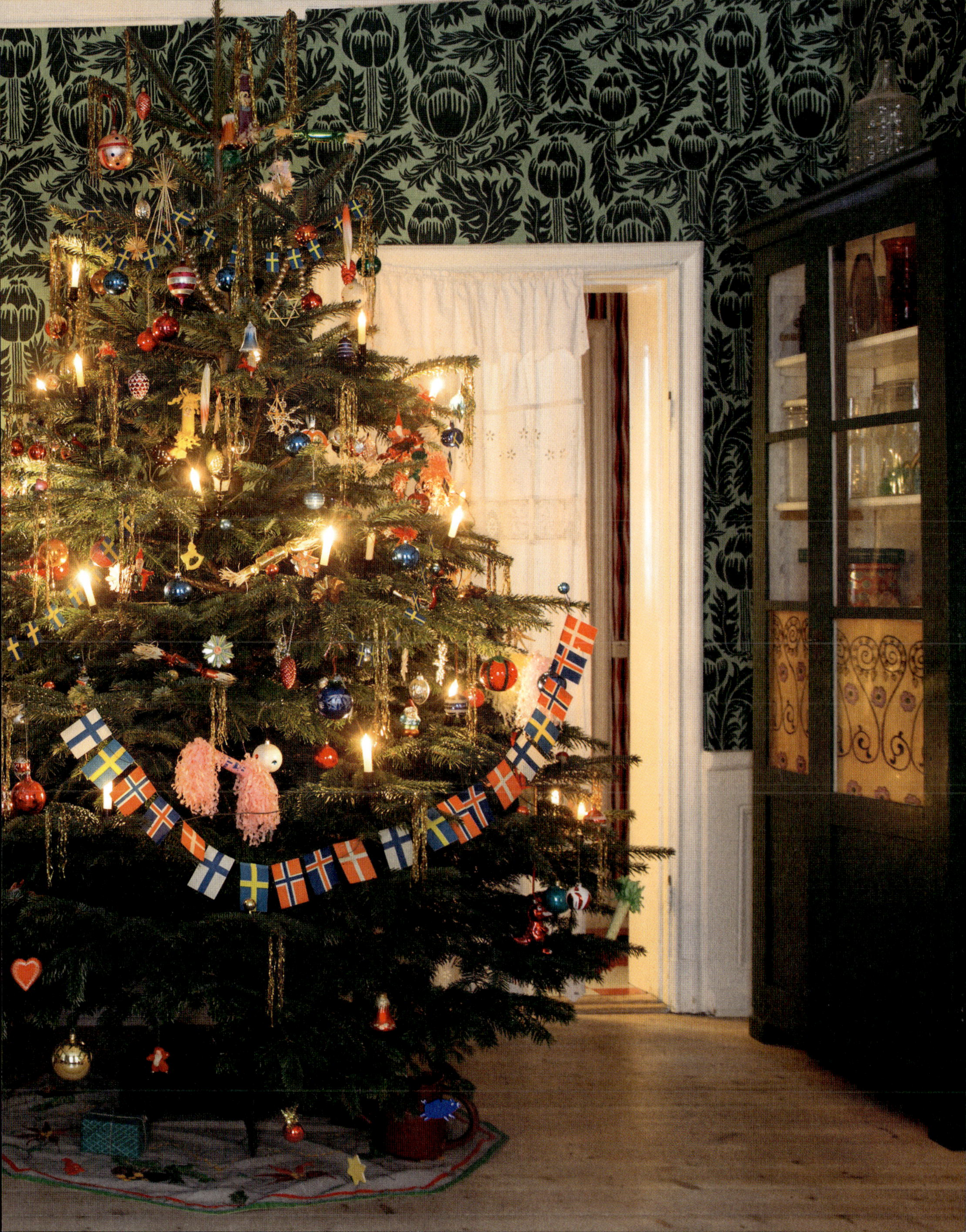

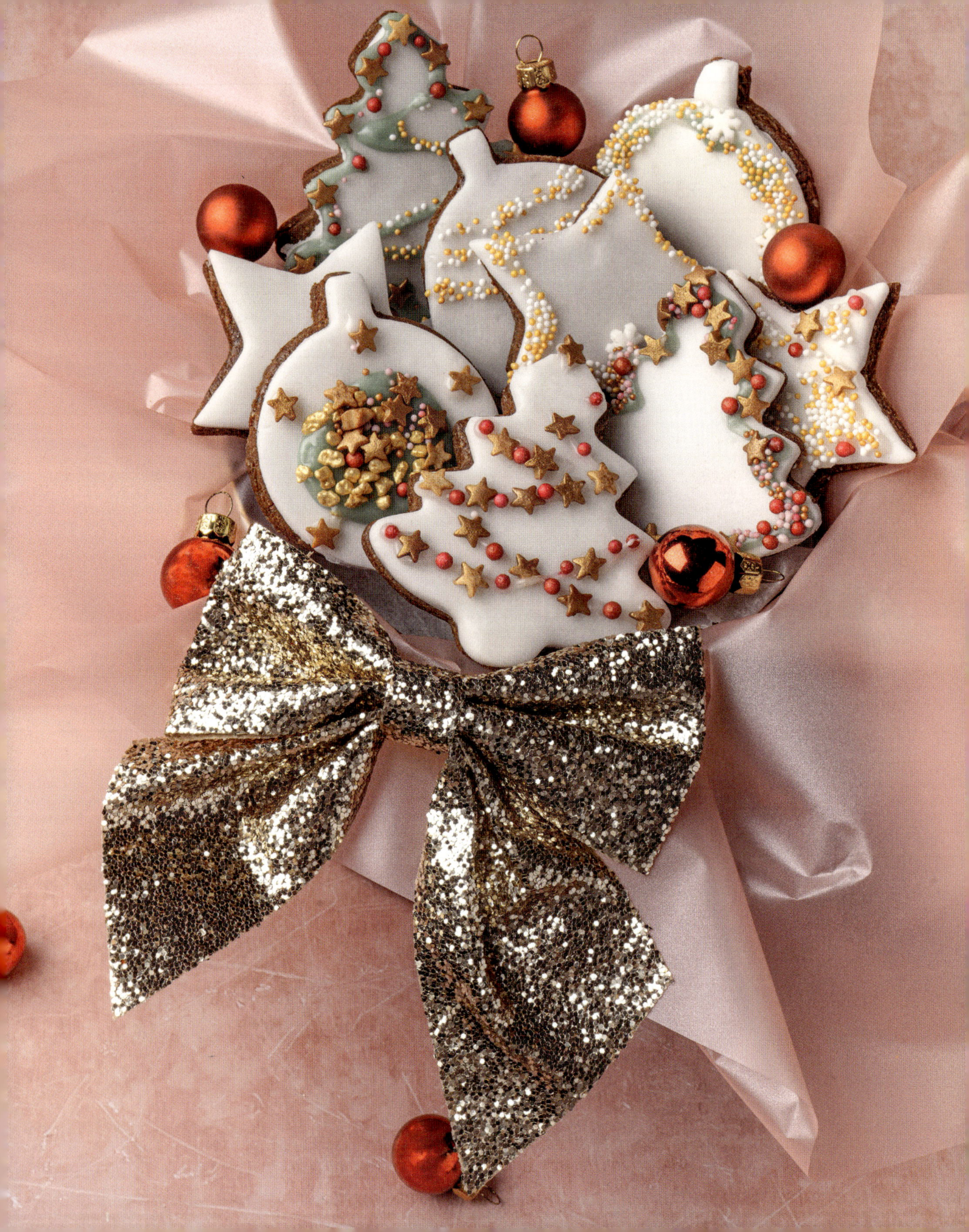

Foodie Christmas

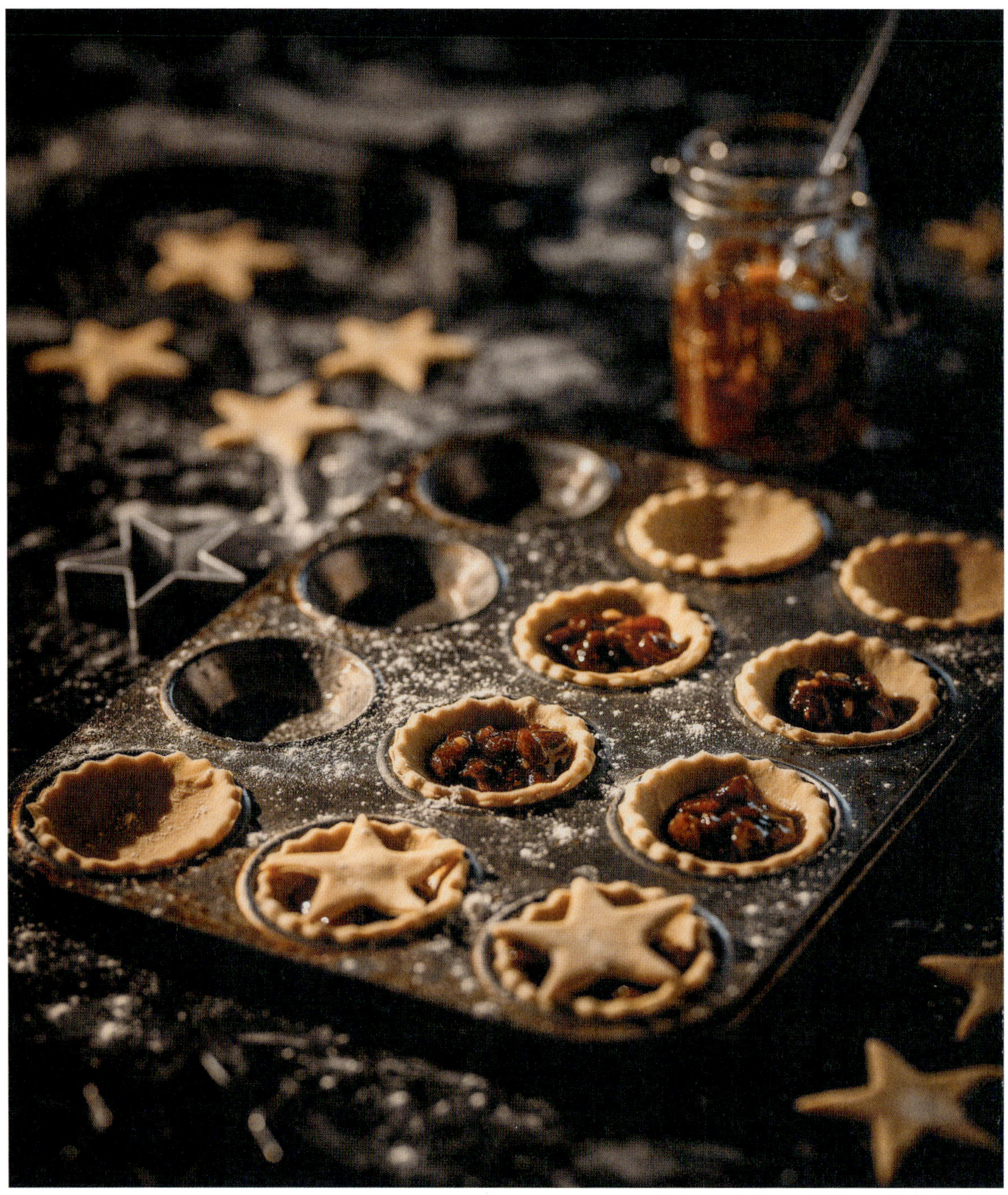

Mince pie is a beloved British pastry featuring a crust made of shortcrust or puff pastry, filled with a rich mixture of dried fruits, nuts, and spices. In contrast, Spanish-speaking countries celebrate Christmas with buñuelos, which are deep-fried pastries or balls.

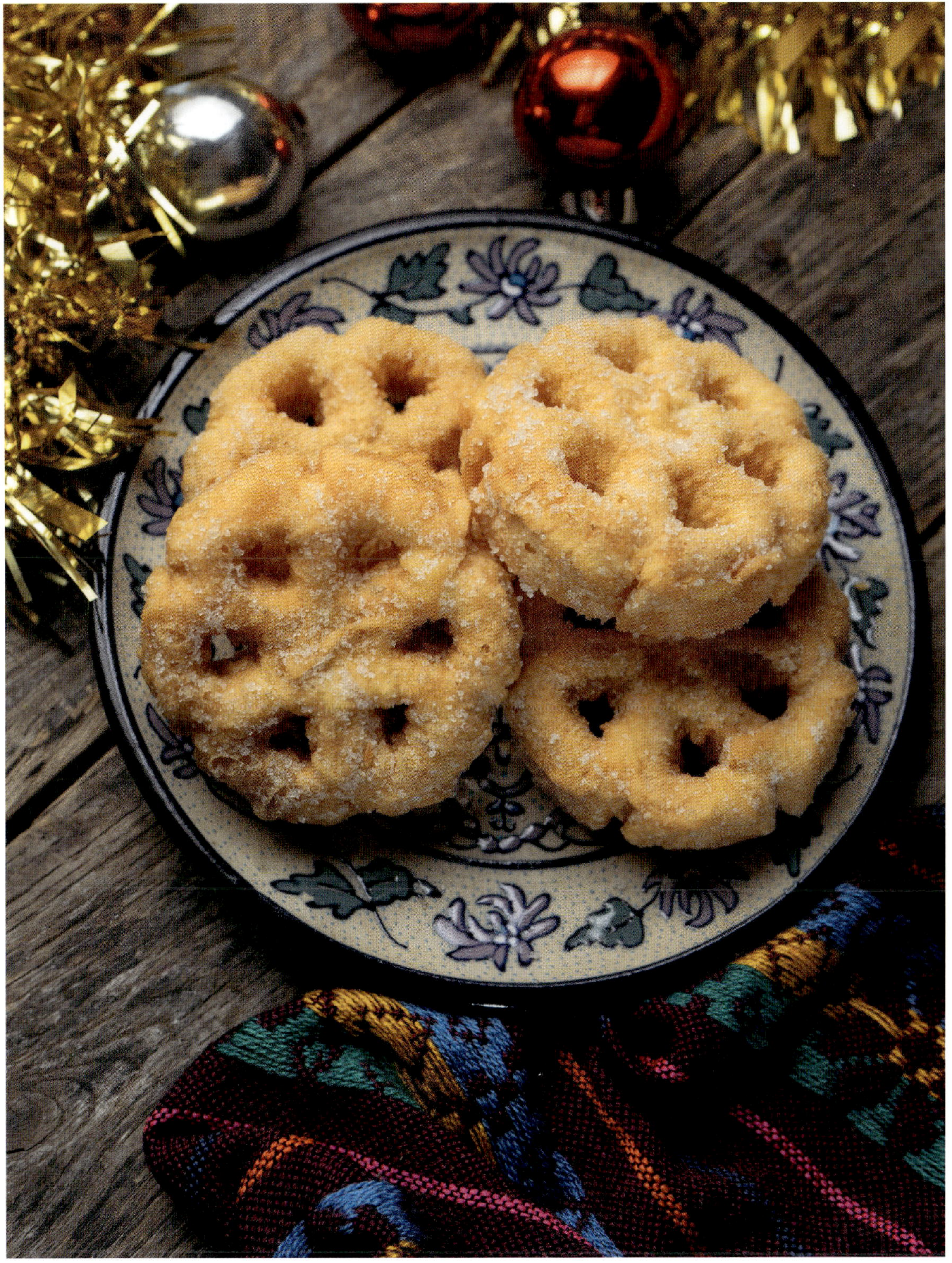

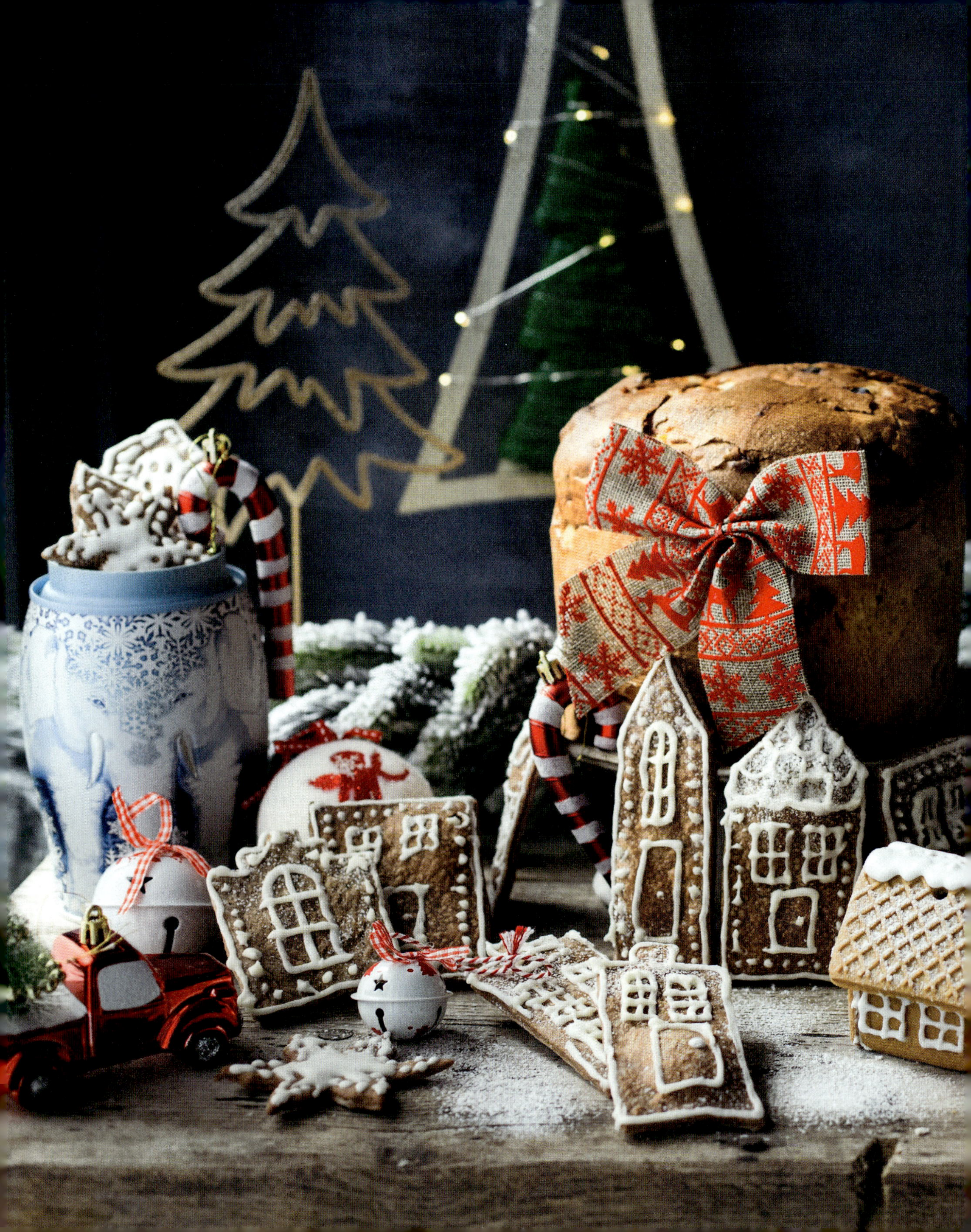

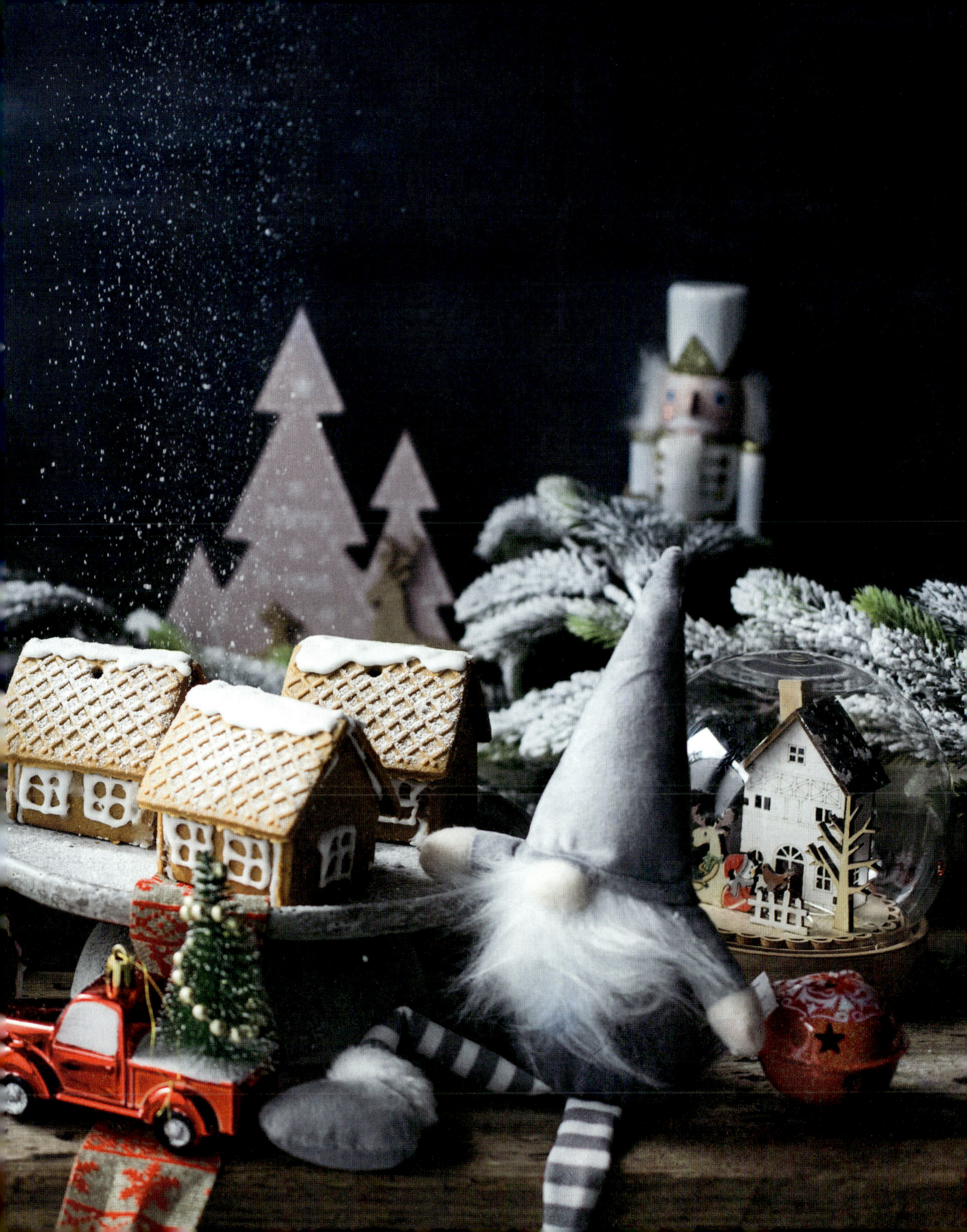

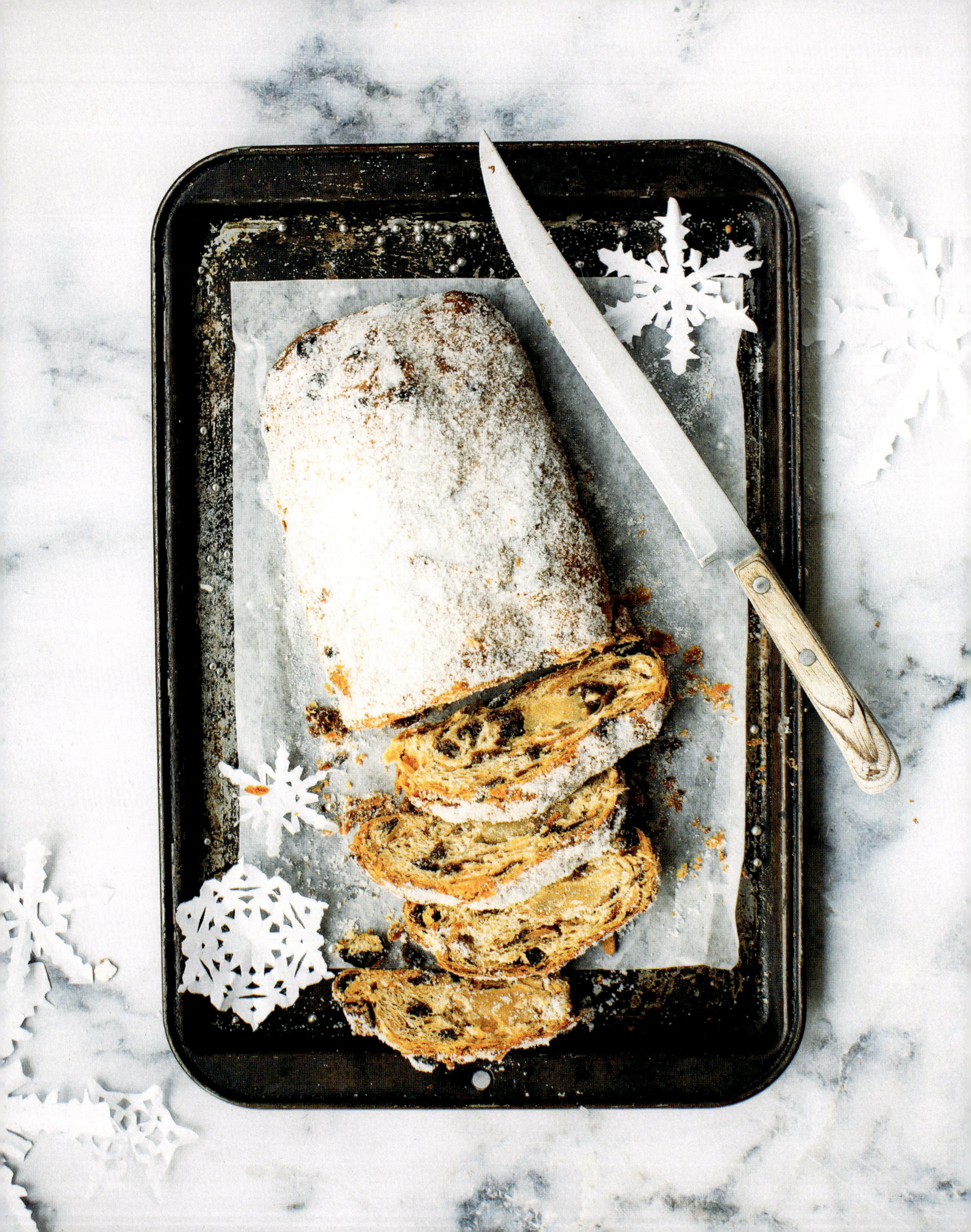

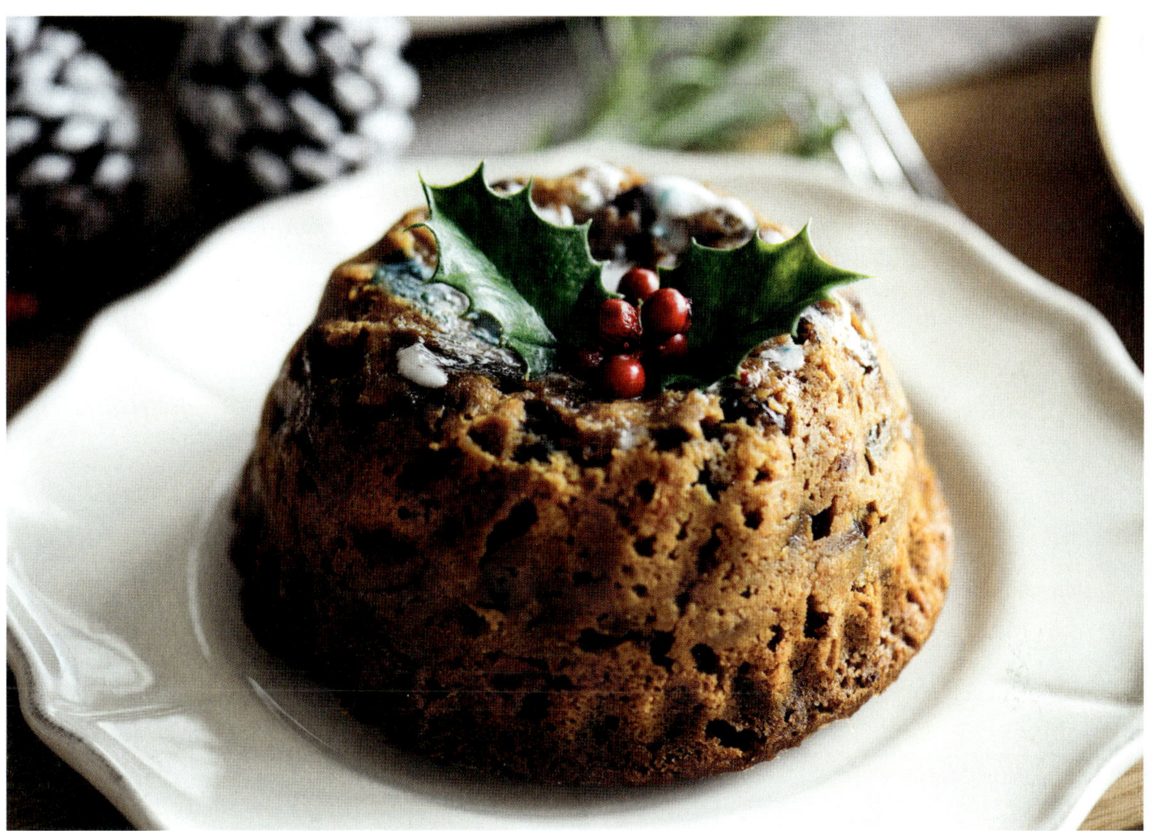

Classic Christmas treats include gingerbread, stollen, and British Christmas pudding, all renowned festive desserts. Stollen, a dense yeast cake infused with almonds, marzipan, and dried or candied fruit, can be traced back to the Middle Ages. Notably, only stollen made in the Dresden region following strict regulations can use the name "Dresdner Stollen." Christmas pudding also dates back to medieval times, originally serving as a beef dish. Today, it typically combines beef suet, nuts, spices, dried fruit, and brandy (or sherry), with the solid pudding traditionally enjoyed on Christmas Day.

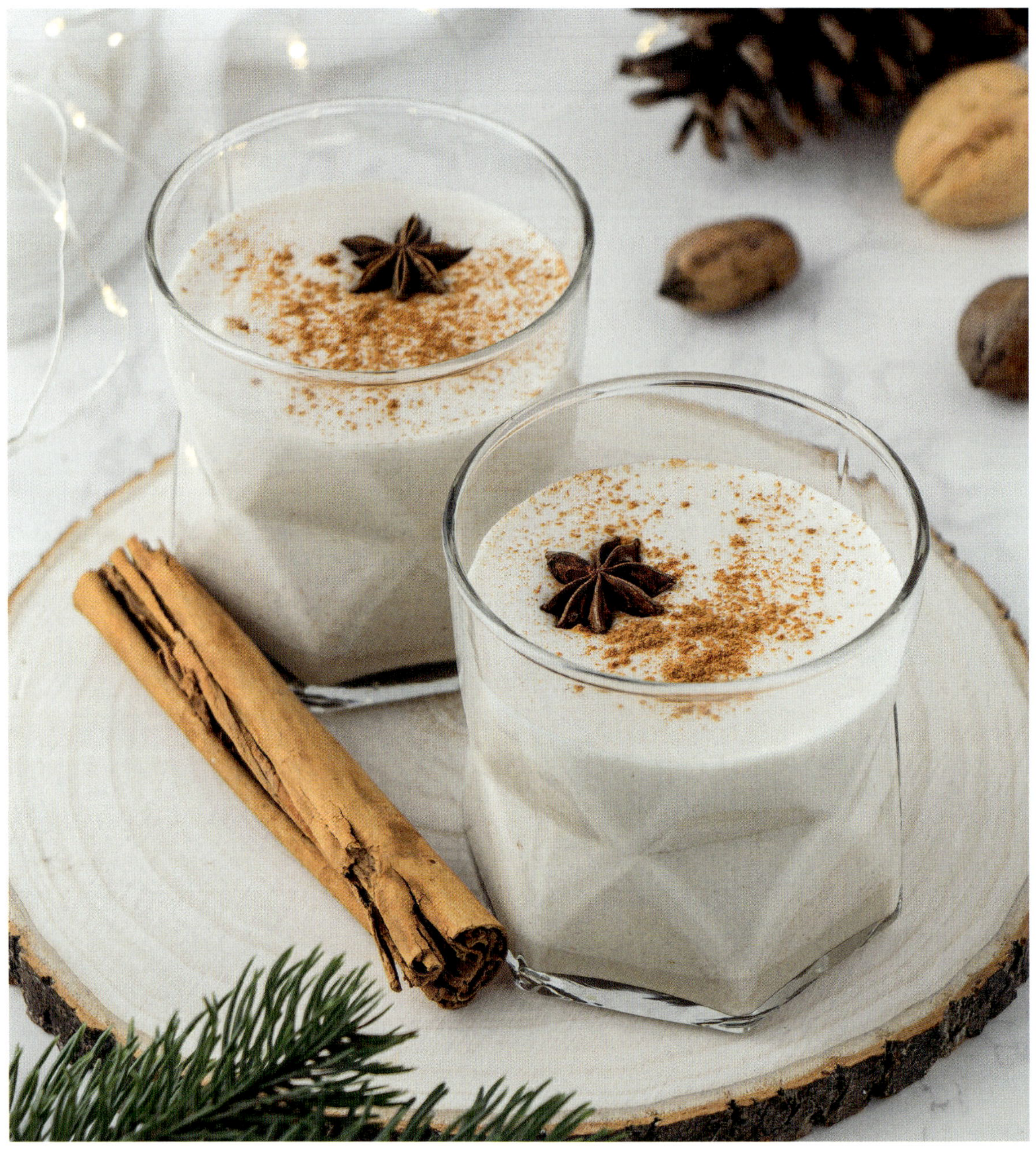

Eggnog, coquito, and hot chocolate are among the most cherished holiday beverages. While eggnog originated in the UK, it has become particularly popular in the USA and Canada, where it is typically served chilled and often contains alcohol. Coquito is a traditional Puerto Rican holiday drink made from coconut milk, sweetened condensed milk, rum, and spices. Hot chocolate, especially topped with marshmallows and a dash of cinnamon, is a festive favorite that excites not only children's hearts during Christmas time.

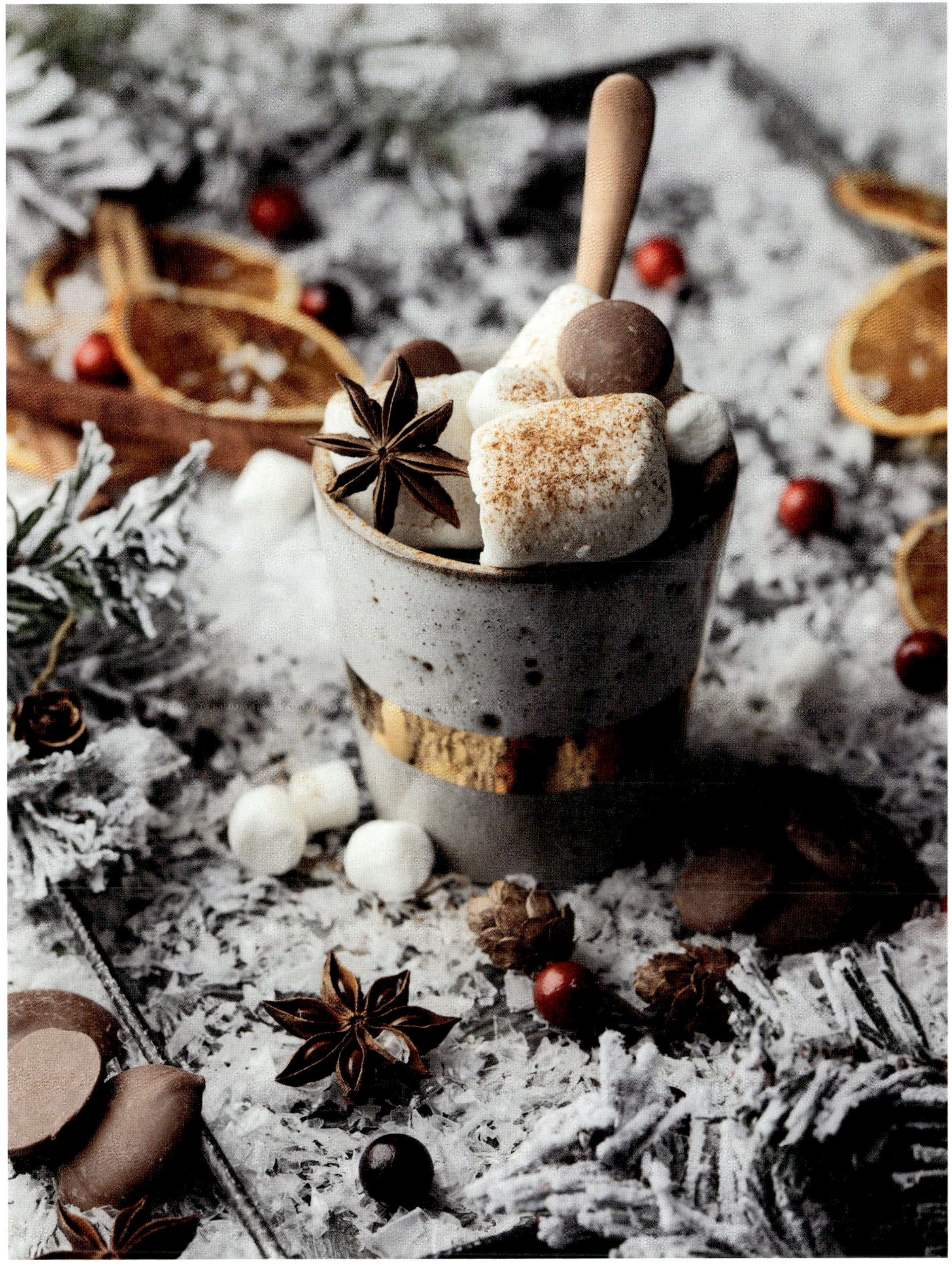

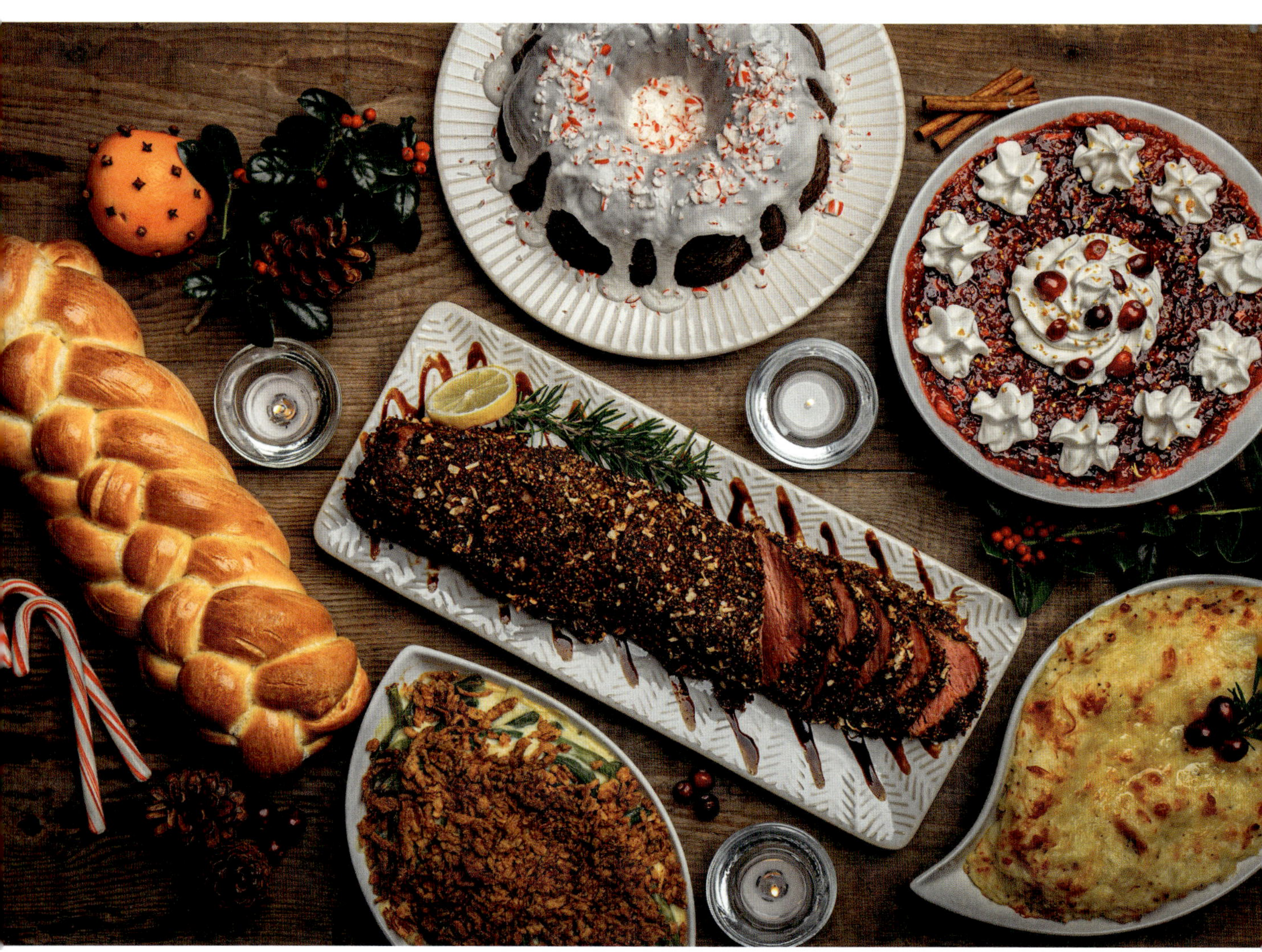

Christmas menus around the globe highlight the diverse cultural traditions of various countries. In Germany, a festive meal often includes a succulent roast or poultry paired with red cabbage and dumplings, while the classic UK Christmas dinner features stuffed poultry, Brussels sprouts, and crispy potatoes. Americans tend to enjoy roast meat with green beans and mashed potatoes. In Italy, Christmas Eve is marked by an array of fish dishes, while Mexicans celebrate with festive fare like tamales and bacalao.

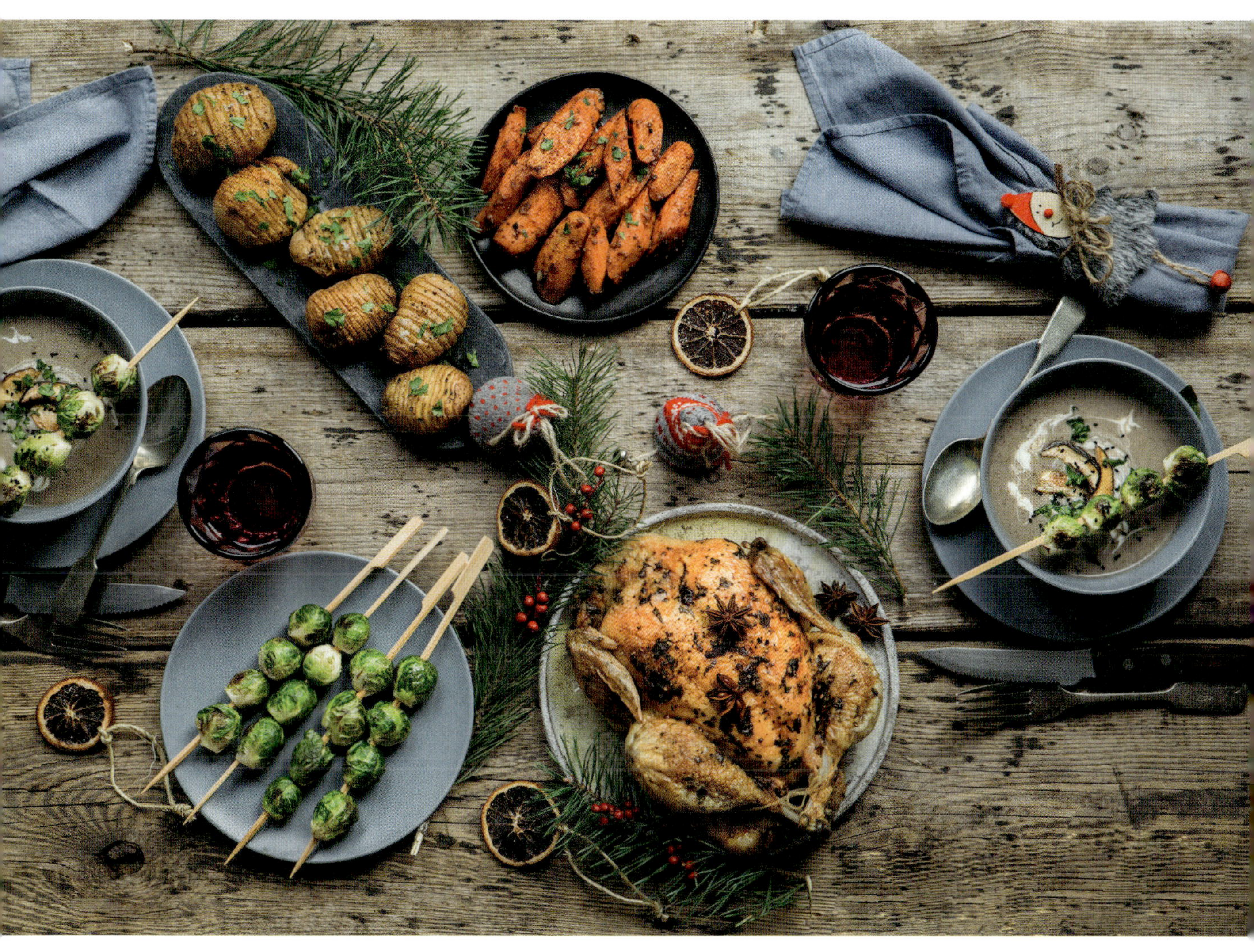

FEATURE

CHRISTMAS IN BYRON BAY

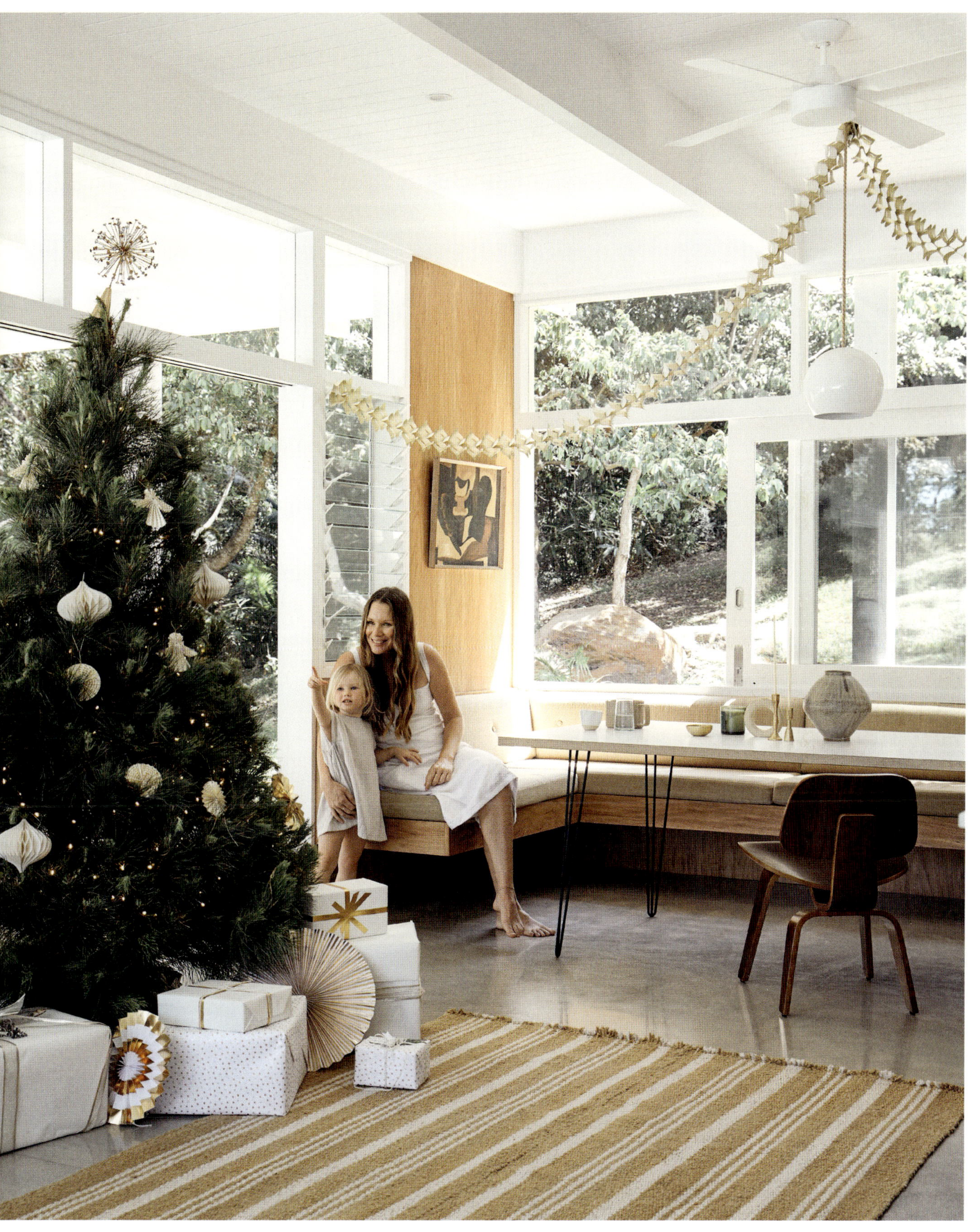

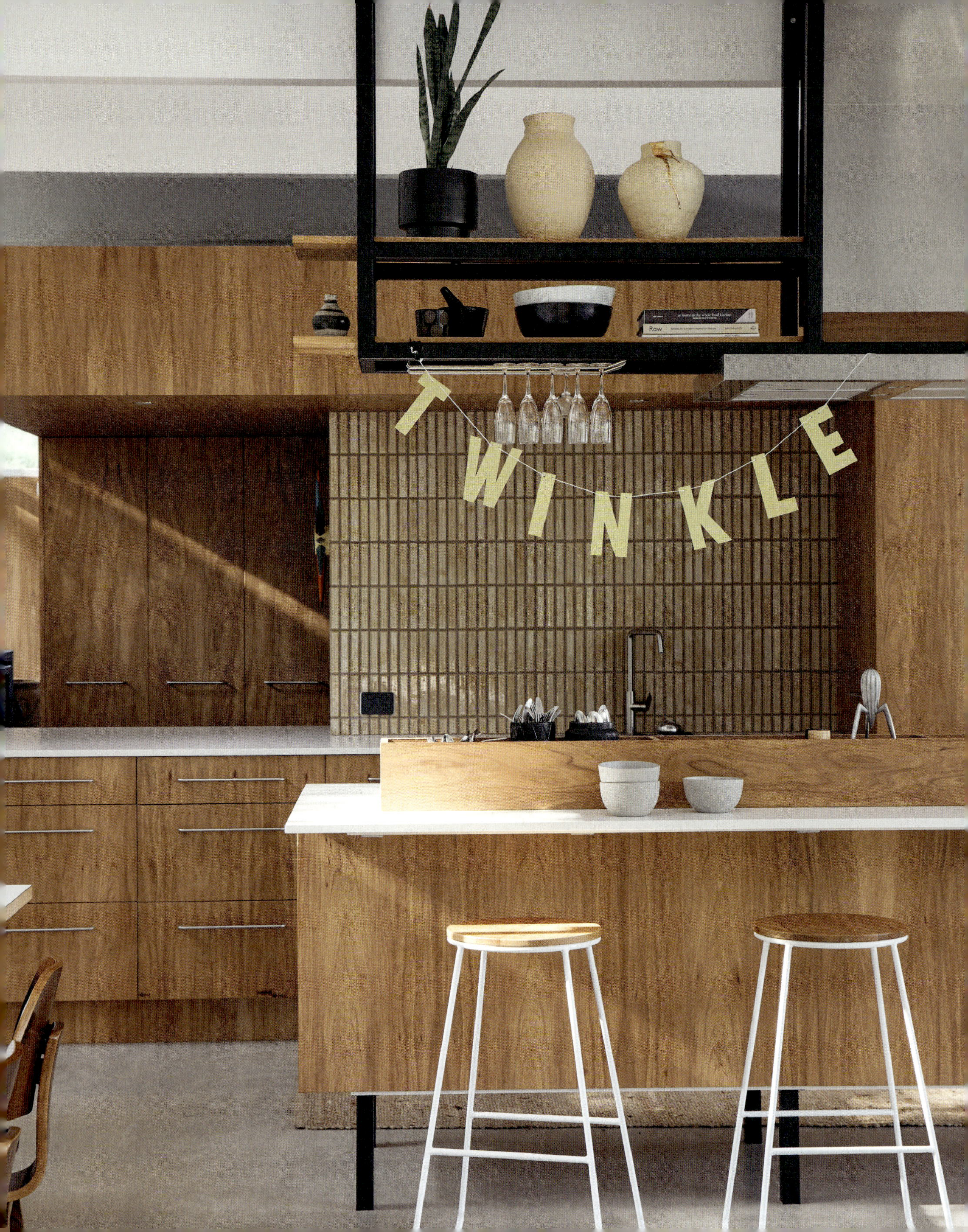
TWINKLE

Natural Festive Charm

High among the gum trees, this three-bedroom, Modernist-style house, nestled in the serene coastal bushland just south of Cape Byron, embodies tranquility and a strong connection to nature.

Megan, a former model from California, and Mike, a fashion design manager, have called this area home for 12 years. After renovating their previous house, they embarked on a new adventure in 2017 when they discovered this hidden plot surrounded by native trees. "It offers privacy and space while remaining just five minutes from town," shares Megan, highlighting their special community.

Throughout their eight-month journey living in a camper van with their three daughters, the couple maintained focus on creating a home that reflects their love for iconic Modernist architecture. "We love the fact that everything from the mid-century design era has a purpose," Megan explains. The home features organic timber, notably Australian blackwood, which adds warmth and moody texture. Sandstone rock walls and a handcrafted seat by their stonemason friend Paul Squires enhance its charm.

Their design allows sunlight to flood the rooms, seamlessly connecting indoor and outdoor spaces, which is a source of pride for Megan. "Mike managed most of the construction himself, which was a testament to our collaboration," she notes. Though there were challenges—like a pool construction mishap and storm damage—they persevered, knowing they would eventually create a space to make lasting memories in.

As they prepare for Christmas, the festive spirit is palpable. The family happily decorates their Christmas tree, and the girls create special touches for their rooms. "But Christmas for us is really just a day at the beach at Wategos with friends and family. We set up our spot on the sand and the kids open their presents, then we hang out there for hours, playing games and eating. It's low-key, relaxed and natural," Megan shares.

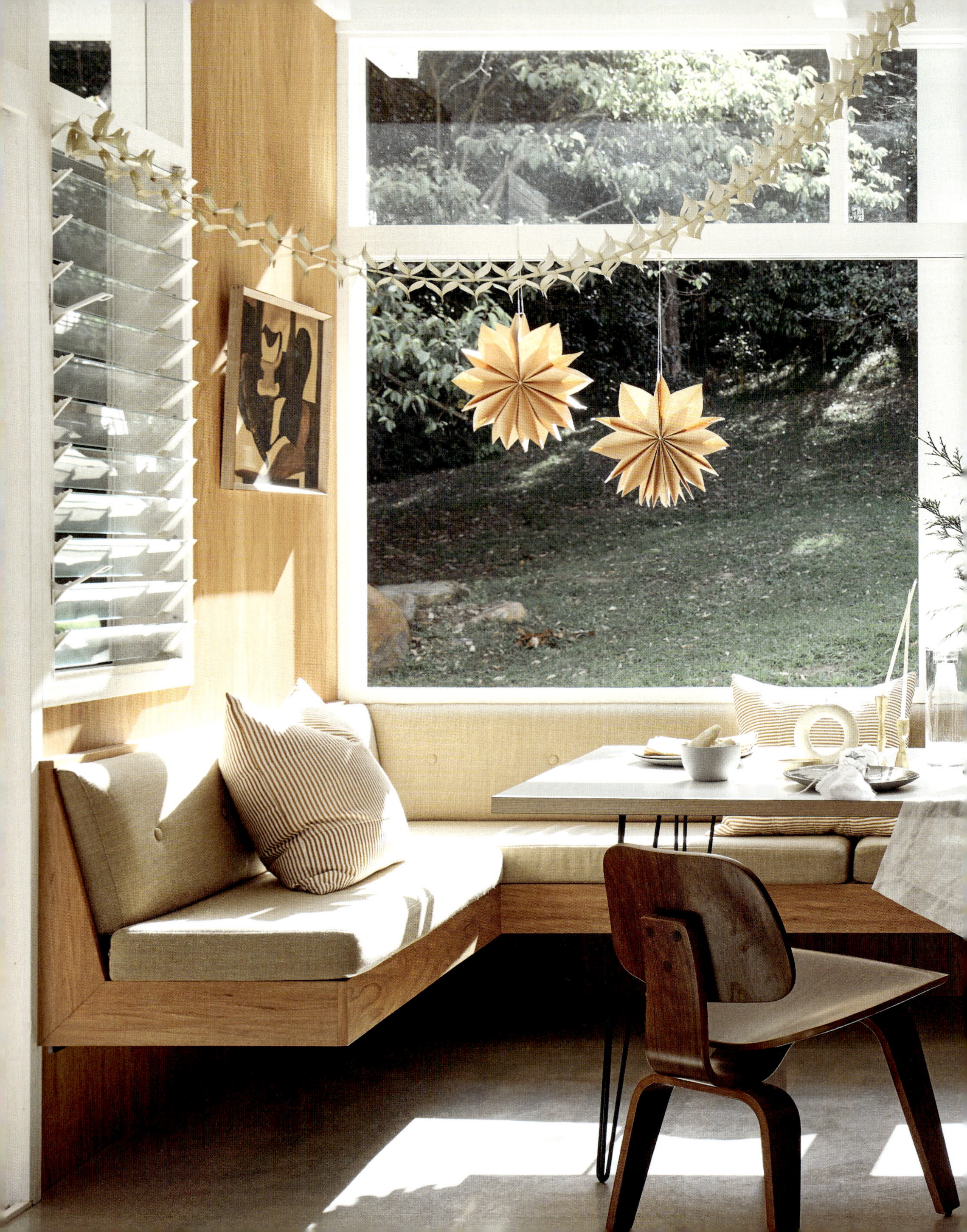

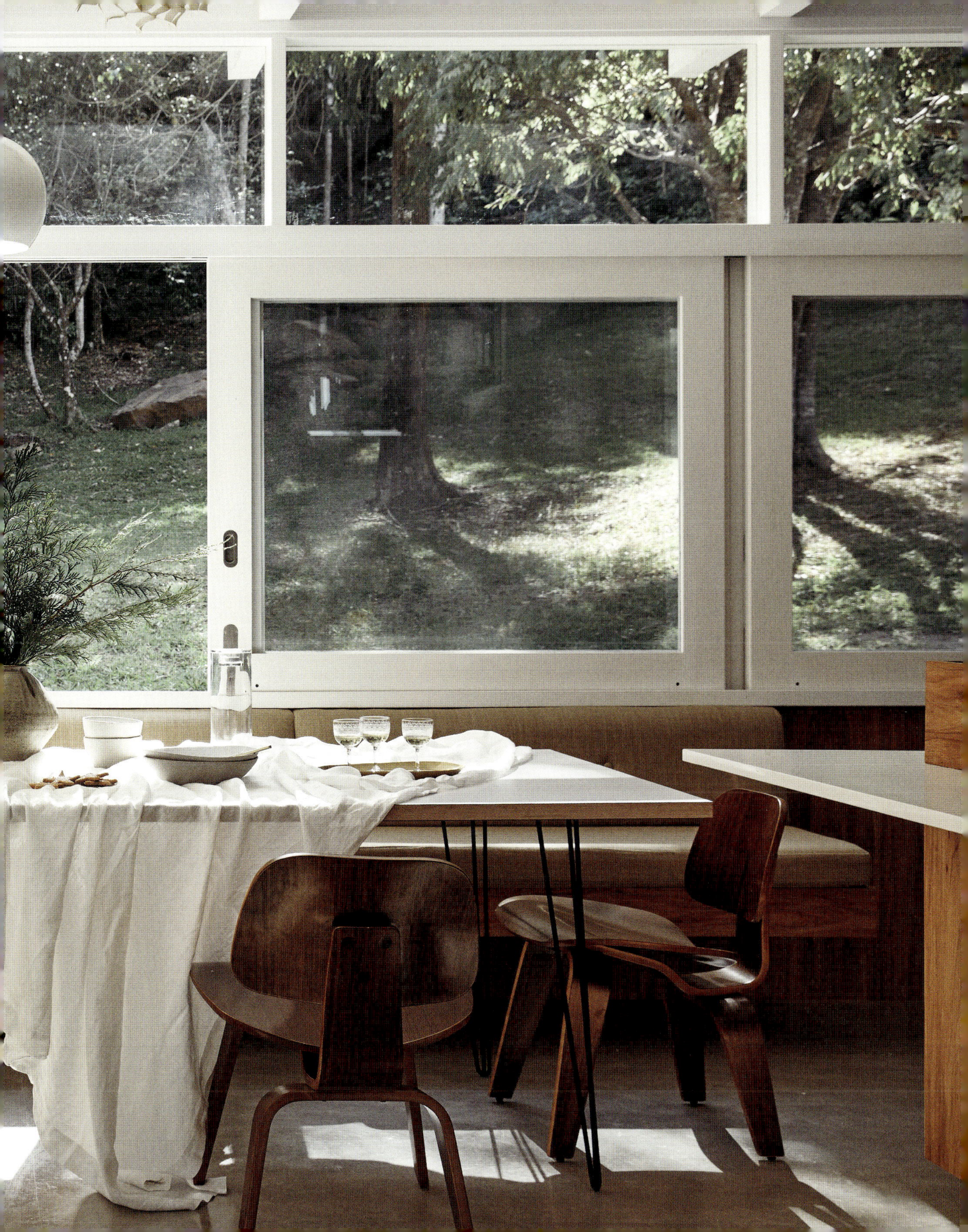

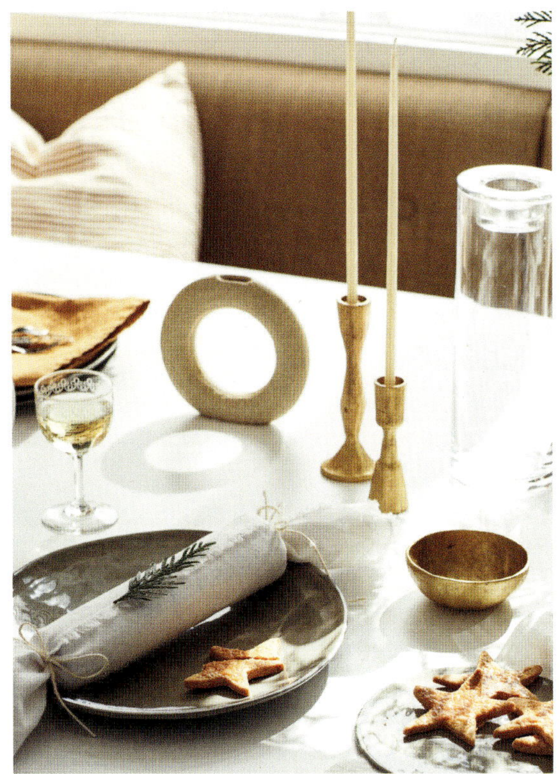

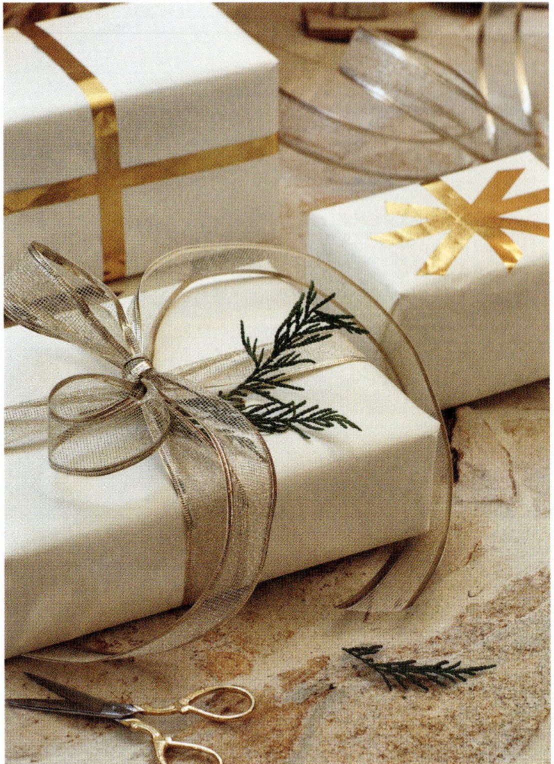

The family embraces a minimalist and natural approach to Christmas decor with charming paper stars and garlands. Gifts are adorned with twigs and golden *washi* tape. Fabric Christmas crackers provide a sustainable twist to the table. A simple golden star hanging from the bedside wall lamp adds minimalist festive charm to the bedroom (see next page).

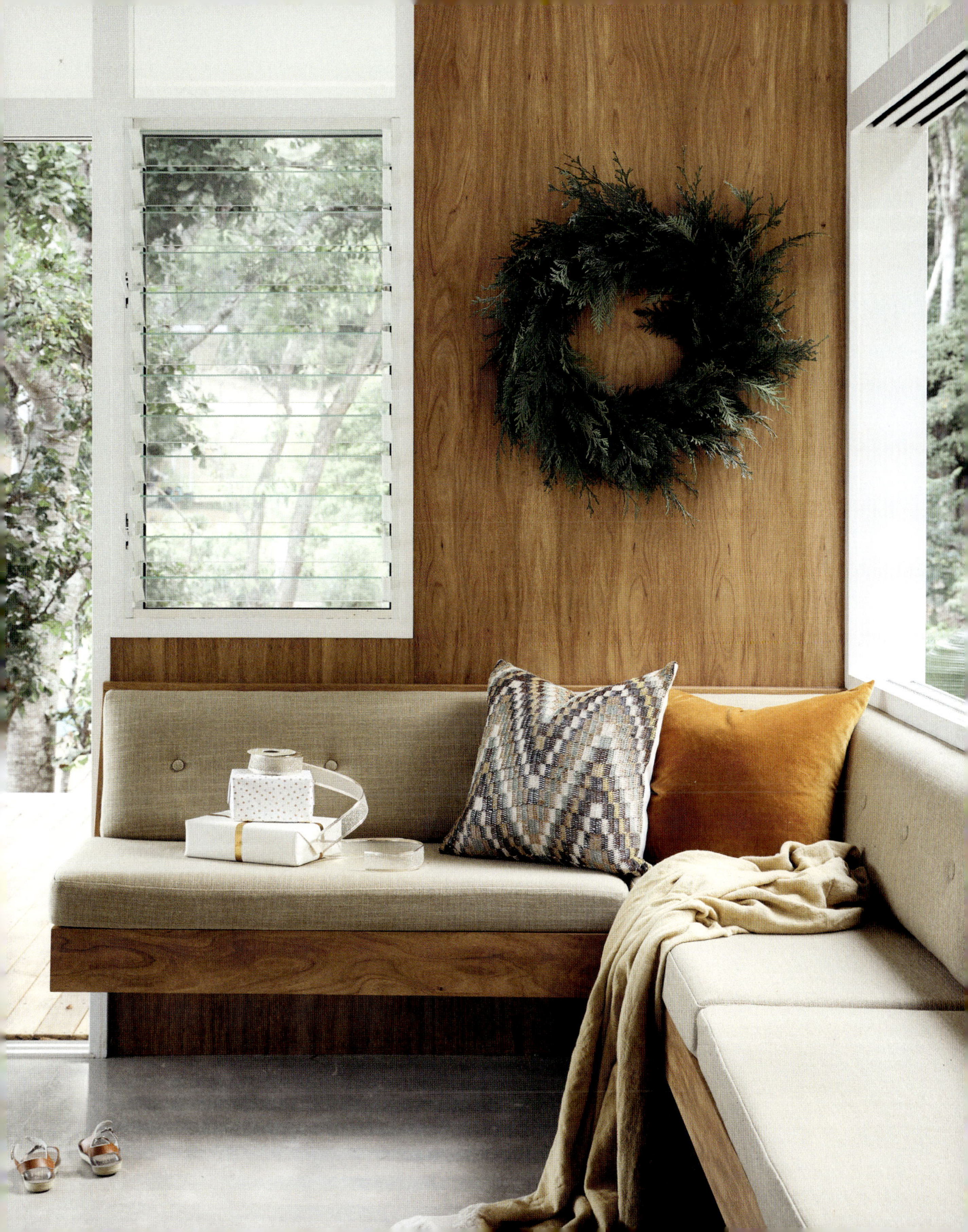

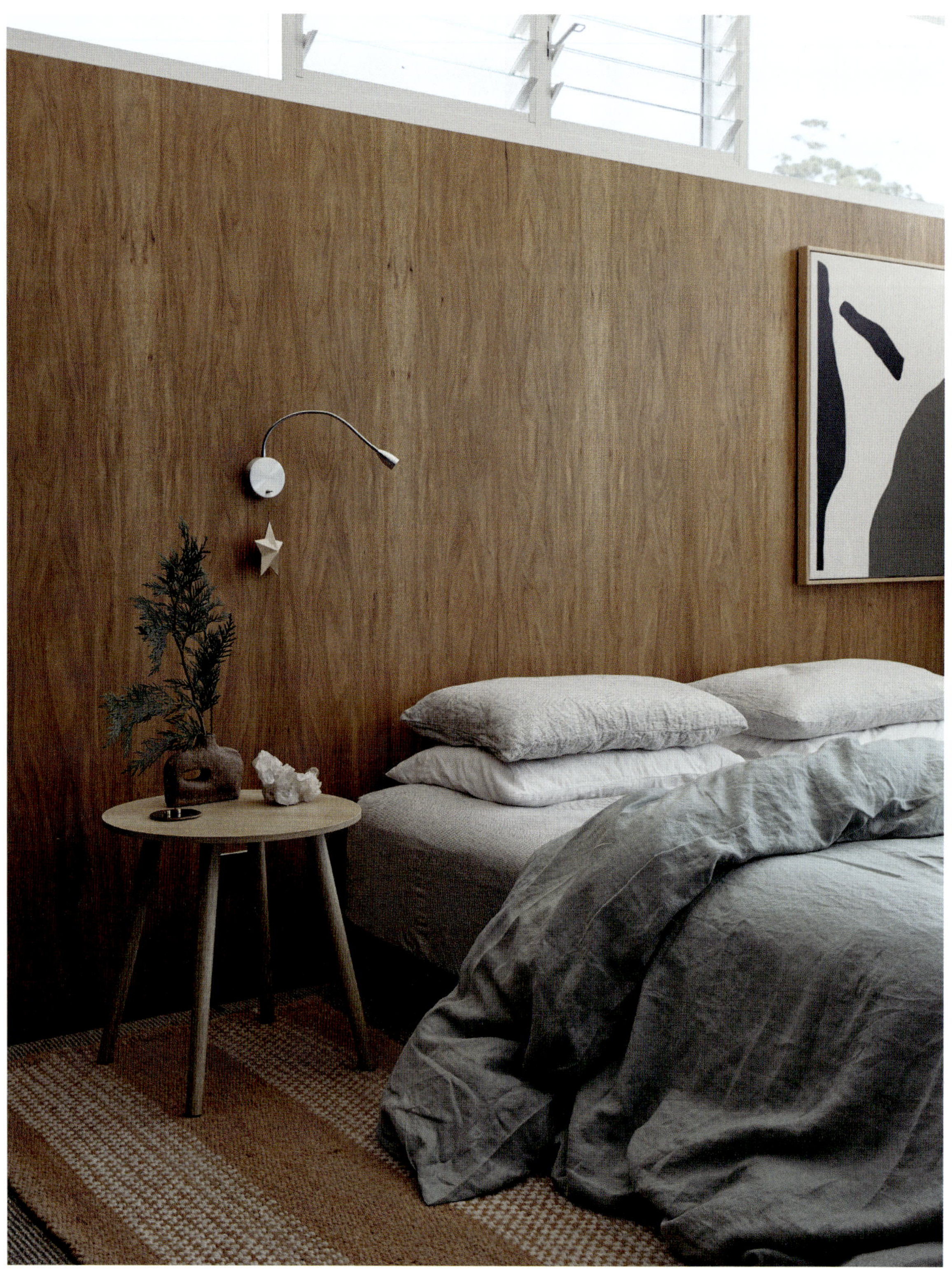

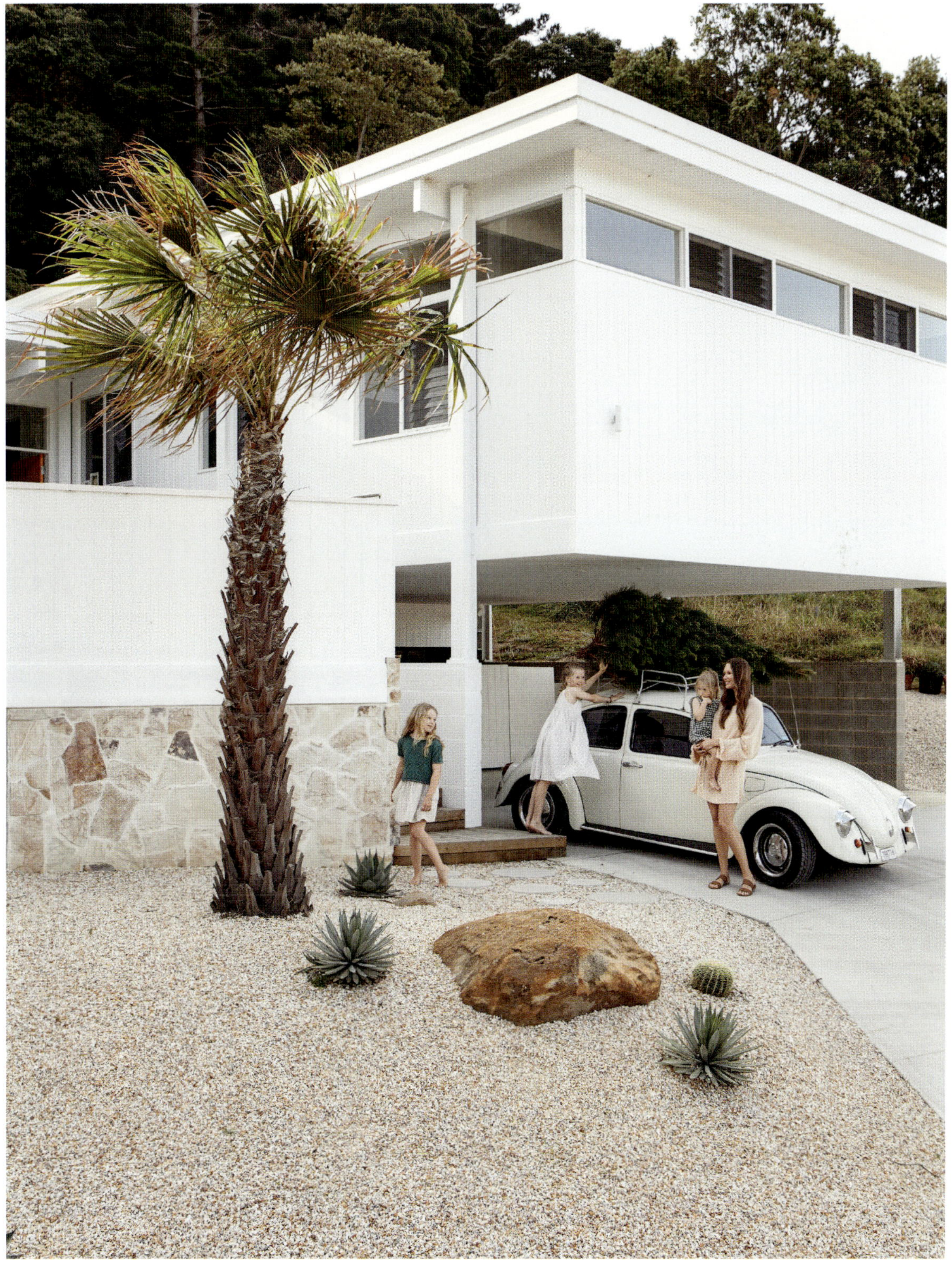

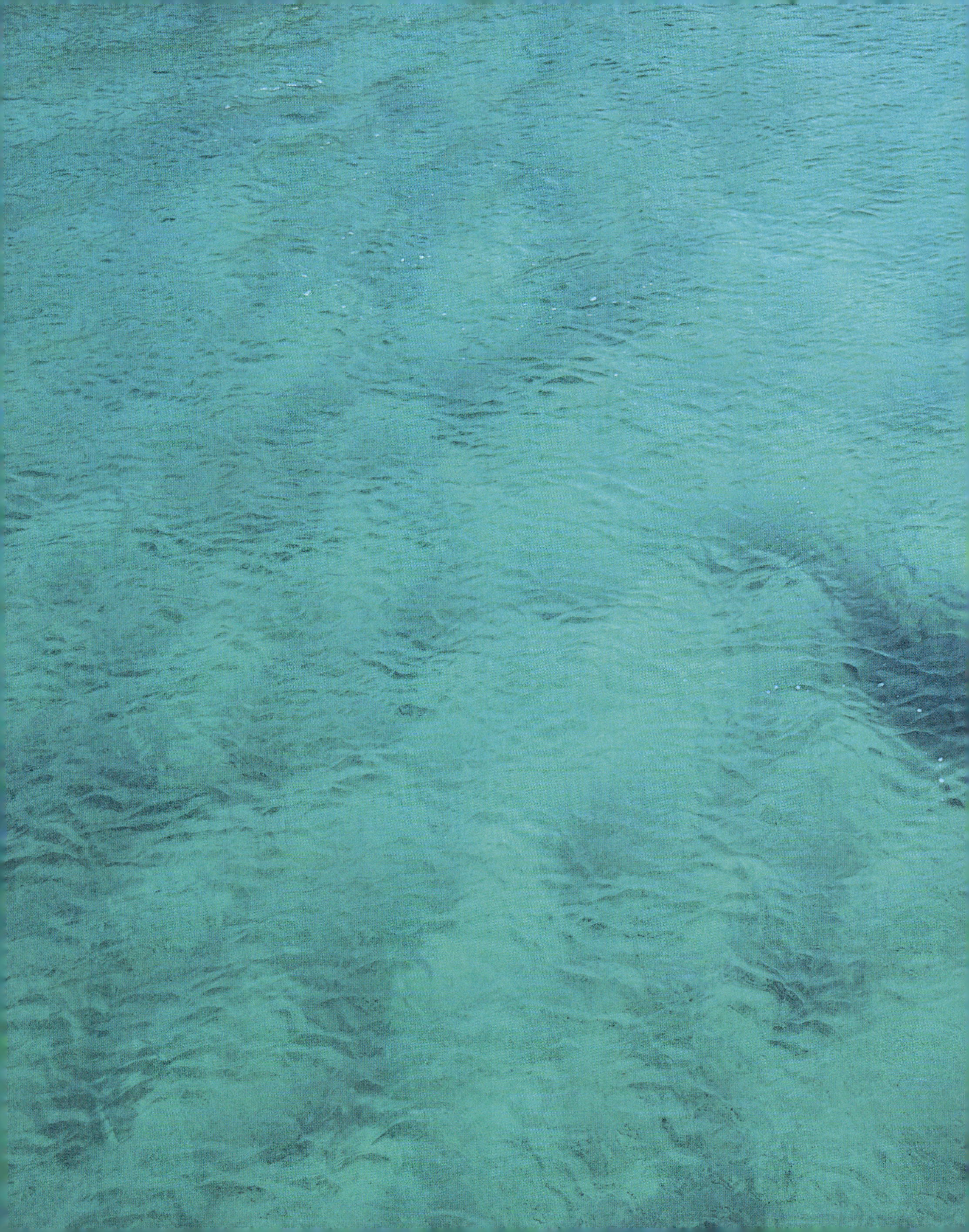

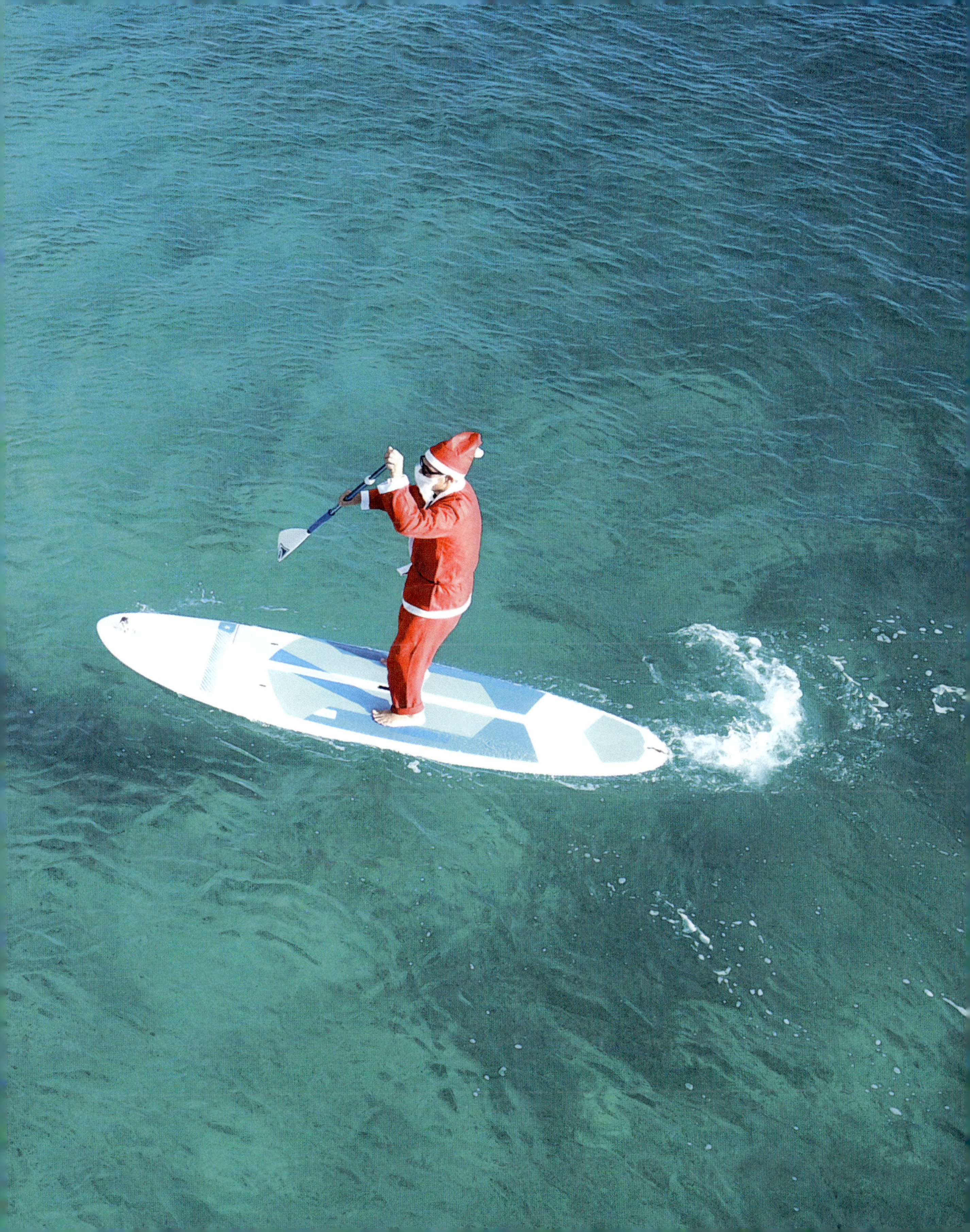

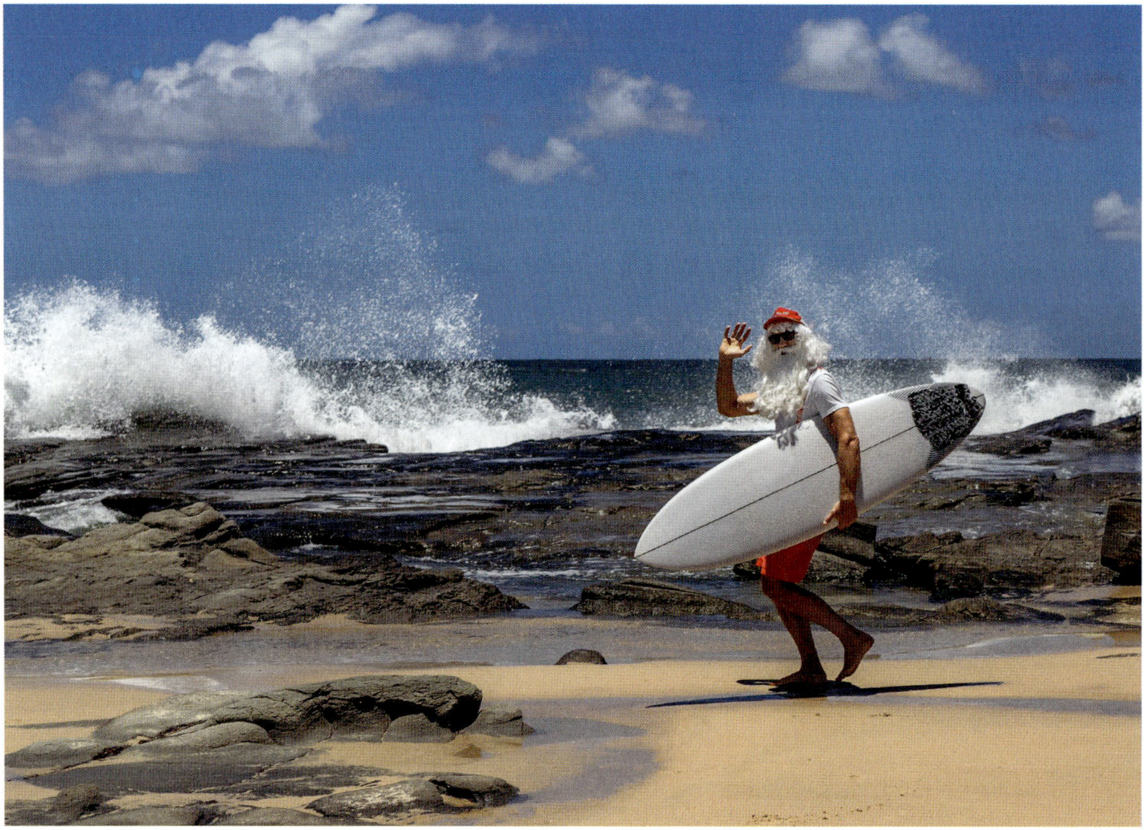

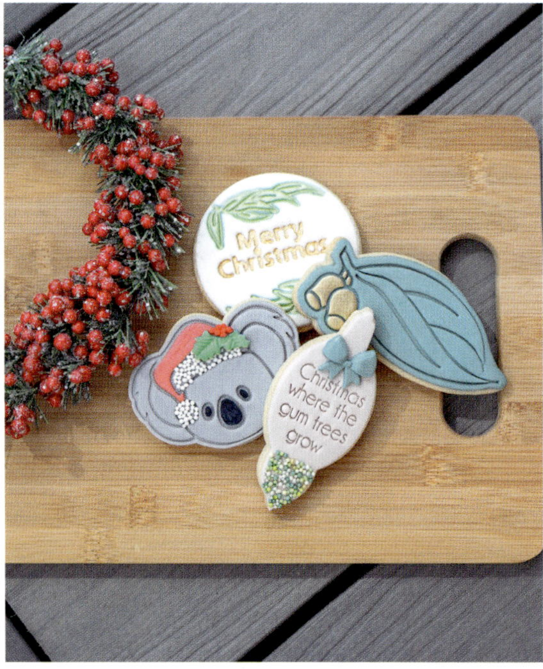

Christmas in Australia is largely celebrated outdoors, featuring picnics and barbecues on the beach, with creatively decorated cookies and Christmas trees, such as the one seen at Coogee Beach in Sydney. And Santa swaps reindeer for a surfboard.

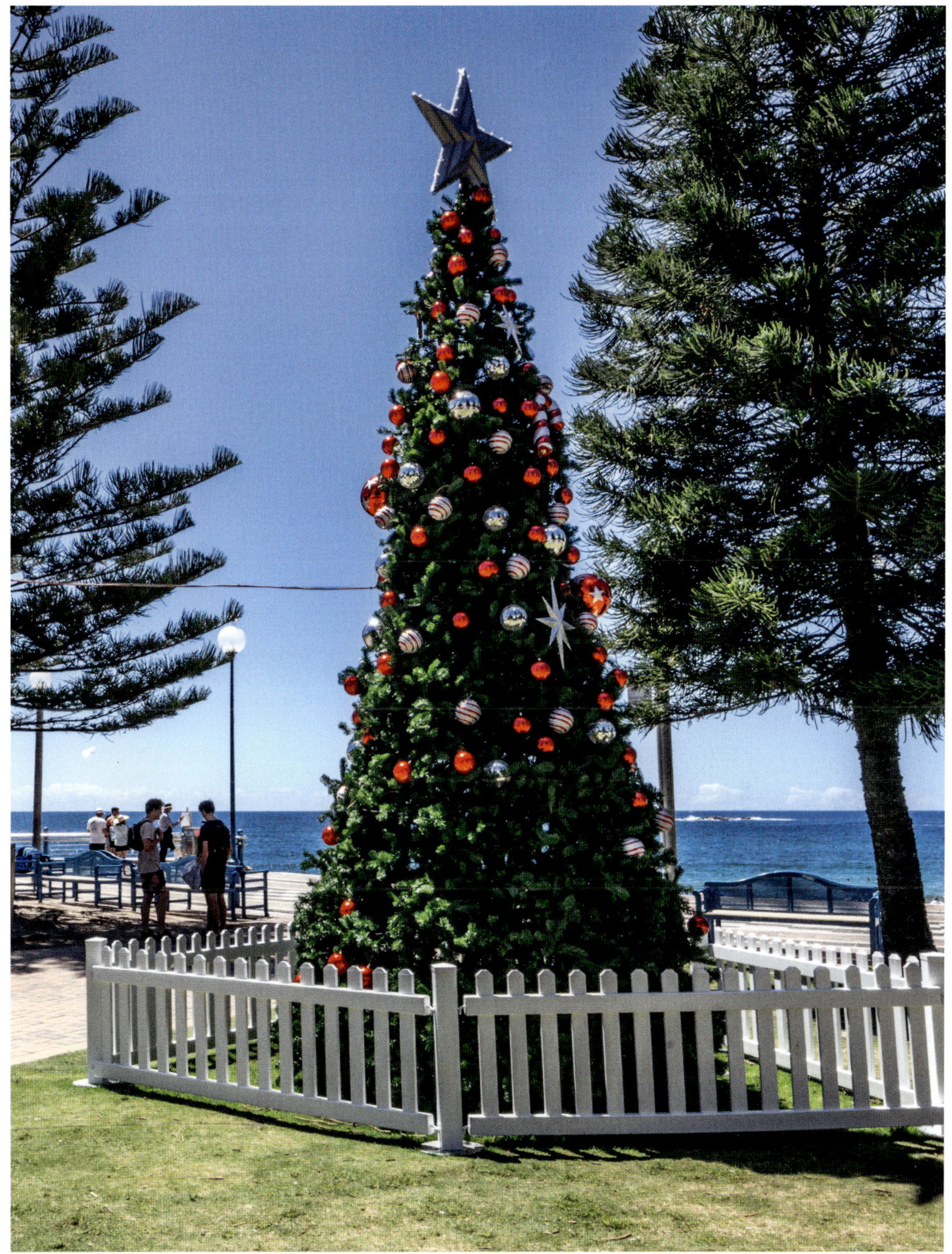

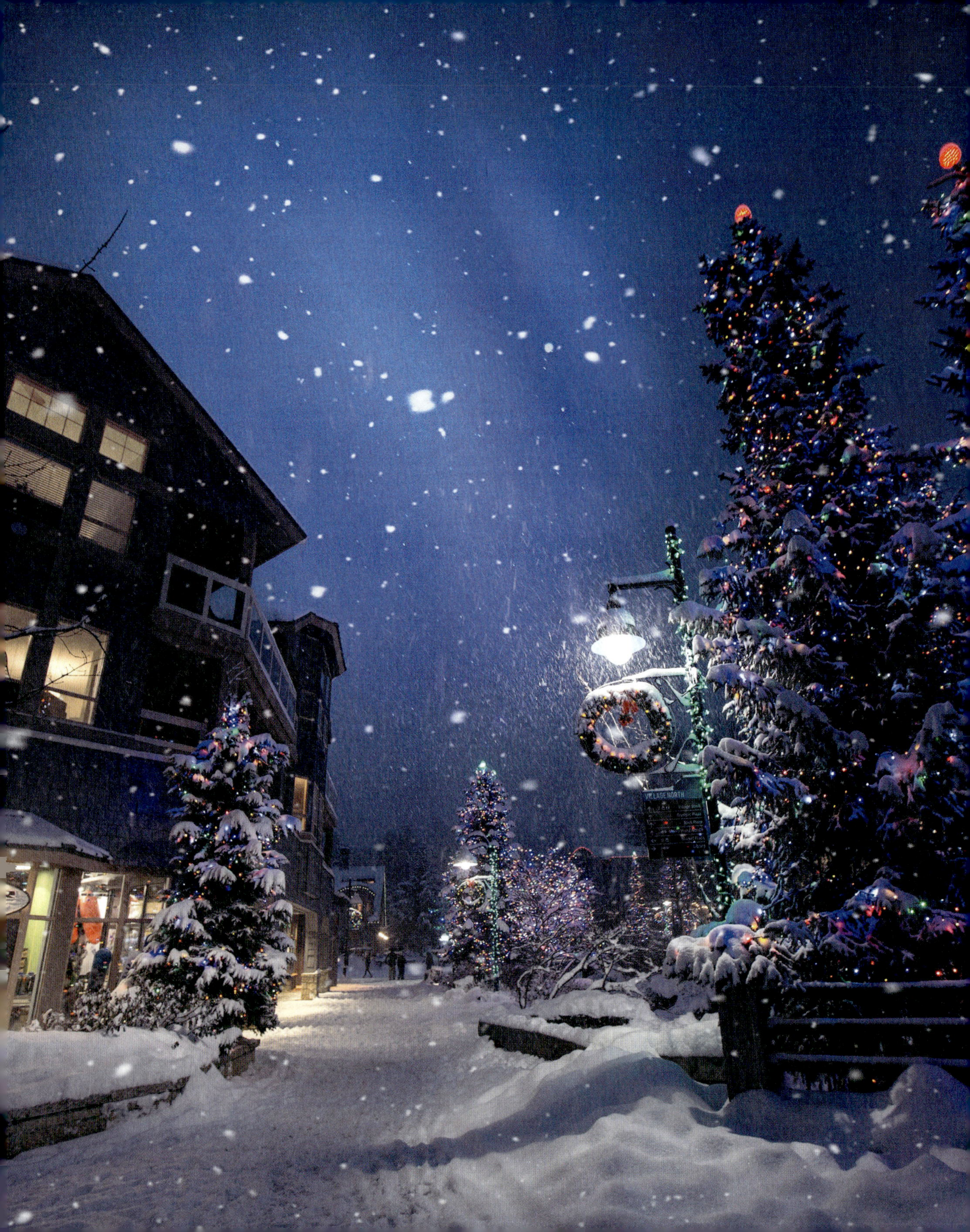
VILLAGE NORTH

Decorating the Outdoors

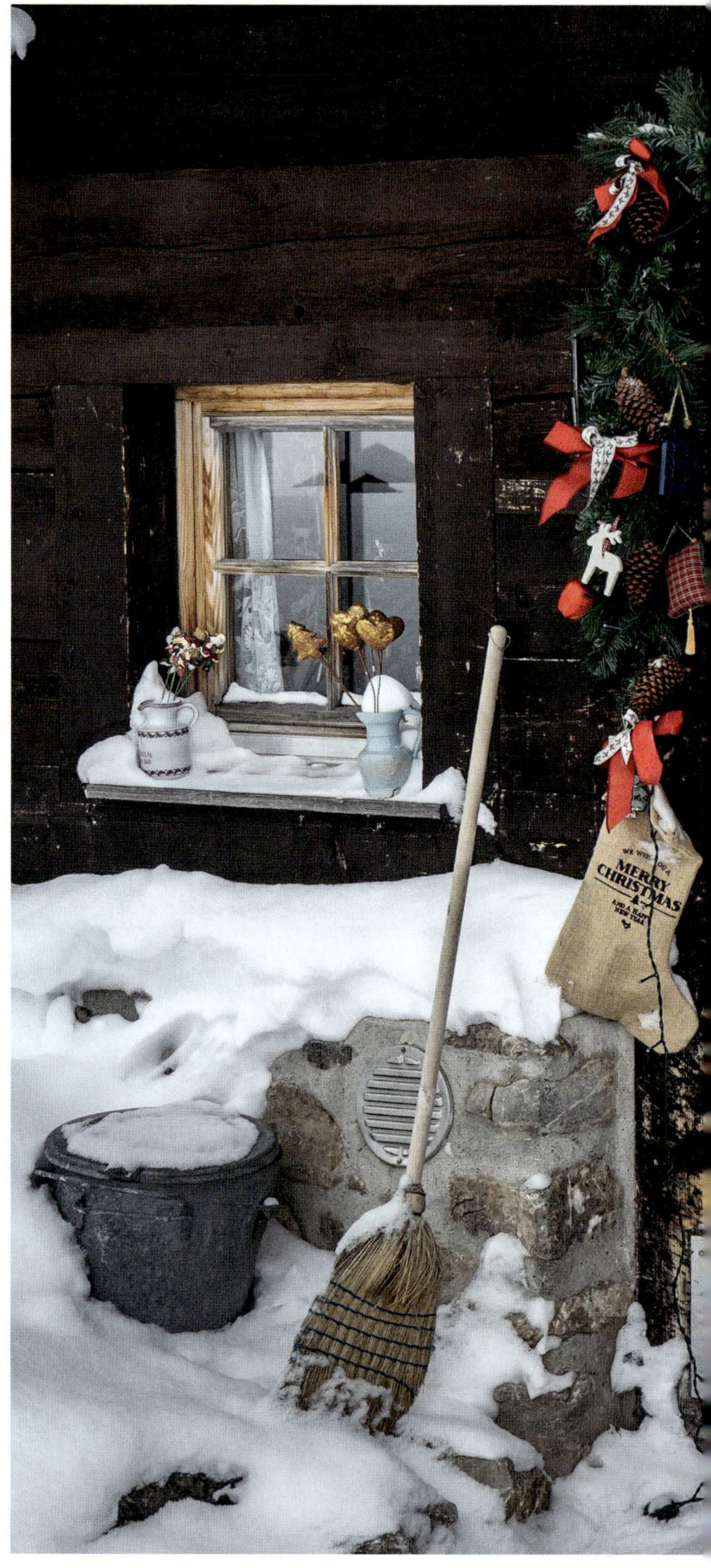

During the festive season, front doors and verandas become especially inviting, adorned with extravagant bows, ornaments, and festive wreaths and garlands that enhance the holiday spirit.

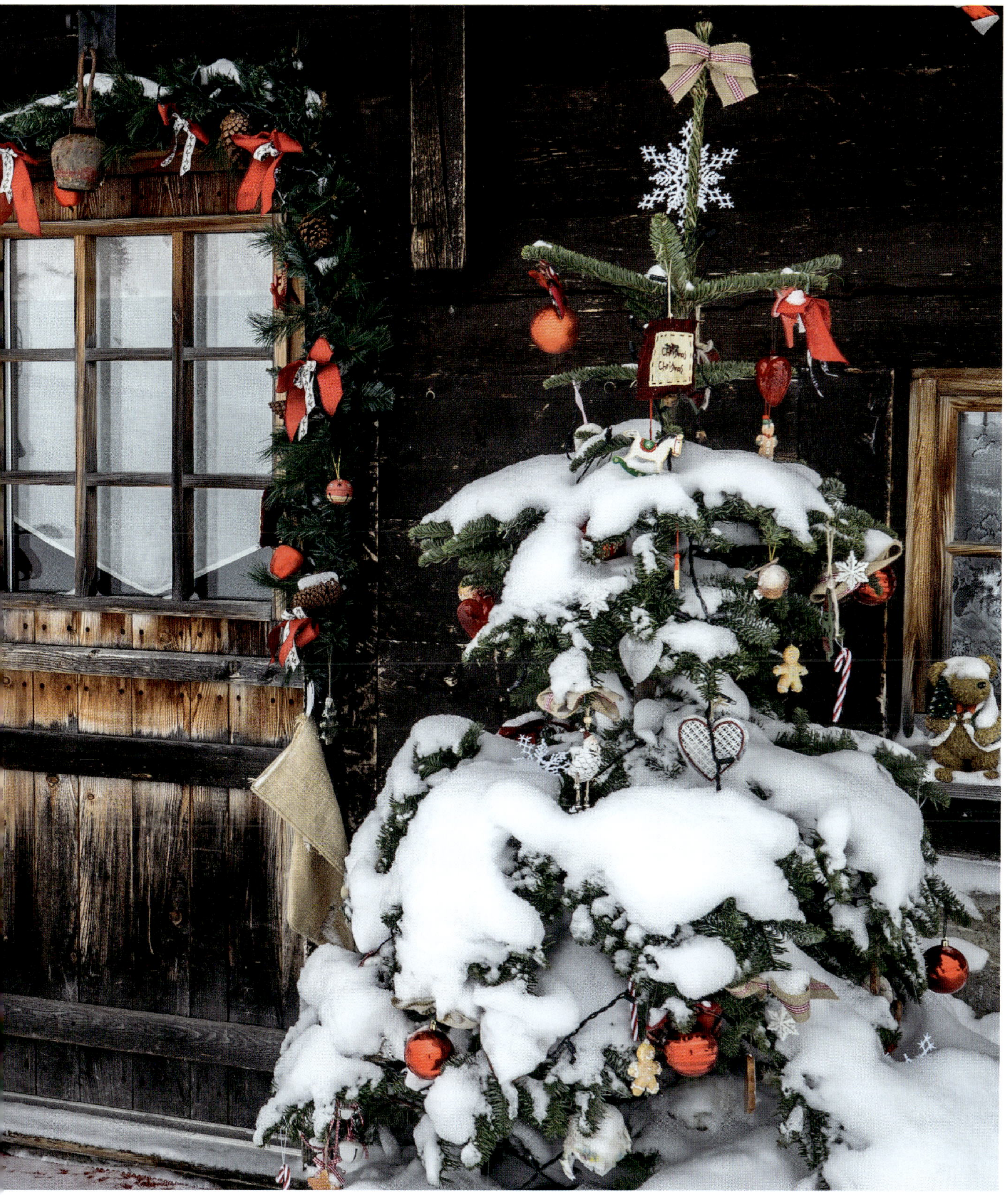

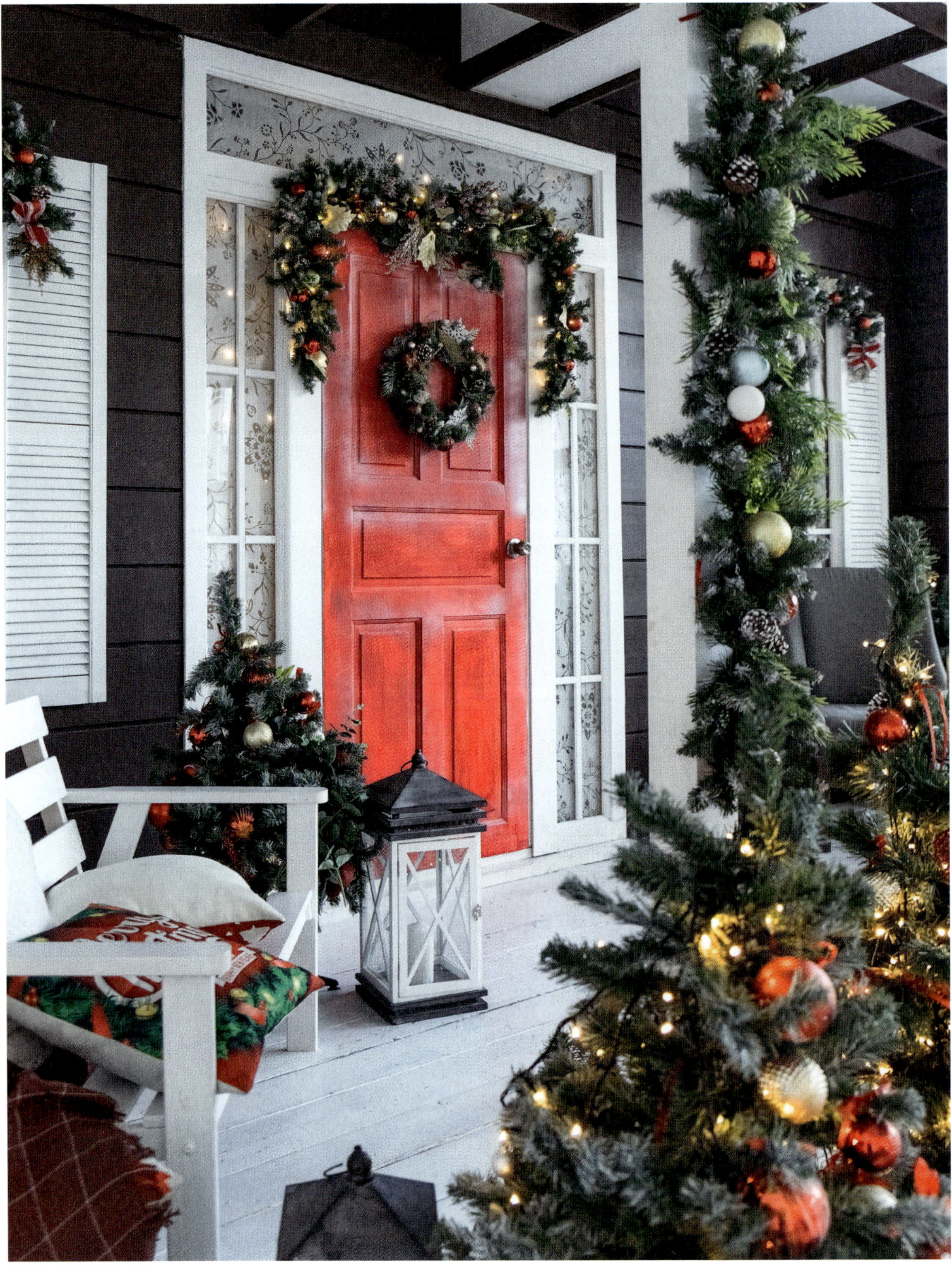

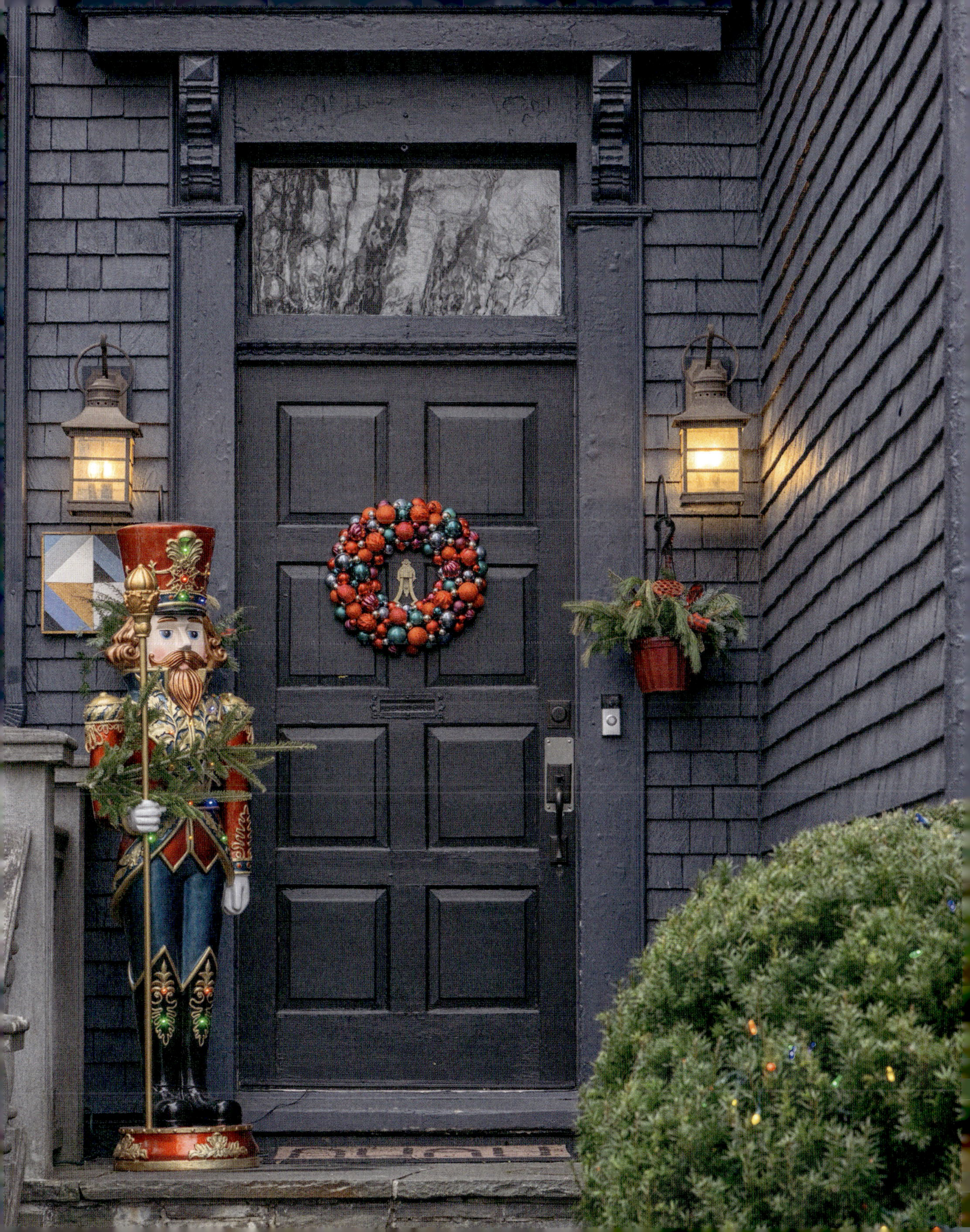

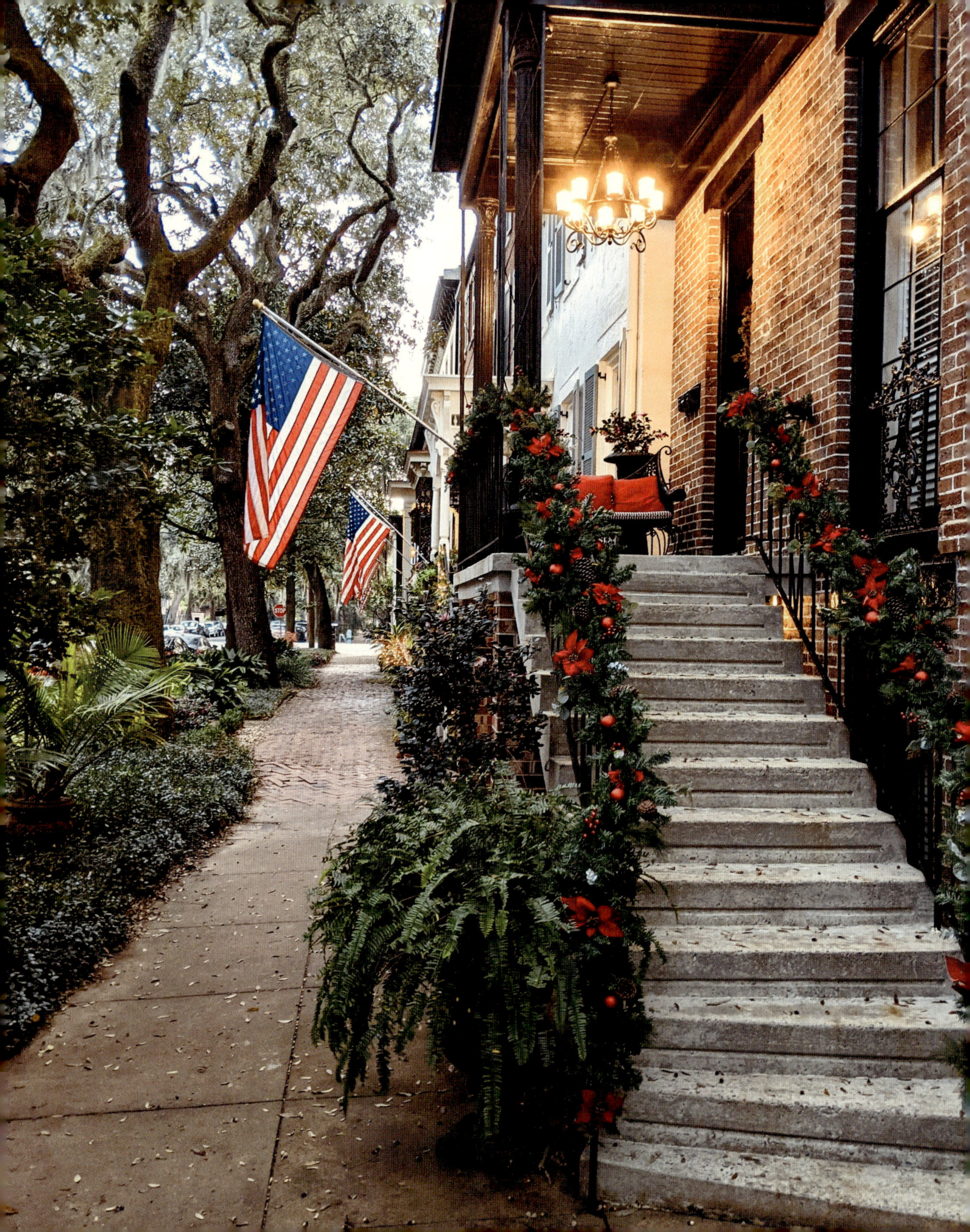

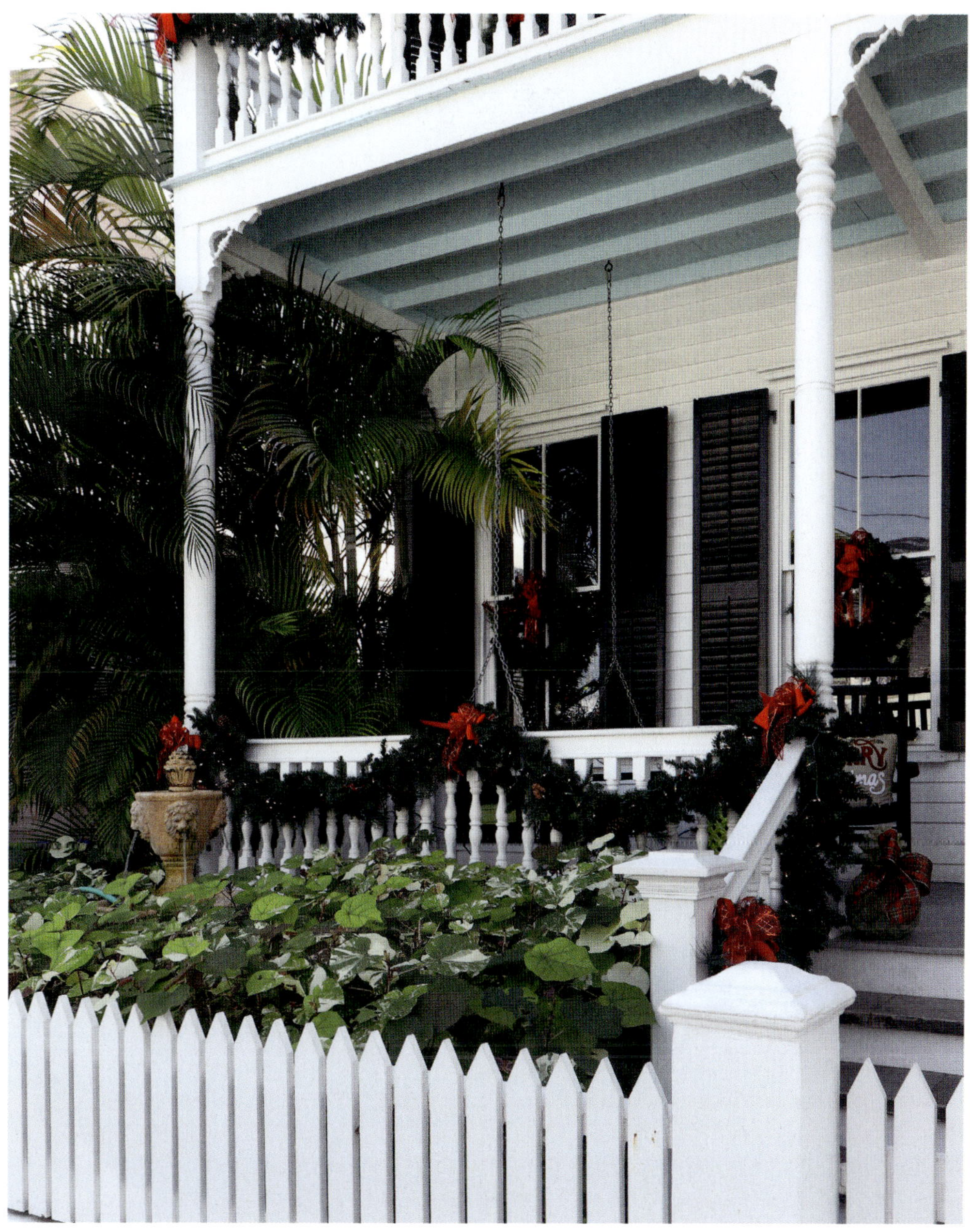

The vibrant red poinsettia adds a cheerful touch to banisters and balustrades. Kids love illuminated decorations for the garden and sparkling fairy lights that brighten up homes and entire streets, creating a magical atmosphere.

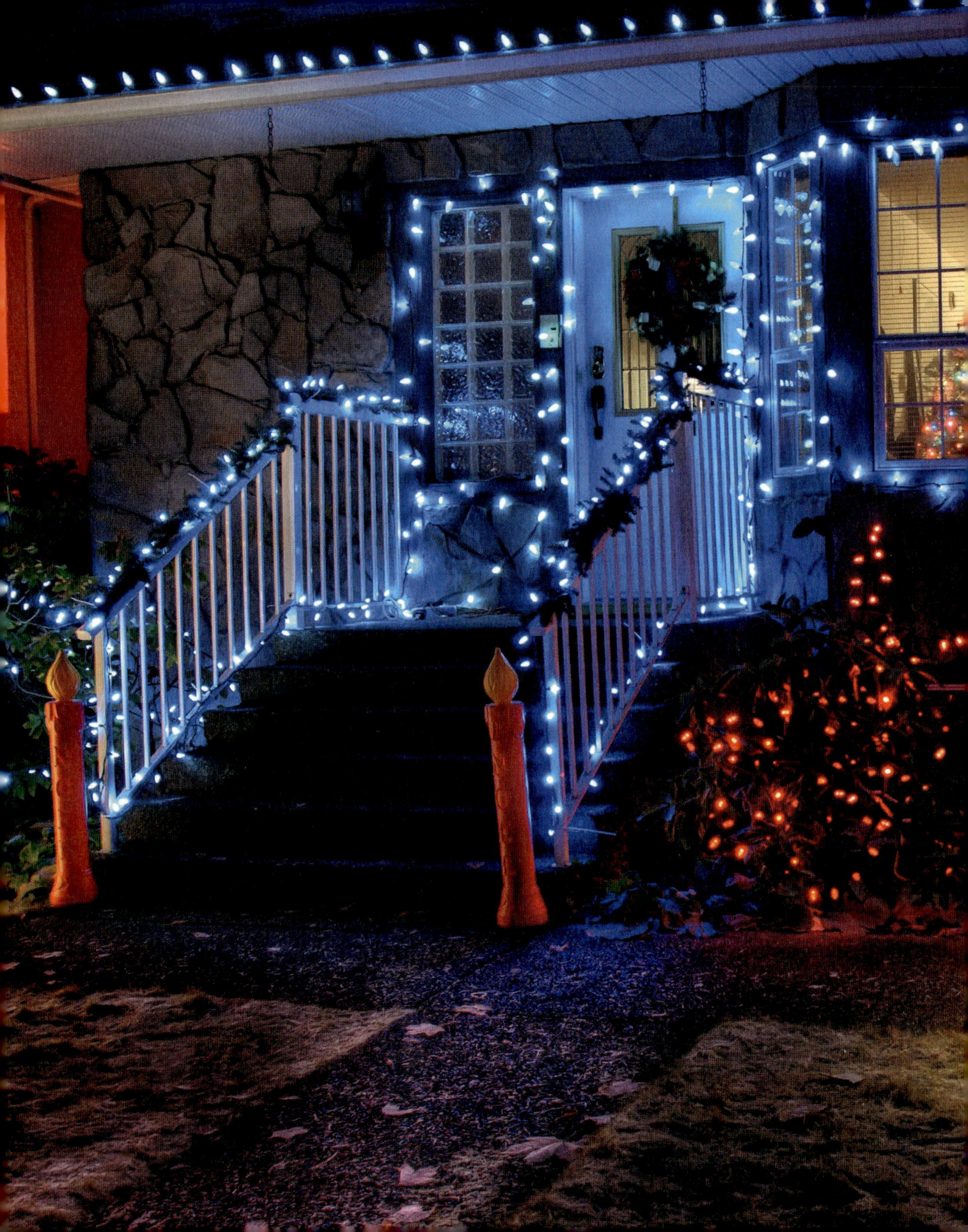

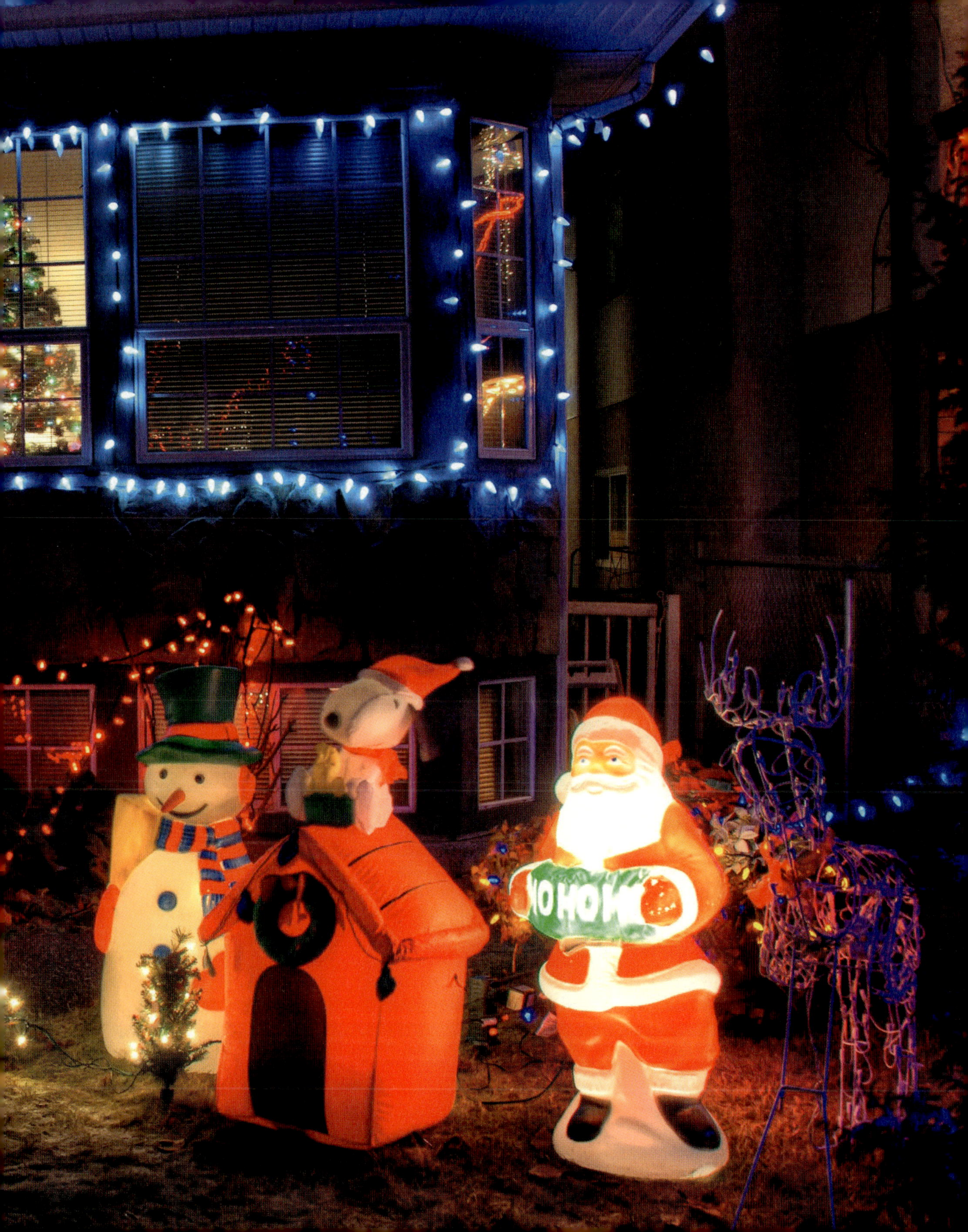

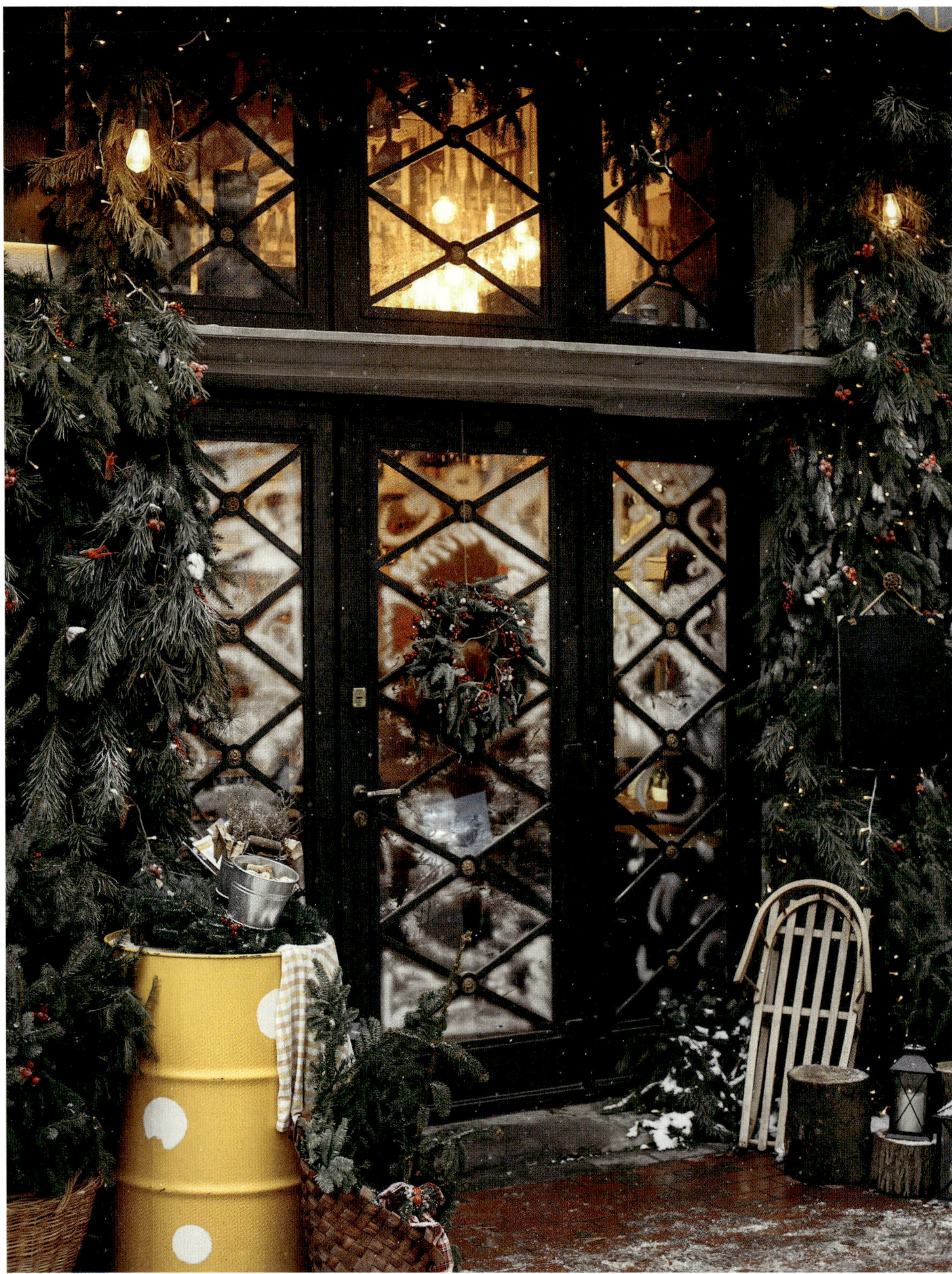

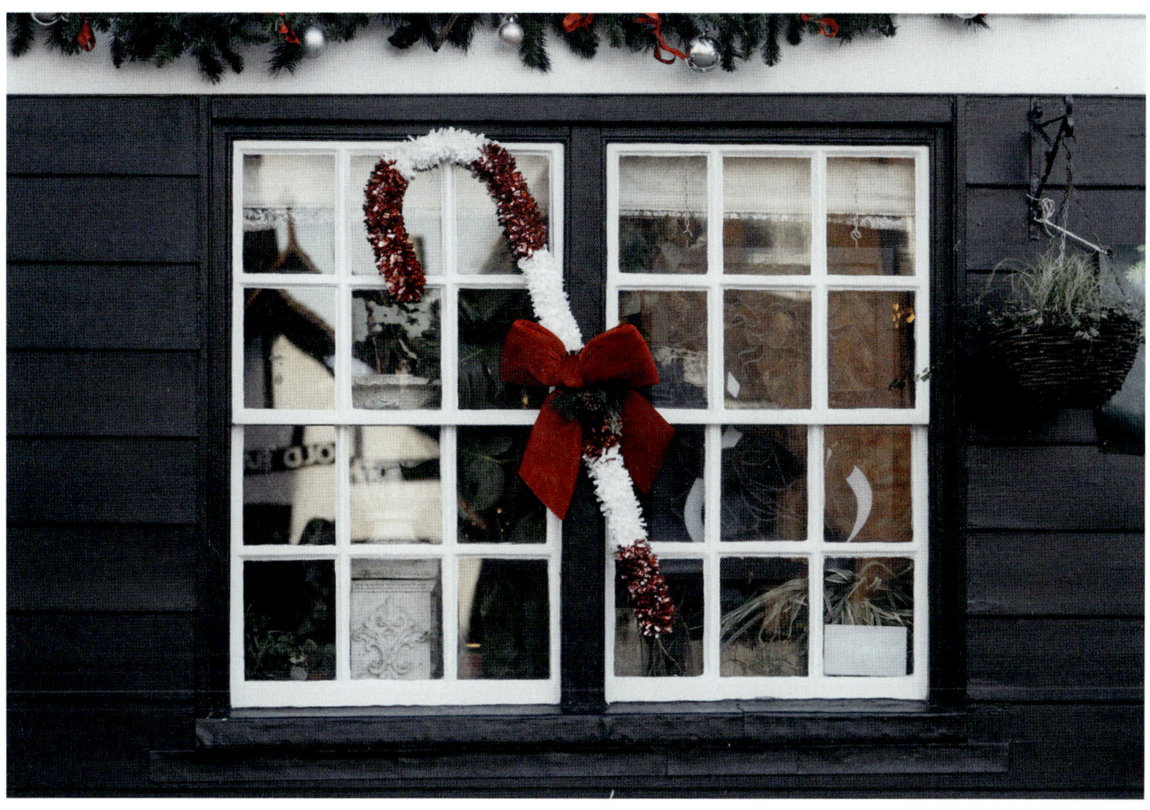

You can easily create a cozy Christmas vibe using spray snow from a can, which adds a festive touch to Christmas trees or window panes. Oversized holiday decorations hung in windows also captivate the admiration of passersby.

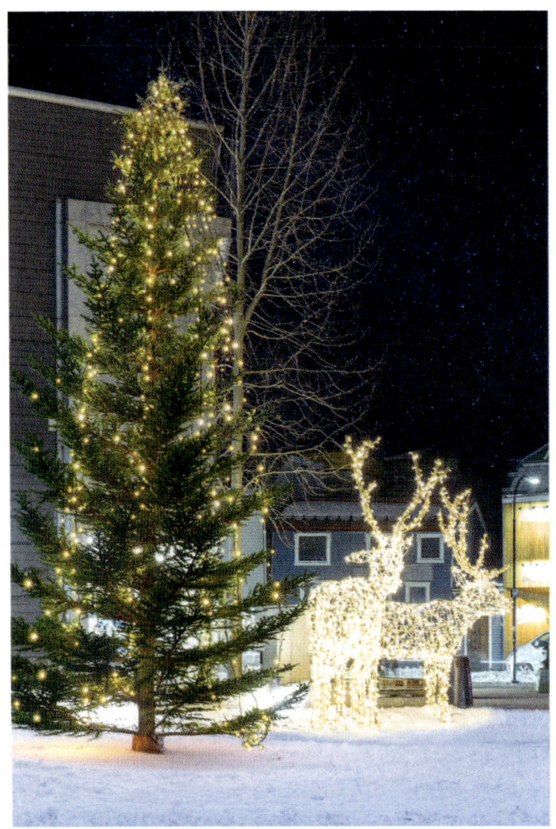
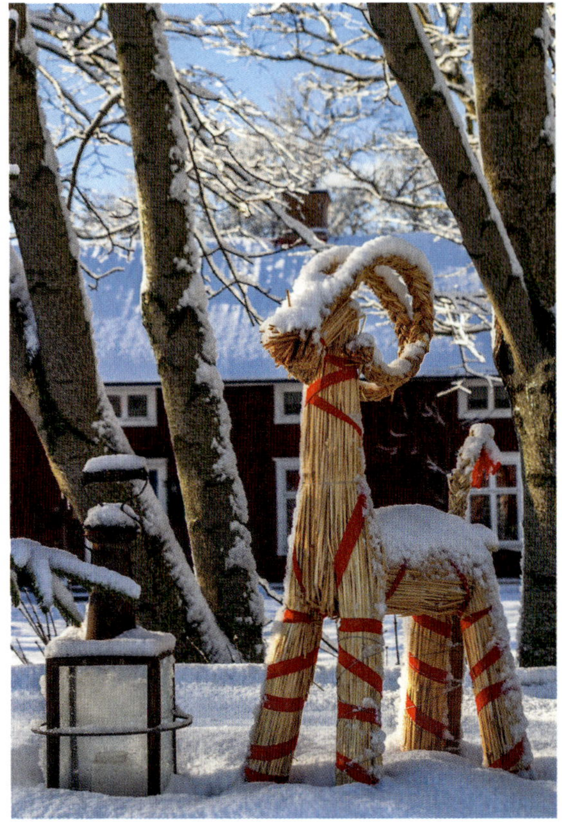

In Scandinavia, outdoor Christmas ornaments include glowing reindeer and traditional Yule goats made of straw, with smaller versions often adorning Christmas trees as charming accents.

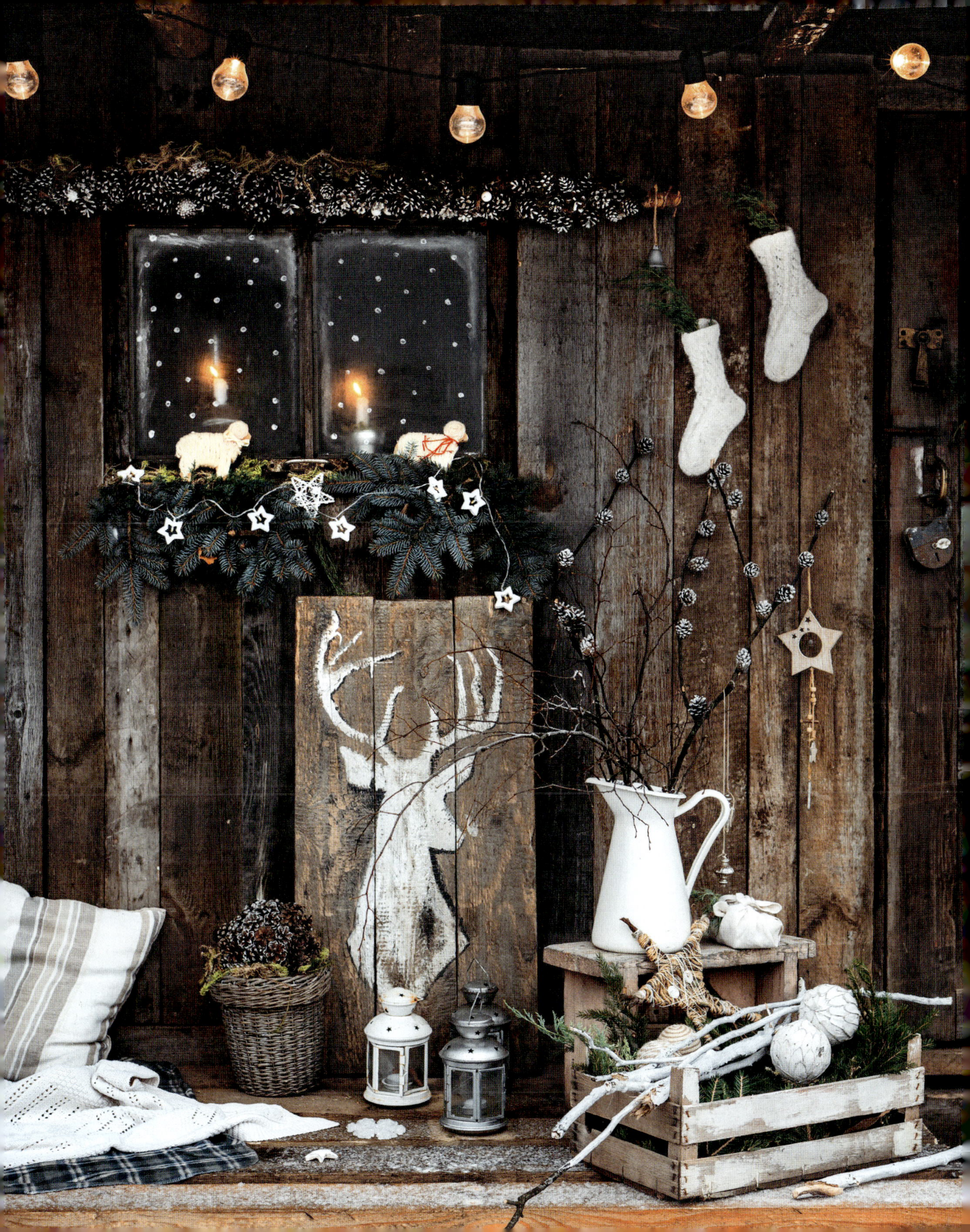

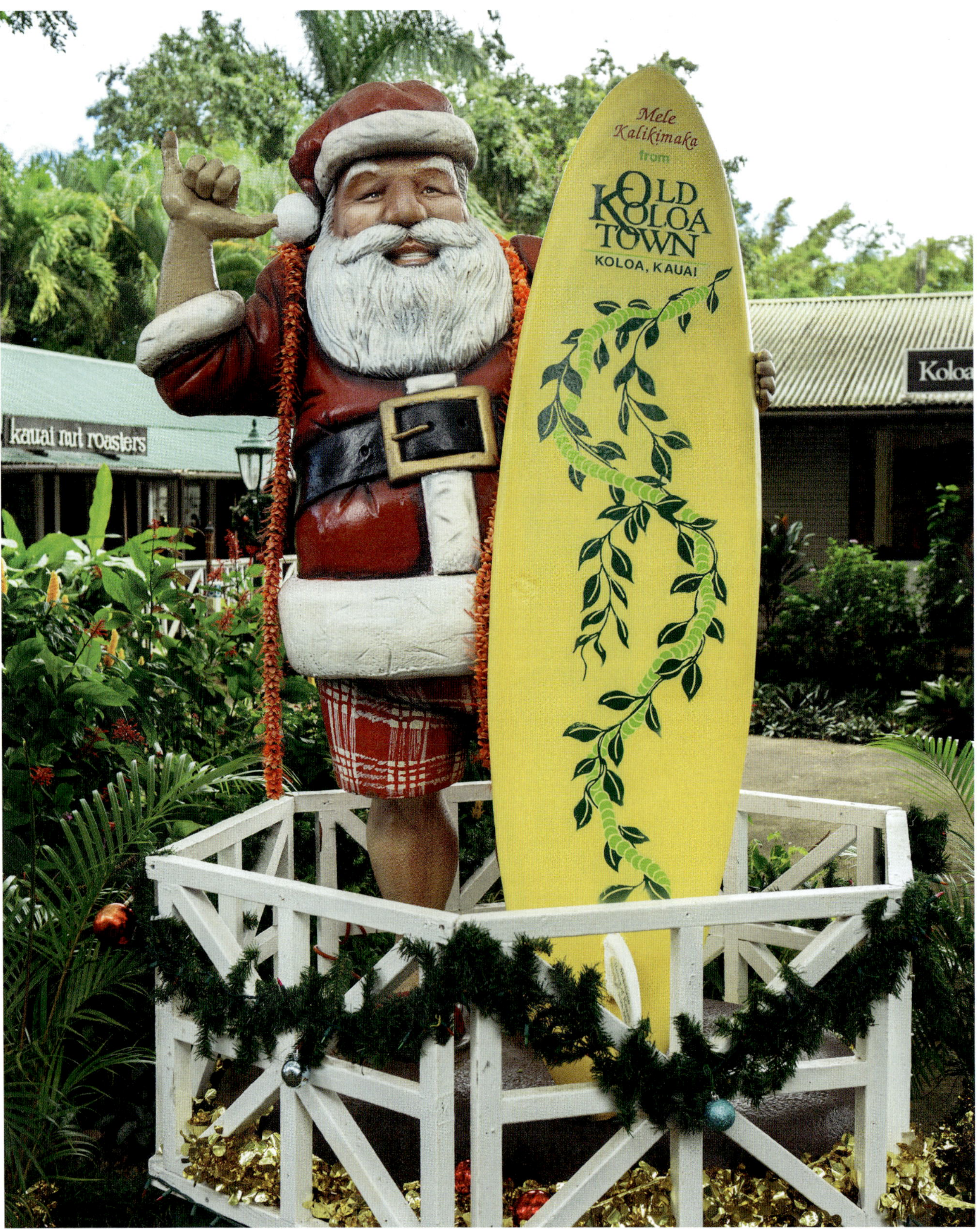
Mele
Kalikimaka
from
OLD
KOLOA
TOWN
KOLOA, KAUAI
kauai nut roasters
Koloa

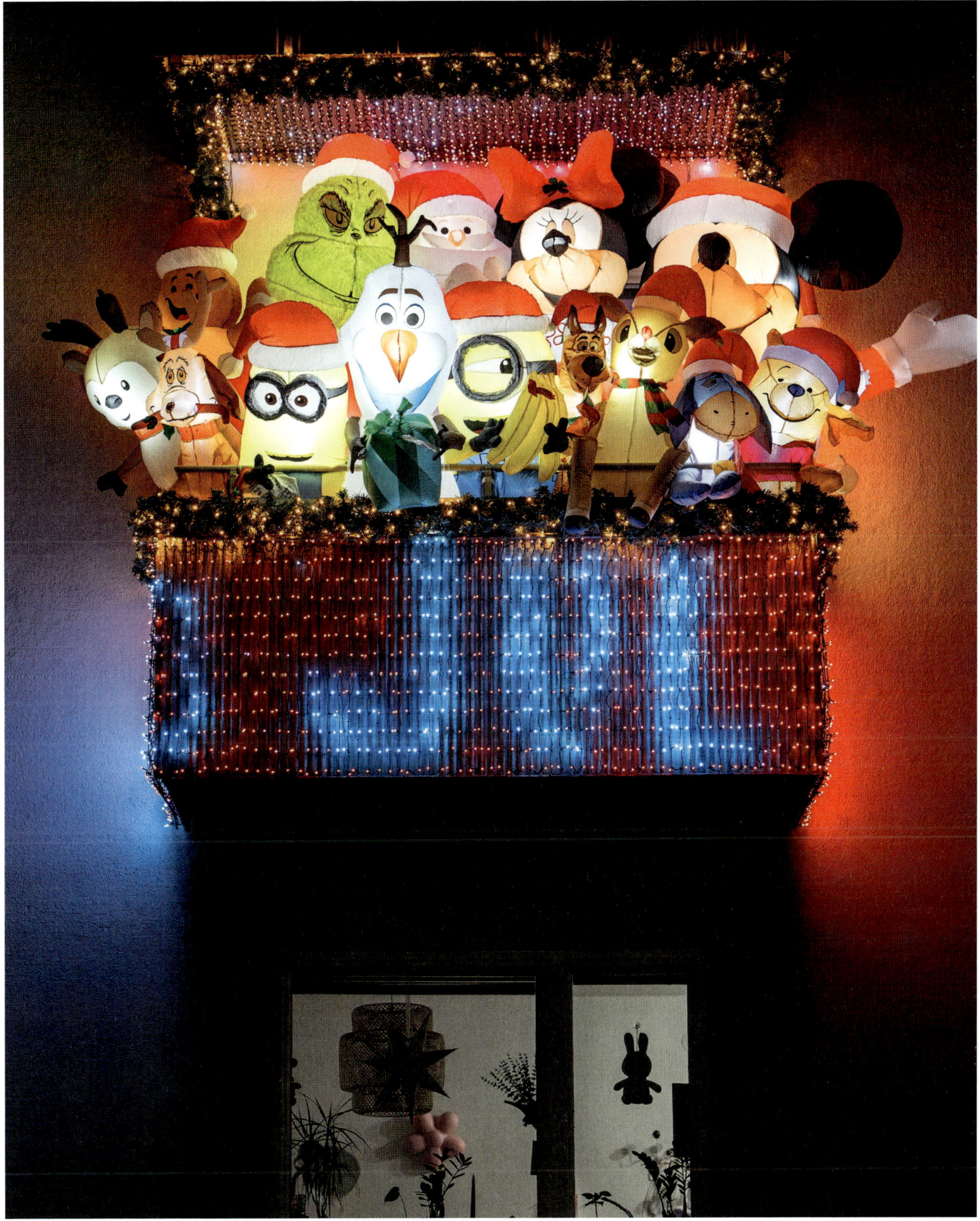

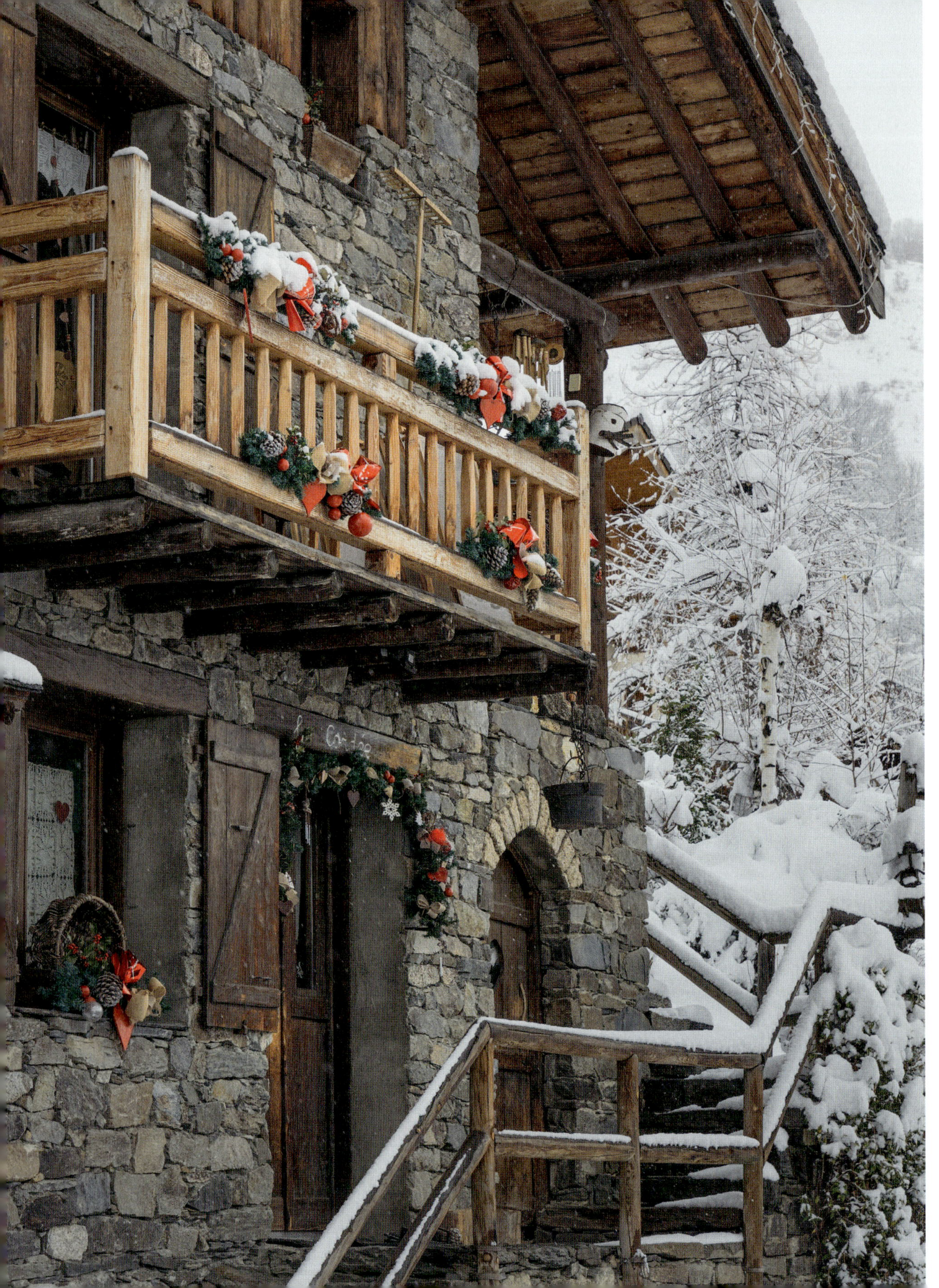

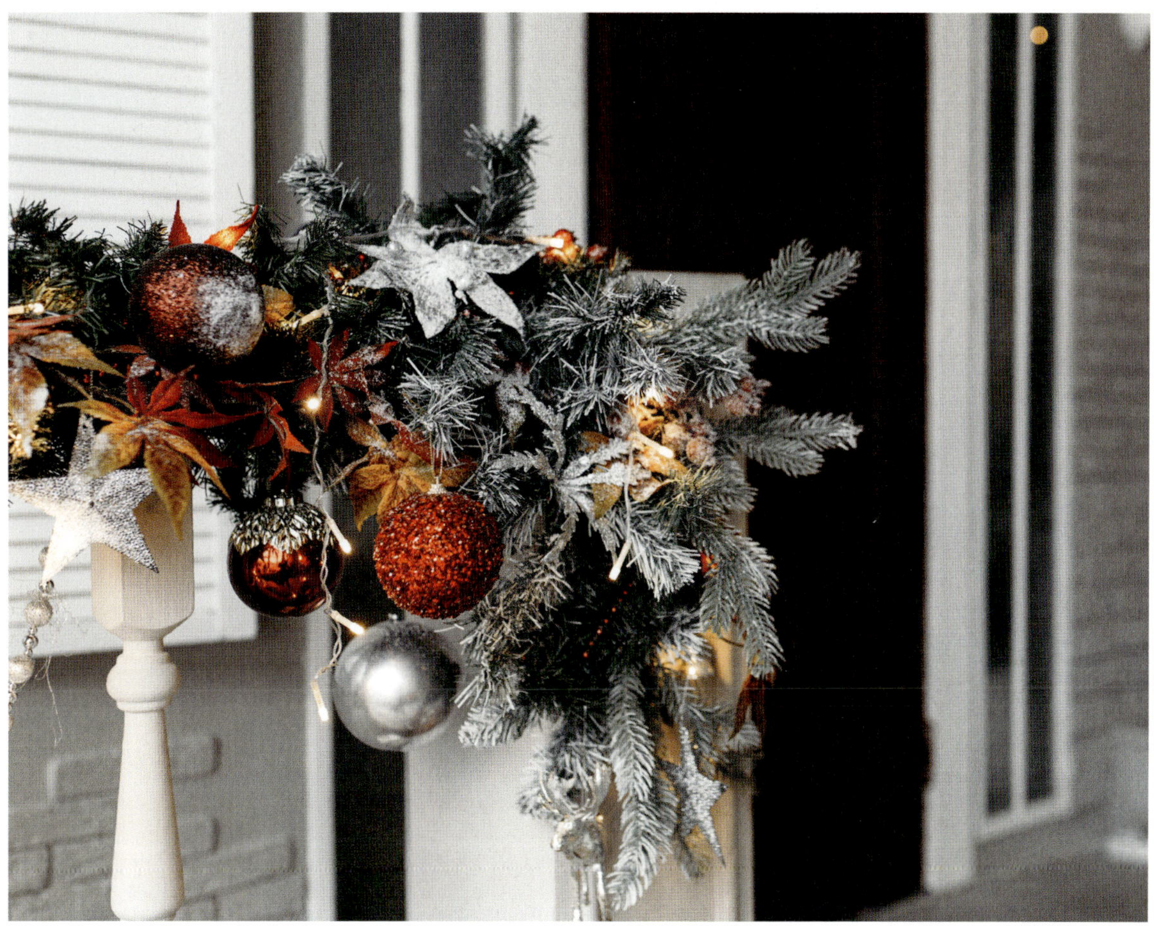

Previous spread
From a life-size Santa with a surfboard in Hawaii to a Stockholm balcony decorated with inflatable cartoon characters, the possibilities for Christmas decoration are endless and creative.

Regardless of where you are in the world—whether in snowy mountains, warm Caribbean beaches, or bustling cities—Christmas decorations share a common goal: to evoke feelings of coziness and joy. Beautifully adorned trees, hand-crafted wreaths, and twinkling lights come together to create inviting environments, showcasing a universal spirit that connects cultures during the festive season.

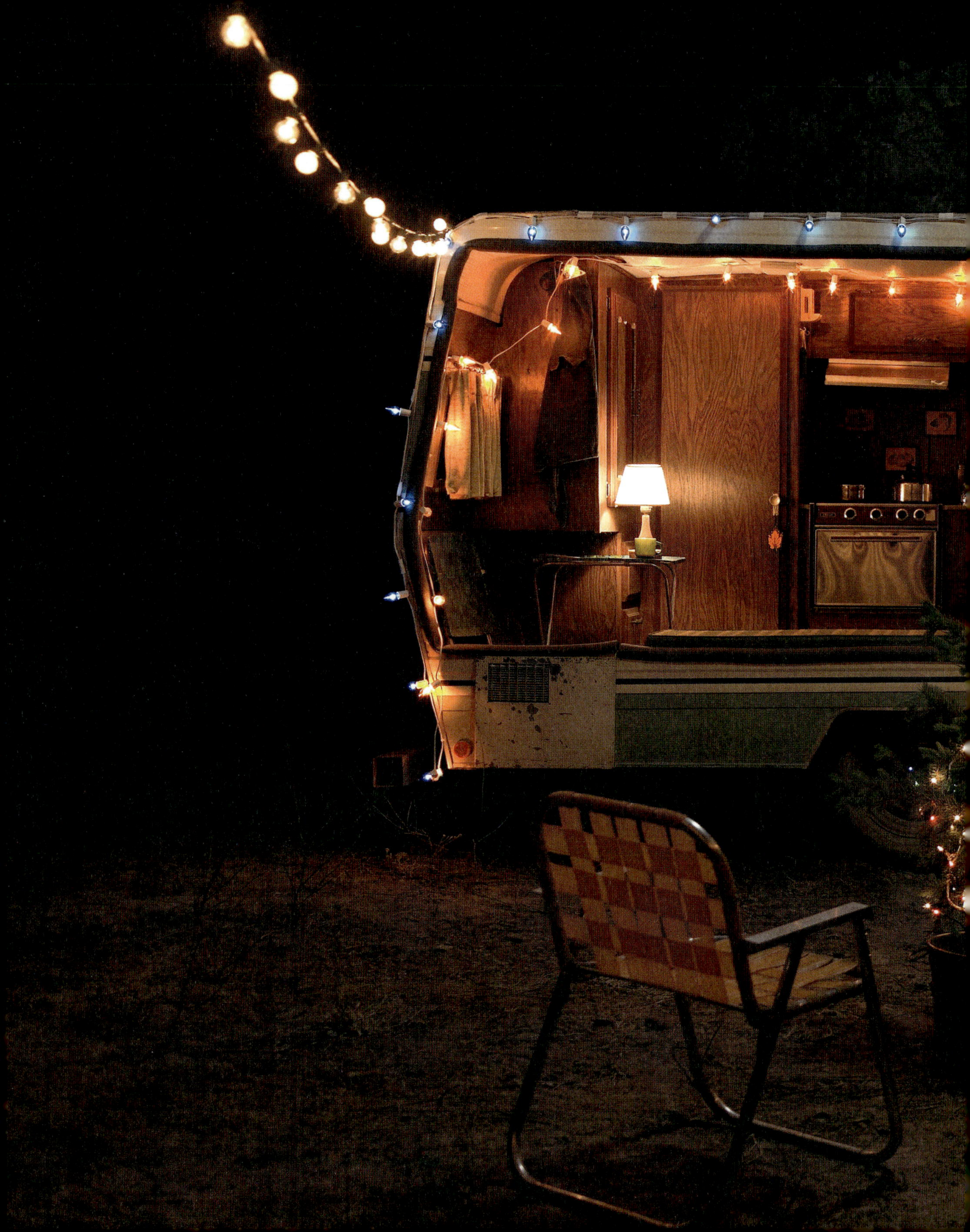

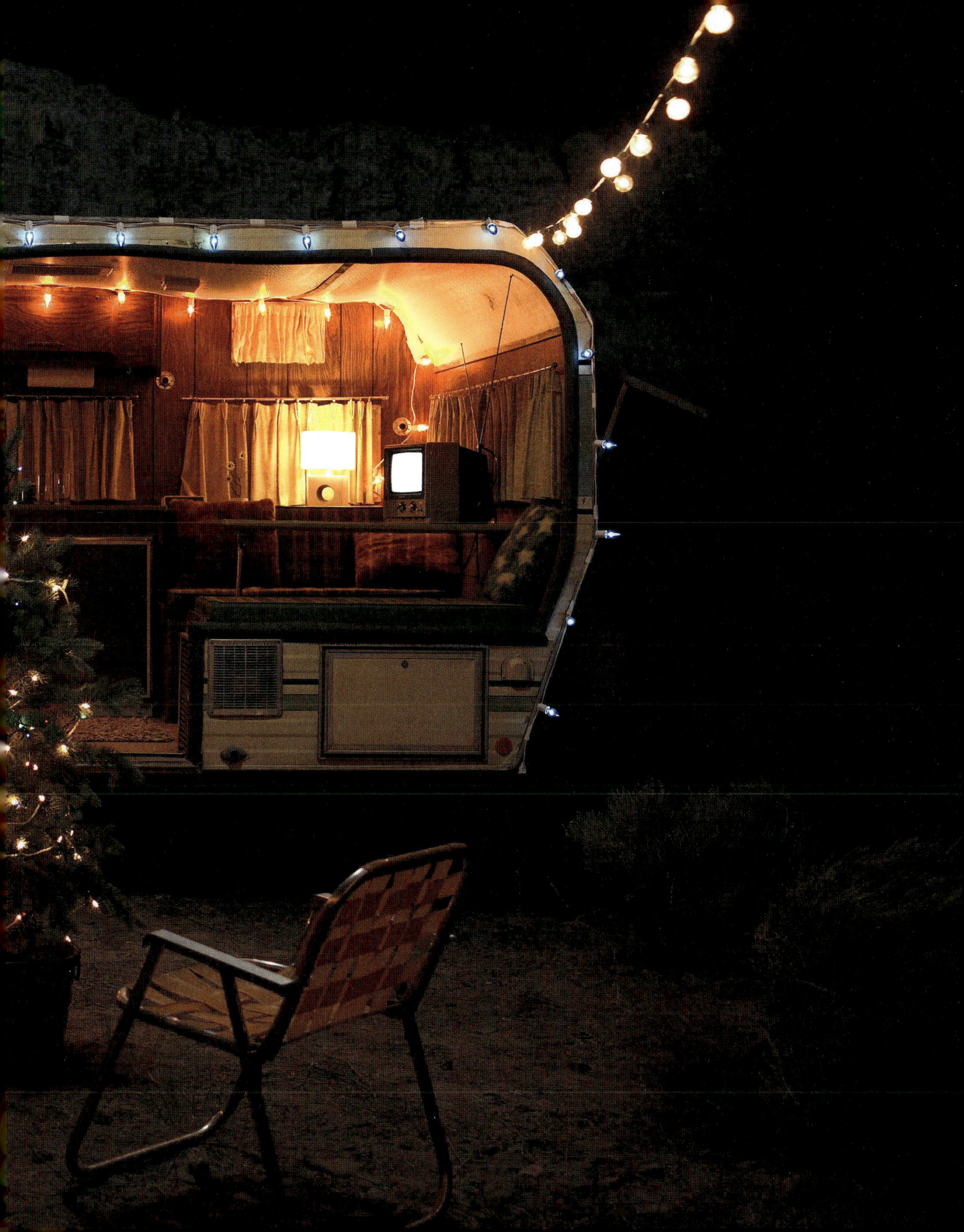

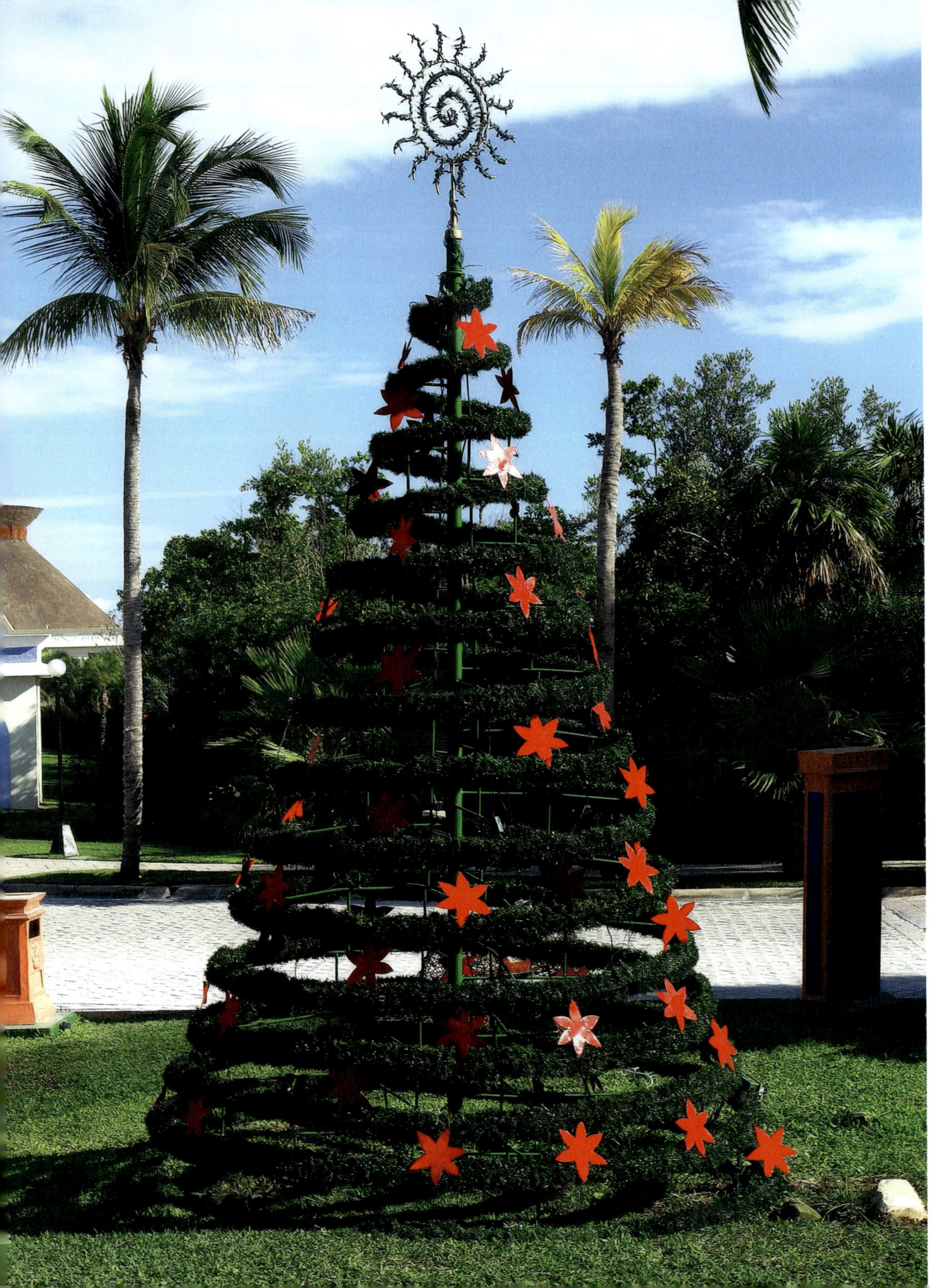

Christmas Trees around the World

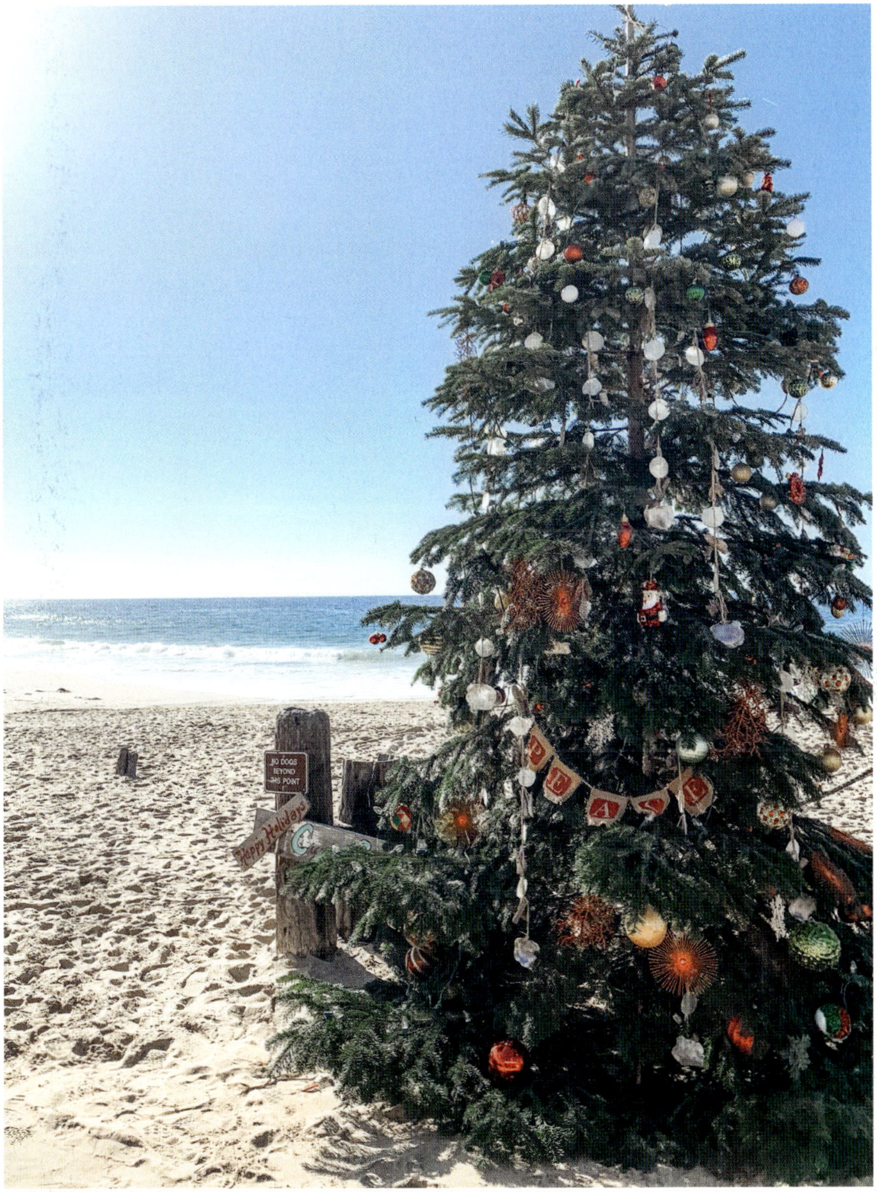

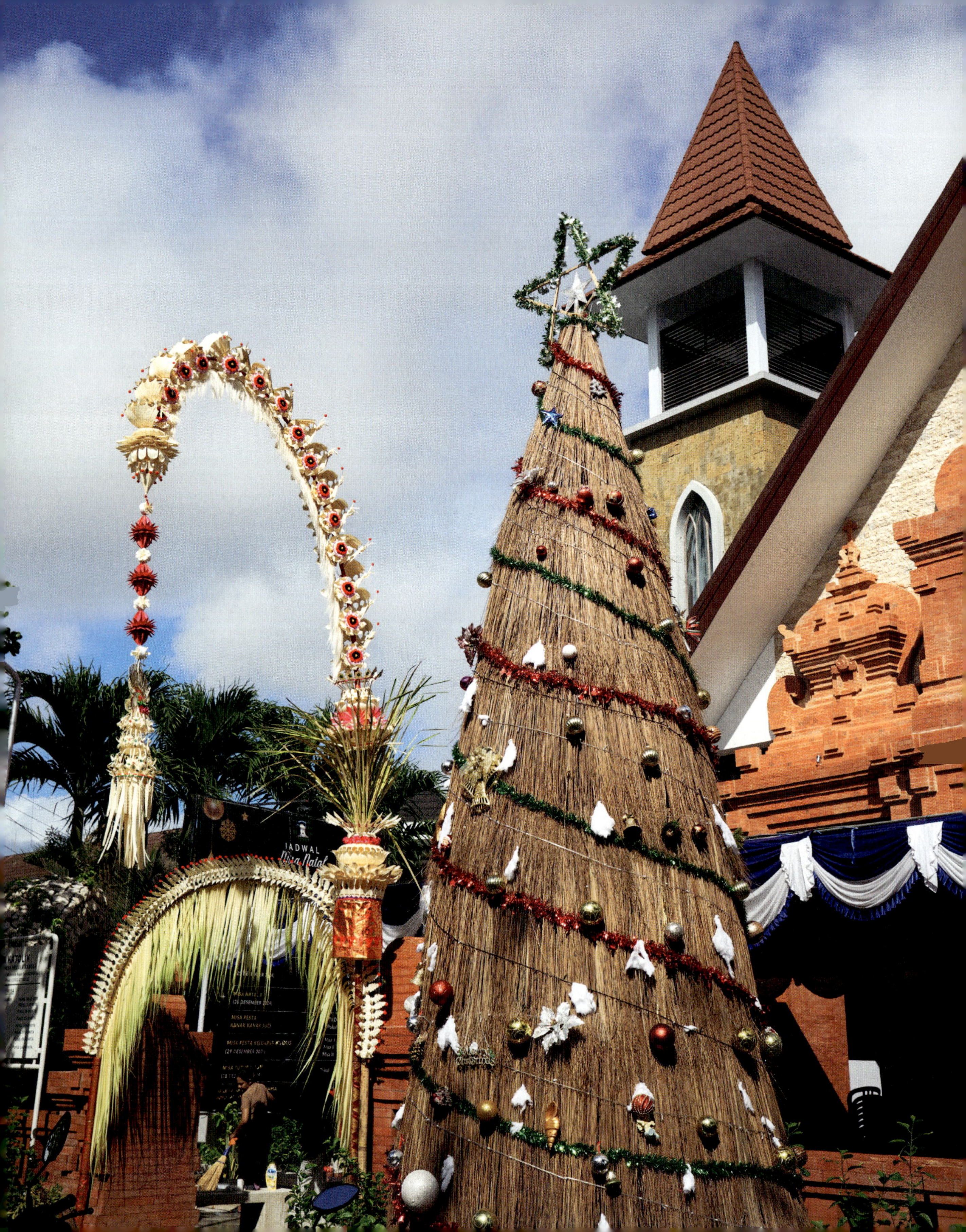
JADWAL
Misa Natal
MISA PESTA

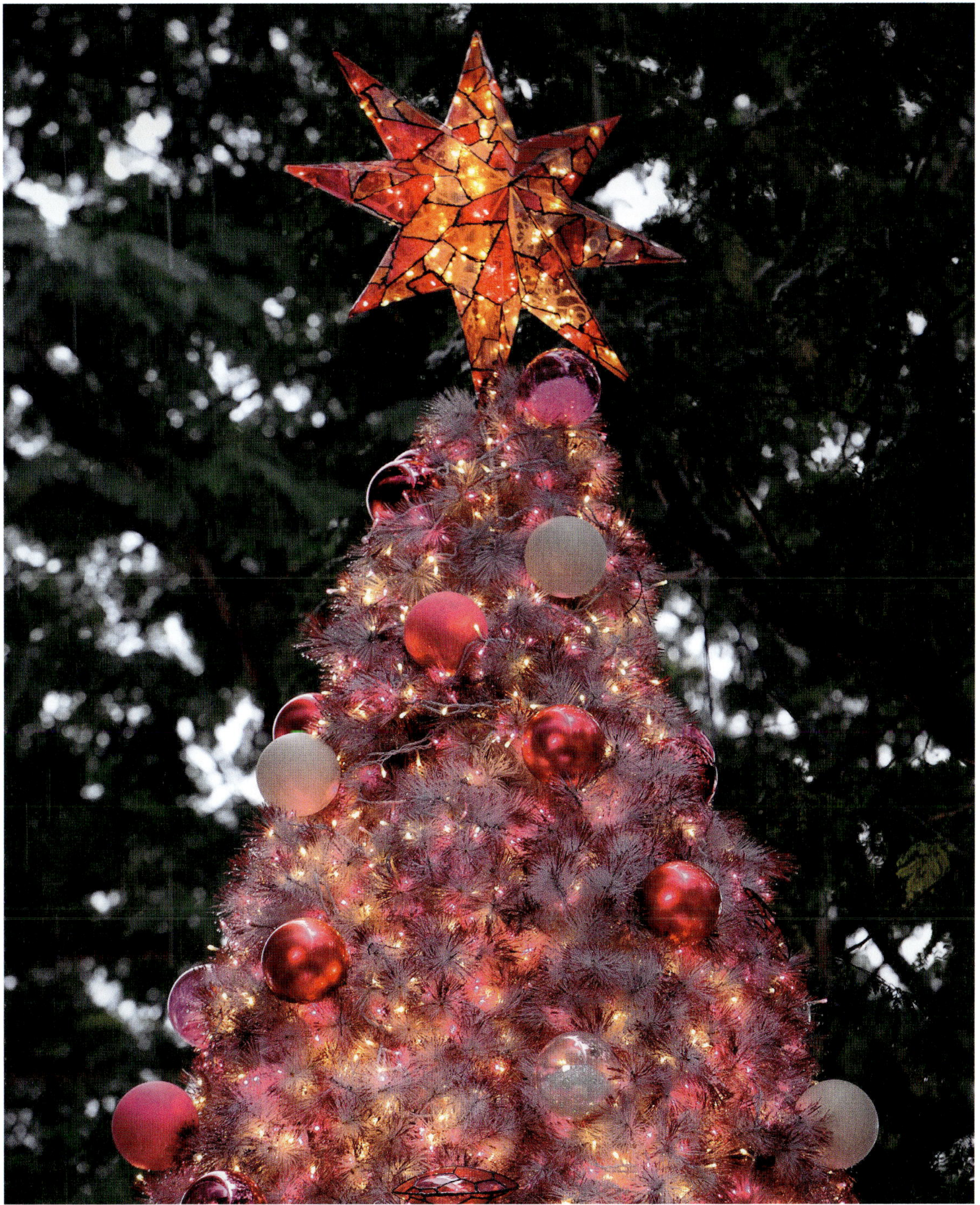

Christmas trees come in all shapes, colors, and styles, from spiral specimens found in tropical regions to beach trees in Southern California and straw trees in Bali. Notably, the pink tree displayed on Orchard Road in Singapore and the famous floating Christmas tree in Rio de Janeiro exemplify the creativity and variety of holiday celebrations worldwide.

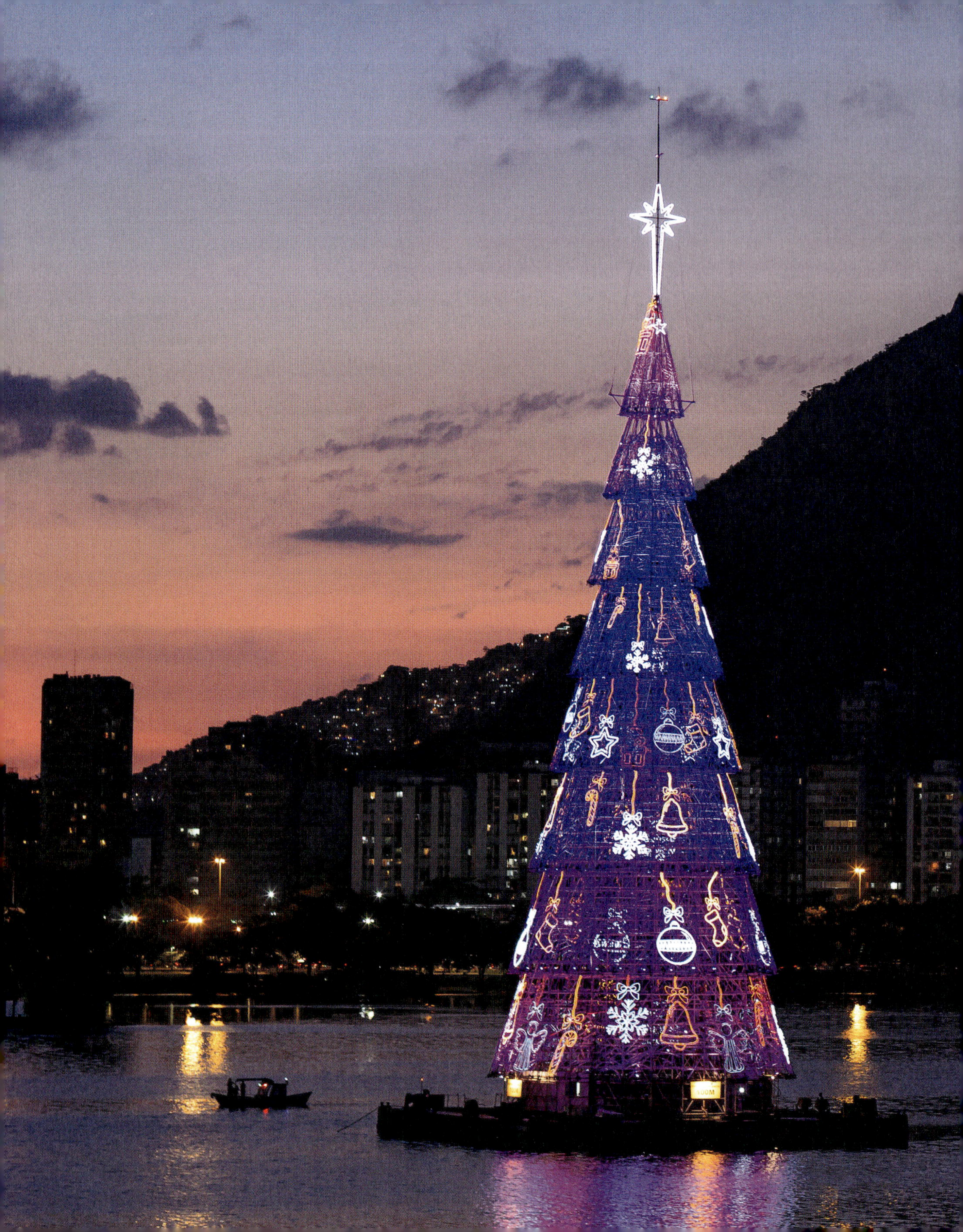

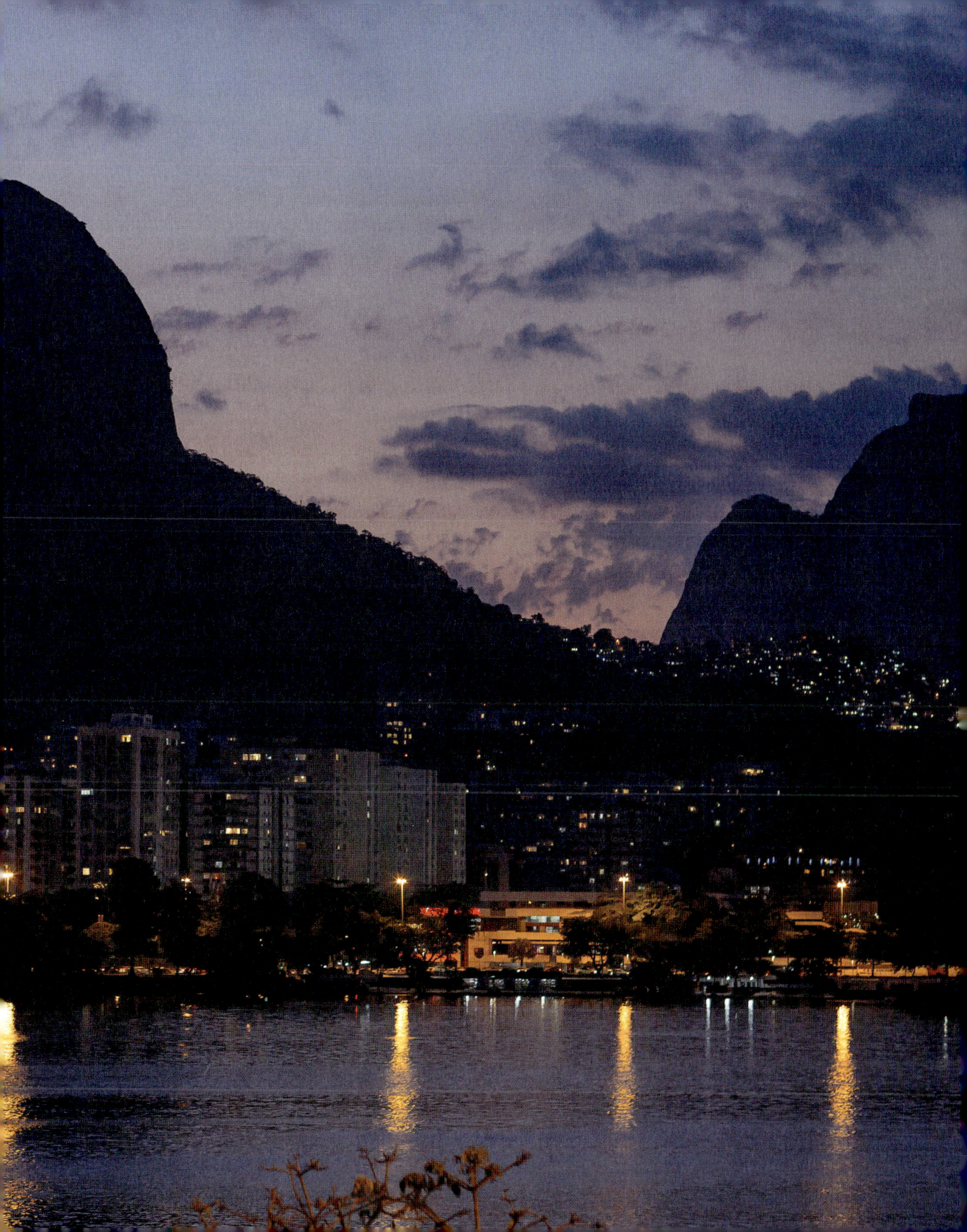

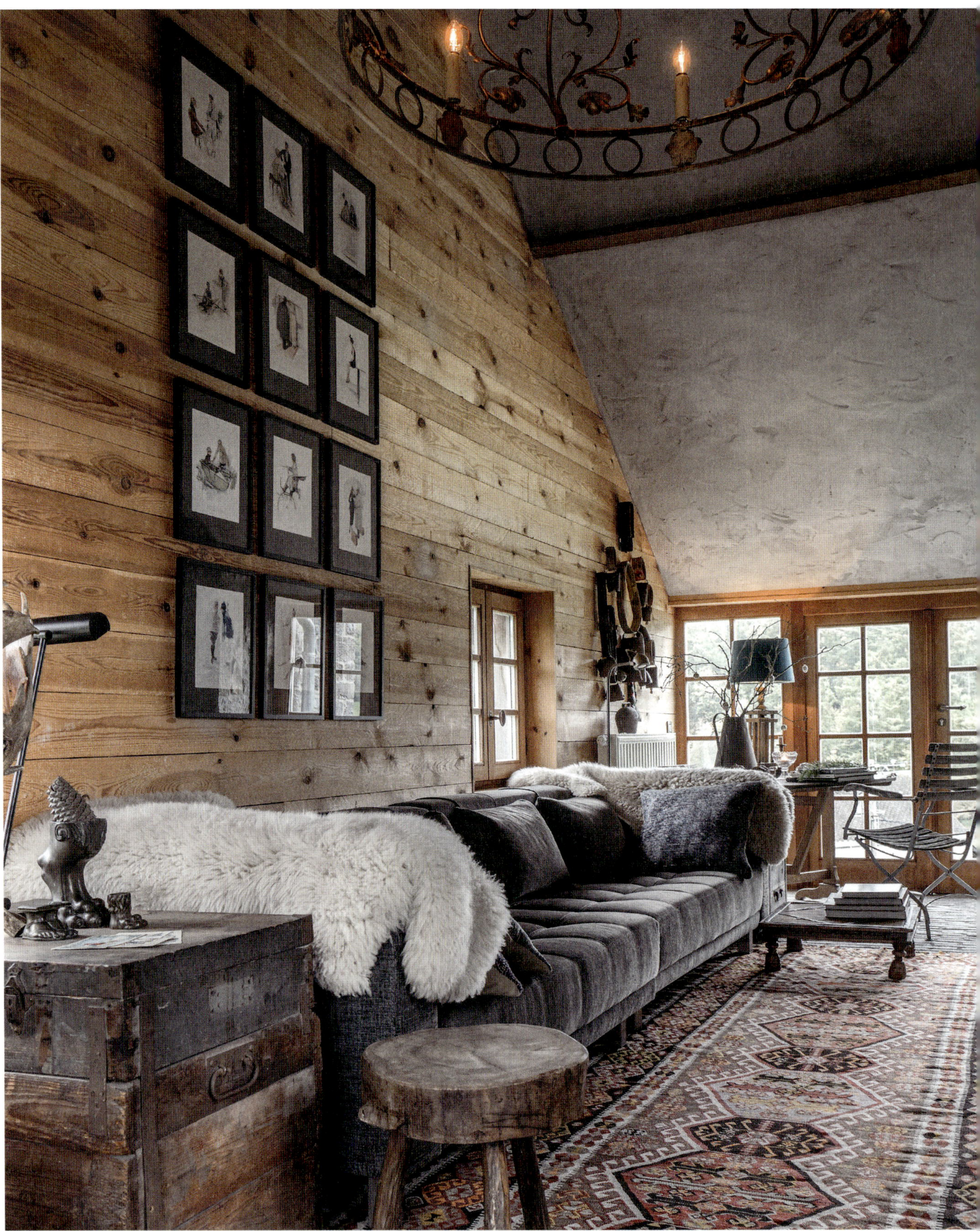

FEATURE

A COZY CHRISTMAS IN BELGIUM

A Home Full of History

Almost a decade ago, Magda and Claude purchased a charming country house near Maredsous, nestled between the Sambre and Meuse rivers. Dating back to around 1900, the house was originally part of a tobacco farm and served as a stable. Today, aside from a collection of cowbells and the gentle rolling hills, there's little trace of its past, creating a warm and cozy atmosphere year-round.

Christmas magic begins at their front door with a wicker star tied with a ribbon. The garden table is adorned with large metal stars and tea lights, while Magda has creatively draped Virginia creeper branches and Christmas lights around the steel frame. Upon entering the dining room, guests are greeted by a warm fireplace and a beautifully decorated Nordmann fir Christmas tree, its gray-green branches adorned with glass ornaments. The long wooden dining table features colorful Moroccan pottery, antique glassware, and stars made of birch bark, adding to the festive ambiance.

Magda excels in color combinations, using unexpected pairings like ox-red and "Majorelle" blue in the kitchen. The house retains its soul, with a stone wall preserving the region's characteristic gray stone. The weathered staircase and thick walls enhance its historic charm.

Despite its modest size, the home accommodates 10 guests, including their own cozy bedroom, two guest rooms, and an enchanting space under the roof with four neatly lined beds draped in red checkered blankets, perfect for the grandchildren. A Christmas book is always ready for Magda to read festive stories to her family.

Magda and Claude are inseparable, both in their professional lives—she as a stylist and he as an interior photographer—and their weekends are spent exploring local flea markets. Their home is filled with unique finds that have been given new life, showcasing their shared passion for creativity and design.

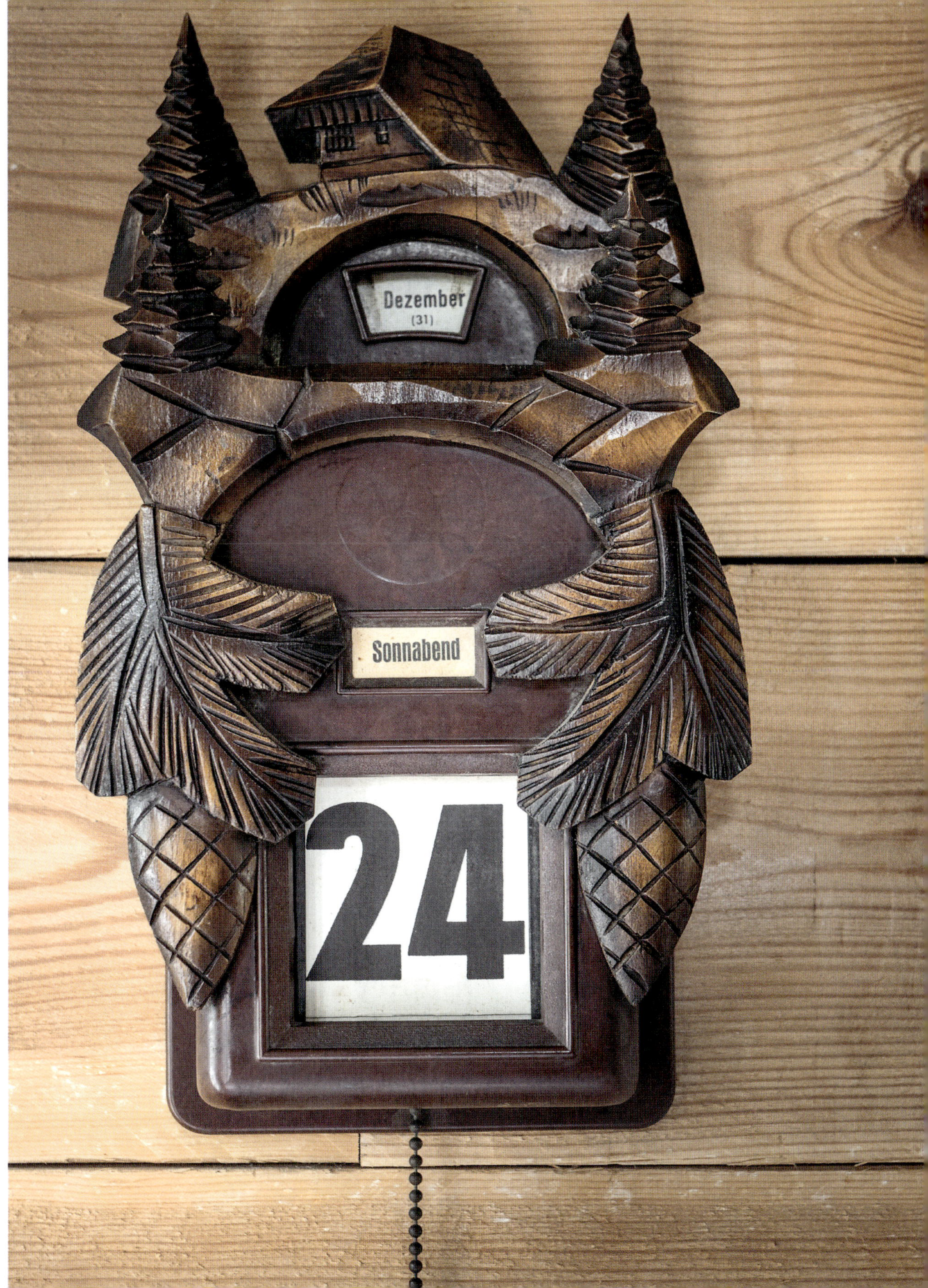
Dezember
(31)
Sonnabend
24

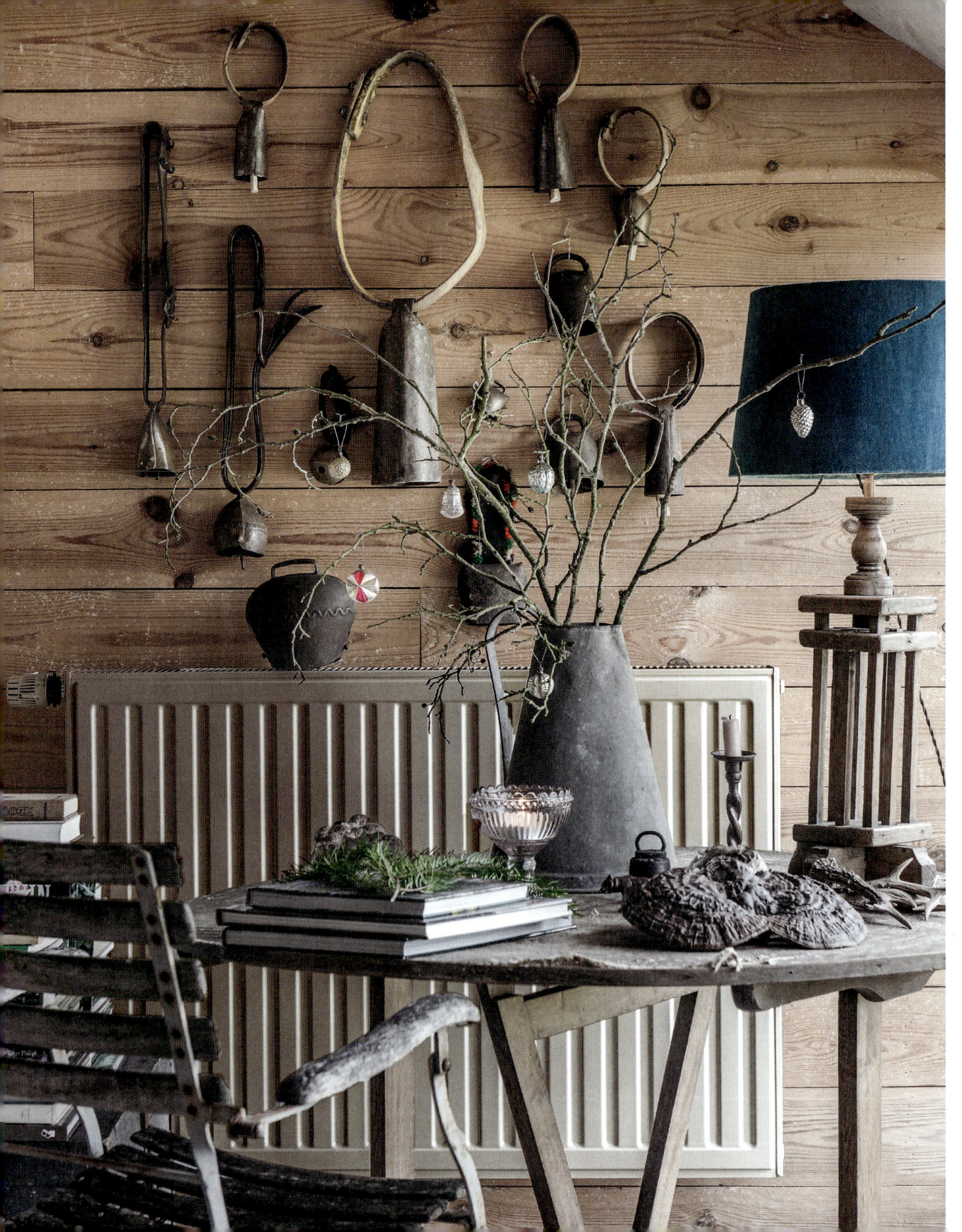

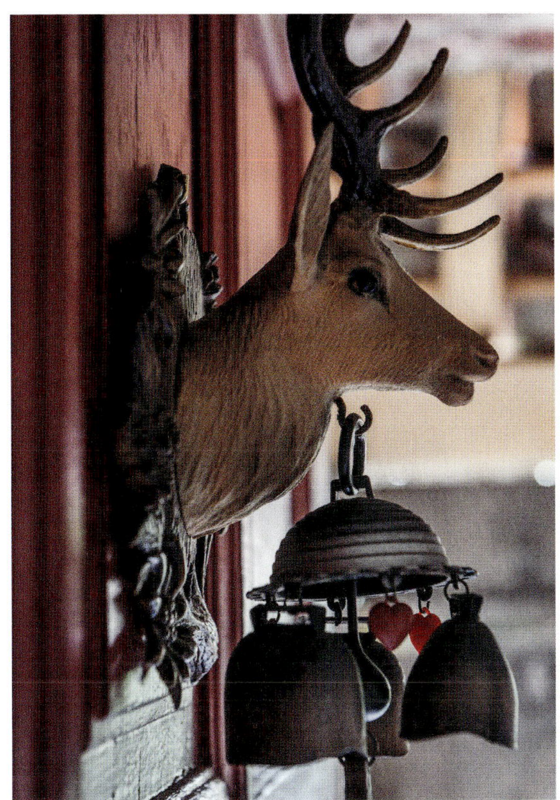

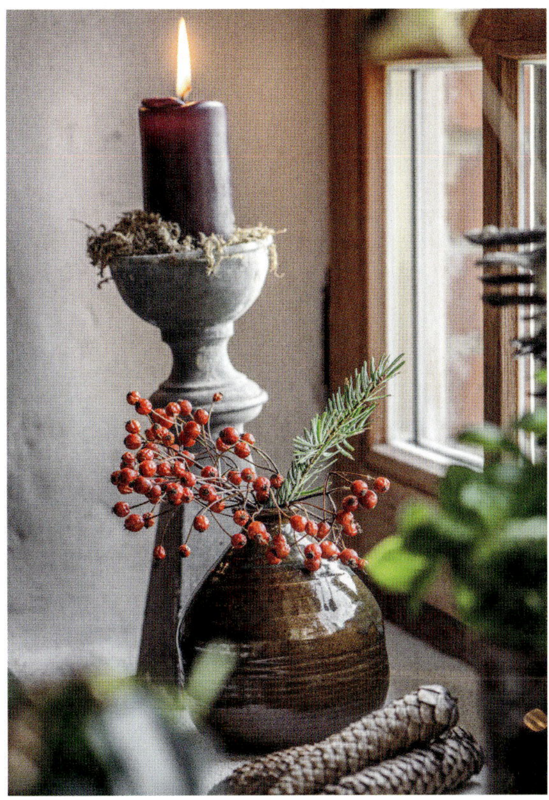

Magda is an avid collector. Her collection of cowbells is displayed on a wall in the living room.

MAGDA'S IDEAL CHRISTMAS ATMOSPHERE

"Christmas is different every year, it depends on where you experience the Christmas party. Because we are surrounded by nature here, I use branches and mosses that I find in the forest. While it's dark outside, I make it cozy inside with greenery and lots of candles. A Christmas tree is not always necessary for me."

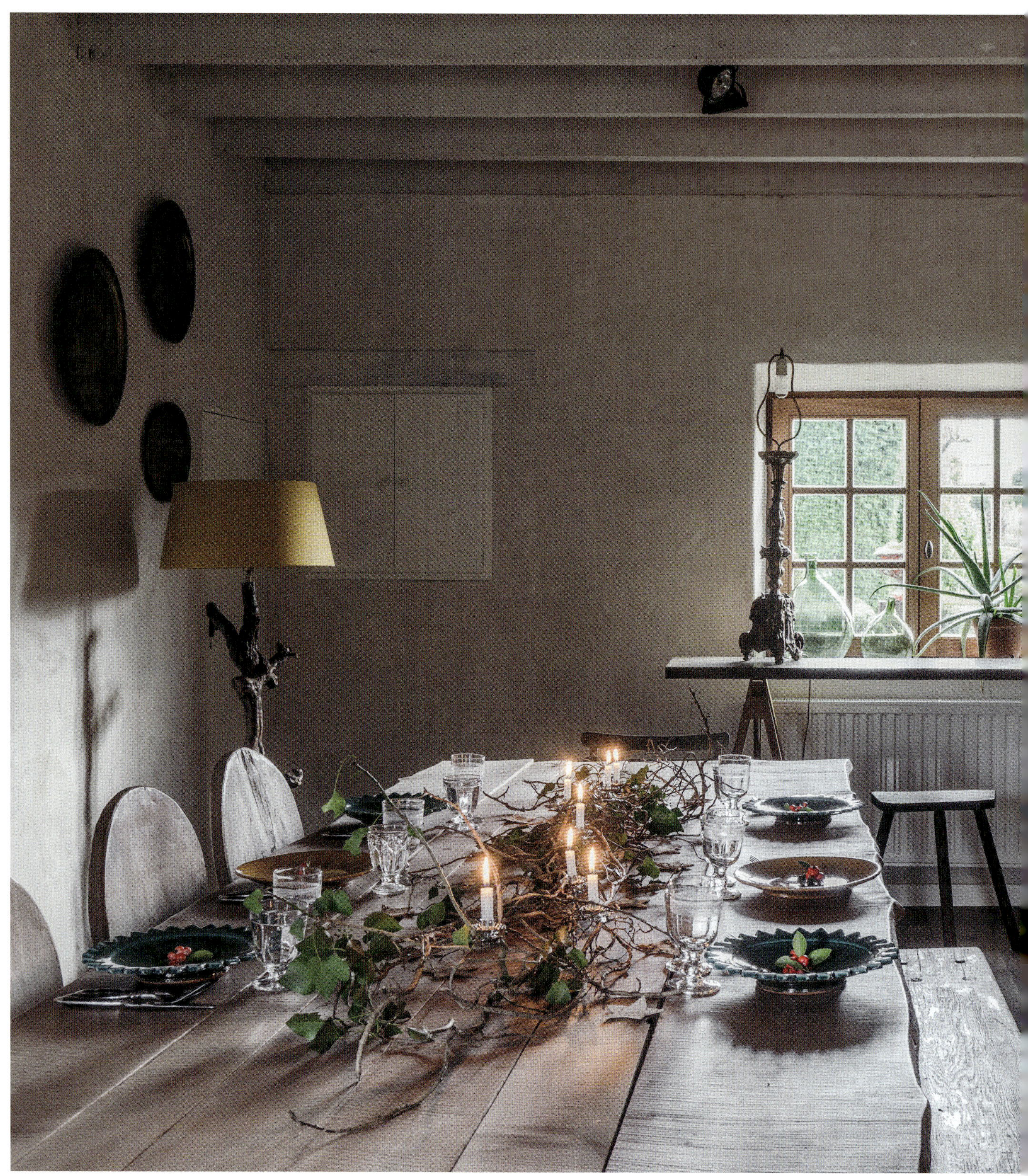

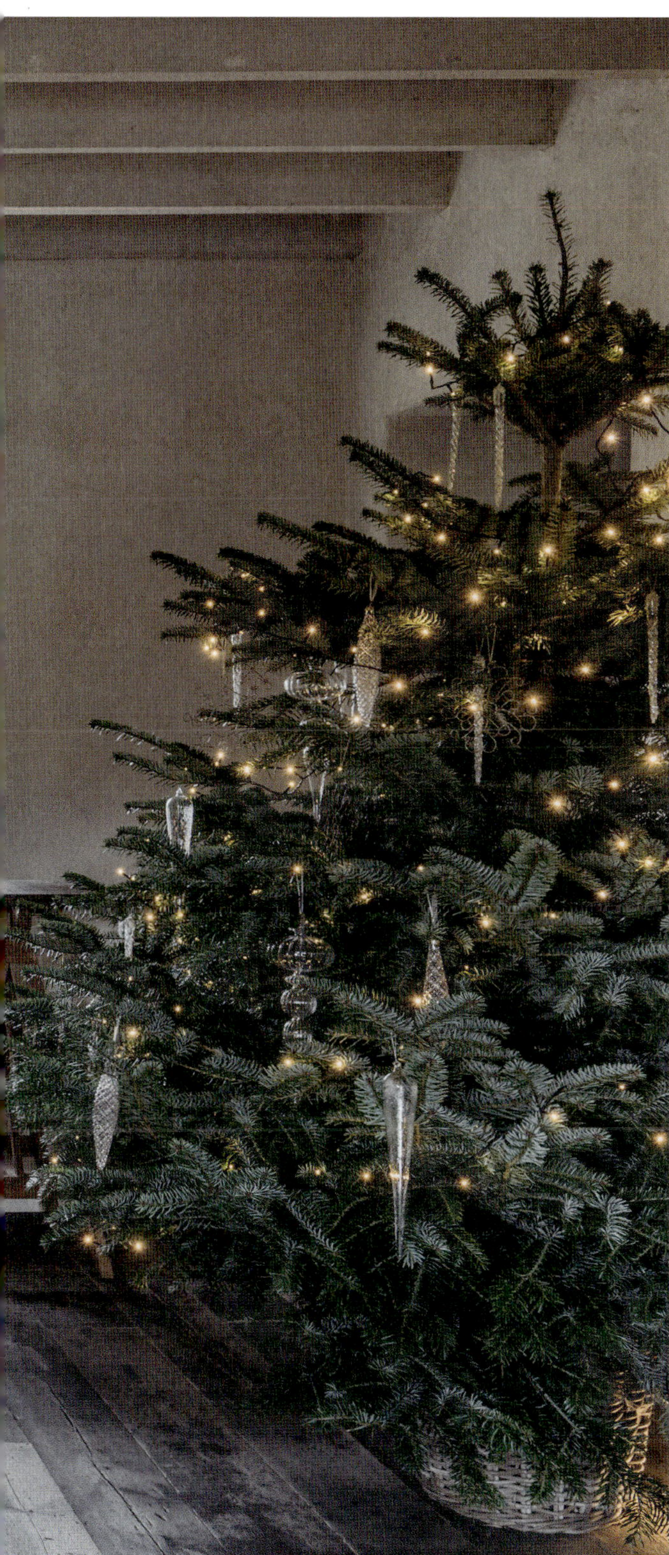

The atmosphere in Magda and Claude's dining room is very natural, with its lime and sand walls and a rustic wooden table adorned with candles, pottery, and foliage. The roughly hewn wooden chairs perfectly complement the room's pared-back charm. Meanwhile, the beautifully decorated Christmas tree, twinkling with glass ornaments, makes this the perfect place for festive family gatherings!

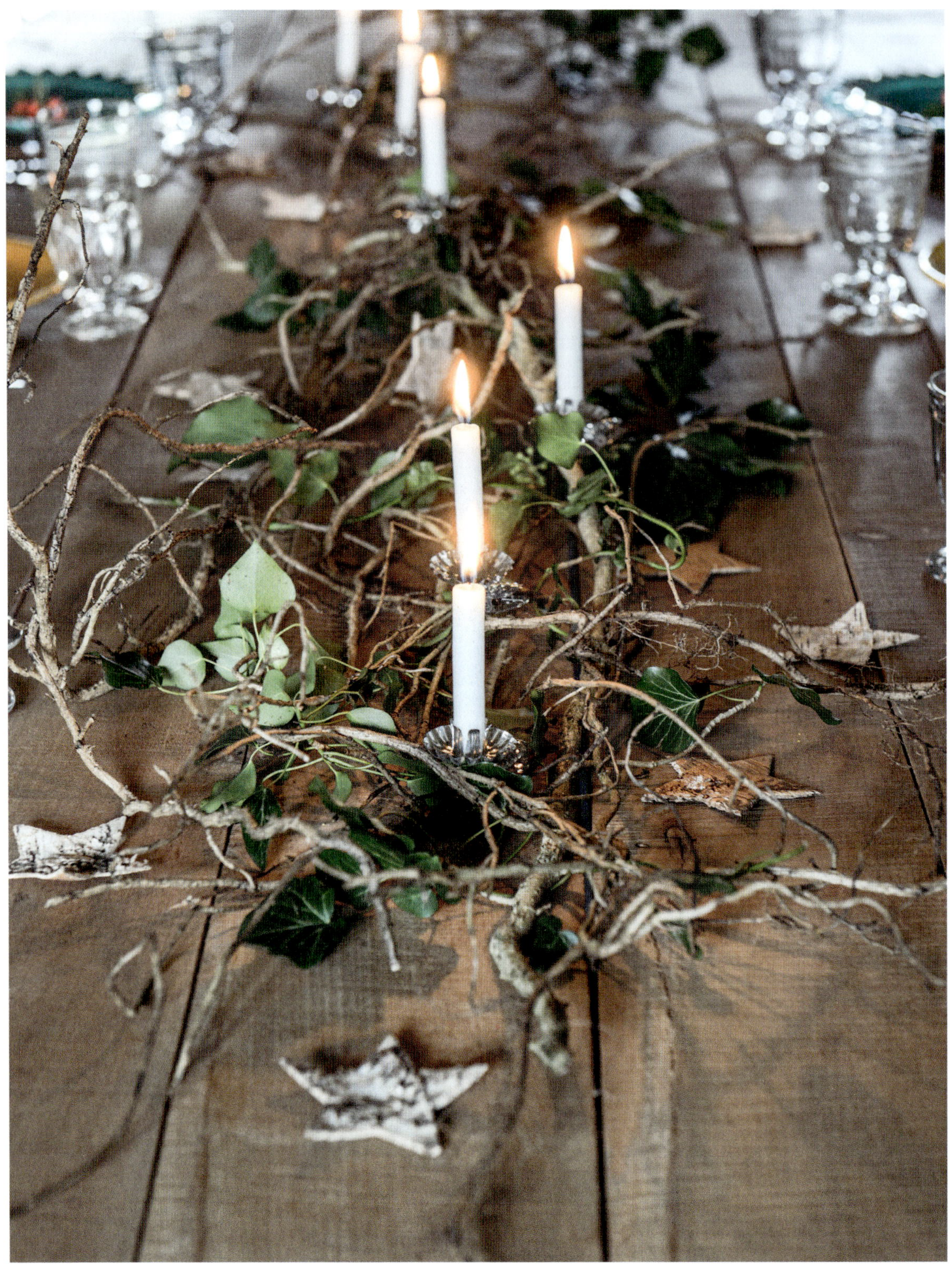

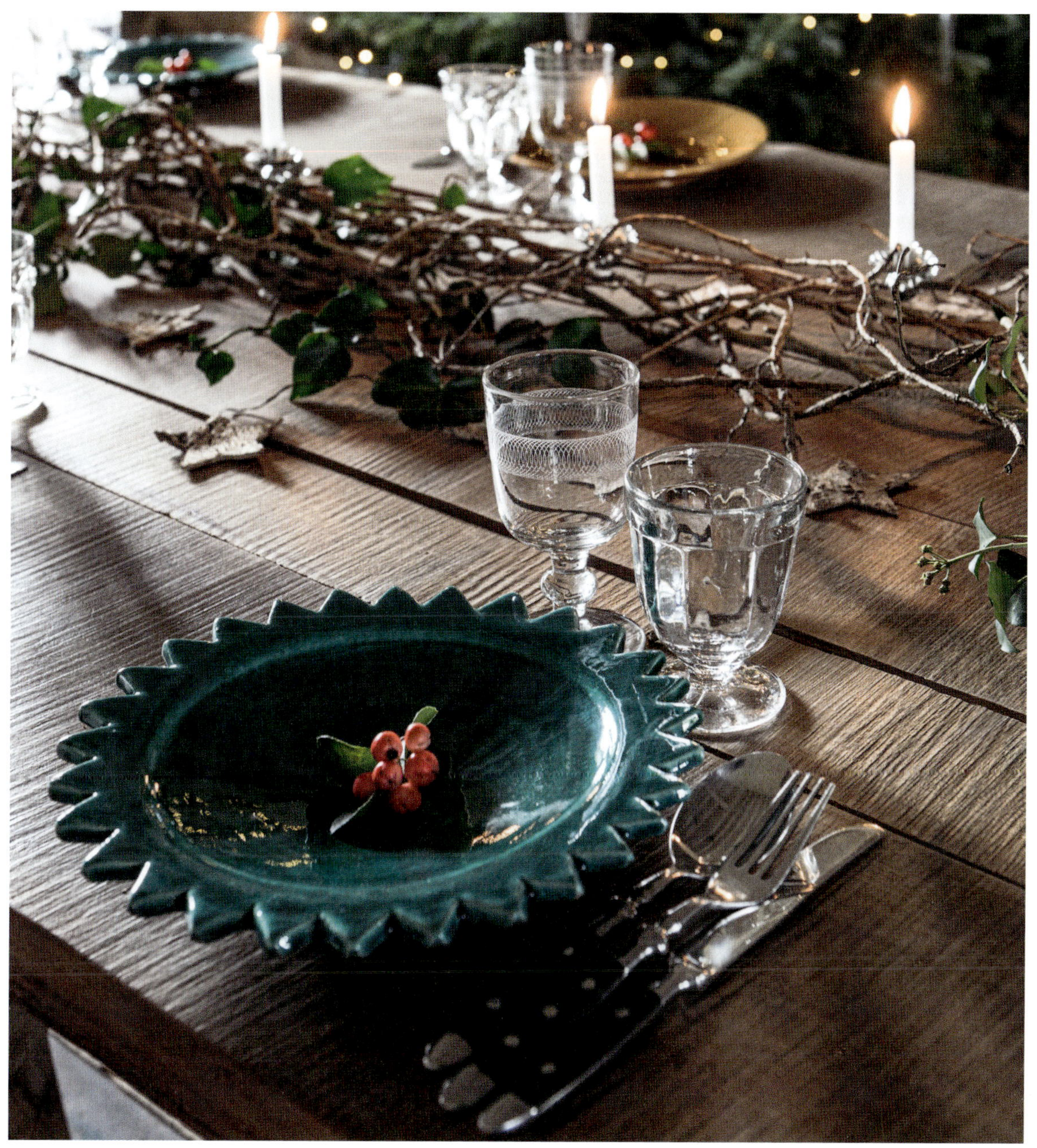

The dining table is set with candles, colorful plates from Morocco and the south of France, antique glassware, and branches and ivy vines from the forest.

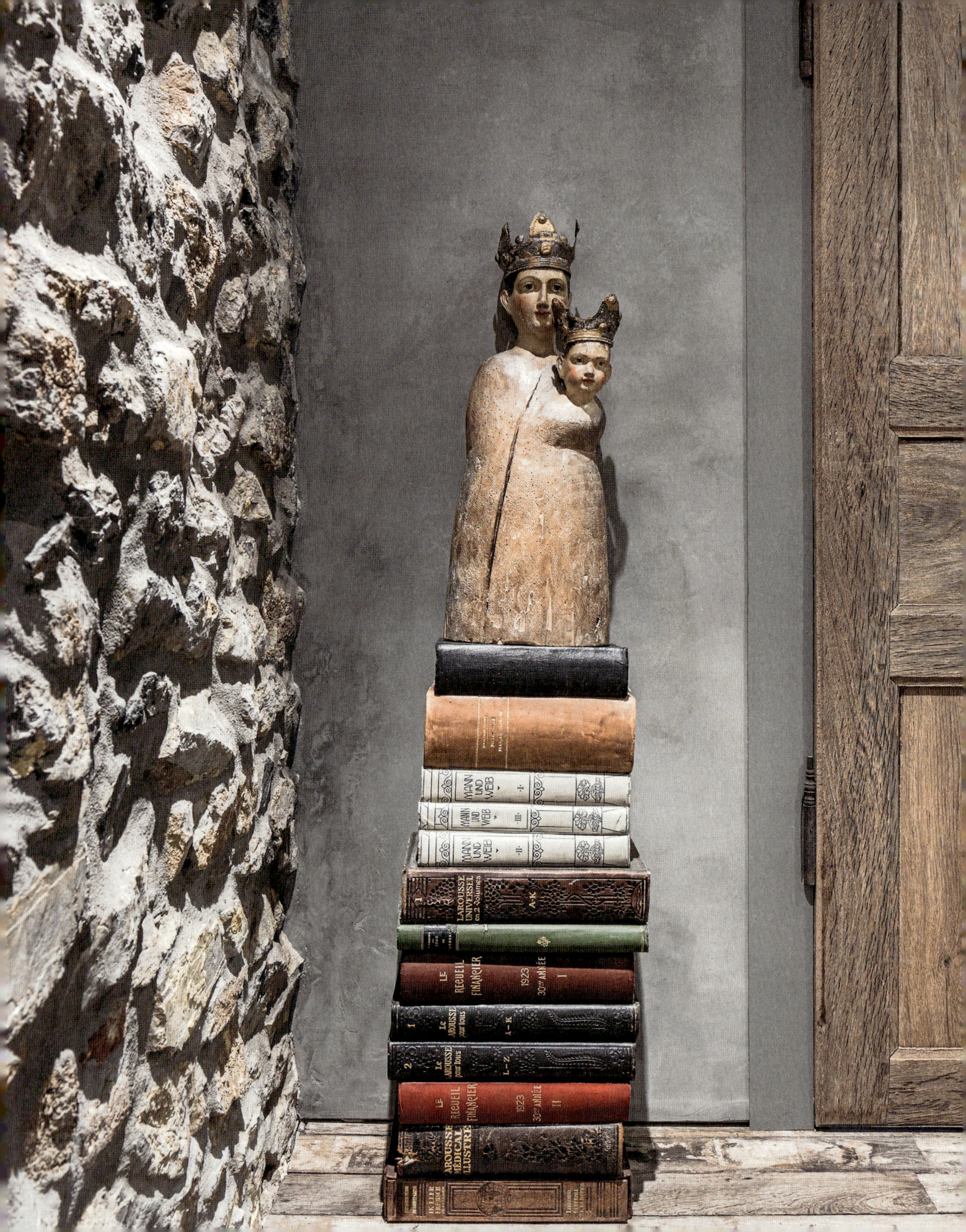

MANN UND WEIB -I-
MANN UND WEIB -III-
MANN UND WEIB -II-
1 LAROUSSE UNIVERSEL en 2 Volumes A-K
LE RECUEIL FINANCIER 1923 30me ANNÉE I
LE RECUEIL FINANCIER 1923 30me ANNÉE II

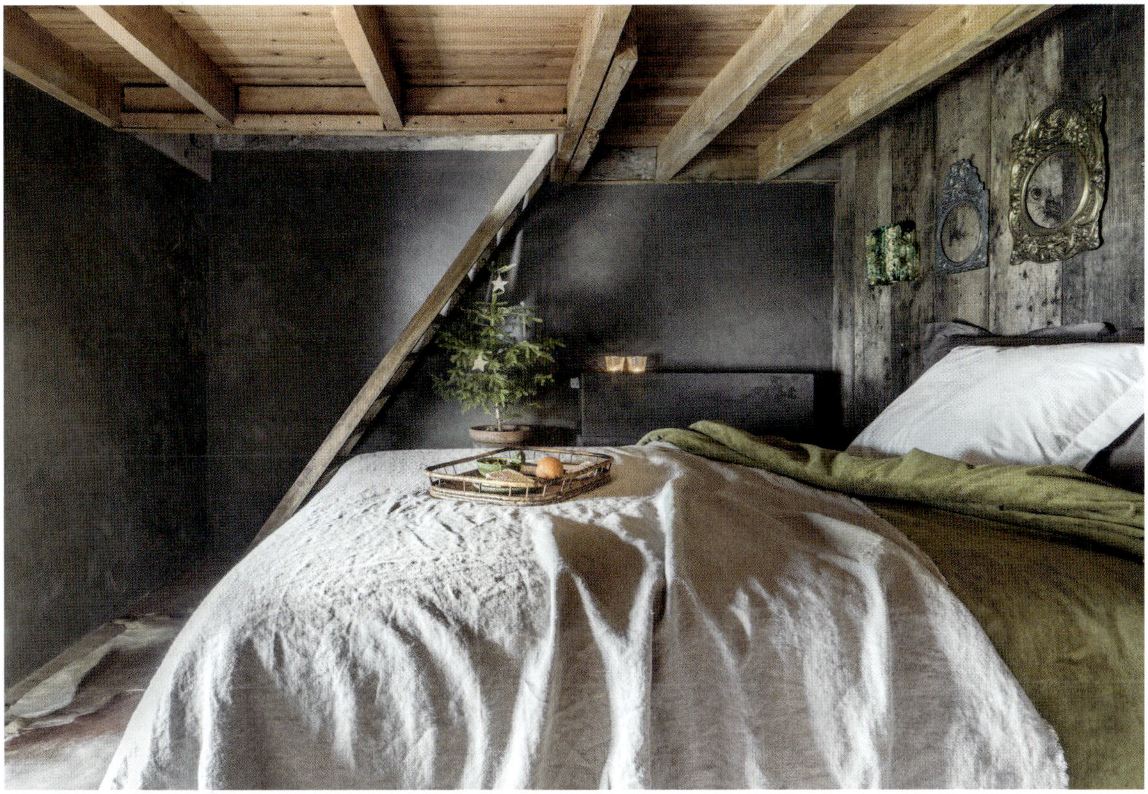

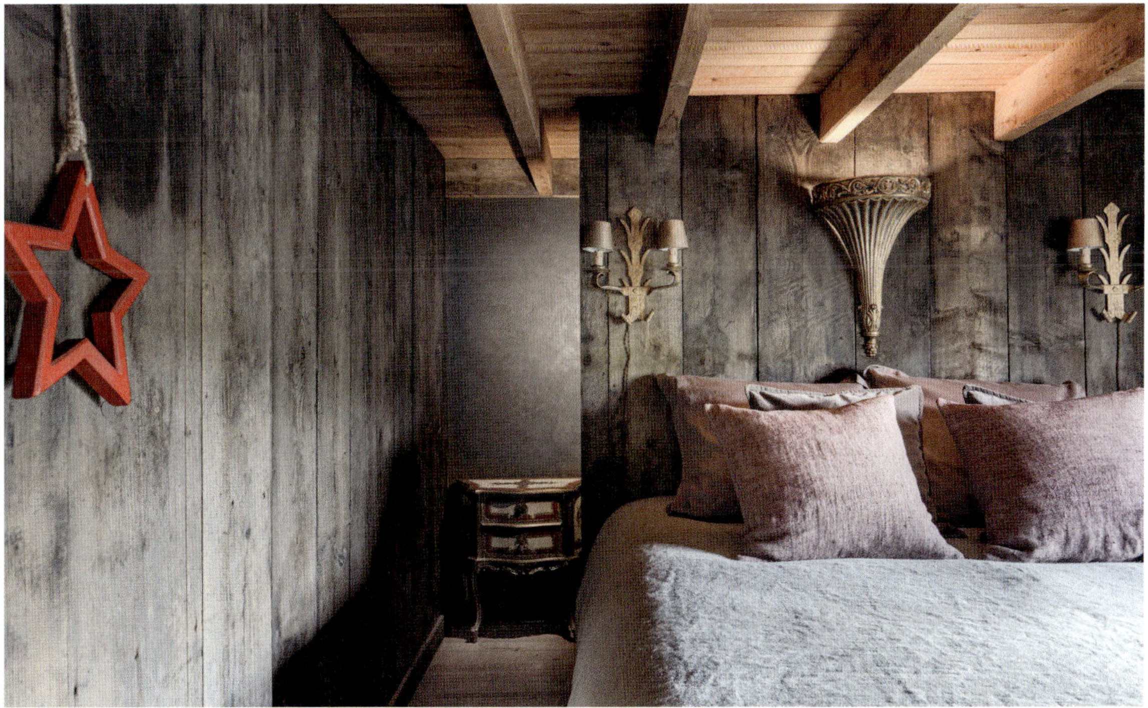

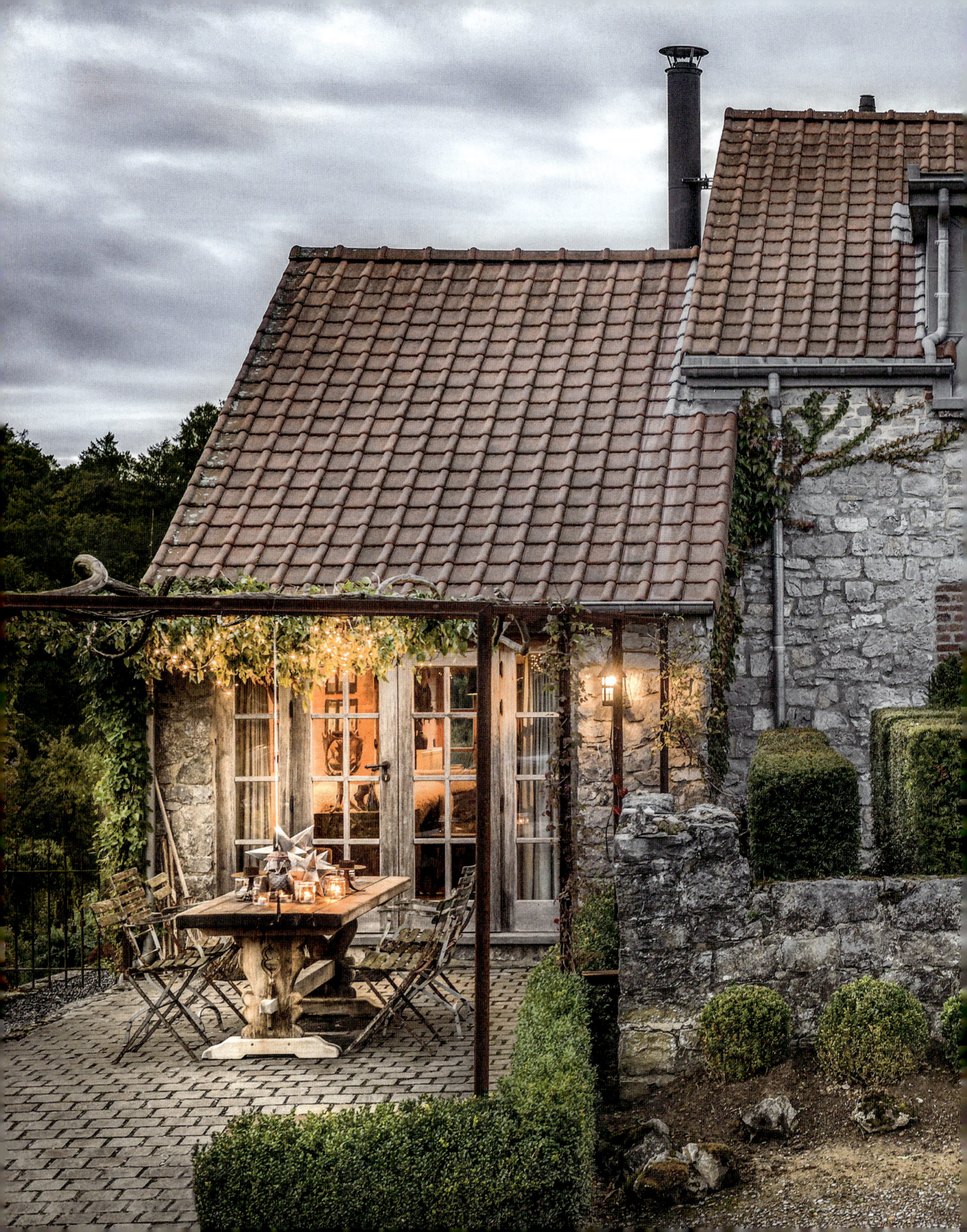

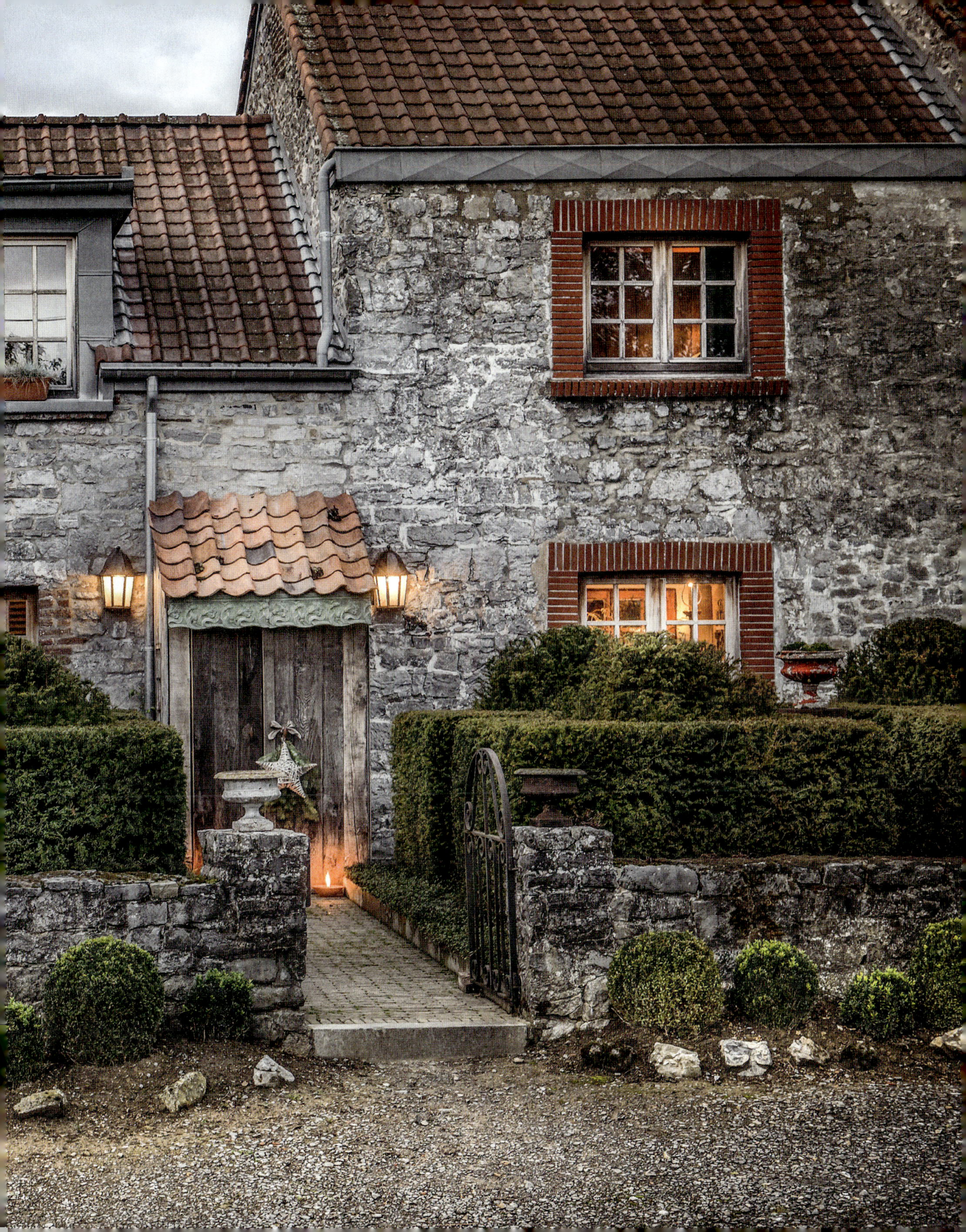

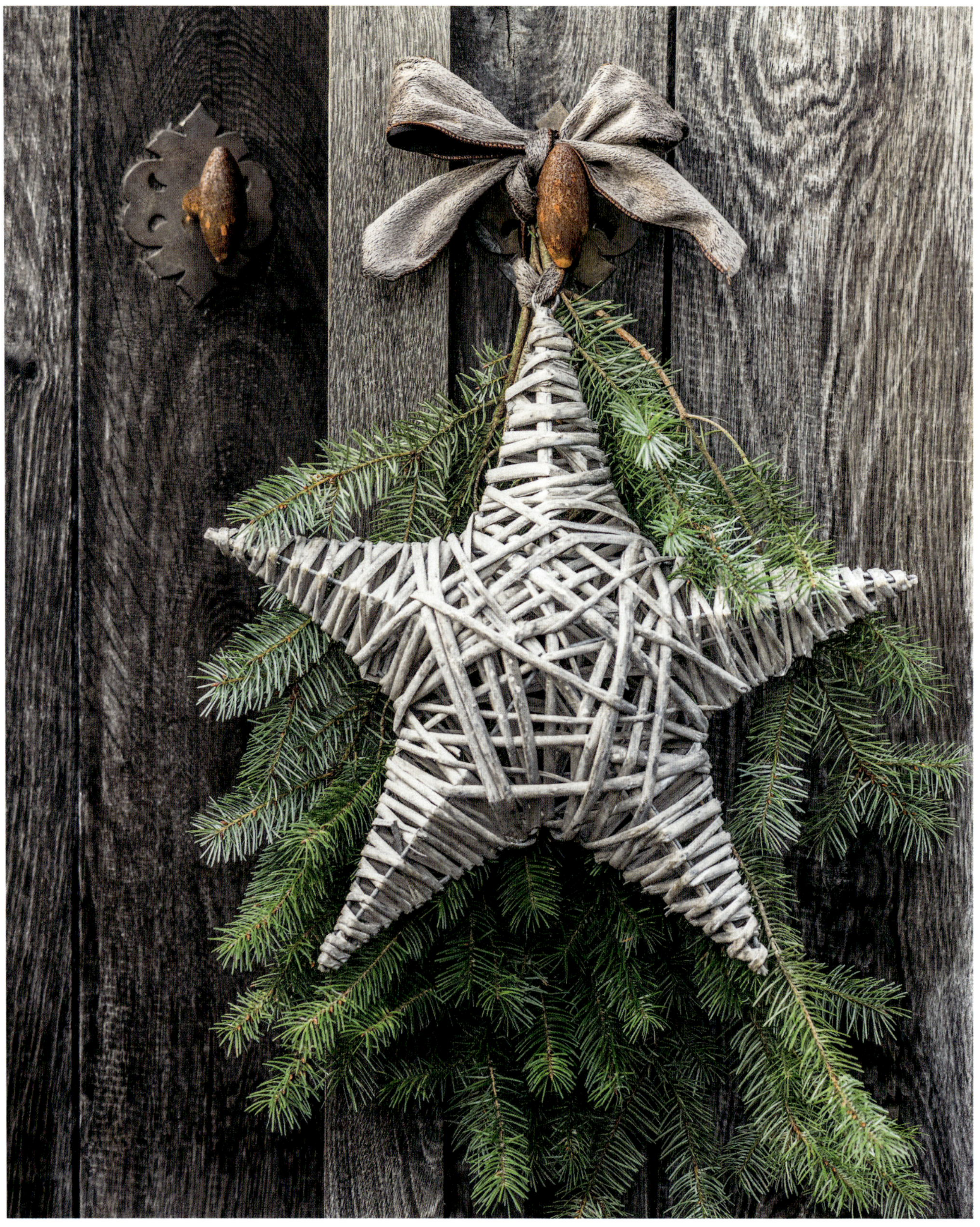

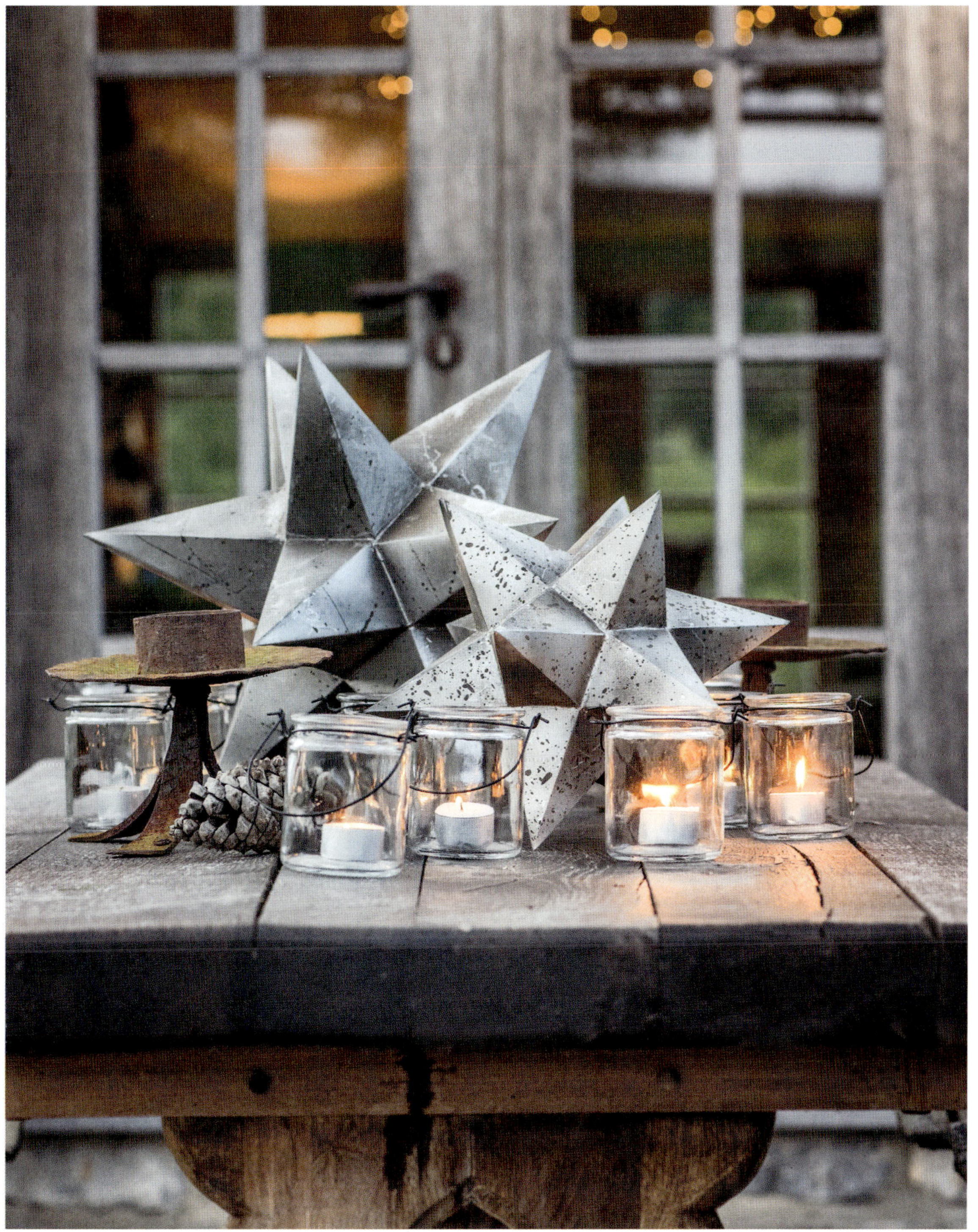

The garden table is strewn with large metal stars and many tea lights.

Creative Trees

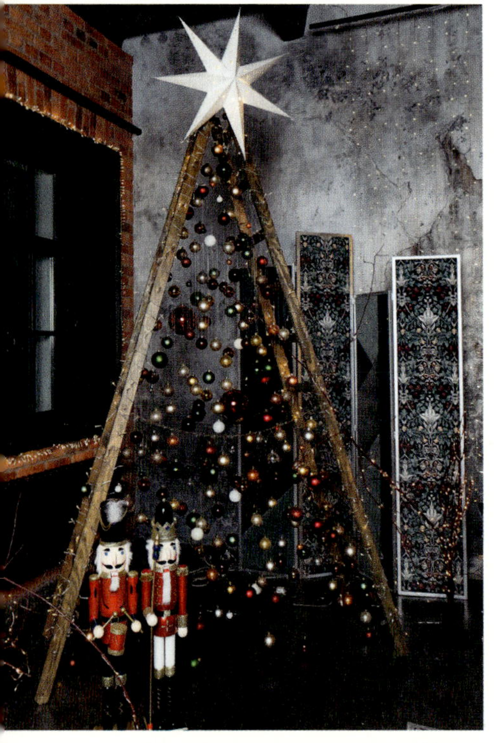

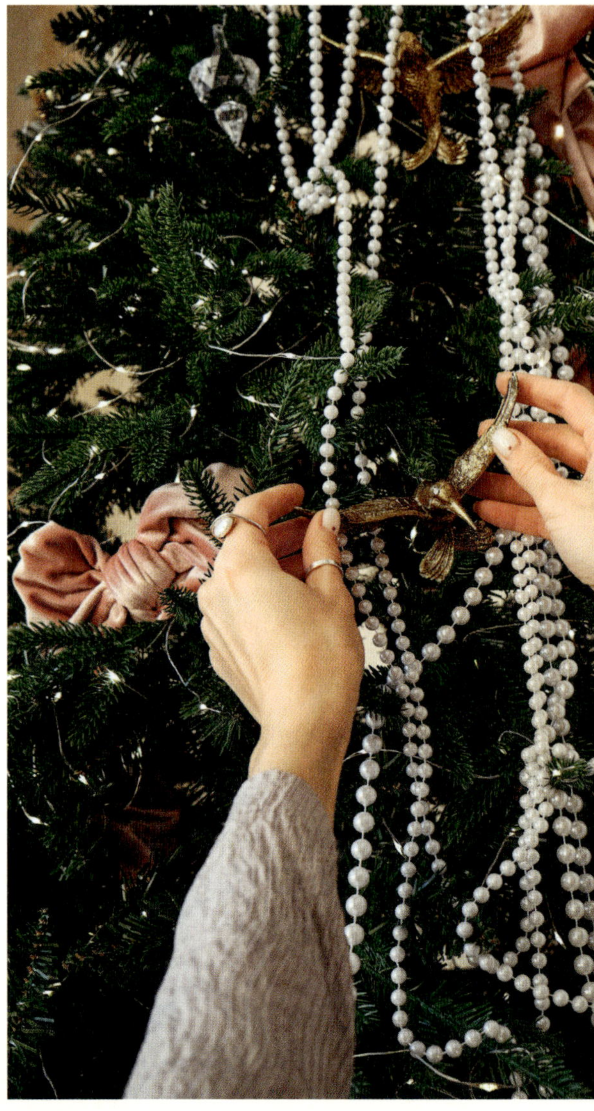

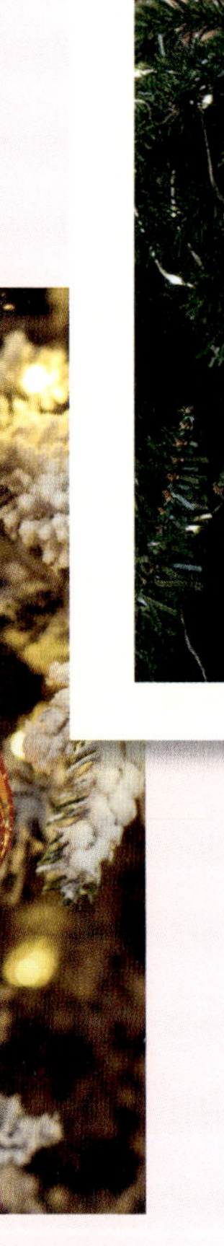

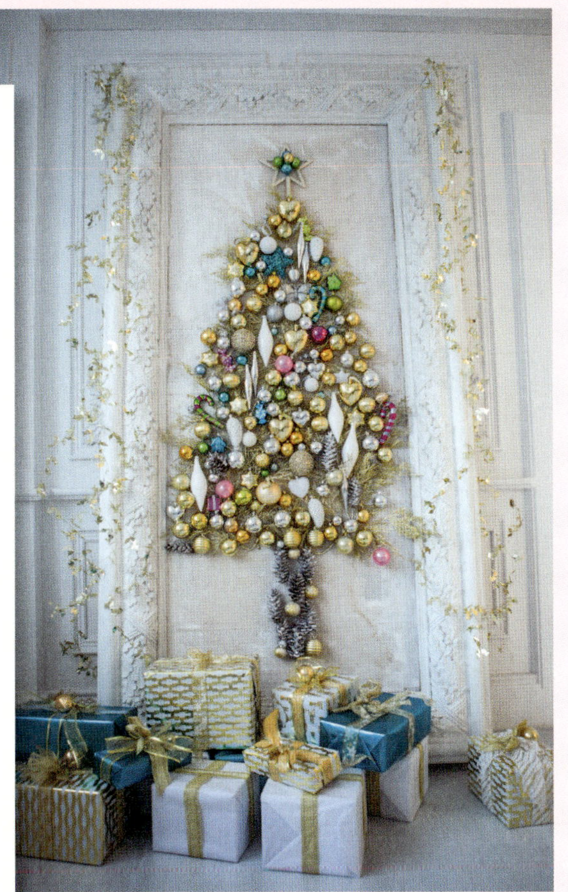

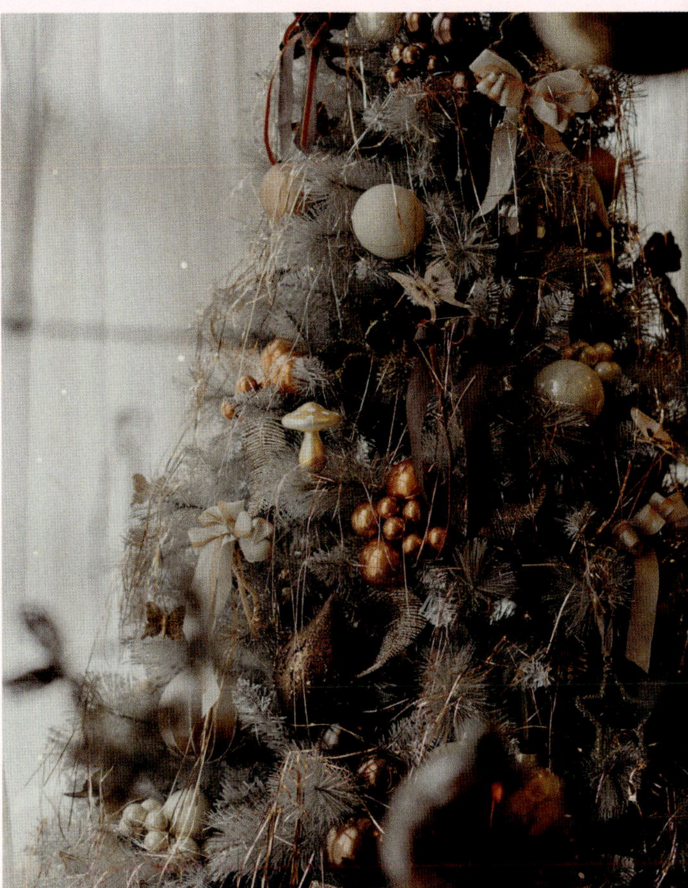

Whether natural or artificial, Christmas trees serve as a central symbol of the festive season, offering limitless opportunities for creative expression. Traditionally adorned with lights, ornaments, and tinsel, these trees can be customized in numerous unique and personal ways. Feathers can impart a sense of airy lightness, while beads, bows, and tassels contribute to a sophisticated appearance. Incorporating natural elements like pine cones or dried fruit adds a charming, rustic flair. For those seeking something a bit unconventional, alternatives such as a decorated ladder in place of a tree or a wall embellished with ornaments can effectively evoke the joyful spirit of a classic Christmas tree.

It's important to note that tree decorating customs vary widely around the globe. As previously mentioned, some traditions include the Christmas pickle and spider's web. In Spain, chocolate figures representing the Three Wise Men are often hung on their trees, while in Denmark, cone-shaped candy bags make festive additions. In the United States, popcorn garlands are a popular choice. Ultimately, edible decorations stand out as the most environmentally friendly option.

FEATURE

A COUNTRY-CHIC CHRISTMAS IN SARZANA

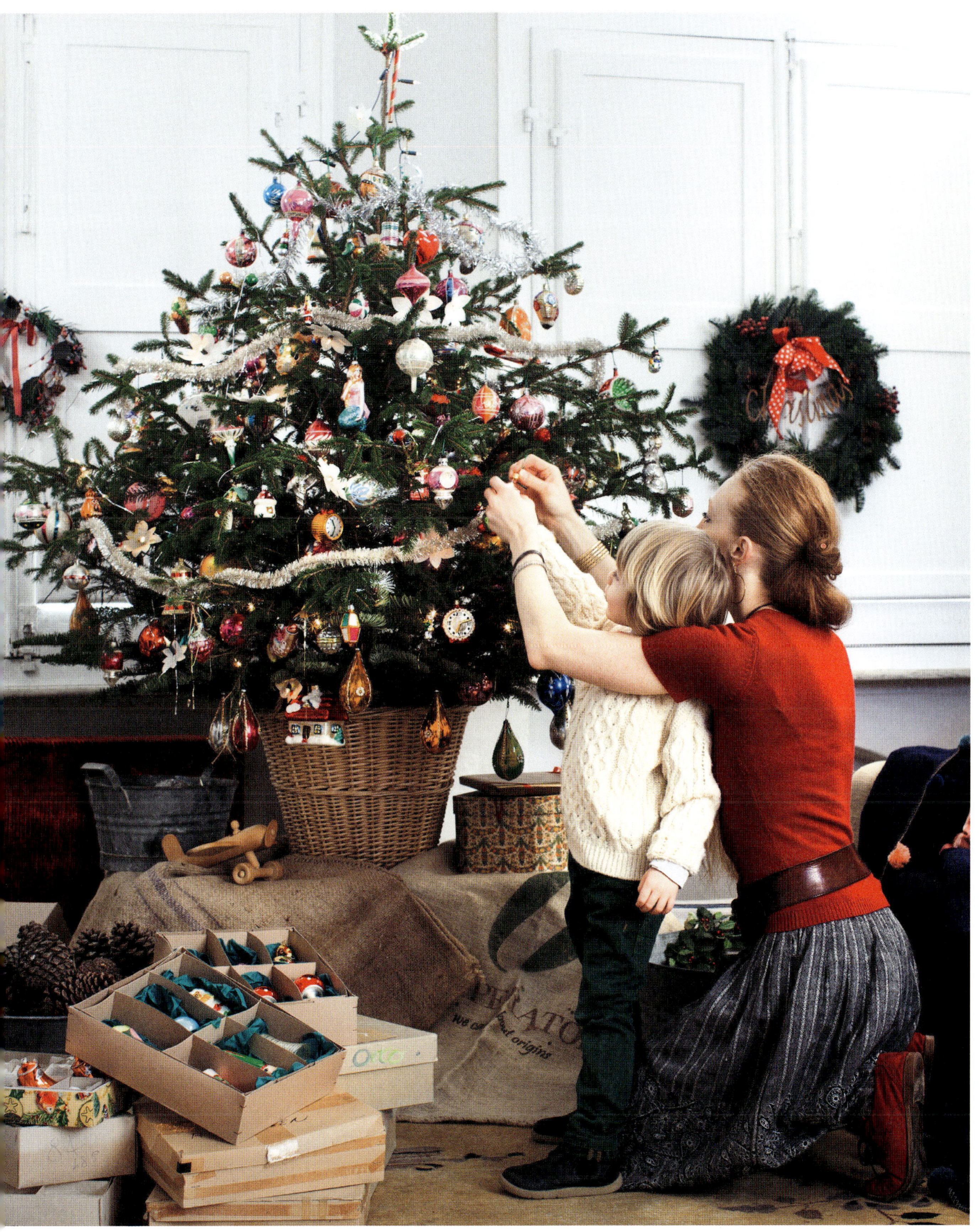

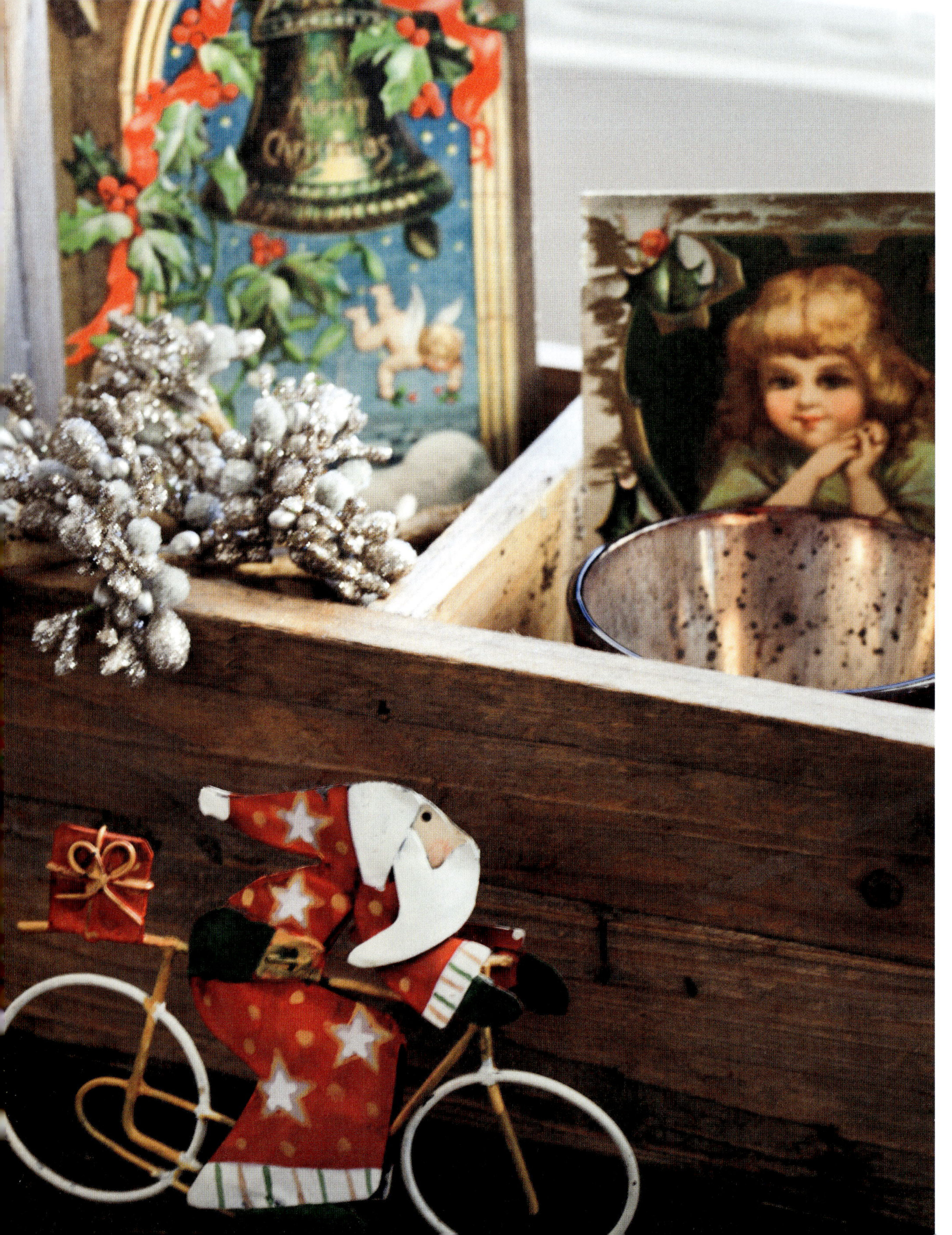

Margherita's Festive Treasures

Margherita lives with her family in a beautifully restored 1500s building in the historic center of Sarzana, Italy, facing the cathedral. Originally the site of the town hall, the space now houses Il laboratorio nell'orto, a unique fabric store run by Margherita and her mother. They create colorful fabric decorations, including aprons, tablecloths, curtains, and custom clothing for children, alongside a diverse range of handcrafted materials from around the world.

Margherita has a deep affection for Sarzana, having cherished this home since first sight. The atmosphere reflects generations of family life, and during Christmas, the holiday spirit bathes the space in a warm, magical light. Her passion for breathing new life into old or abandoned objects is evident throughout her home, which she lovingly curates into a treasure chest of memories.

Perched in the attic, their apartment boasts views over Sarzana's medieval streets. Once a loggia, the room features tall windows that fill the space with natural light. Each Christmas, the traditional tree takes center stage, a cherished tradition for Margherita. Adorned with glass ornaments of various shapes and colors—from family heirlooms to flea market finds—this collection grows each year and is lovingly preserved.

The care Margherita devotes to decorating the tree is reflected in all aspects of her holiday decor. Green garlands, pine cones, and dried floral arrangements—all strictly handmade—create a festive atmosphere throughout the home. Each detail showcases Margherita's dedication to harmonizing colors and textures, making every corner feel special and unique.

The kitchen exudes warmth with a harmonious blend of ancient and modern objects. Large and small cups, boxes, teapots, and vases come together to create a charming tableau. The deep-green cupboard, once a pot holder in a country house, dominates the scene, filled with memories. Unique touches include a shelf made from a beach-found window shutter, a damask tablecloth adorned with poinsettias, and festive aprons featuring Santa Claus and mistletoe.

Margherita's style, much like her home, defies a single definition. It is eclectic yet traditional, combining subjective and universal elements that evoke nostalgic homey feelings. This unique blend creates a deeply personal, distinctive, and inviting atmosphere.

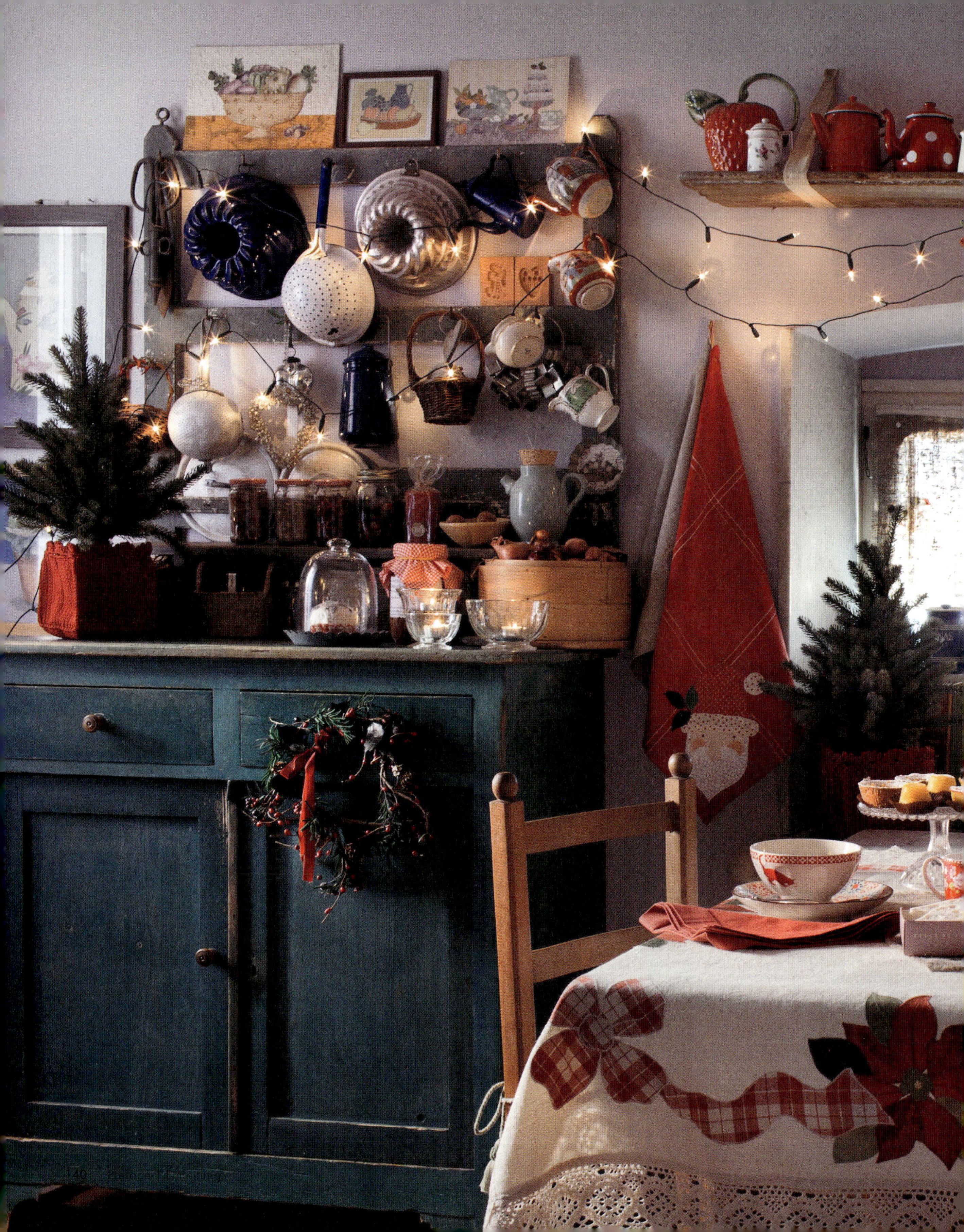

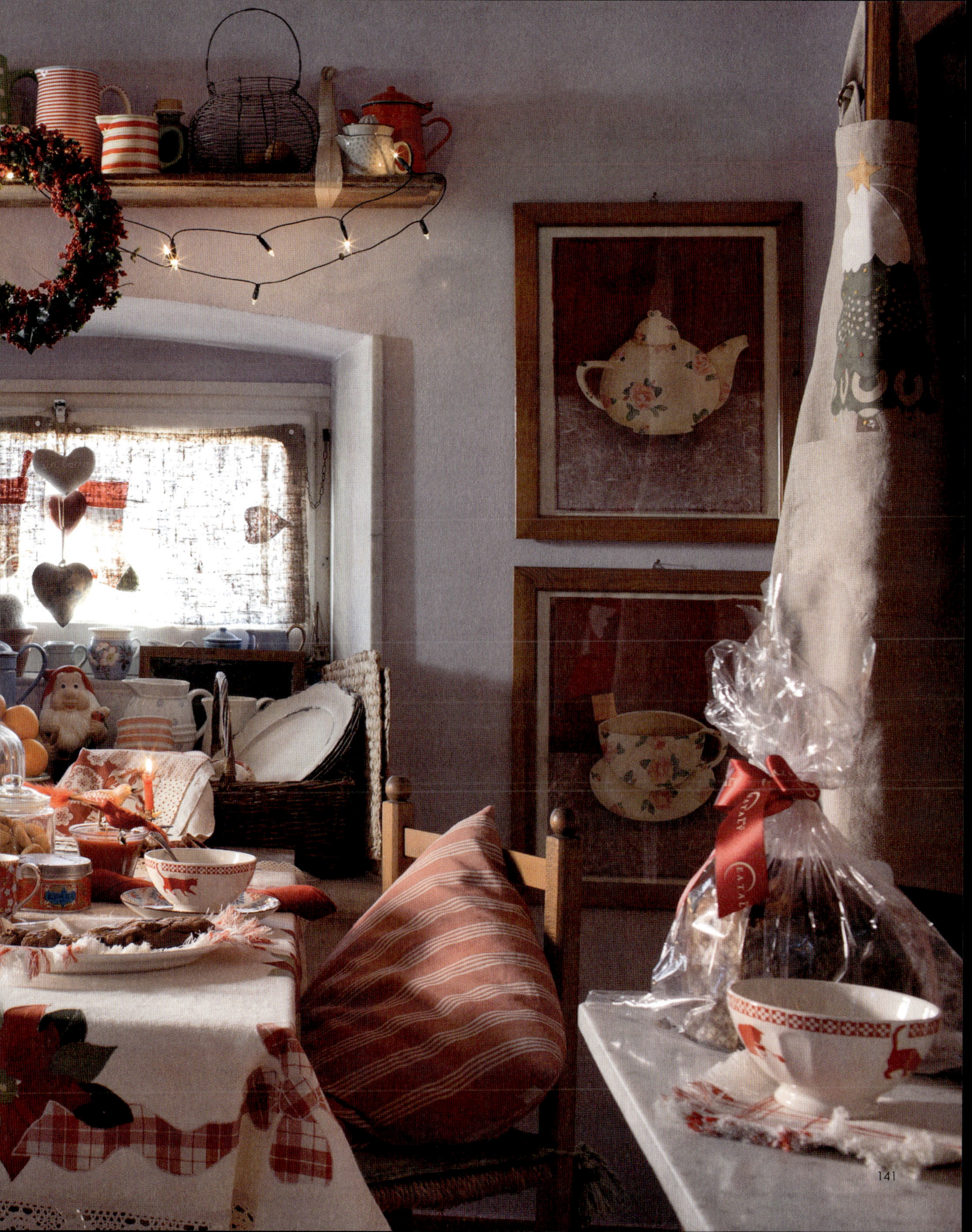

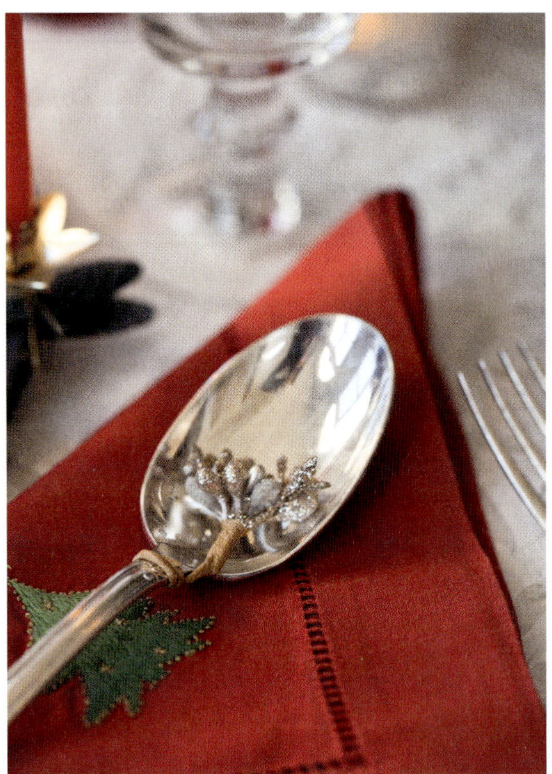

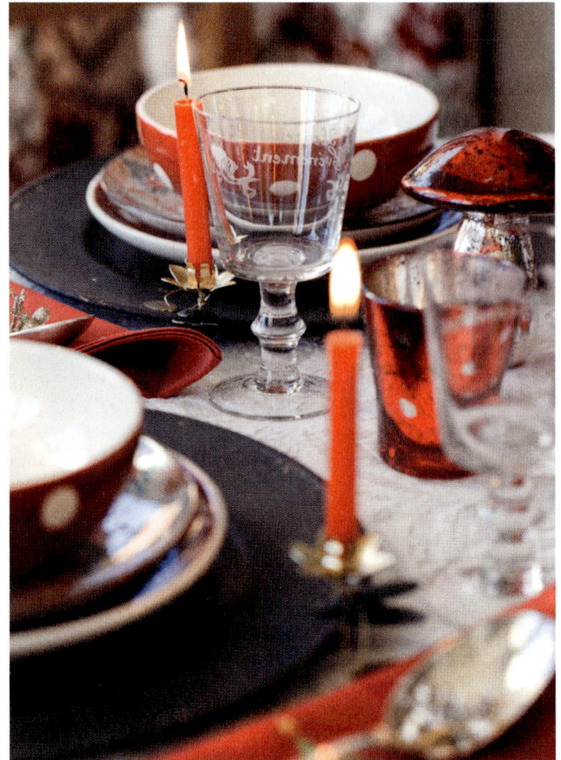

In the intimate dining area, the decor is equally personal. The curtains feature a *mezzero* fabric typical of the Genoa area, and a long bench once found in a billiard room adds character. An old cheese display cabinet now holds Victorian postcards and books, alongside items that reflect Margherita's dreams and wishes. The table setting contrasts a white tablecloth of overlapping Indian gauze with bright red dishes, including polka dot plates and charming Christmas decorations. Adorable glass mushrooms and tealights from Chehoma and little red birds by local artist Giuliano Tomaino complete the scene, creating a festive and inviting centerpiece for holiday gatherings.

The Christmas spirit weaves through every room in the house, and each room features a tree. A large, colorful one graces the hall, small green trees decorate the kitchen, and the primary bedroom features a charming composition by Walther & Co. alongside a large tree on the wall in her son's room.

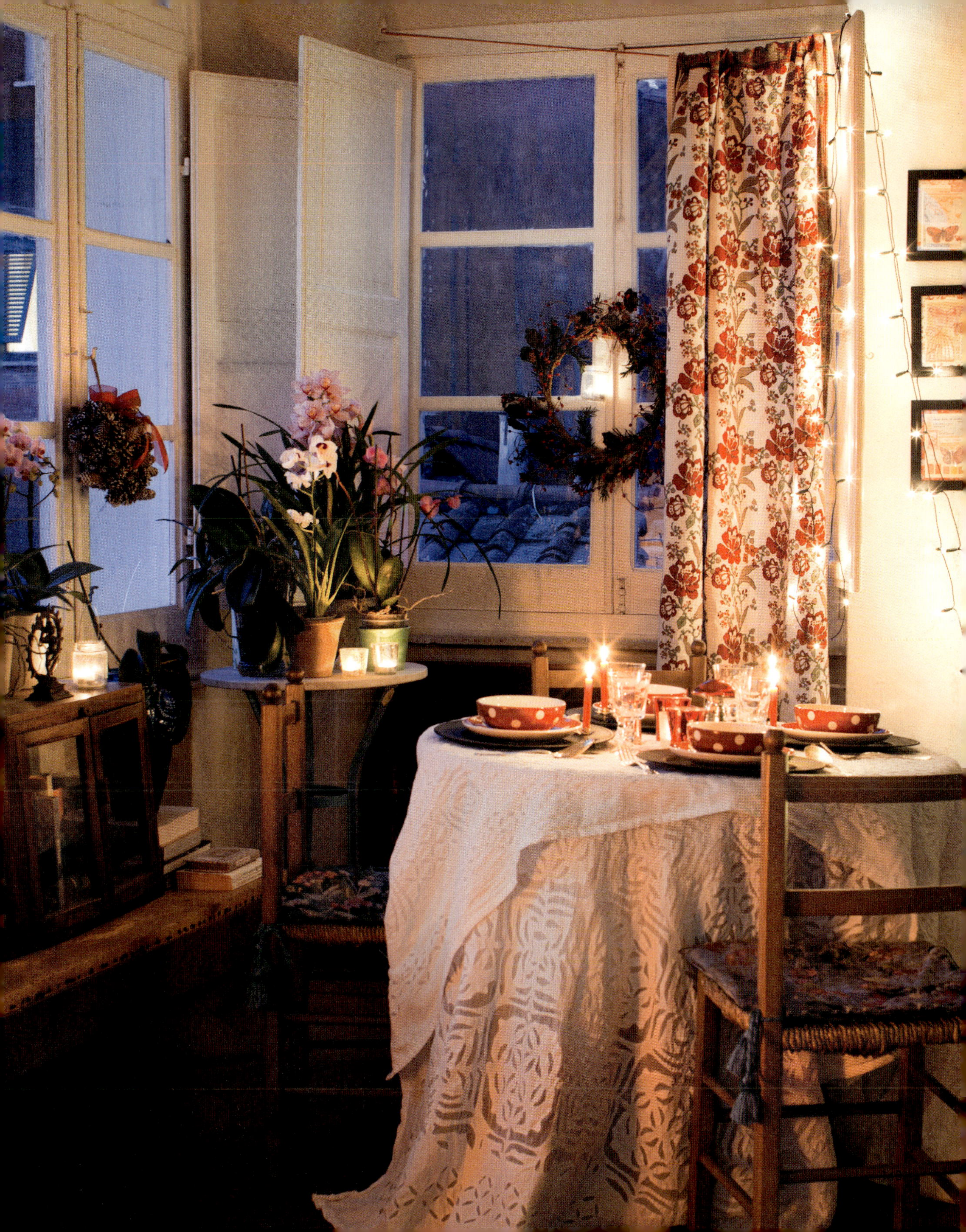

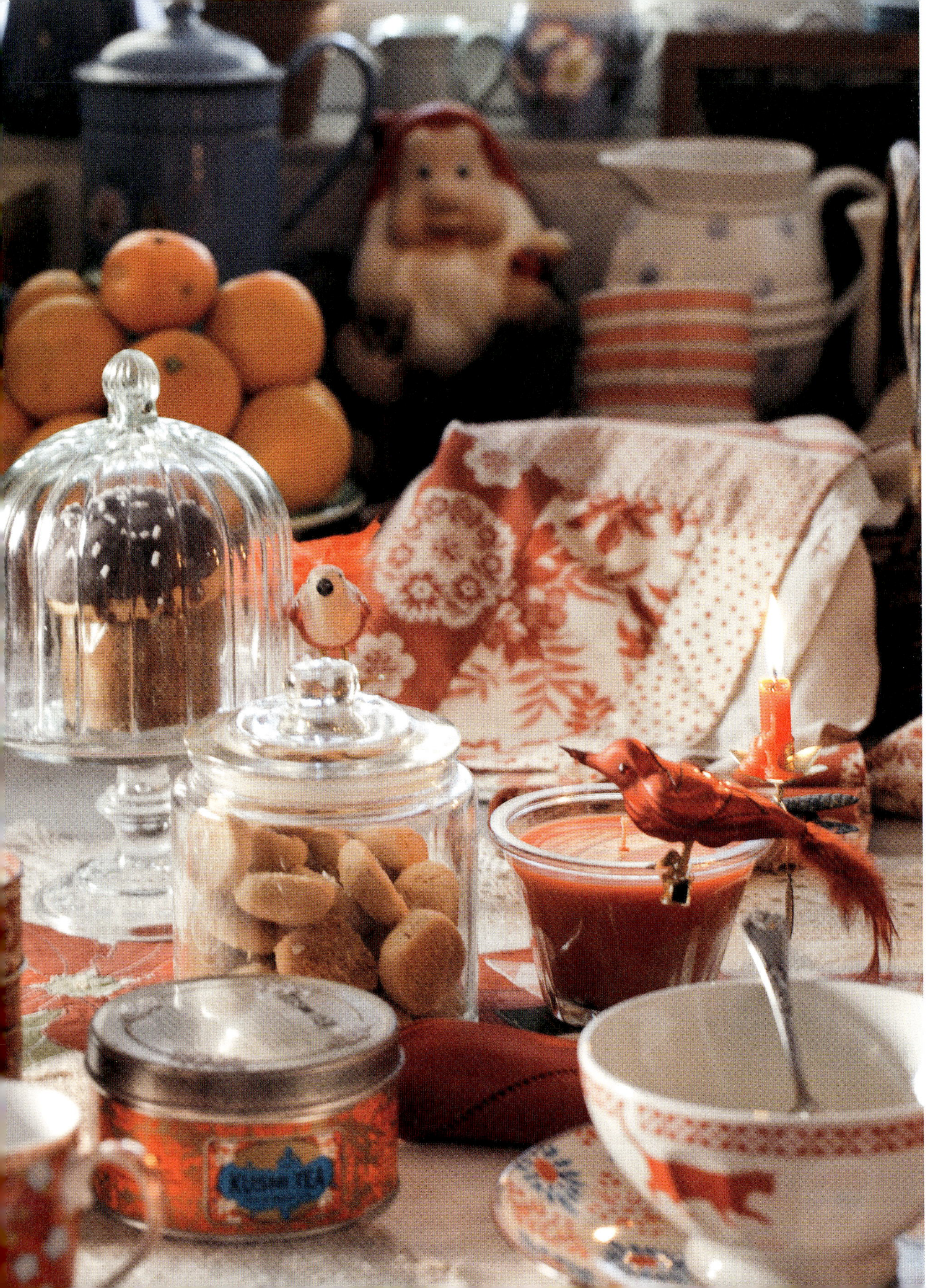
KUSMI TEA

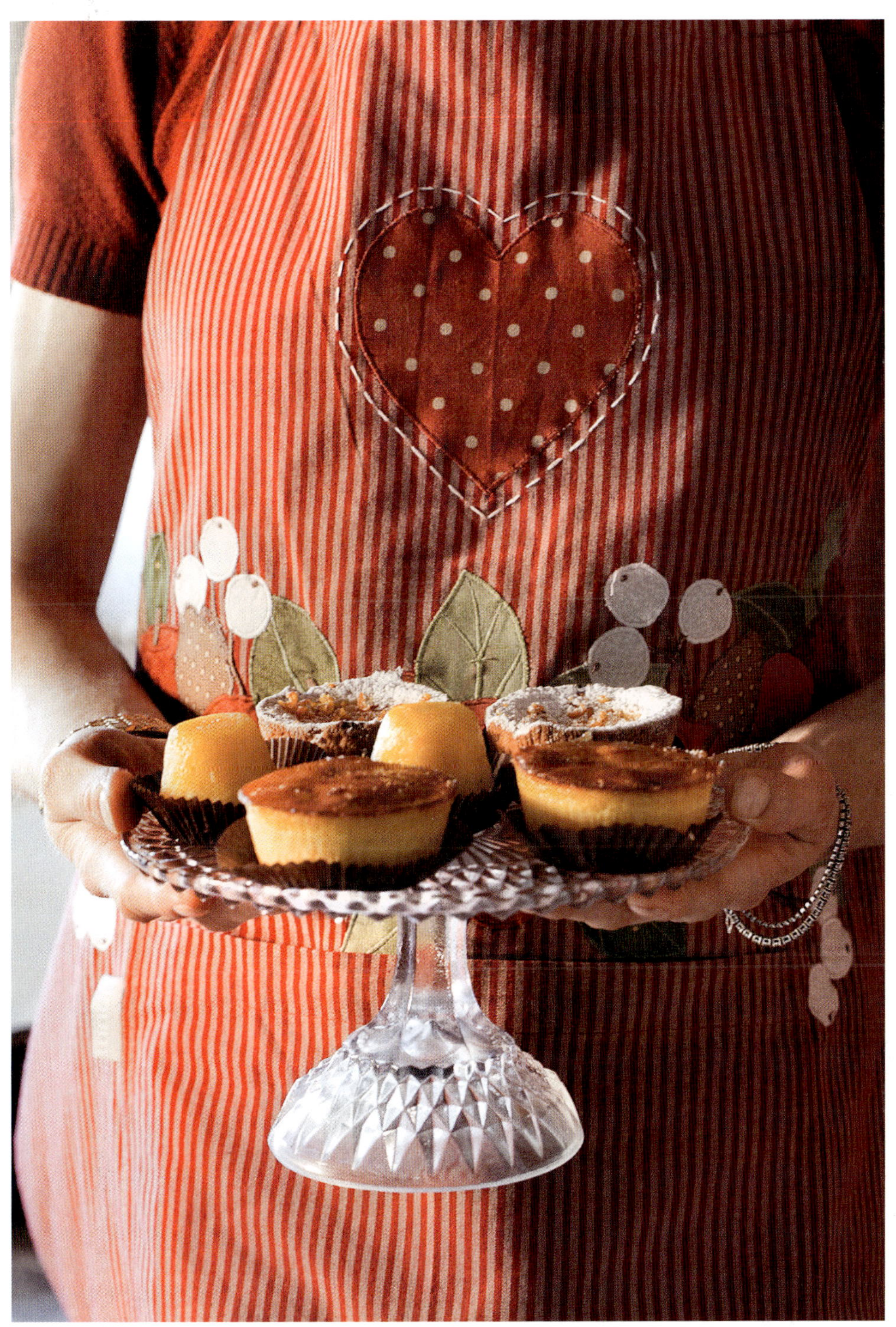

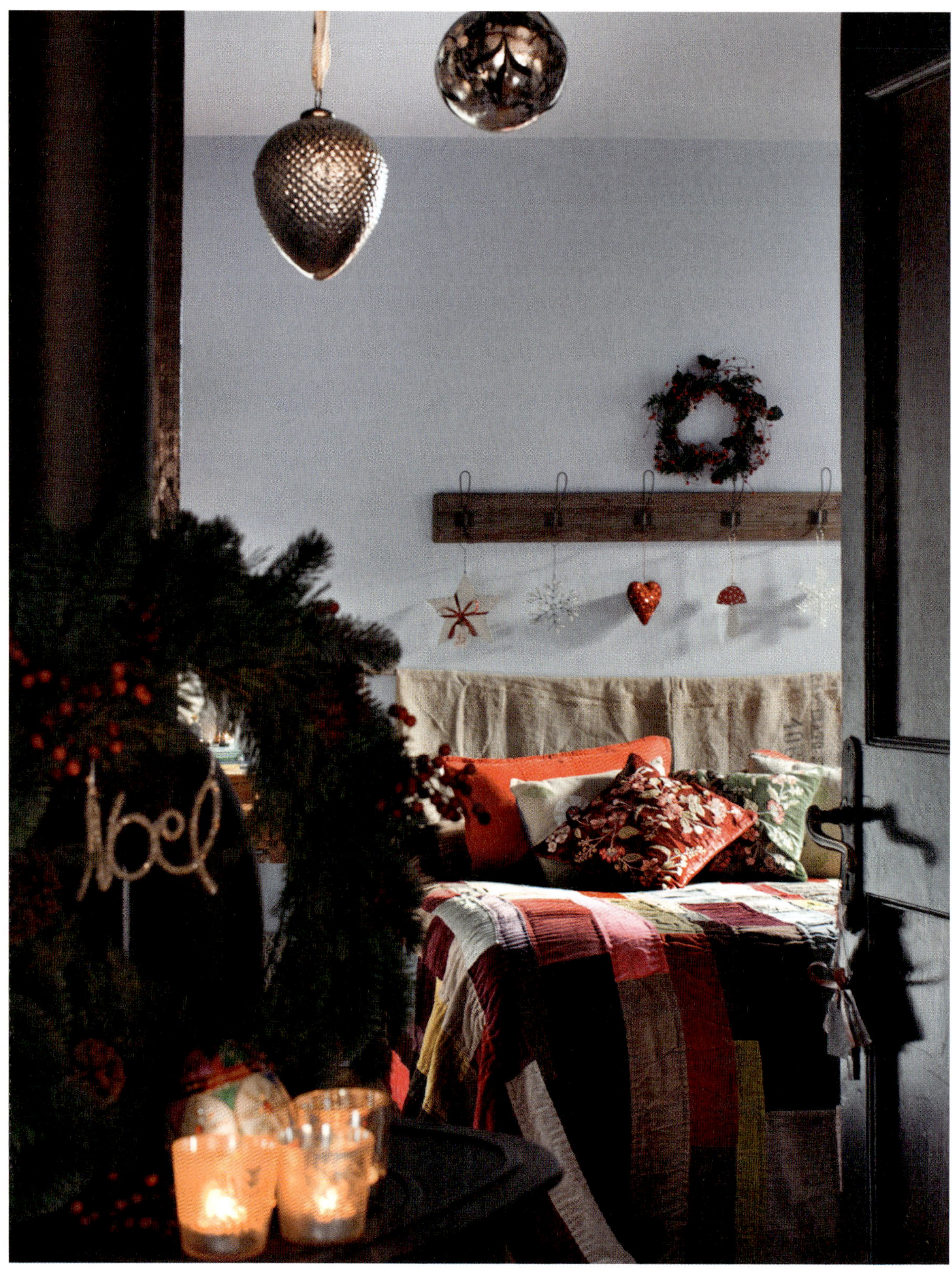
Noel

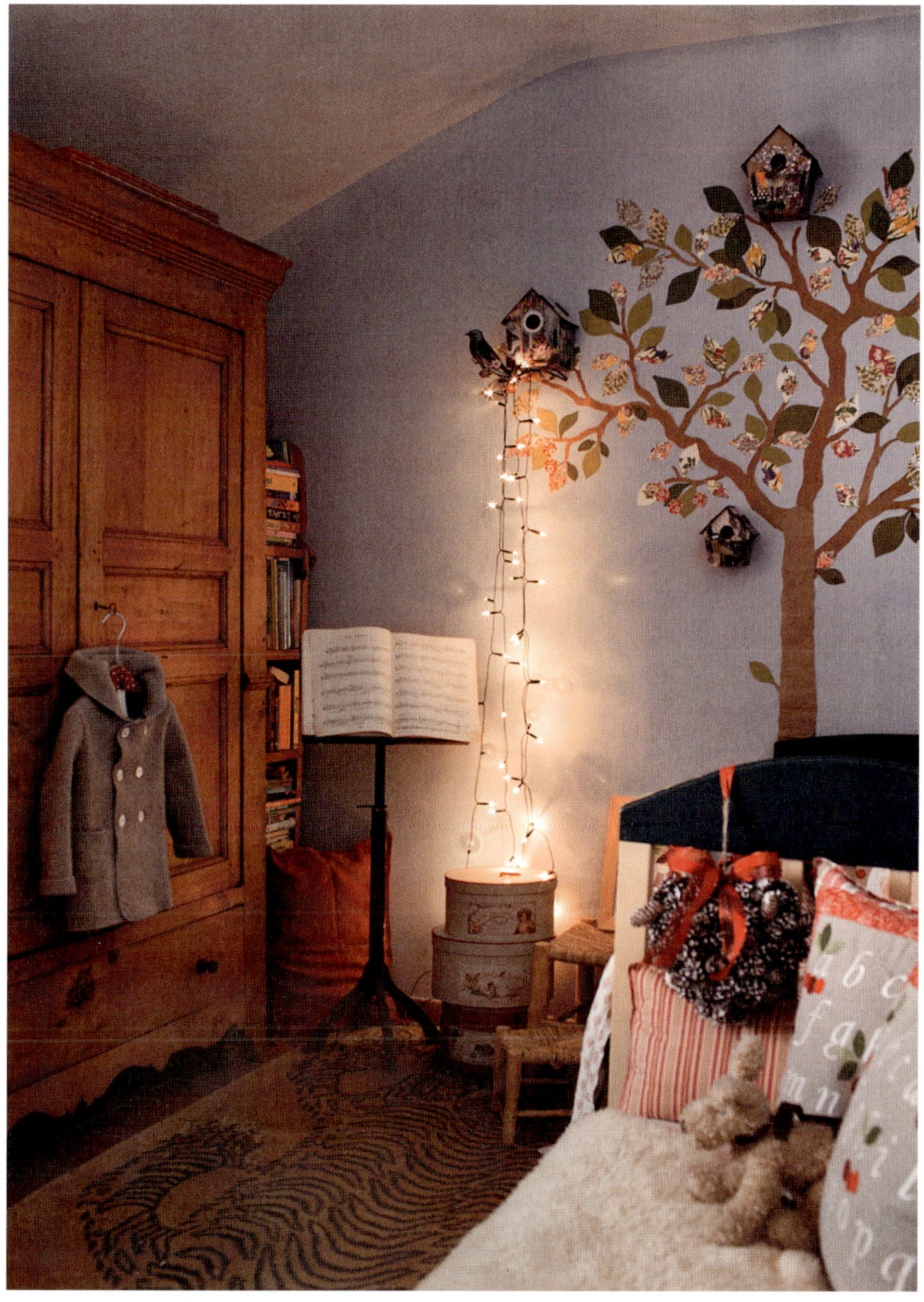

The smaller bedroom is a magical space, featuring a large tree crafted by Margherita for her child from colorful paper and cardboard clippings. Boxes, toys, cushions, and blankets, along with adorable children's clothing, available at Il laboratorio nell'orto, complete the whimsical atmosphere.

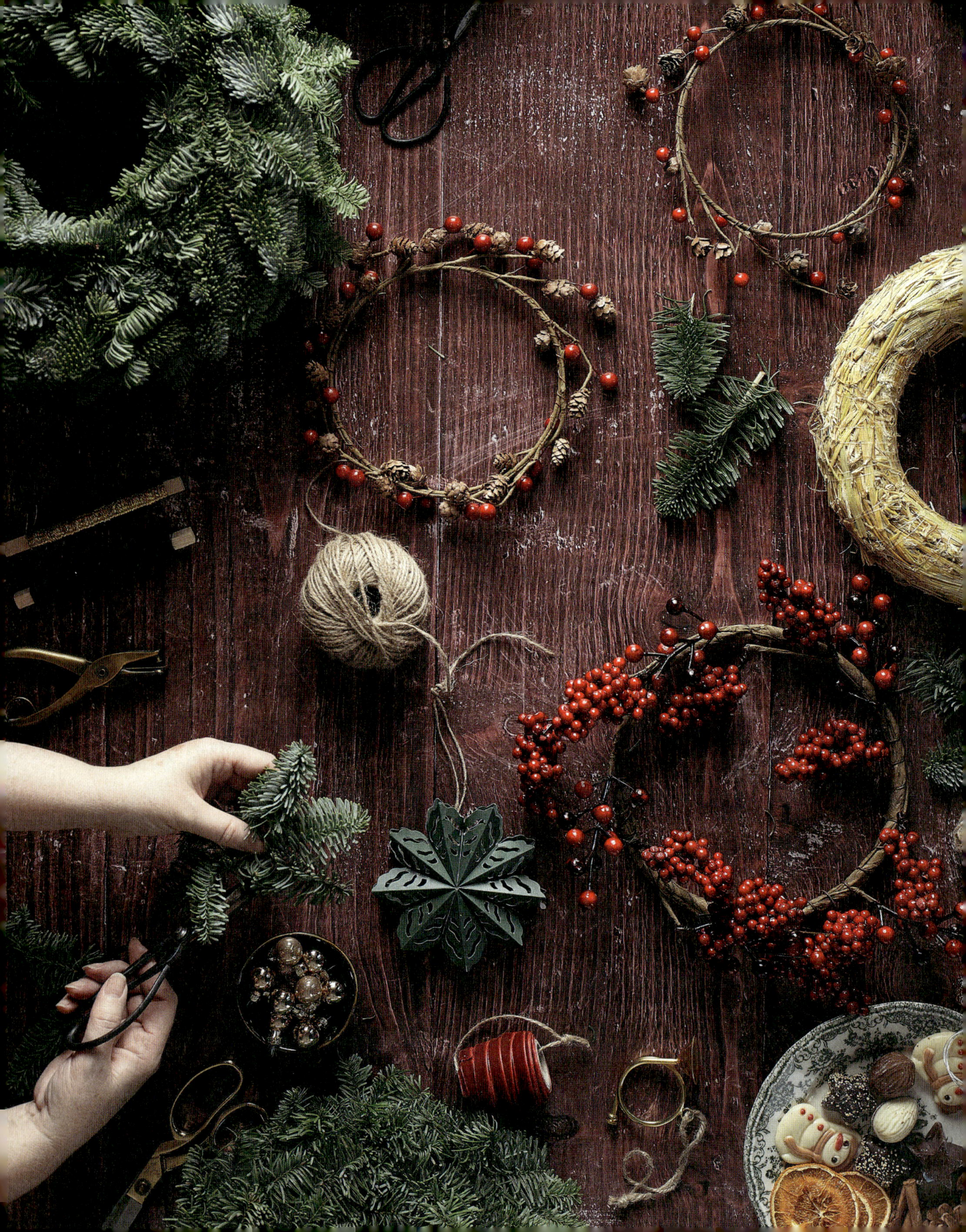

Fir Greenery, Twigs, and Cones: Decorating with Plants

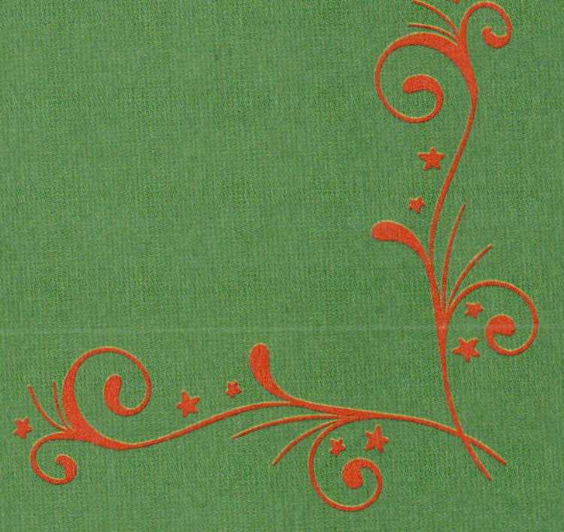

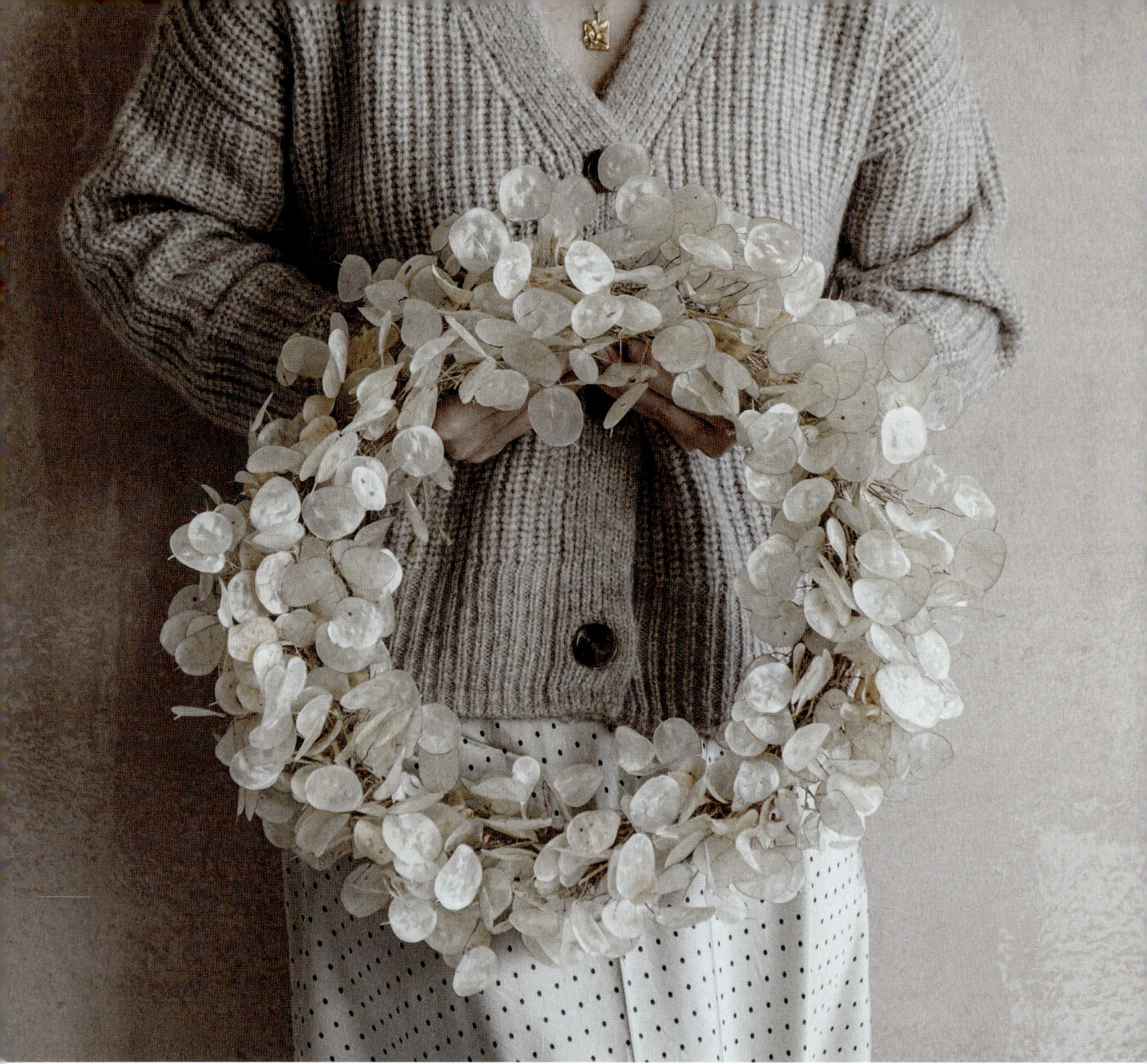

While wreaths typically feature lush greenery, this elegant version made from Lunaria offers a refined touch that complements minimalist decorations beautifully.

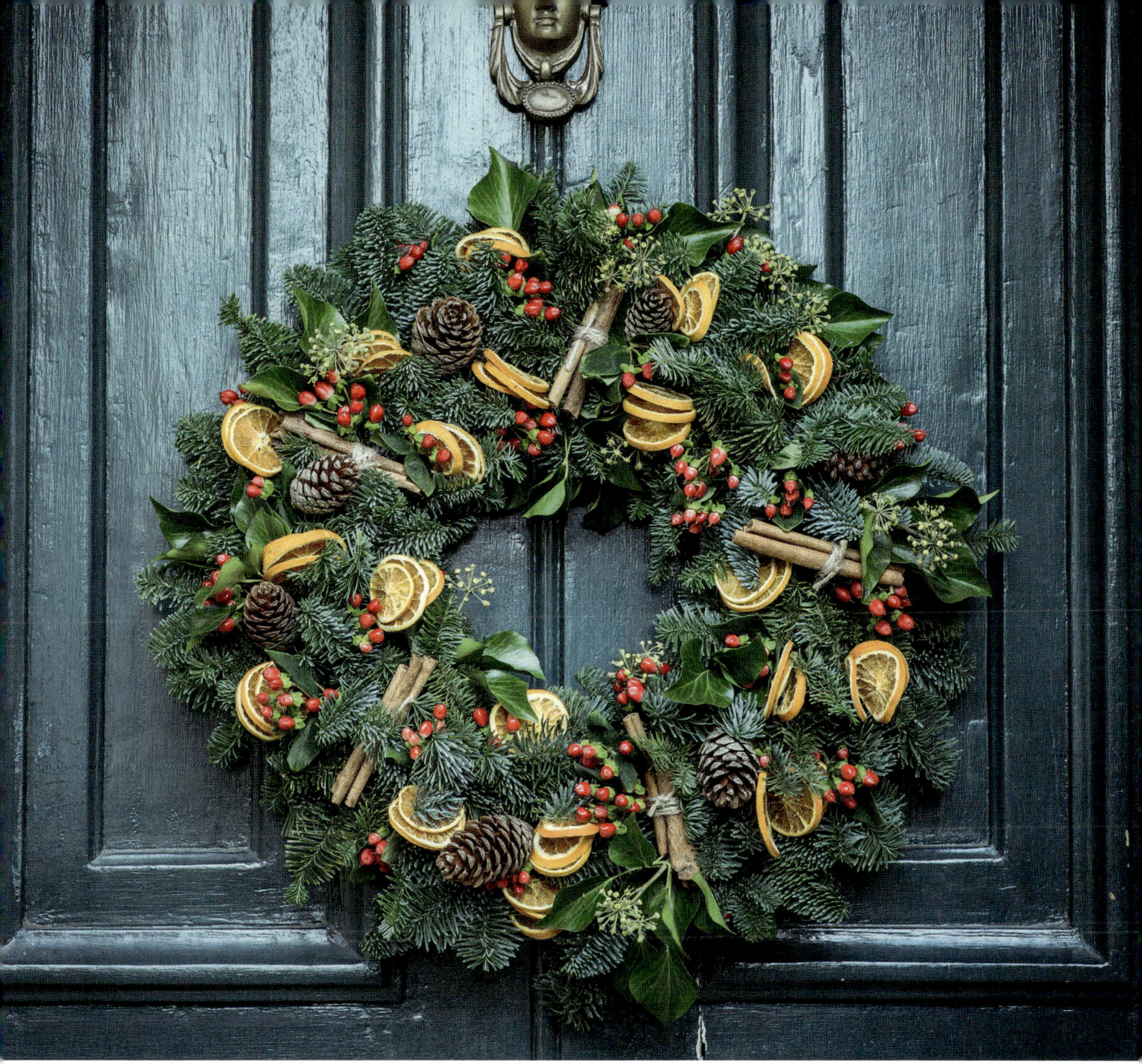

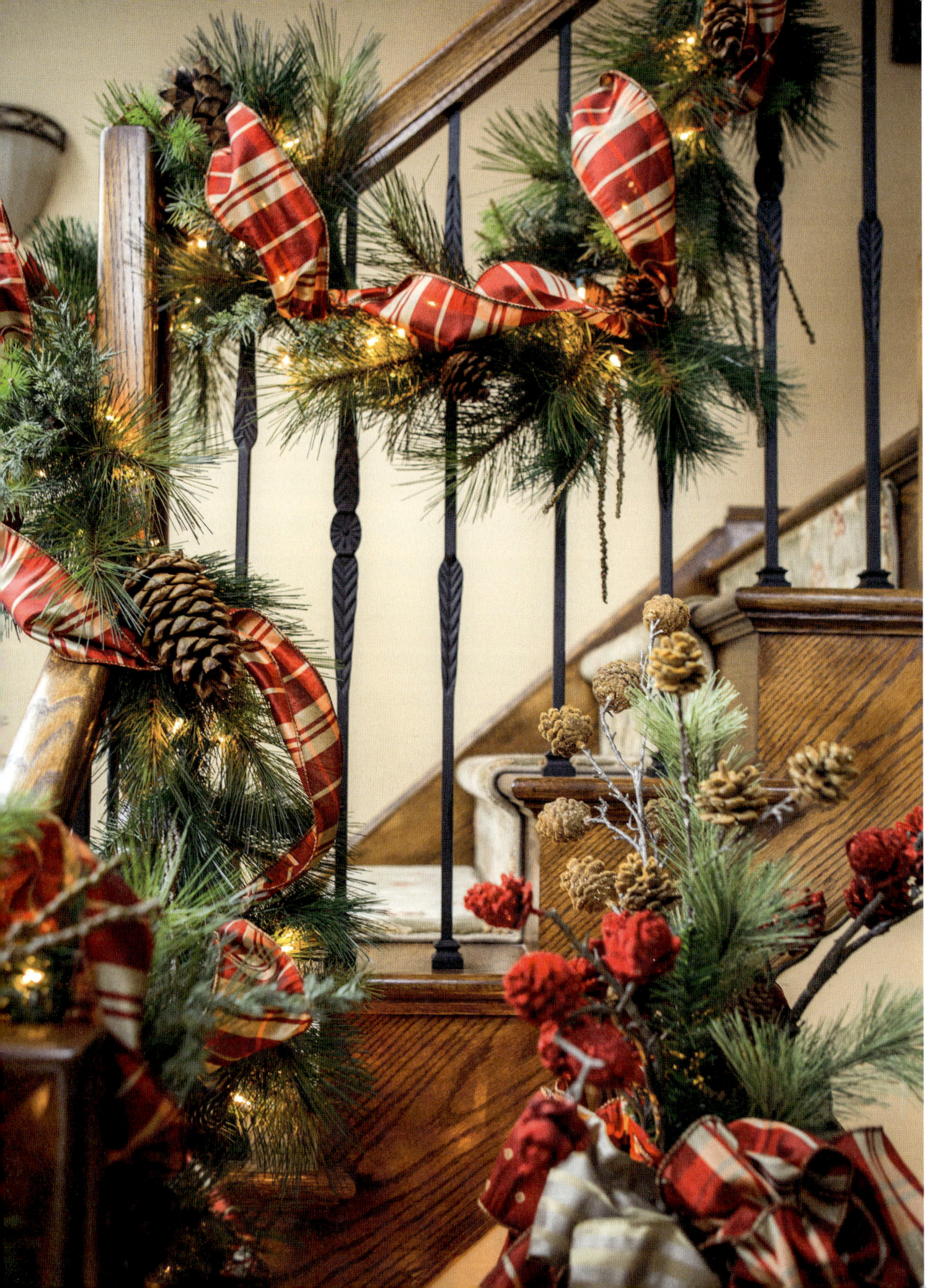

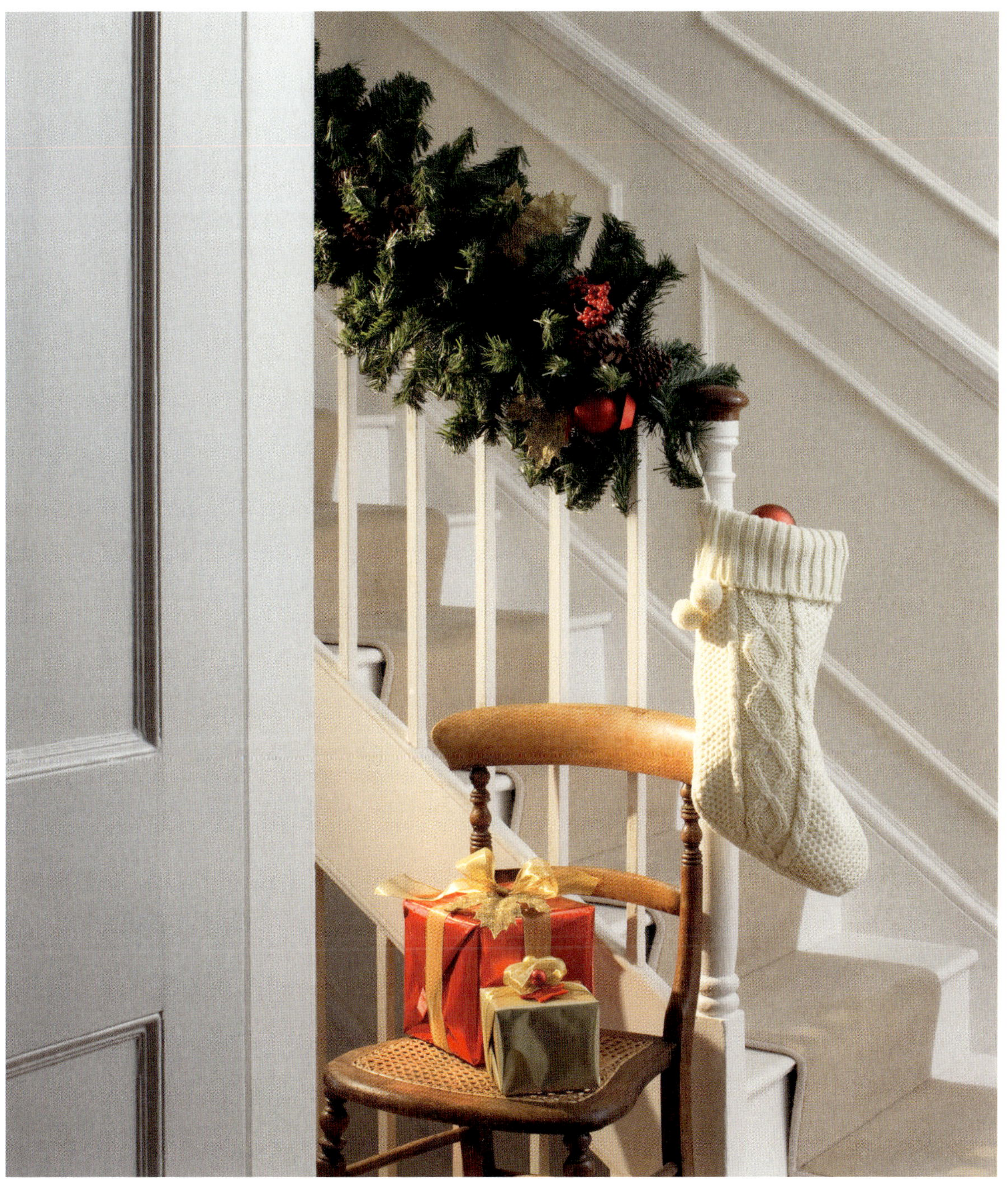

Fir garlands can enhance any home's festive atmosphere, whether they are festooned with colorful Christmas ornaments or casually draped along a banister adorned with bows and pine cones, creating a joyful ambiance in the stairwell.

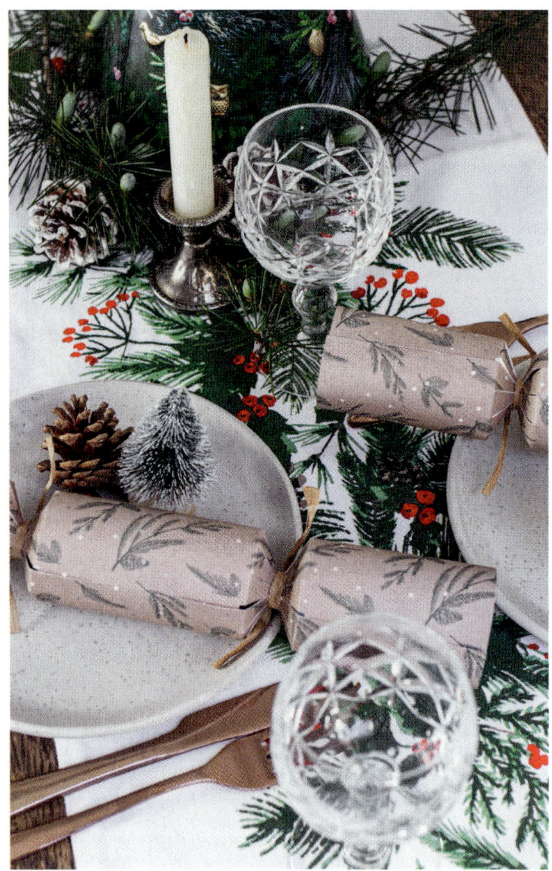

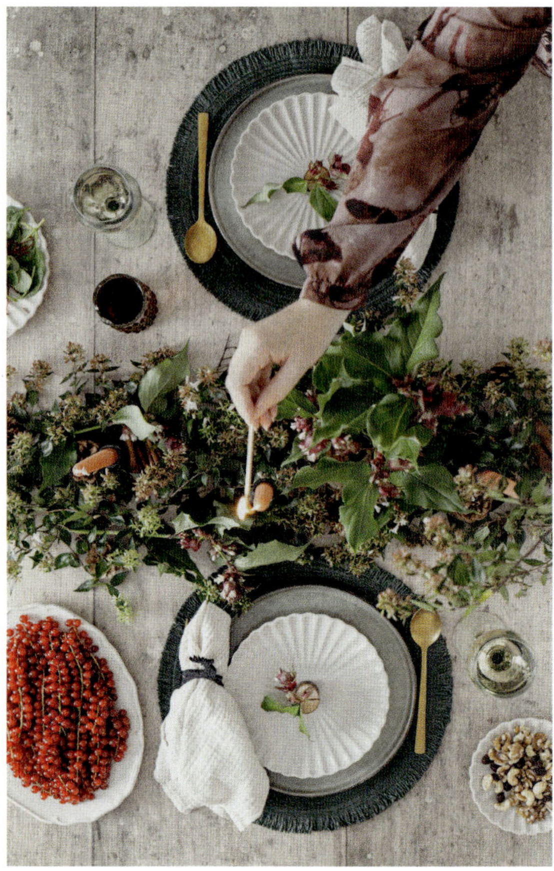

For the Christmas table, a lovely flower arrangement can serve as a stunning centerpiece. A vase filled with seasonal blooms grabs attention, while a floral tablecloth adds charming accents. A thoughtful selection of festive flora can elevate the elegance of the tabletop, leaving a lasting impression and fostering a warm, welcoming environment.

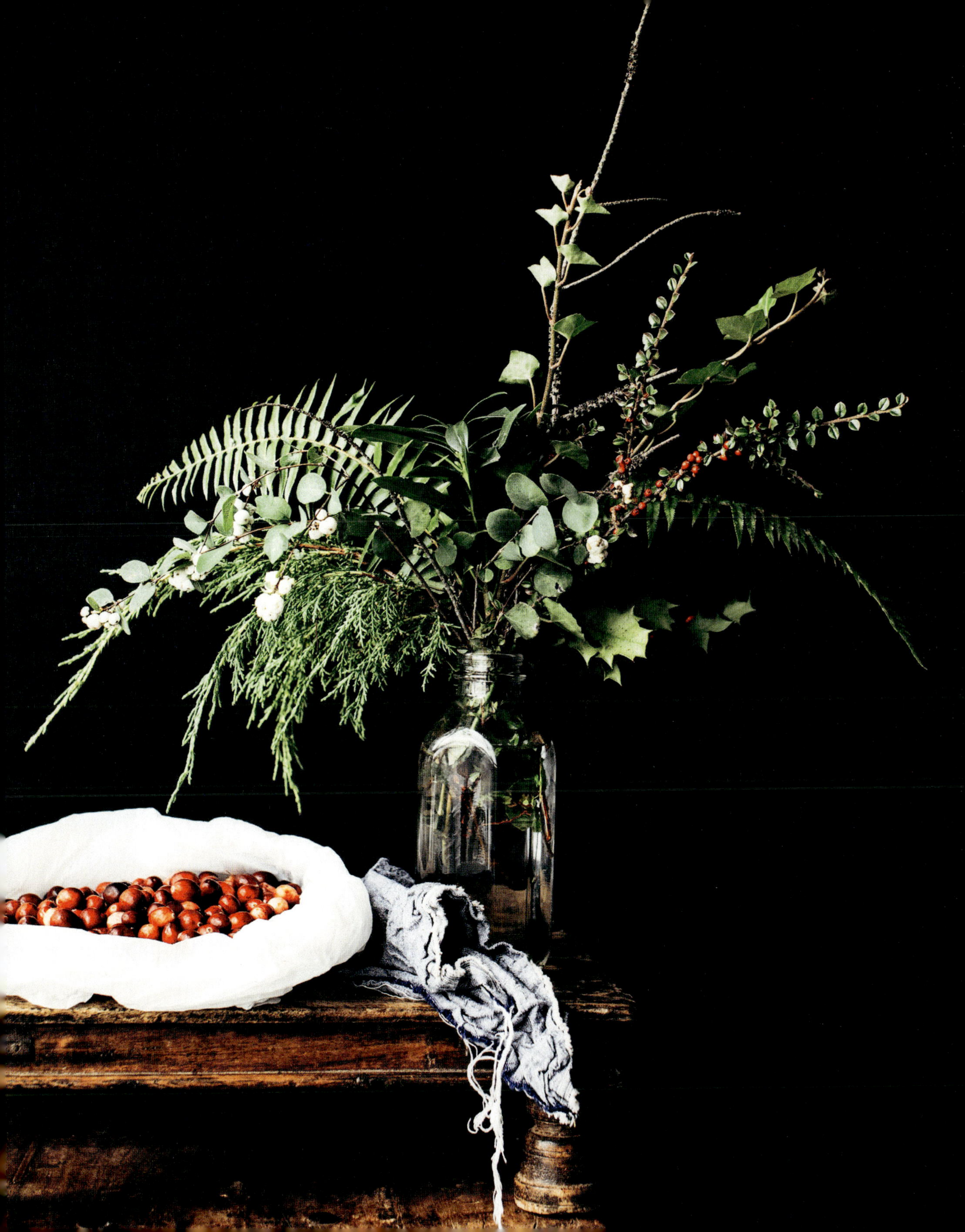

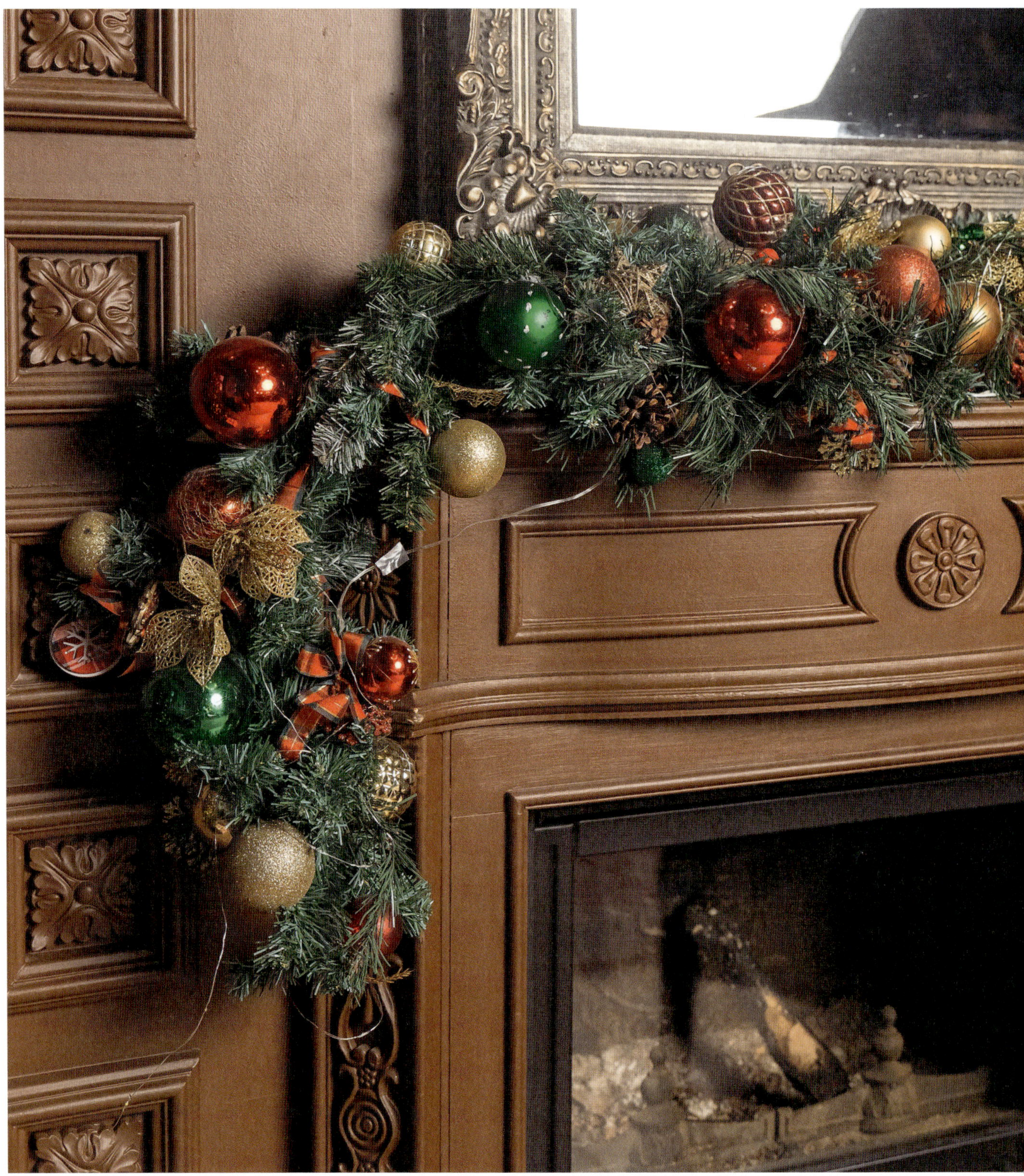

The fireplace is an ideal spot for Christmas decorations, as it often serves as a gathering place for family and friends. Adorned with fragrant branches and cherished ornaments—some possibly hung each year for generations—this area becomes a special focal point.

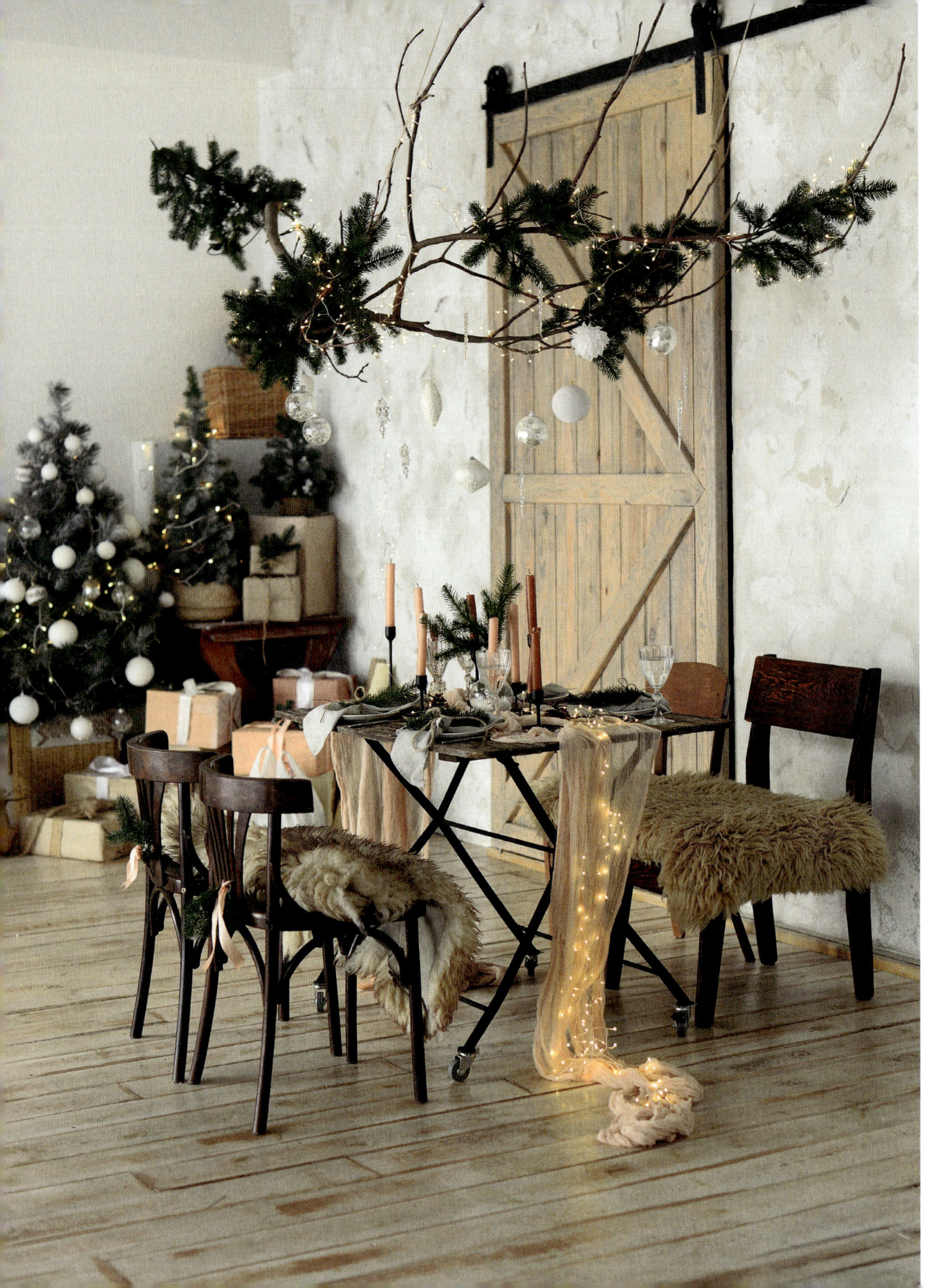

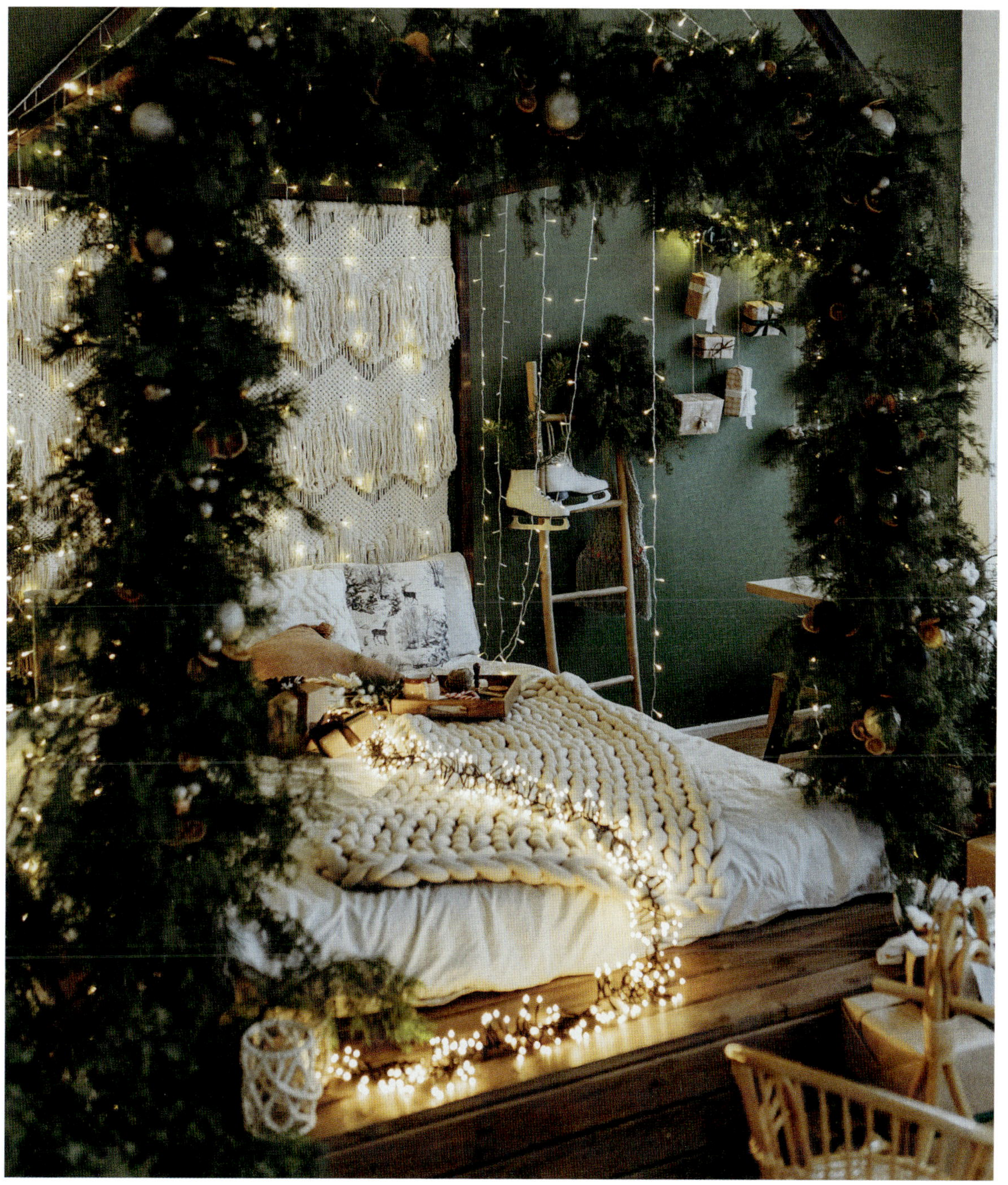

For those seeking uniqueness, consider hanging a decorated branch above the dining table or draping an ornate fir garland around the bed to make your Christmas decorations truly distinctive and memorable.

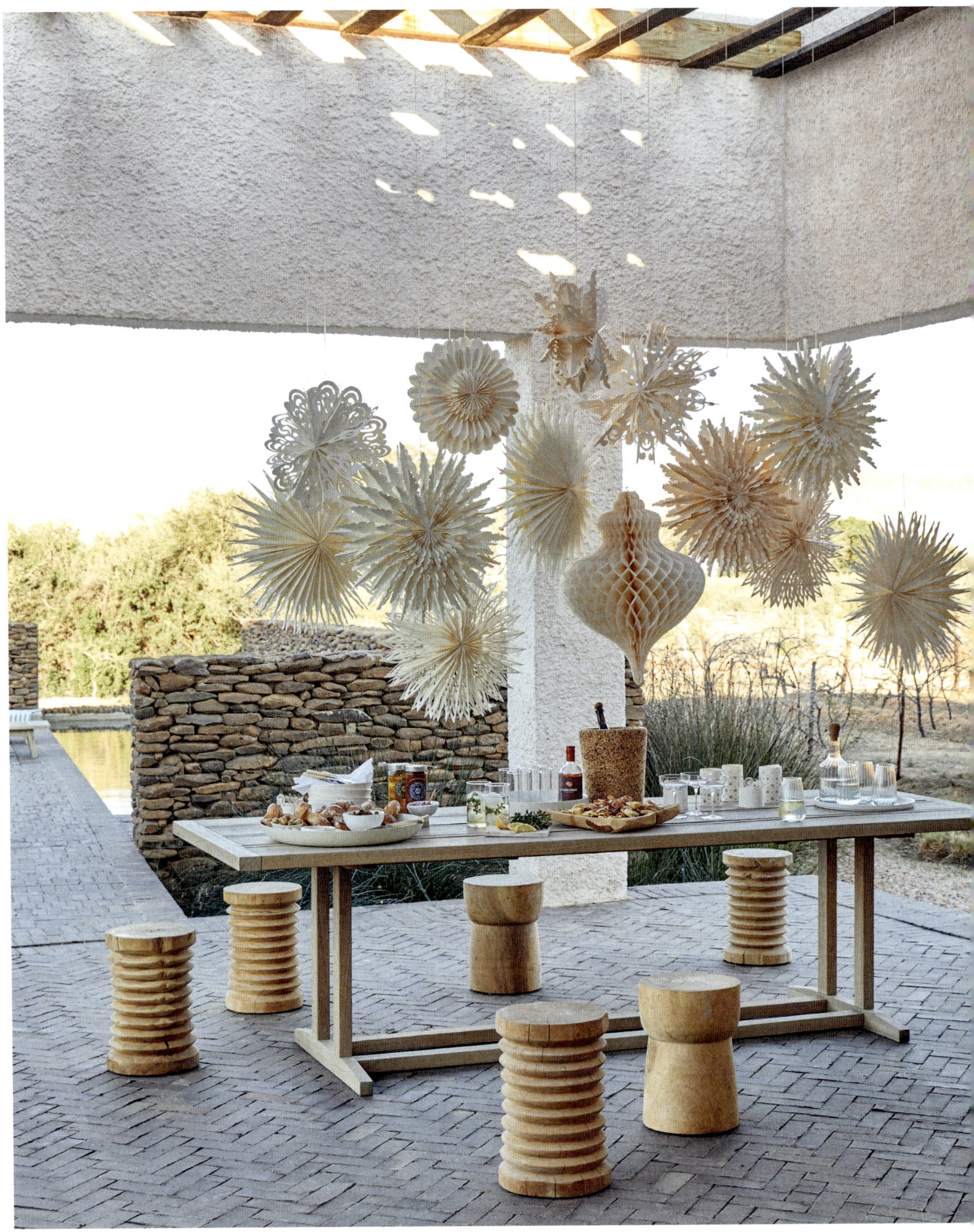

FEATURE

CHRISTMAS IN THE SOUTHERN HEMISPHERE

Discovering the True Magic of the Holiday Season

How many of us travel during the holidays to escape the Christmas grind at home, only to find ourselves missing the very traditions from which we sought refuge?

Often, our desire to escape falls short of deep-rooted holiday expectations. Yet, there are myriad ways to create a sense of festive tradition in a place far from home. A semi-arid region in South Africa may seem an unlikely spot, but the quietude, majestic mountains, and starry nights provide a profound connection to nature and a unique environment for holiday reflection.

In Prince Albert, nestled at the base of the stunning Swartberg Pass, a family found a serene escape from the hustle of Christmas countdowns and last-minute shopping. This remote town's isolation protects its charm, allowing people to focus on southern-hemisphere traditions that resonate and incorporate festive traditions that translate easily from north to south. Wreaths for example are handmade from local fynbos (see page 166), and plants from the surrounding landscape are used to capture the essence of the season while honoring the natural world. Instead of a traditional Christmas tree, a local alternative like a spekboom tree adorns the living area, infusing the celebration with native charm and ecological consciousness.

The family enjoys this remote home with its possibilities of sundowners (i.e., drinks at sundown) to seamlessly transform into stargazing sessions and storytelling around an open fire, followed by a midnight swim, creating a festive celebration rooted in their surroundings. This experience reveals that the true magic of the season lies not in clinging to the familiar, but in the freedom to create your own and new traditions.

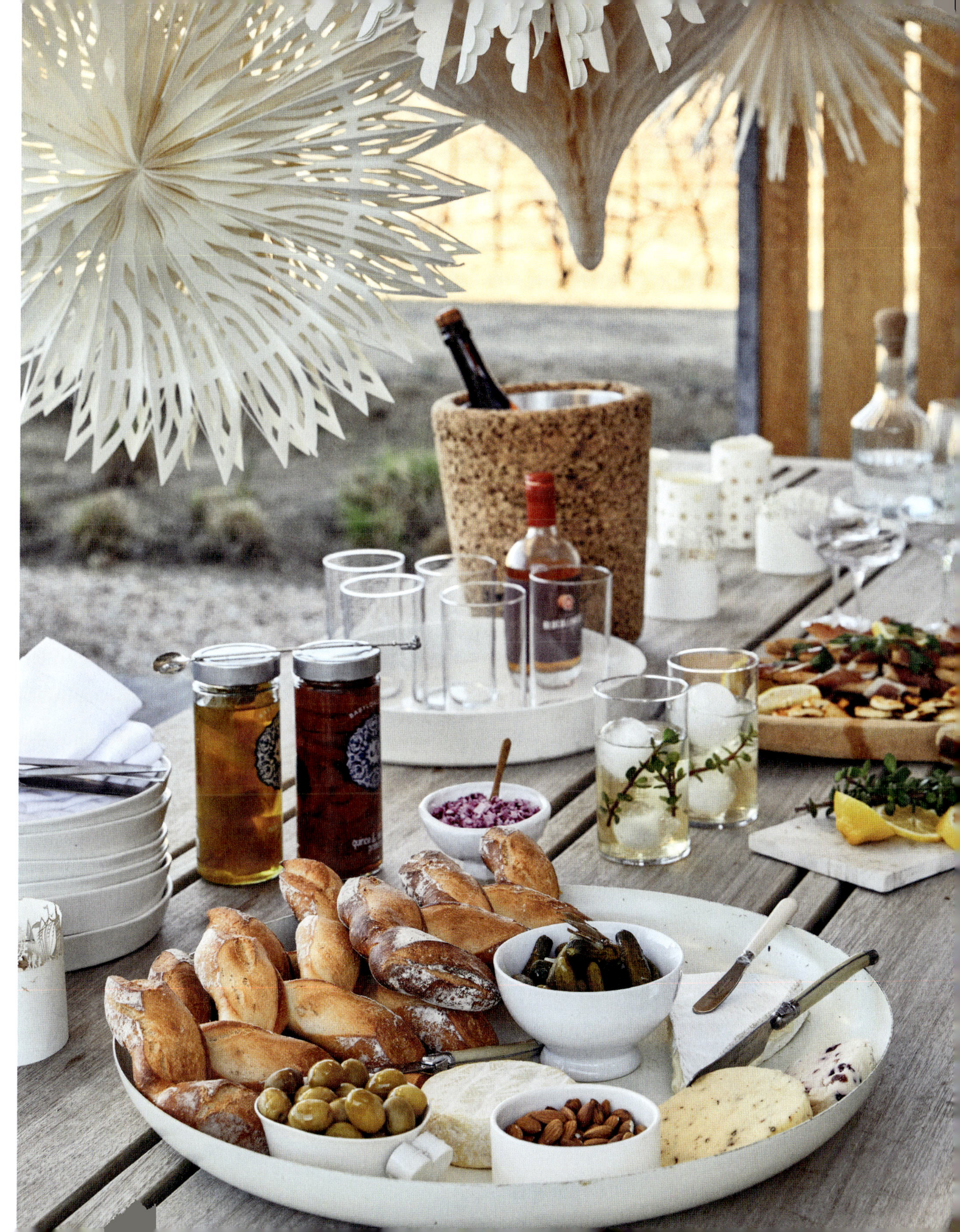

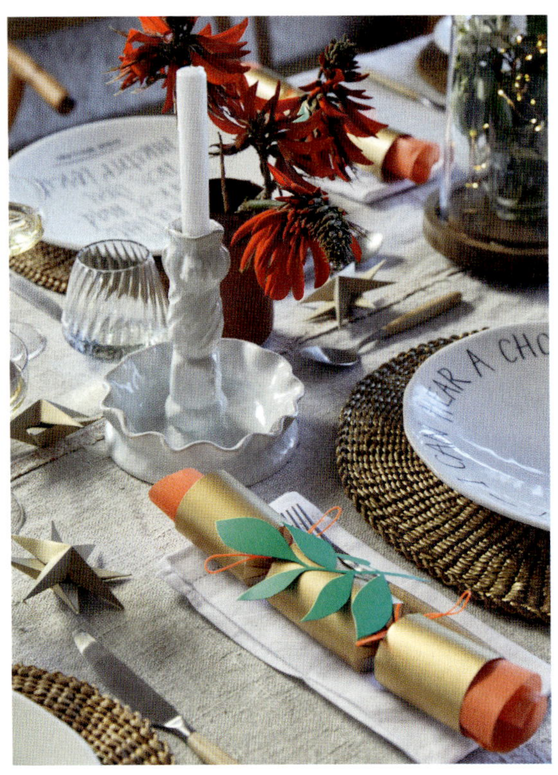

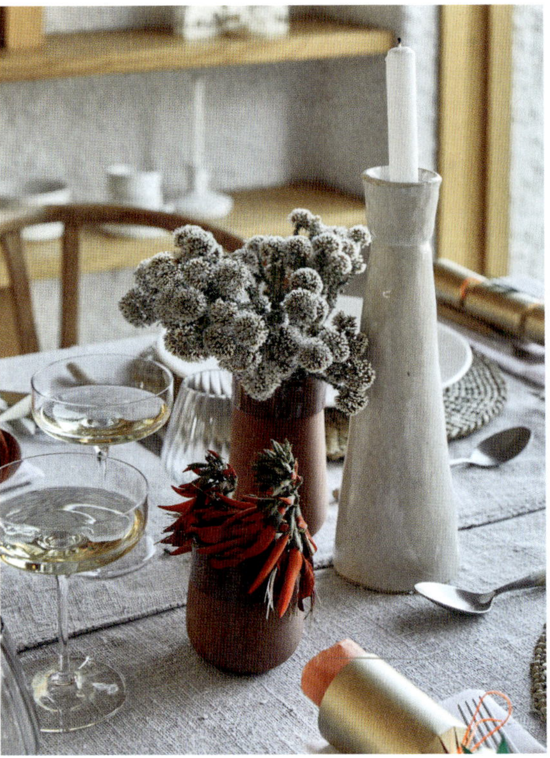

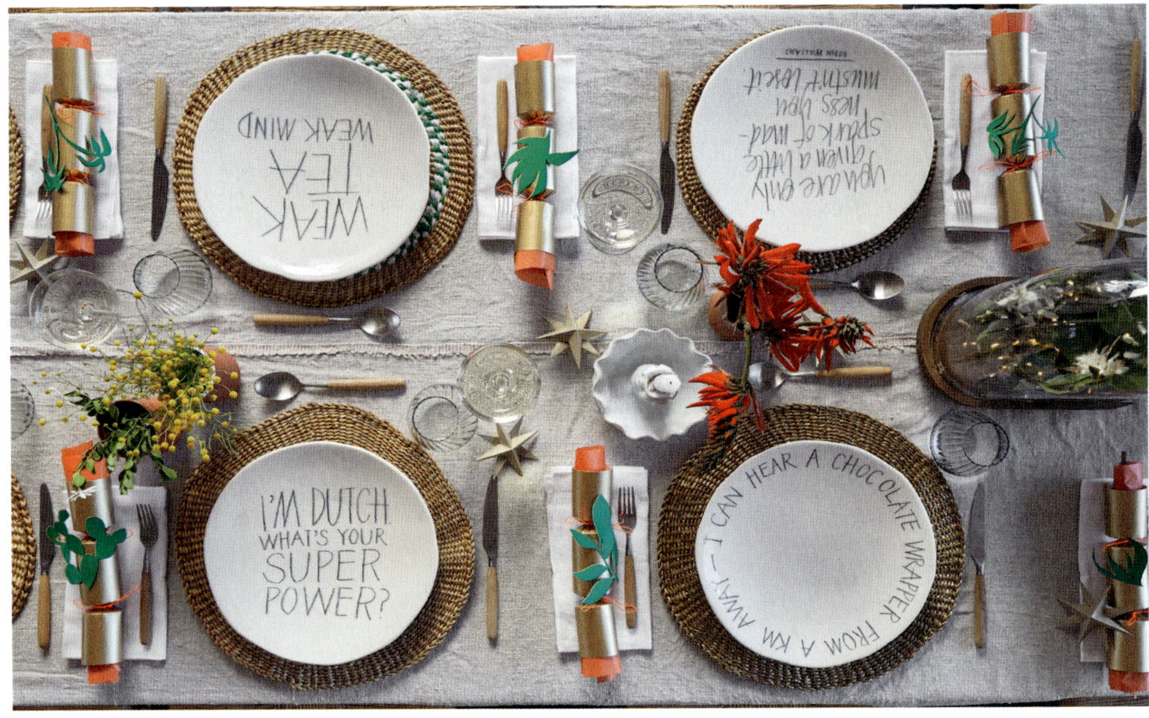
WEAK TEA
WEAK MIND
you are only given a little spark of mad-ness. you mustn't lose it
I'M DUTCH WHAT'S YOUR SUPER POWER?
I CAN HEAR A CHOCOLATE WRAPPER FROM A KM AWAY—

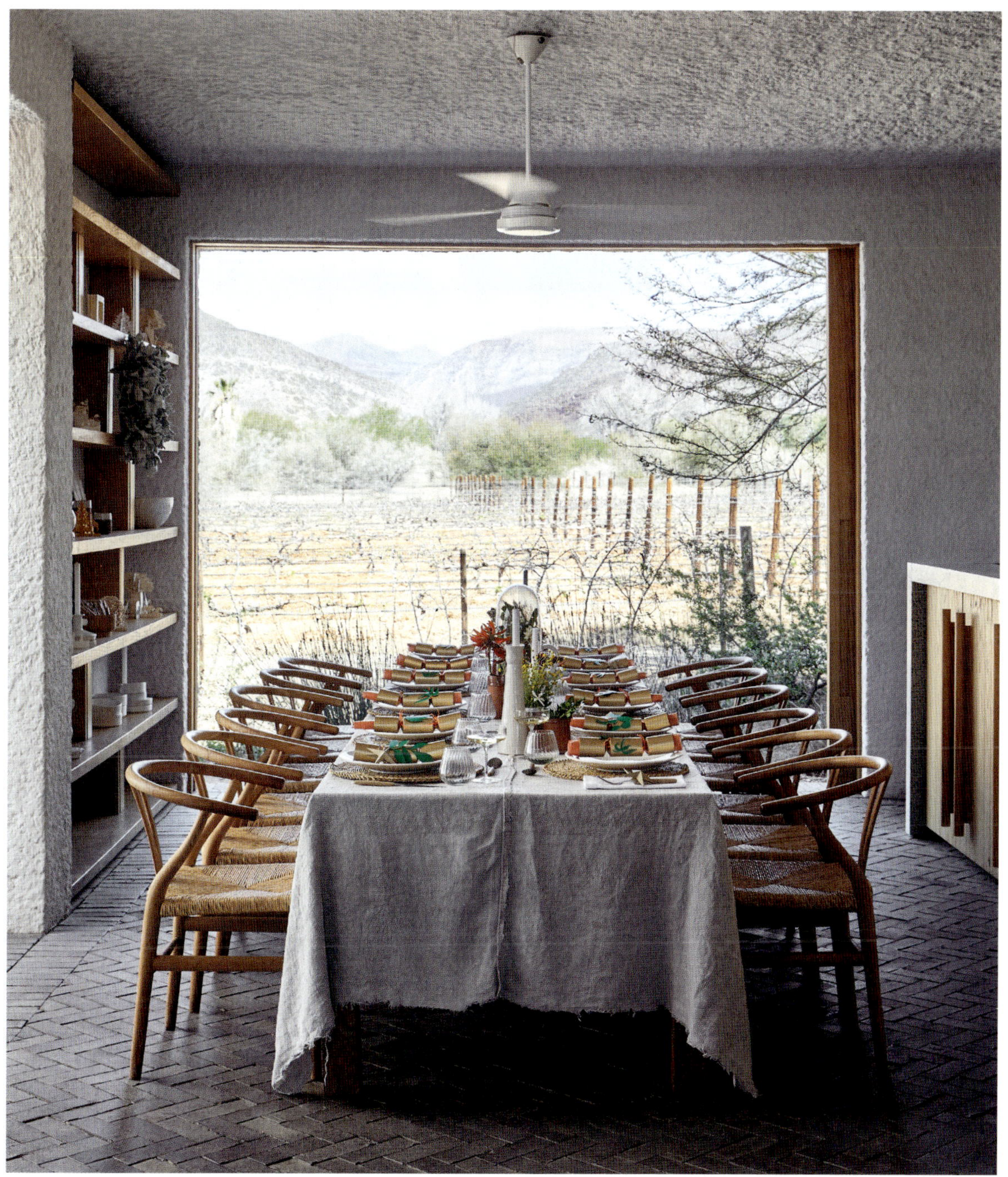

In these spectacular surroundings, the table setting is equally stunning, with plates that feature special messages for each guest that can be taken home as a gift at the end of the festivities.

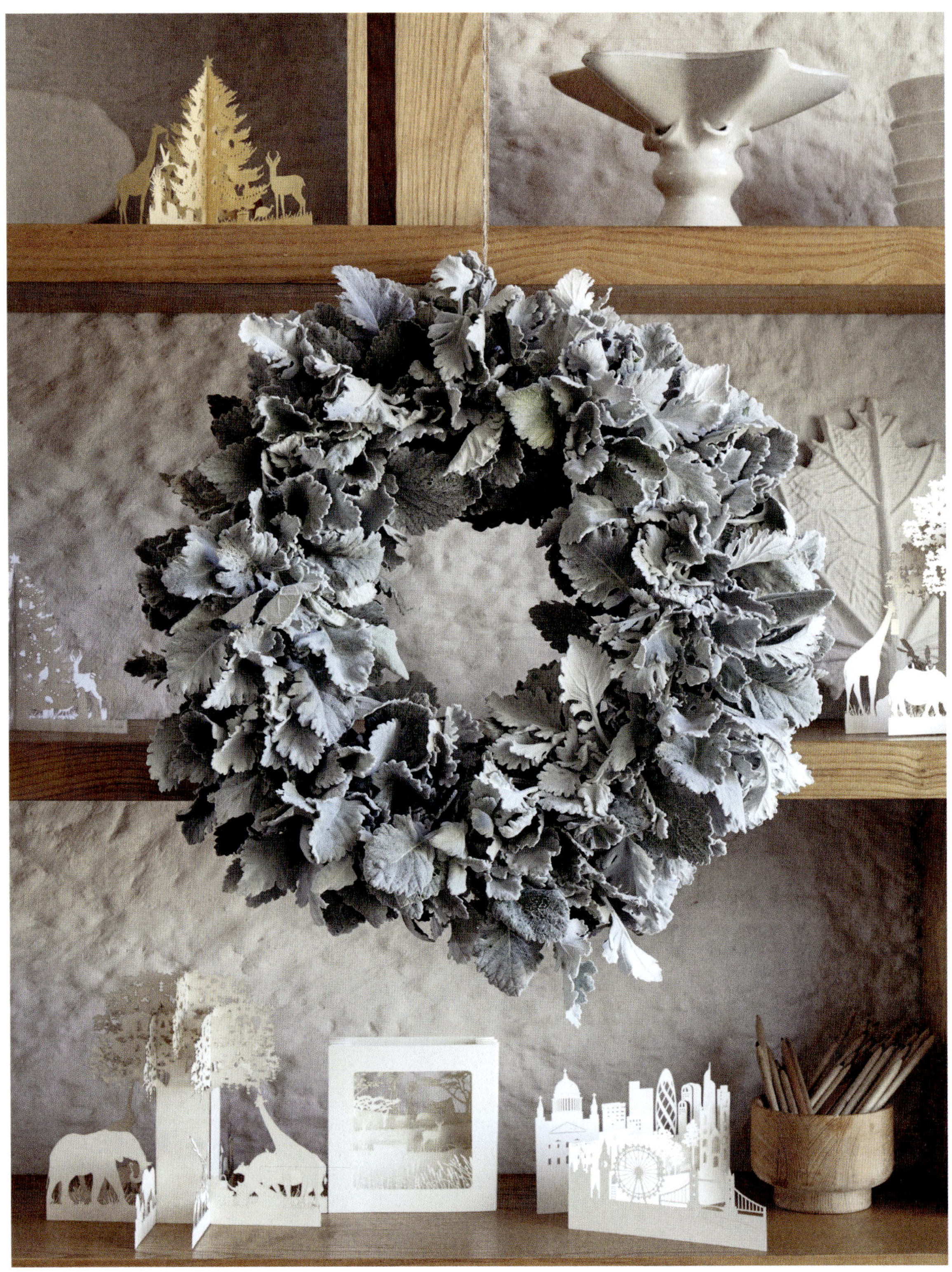

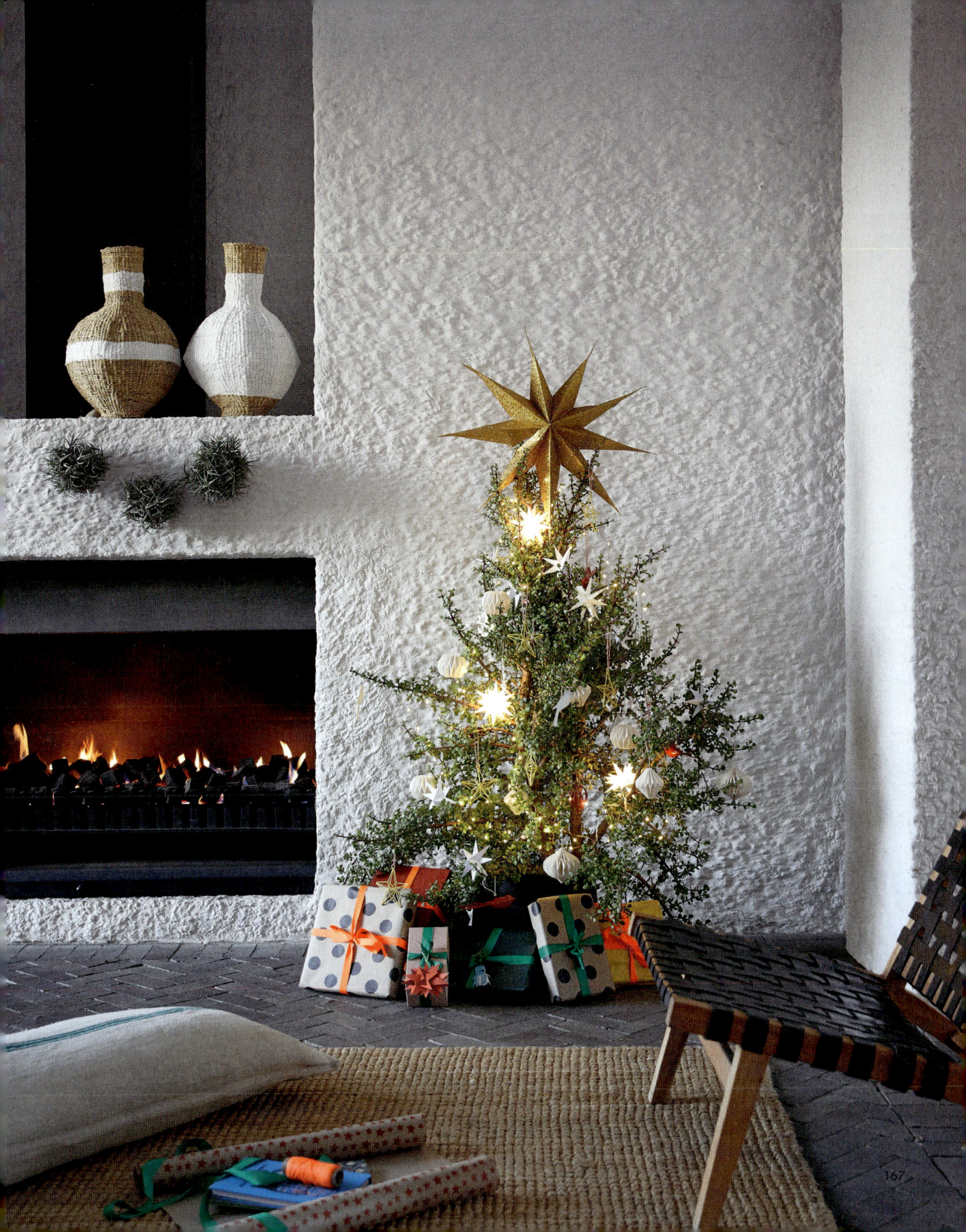

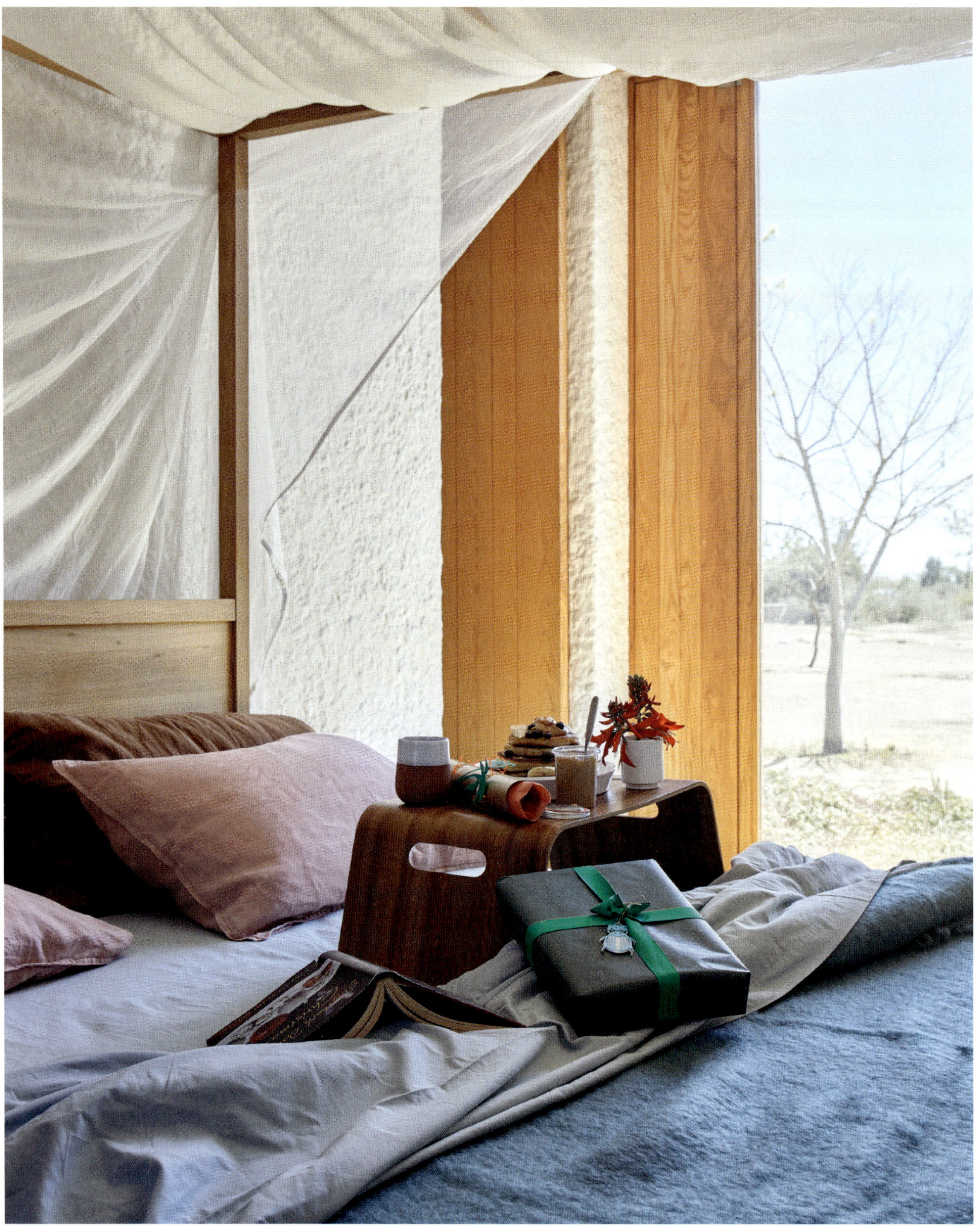

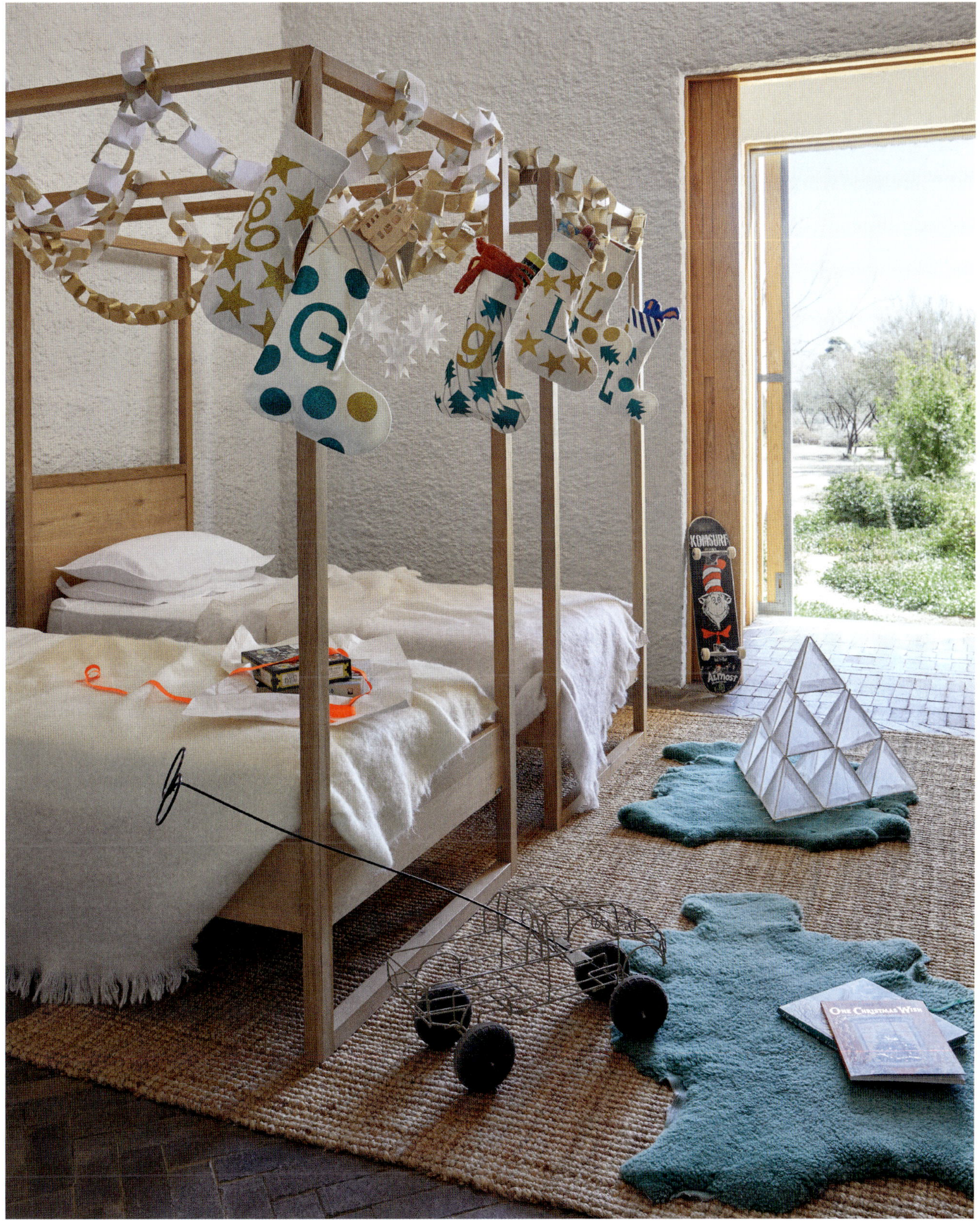
One Christmas Wish

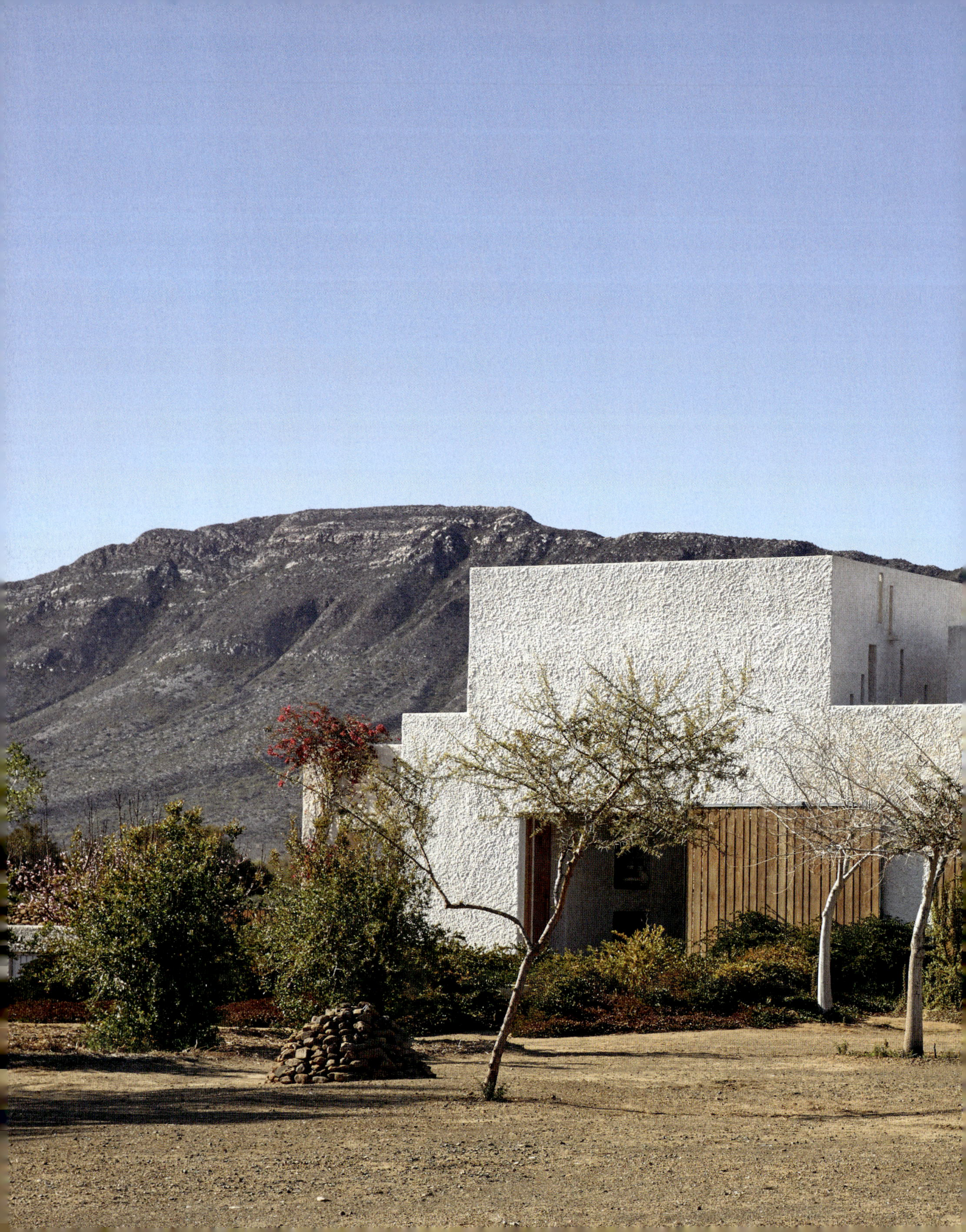

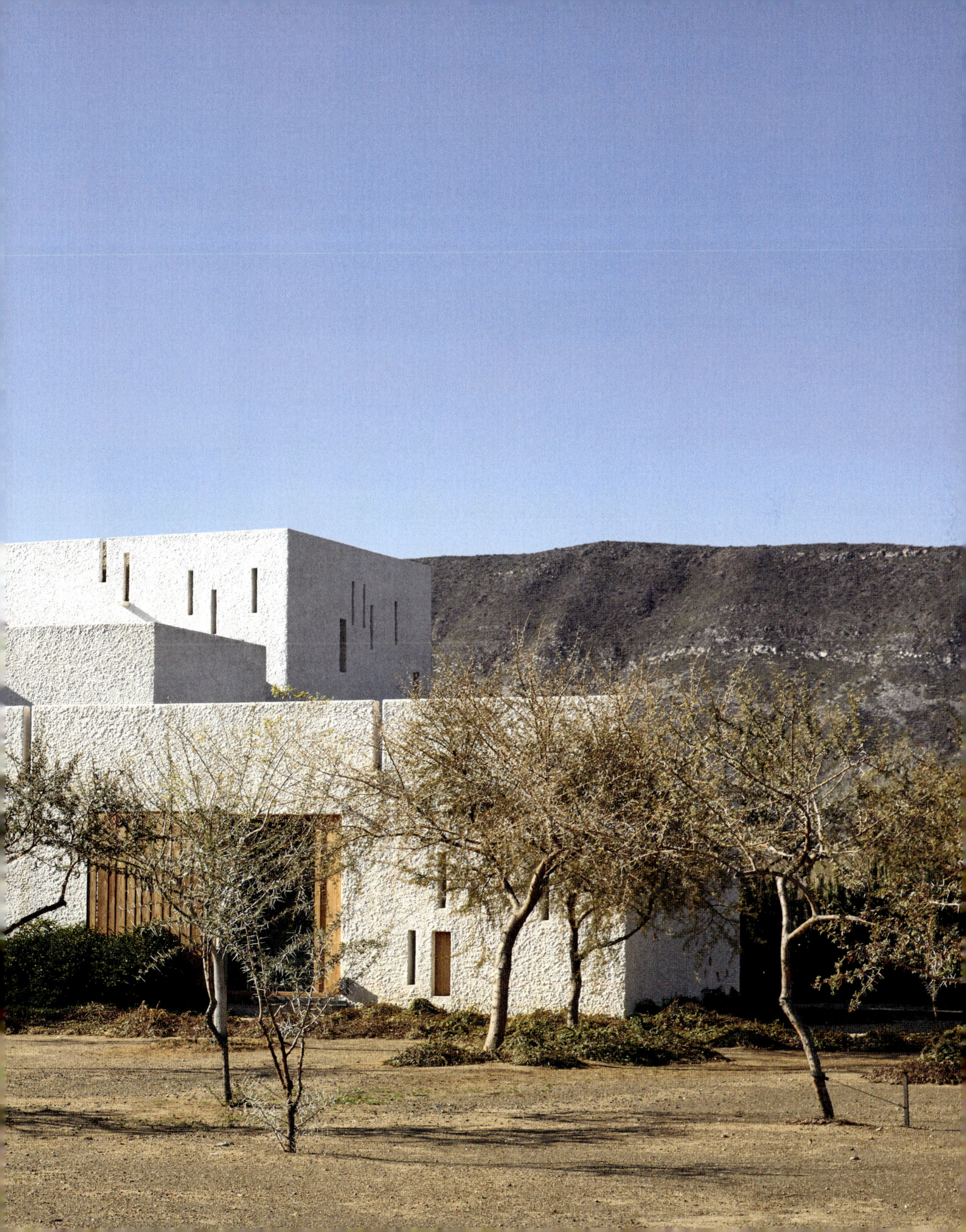

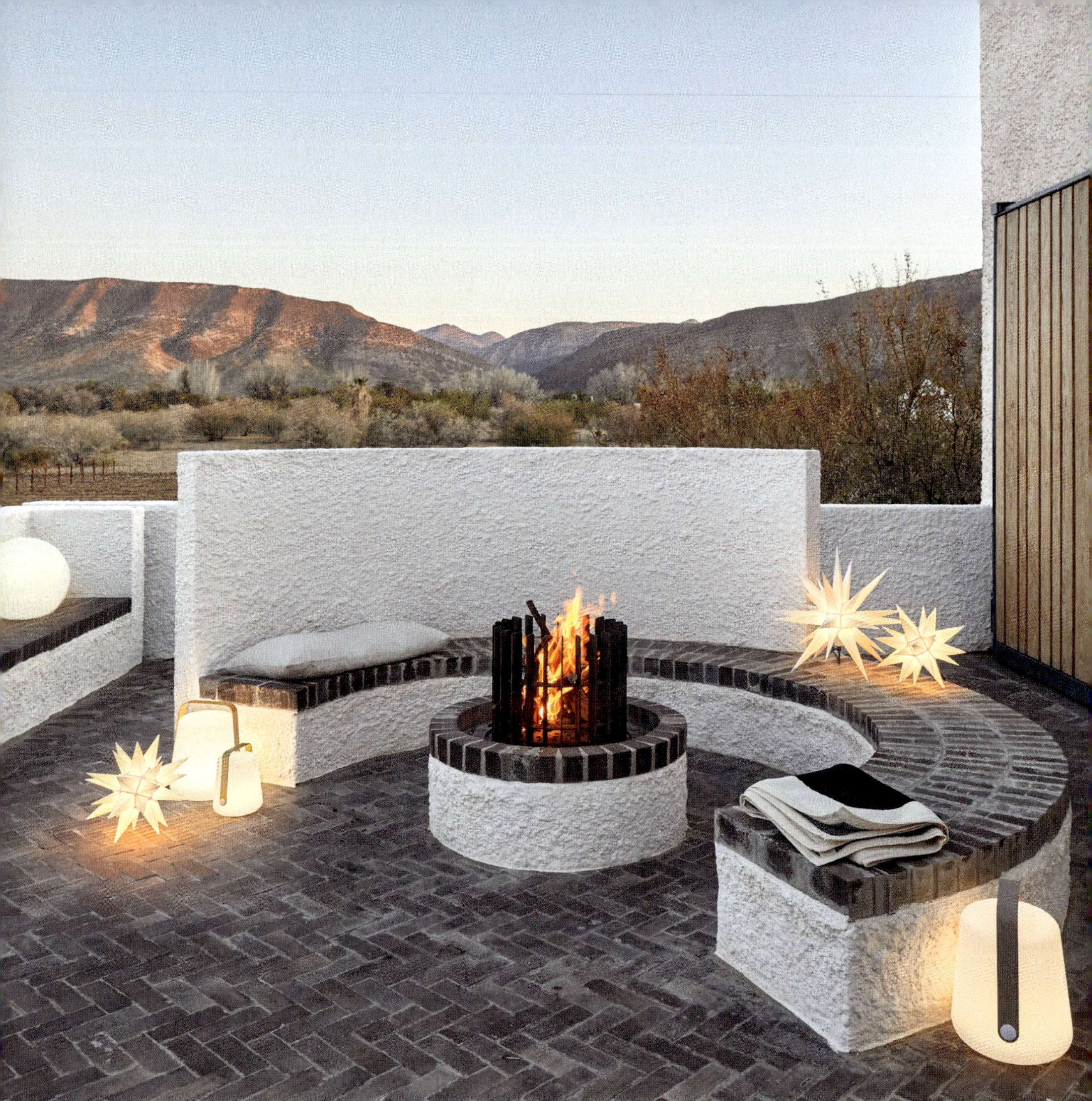

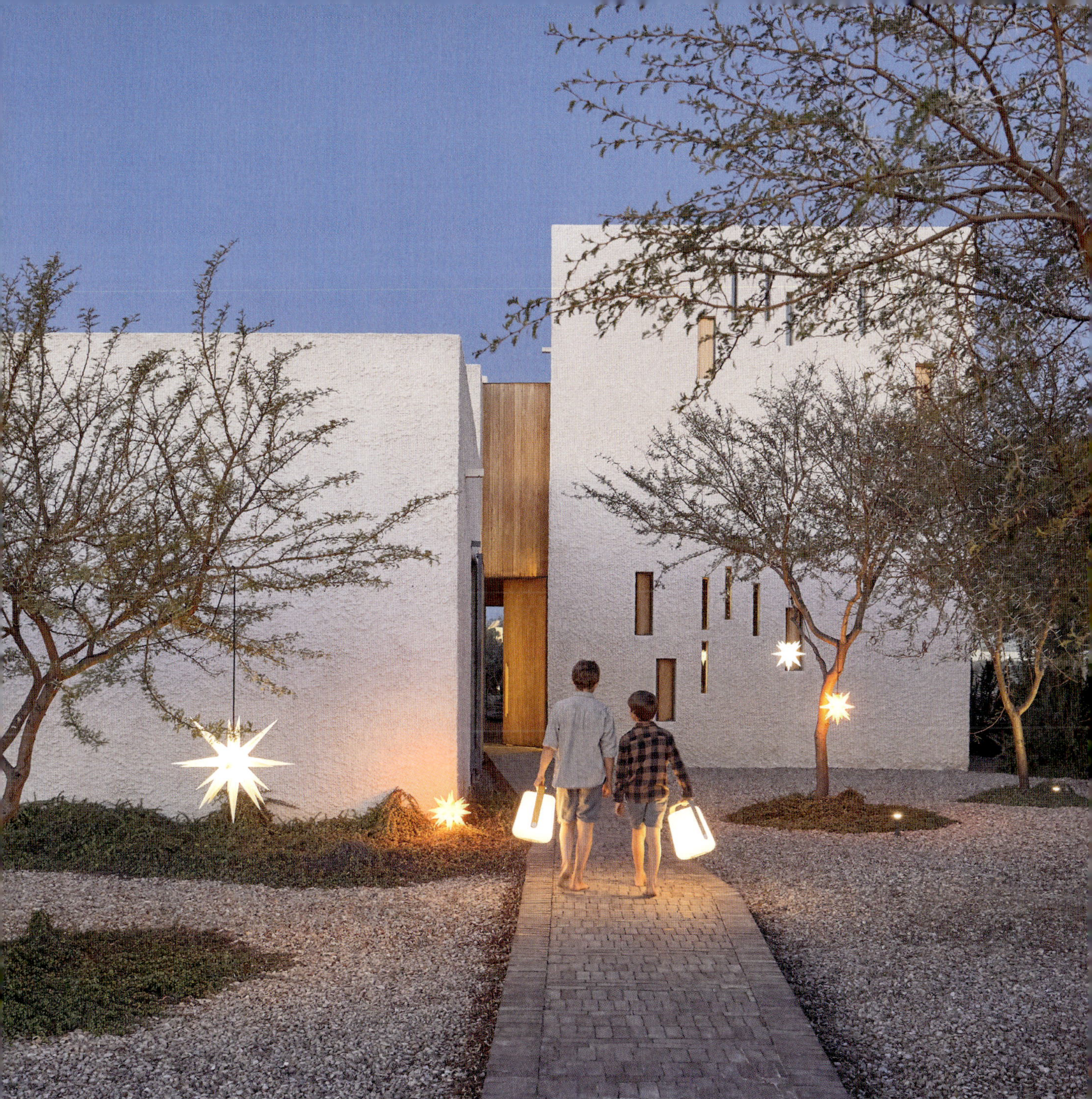

In Prince Albert, summer sundowners are a cherished tradition, kicking off as early as 5 PM when the heat begins to fade. Tables are set with everything needed for a festive gathering. As the sun sets after 8 PM, the fire pit is lit, marking the start of a delightful stargazing safari.

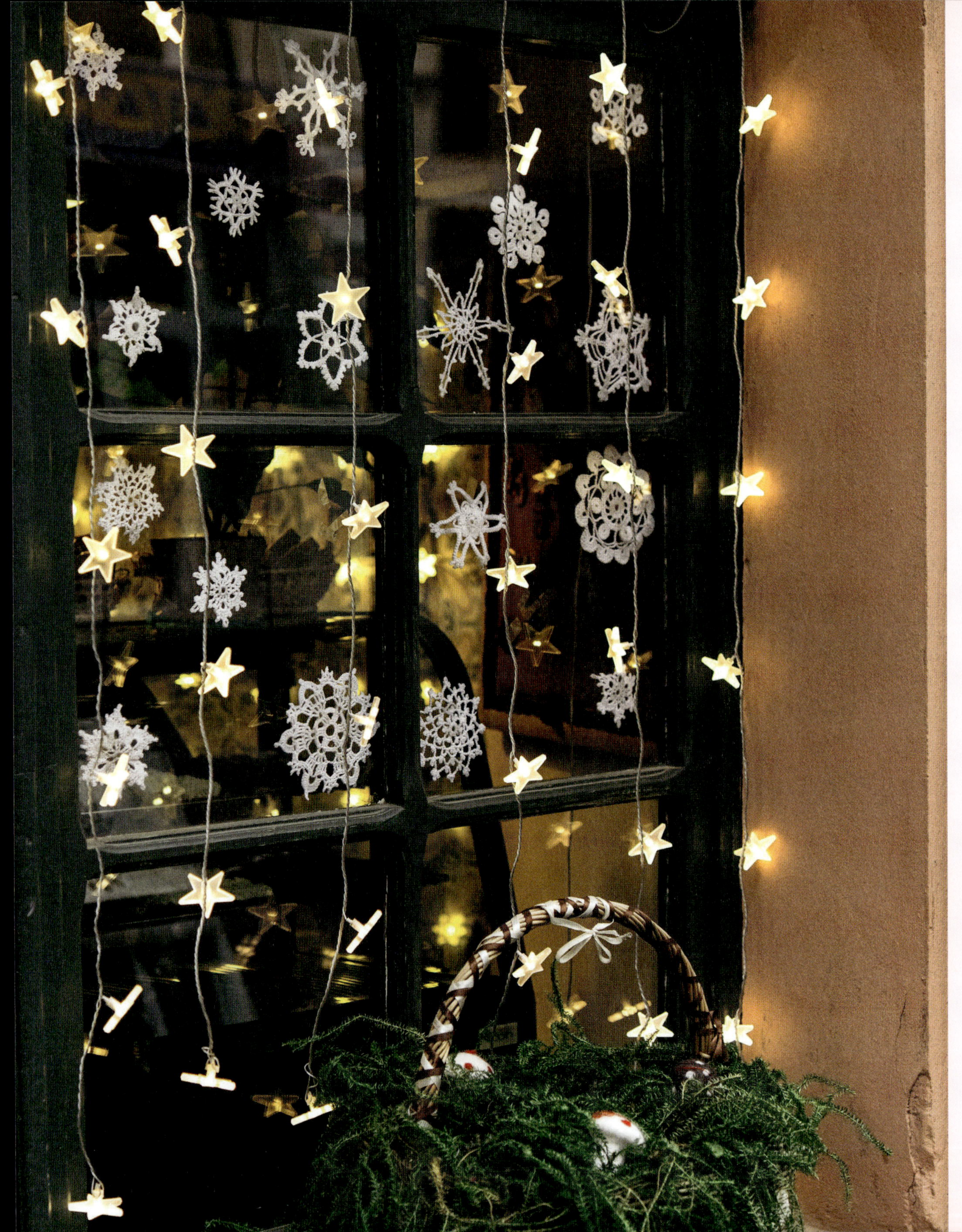

Festive Windows

Windows can be beautifully styled for the holiday season, bringing joy to yourself, your family, and your neighbors. Strings of Christmas lights, artistic crocheted ornaments, and festive window stickers can bring a delightful Christmas spirit to any room.

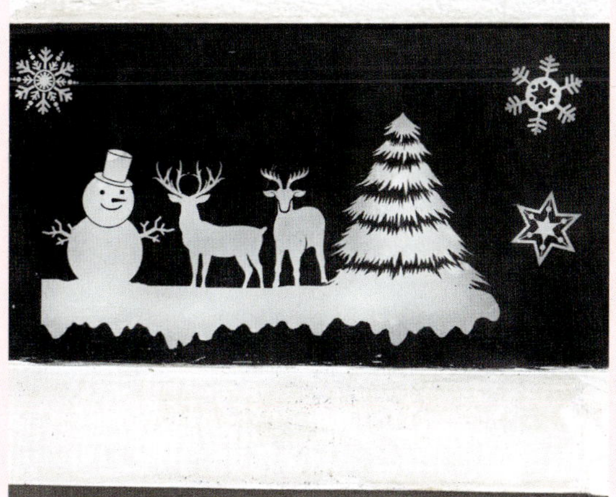

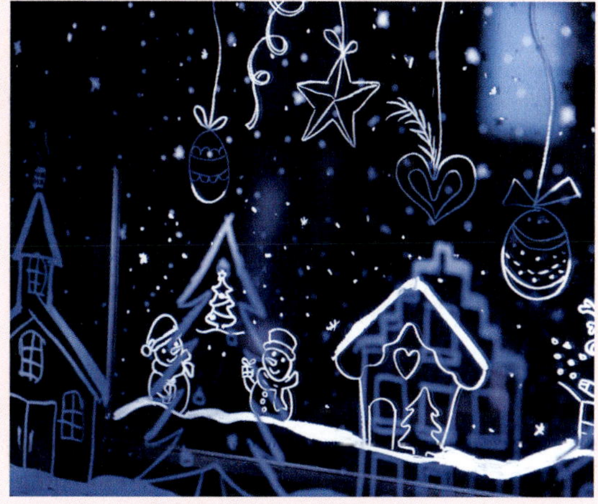

Using chalk pens to create your own designs on the windows adds a particularly imaginative touch.

FEATURE

CHRISTMAS PEACE AND PASTEL POETRY IN DENMARK

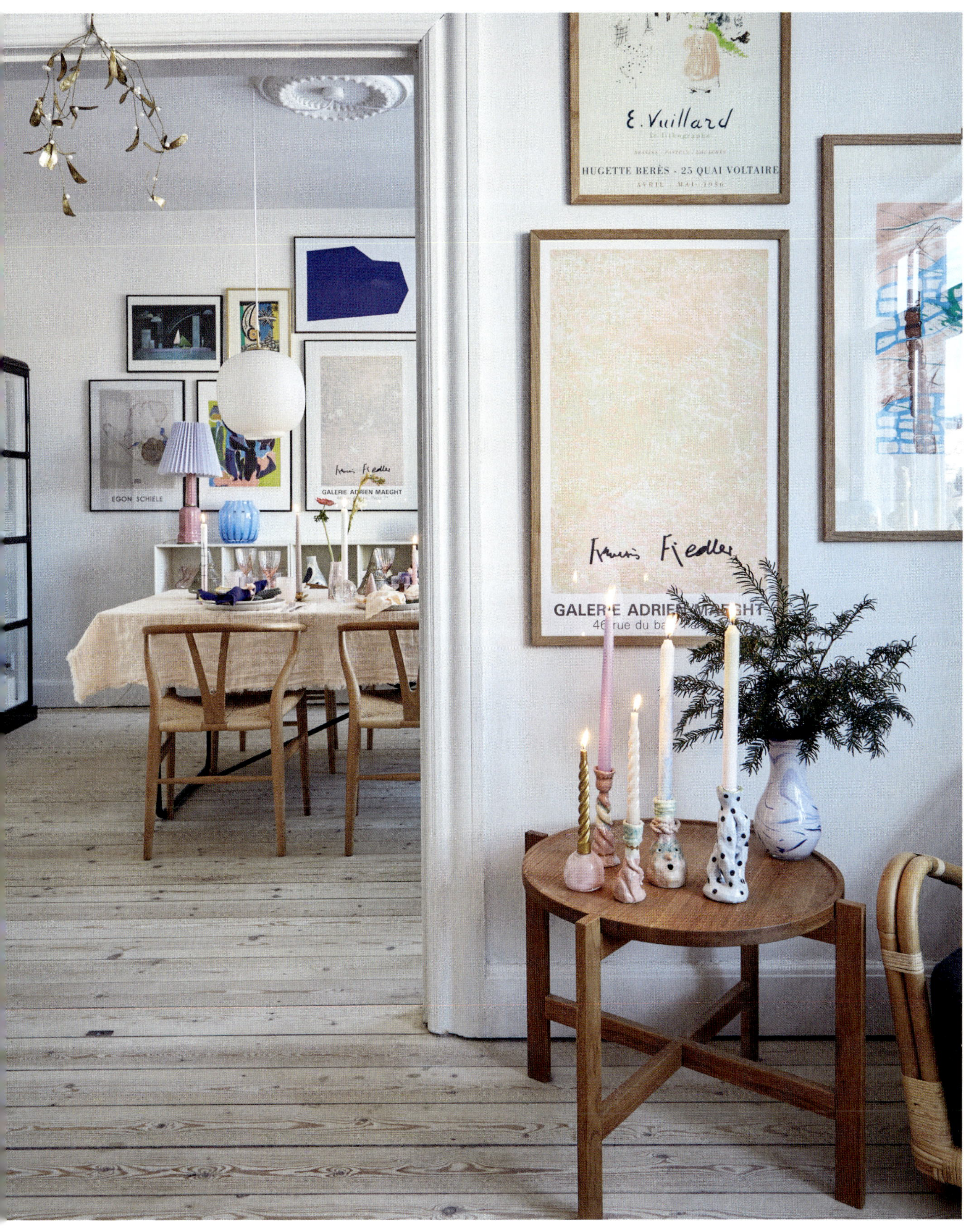
E. Vuillard
le lithographe
HUGETTE BERÈS - 25 QUAI VOLTAIRE
AVRIL - MAI 1956
EGON SCHIELE
GALERIE ADRIEN MAEGHT
Fiedler

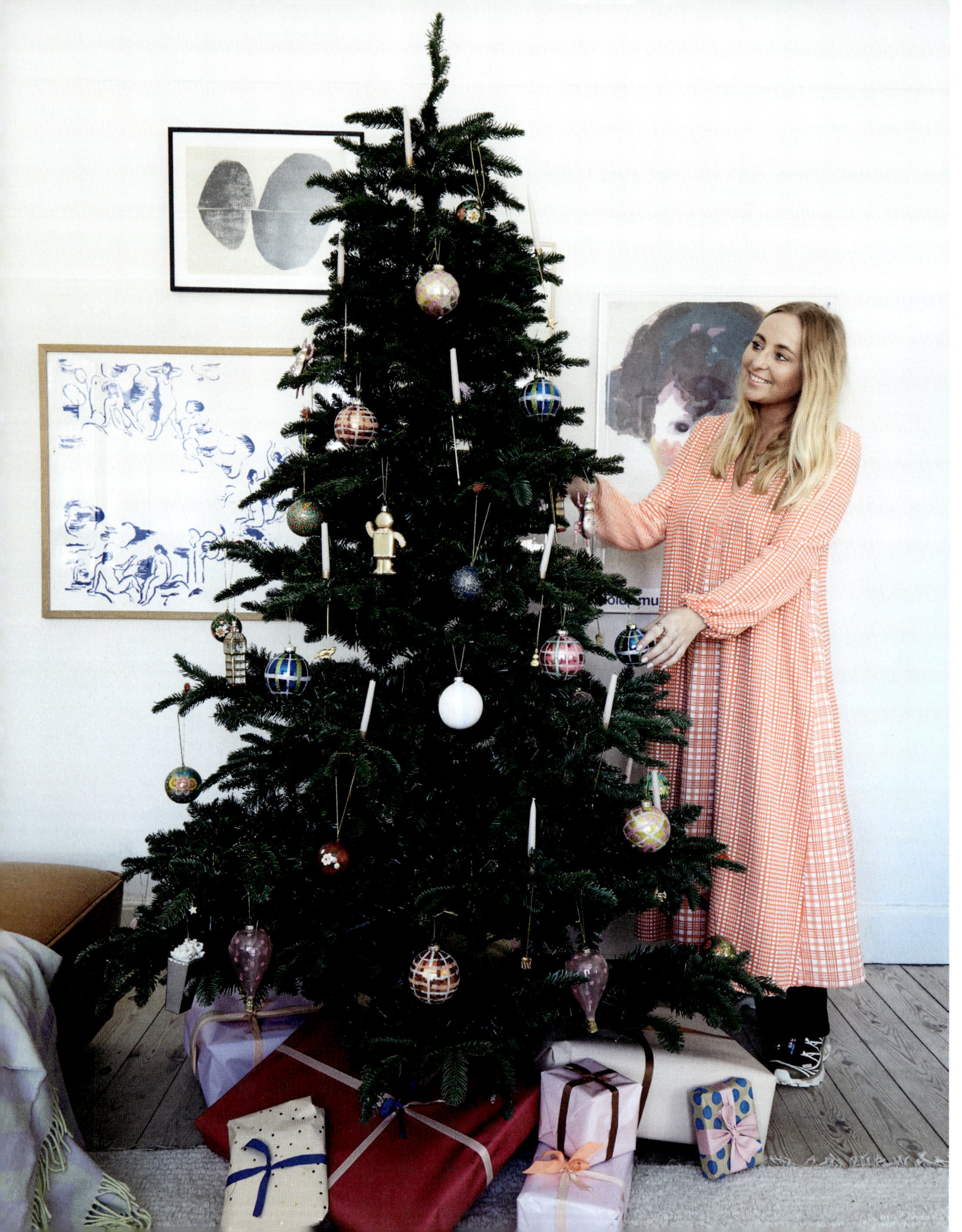

Opposite: Ann-Sophie Ulka is a big fan of Christmas and loves to decorate. Every year she adds new ornaments to the collection.

Ann-Sophie's Cozy Christmas

For Christmas, Ann-Sophie Ulka's home reflects the same positive energy as the rest of the year but embraces cozy and feminine pastels during December. Ann-Sophie, the entrepreneur behind the interior shop FABREK, lives in a charming 1,280-square-foot (119-square-meter) villa from 1925 in Odense, Denmark, with her husband Kasper and their three sons.

Surrounded by a snowy landscape, their home exudes a festive charm, embodying a true Christmas idyll on Funen. Ann-Sophie adores Christmas traditions, and the family begins decorating as early as November. "I love the Christmas days, and to watch the children play with their toys while eating delicious marzipan," she shares. They celebrate Christmas Eve at home every other year, and Ann-Sophie delights in hosting festive gatherings and creating new family traditions.

With her keen eye for color and creativity, Ann-Sophie has transformed her passion into a successful career at FABREK, where she curates a fantastic pastel universe filled with unique home products. Stepping into her masonry villa, guests are greeted by cheerful colors that inspire positivity without overwhelming the senses. Larger furniture pieces are kept in muted tones, allowing decorations, cushions, and art to stand out, resulting in a harmonious and tranquil aesthetic. "If you need renewal in the home, you can always change pillows and posters to create new energy in the room," she advises.

This love of color extends to Ann-Sophie's Christmas decorations. Each year, she adds new ornaments, often sourced from Christmas markets or unique shops, which further enhance the holiday spirit in her home. With every detail thoughtfully arranged, Ann-Sophie's festive decor captures the warmth and joy of the season, making her home a beautiful celebration of Christmas traditions.

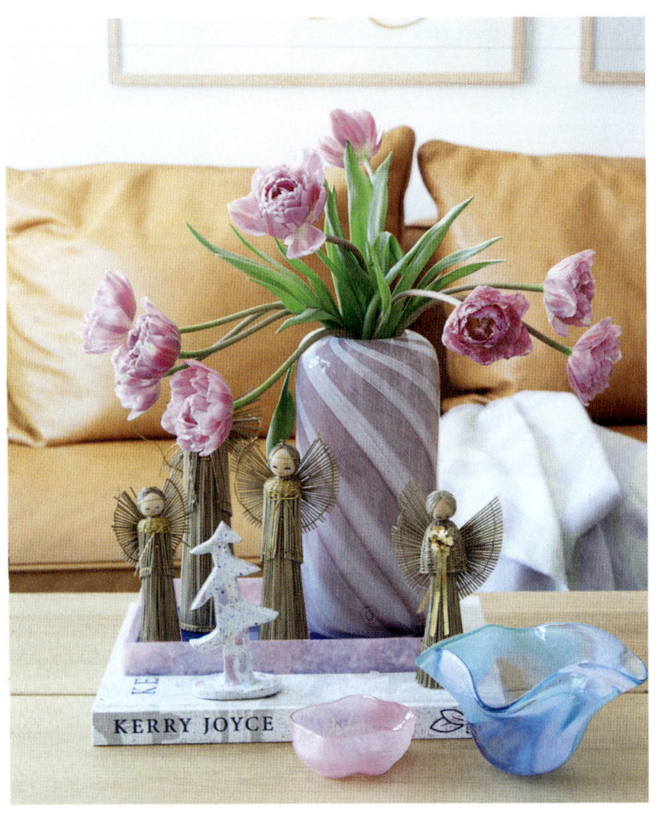

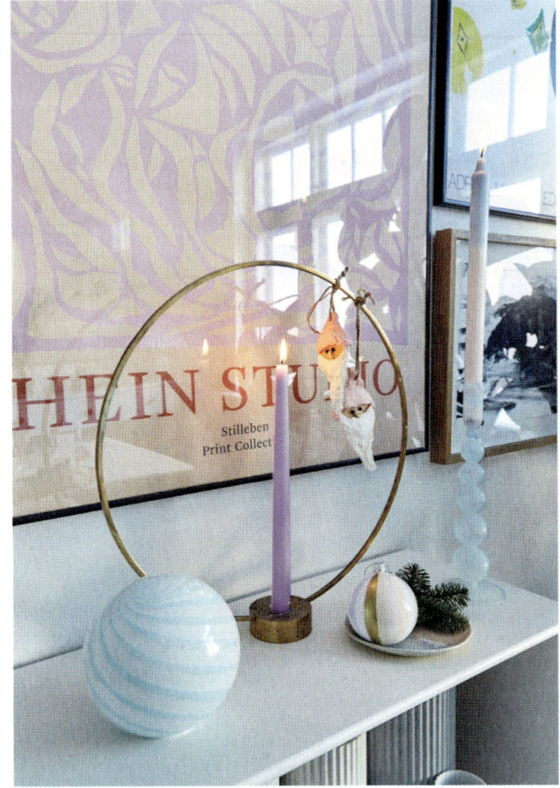

Every detail in Ann-Sophie's home is carefully considered, including her approach to gift wrapping. "I love to wrap gifts, preferably with nice bows; each package is uniquely wrapped," shares Ann-Sophie, who finds joy in showering her loved ones with beautiful gifts. She blends old and new in her decor and Christmas traditions, ensuring they foster family togetherness. The Christmas spirit truly shines during Advent when her family, including her mother, cuts down a tree in the woods. They conclude the day by making confectionery, baking festive treats, and dancing to Christmas music in the living room, creating cherished memories together.

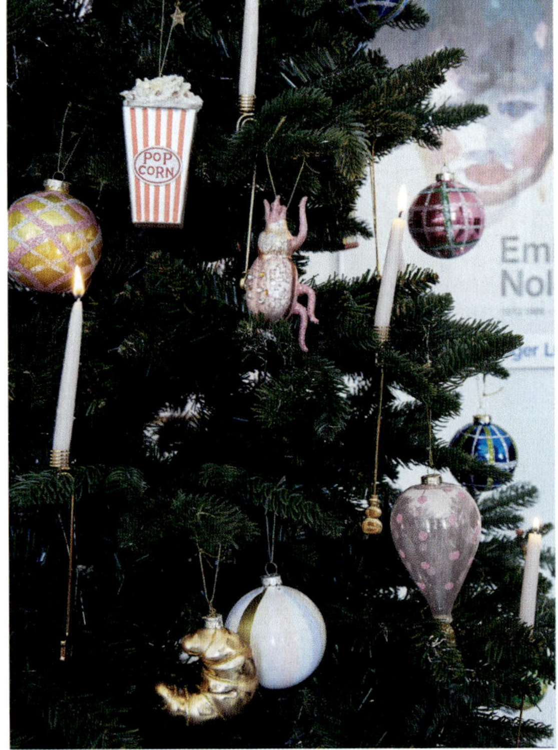

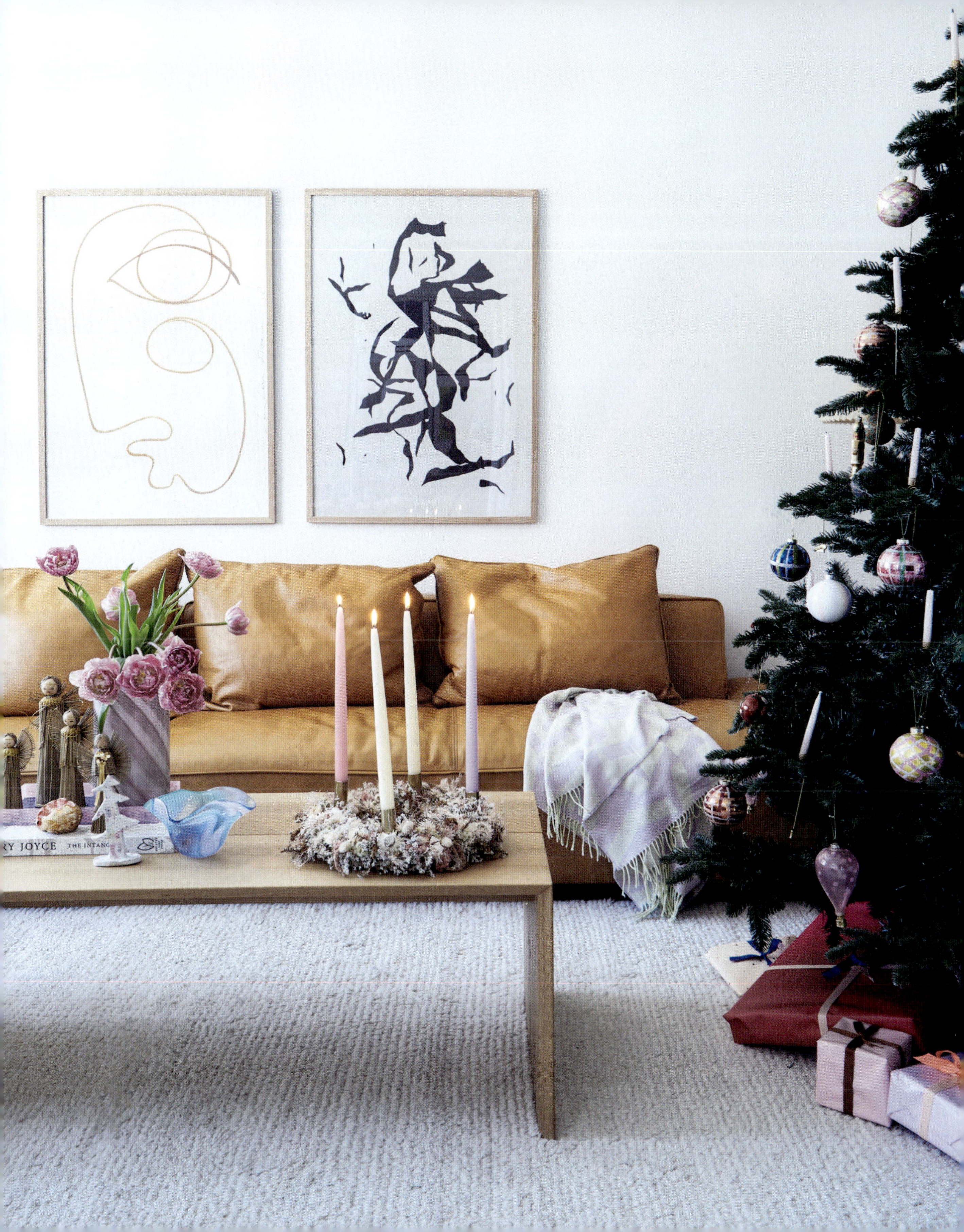

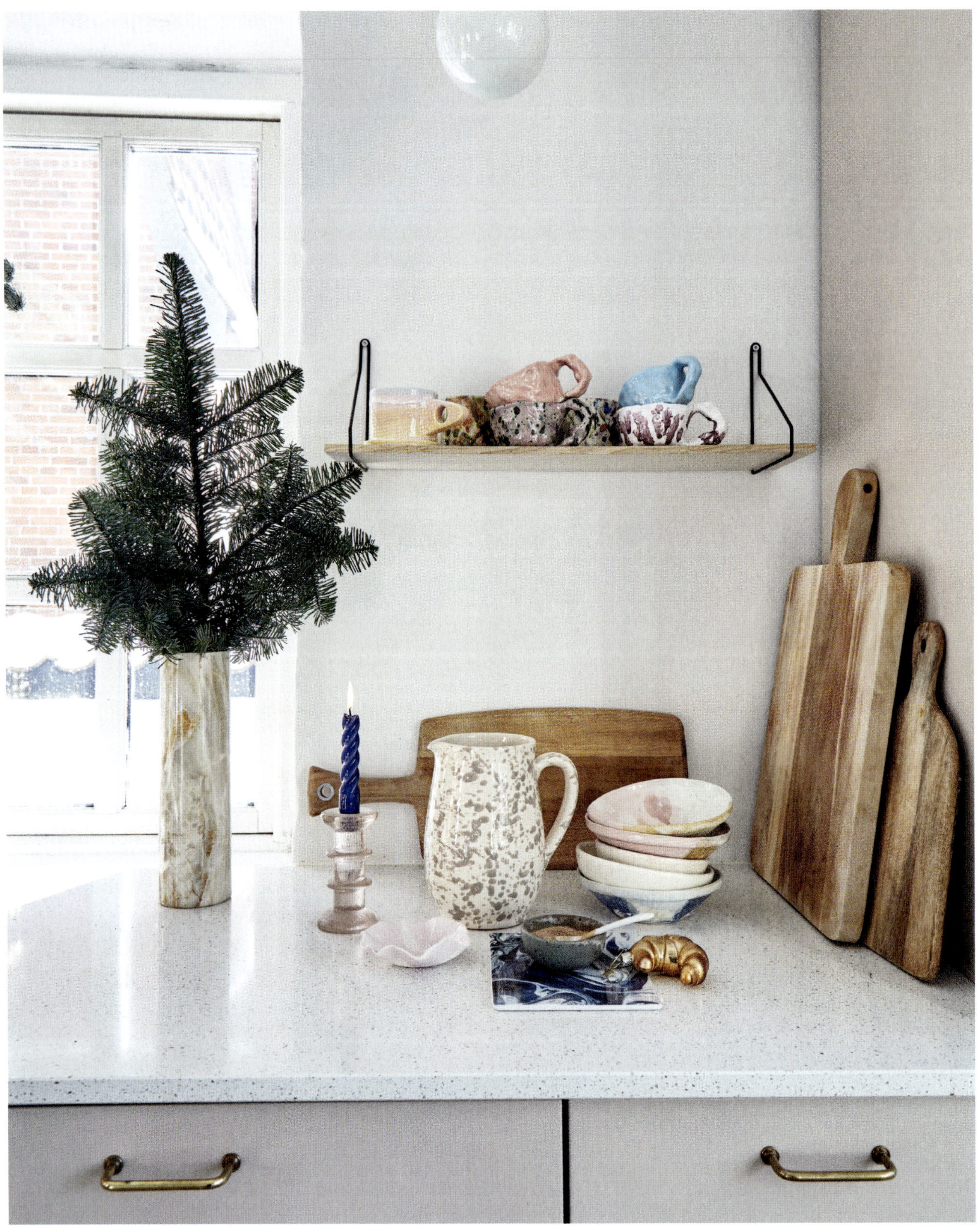

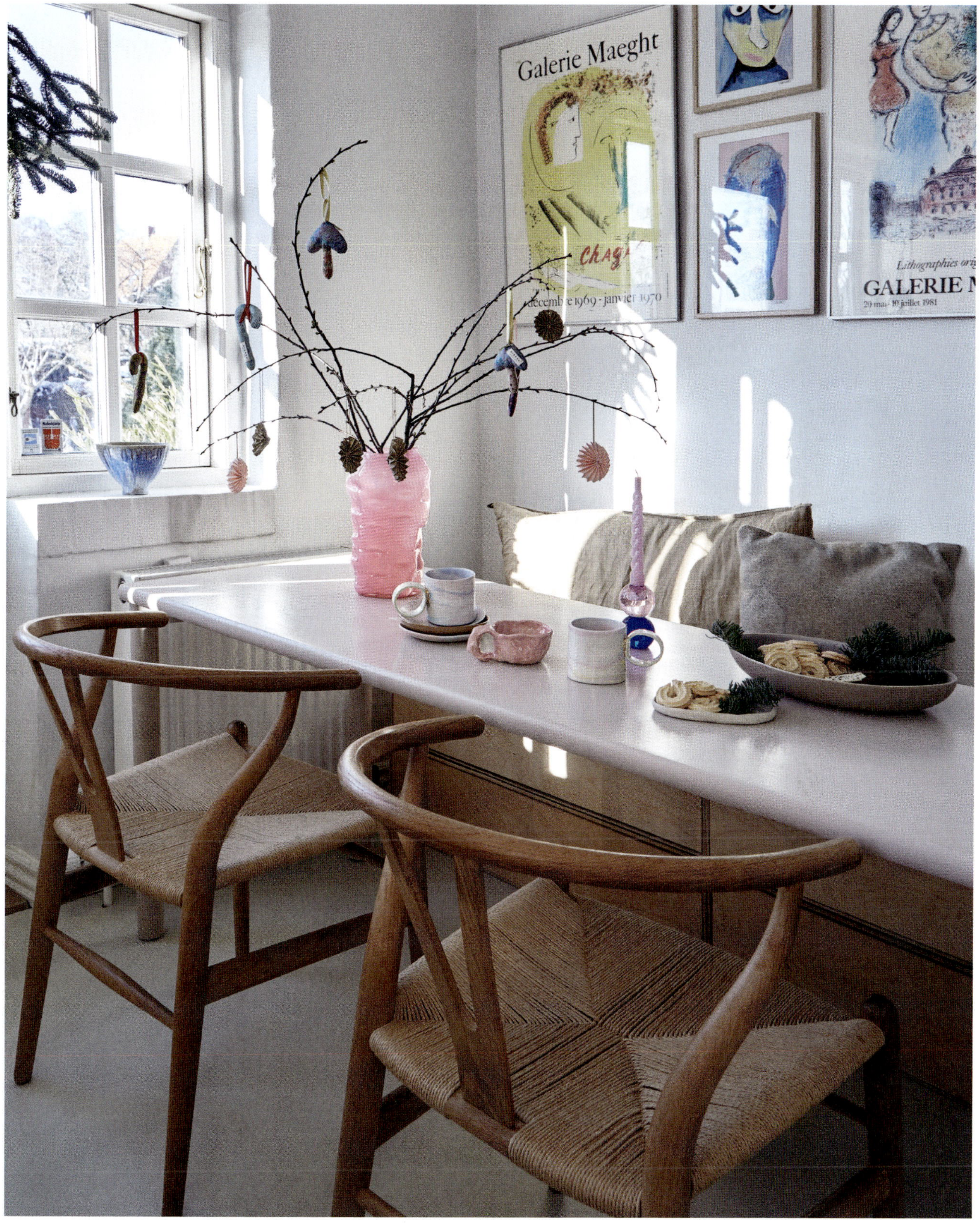
Galerie Maeght
décembre 1969 - janvier 1970
20 mai - 10 juillet 1981

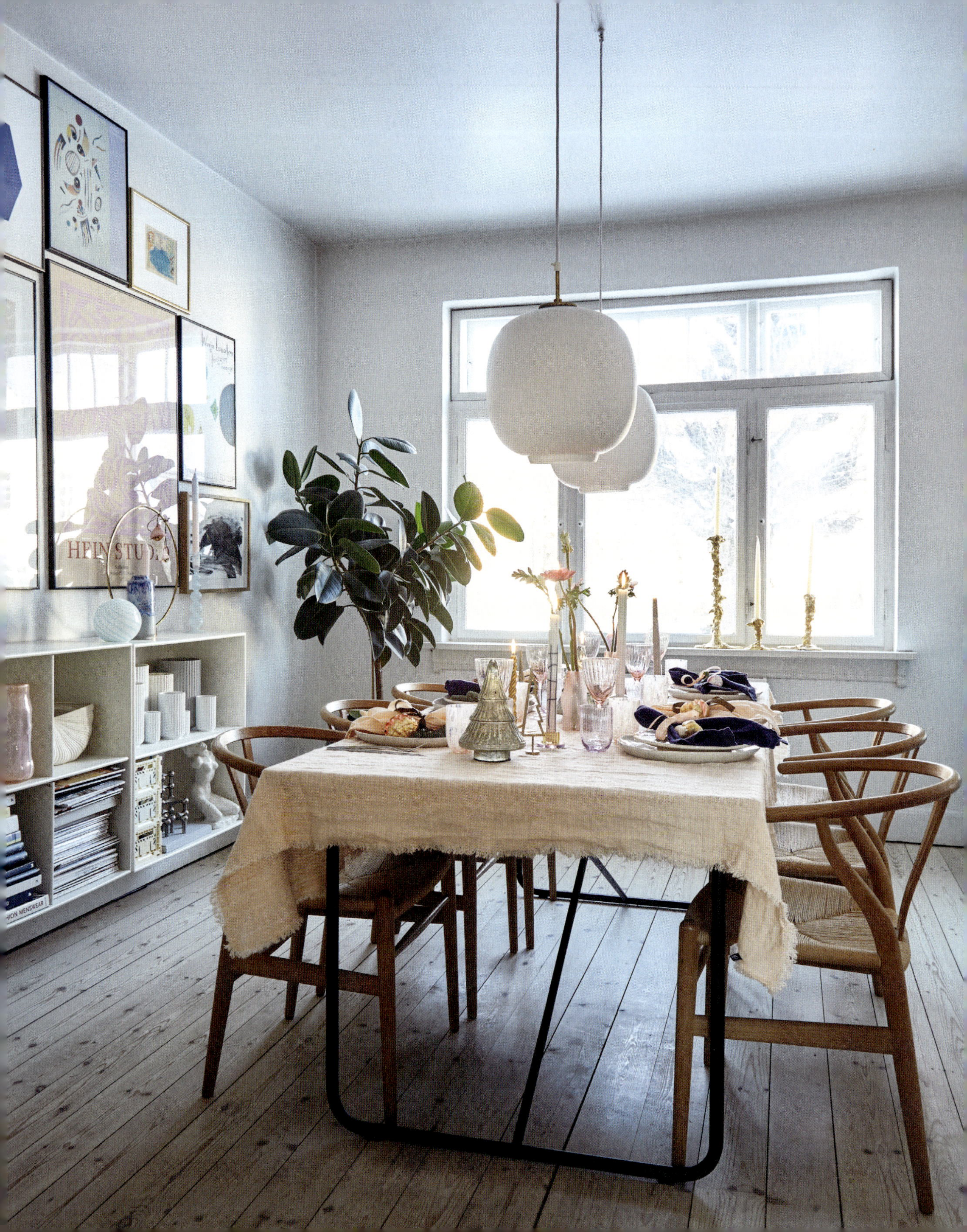

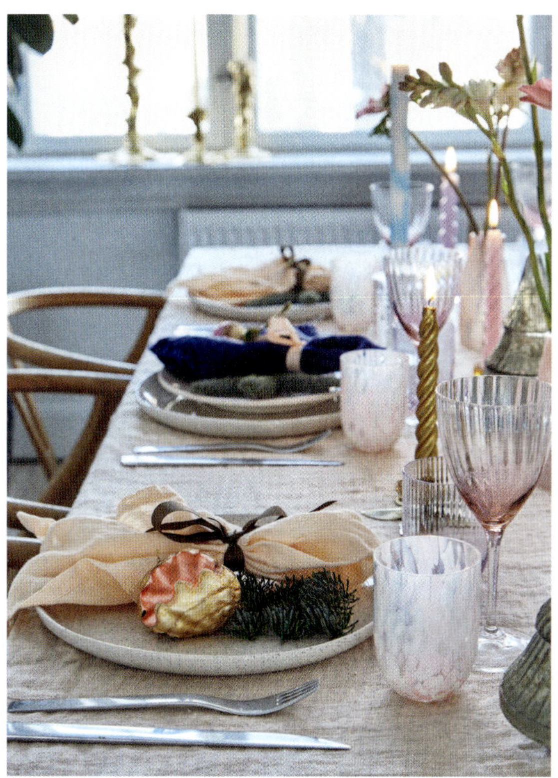

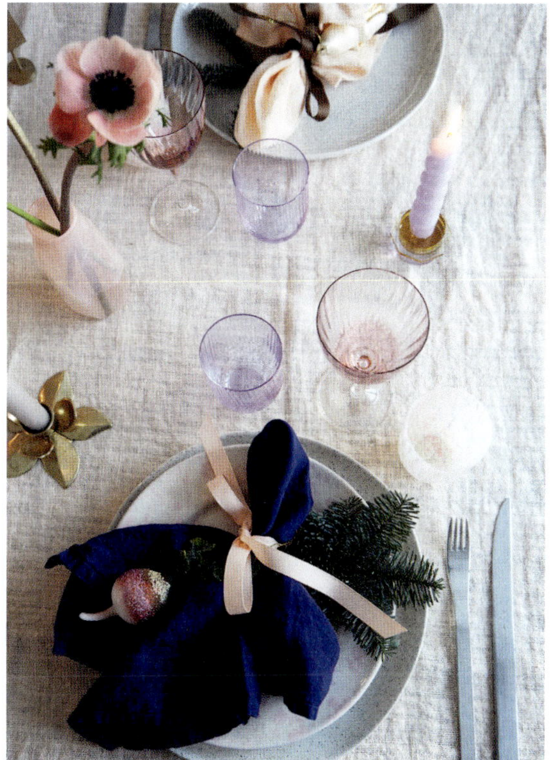

The dining room serves as a cozy gathering spot for family and friends, beautifully decorated for Christmas guests. A vibrant gallery wall sets the stage for the festive table, where Ann-Sophie has thoughtfully echoed the colors in the decorations. This creates a harmonious and serene atmosphere, despite the variety of hues. The wall art features a blend of vintage treasures and prints from FABREK, adding character to the space.

ANN-SOPHIE'S DESIGN AND CHRISTMAS TIPS

◊ Mix candlesticks and candles in different shapes and colors and use it as the decoration in the center of the table. It creates a vivid expression for an otherwise simple table decoration and at the same time gives cozy Christmas lighting.

◊ Choose a tablecloth in a neutral color so that it does not drown out the table decorations. Invest in a high-quality tablecloth that lasts many years, and choose a color that can be used in many contexts and let the table decorations and napkins emphasize the theme.

◊ Decorate the table with lights, colors, and personalized table cards. "I like to decorate the day before so I can enjoy it all day and add a little extra decoration," Ann-Sophie explains.

◊ Live with colors—they give wonderful energy! You can easily renew boring things with a blob of colorful paint and create new energy in the room.

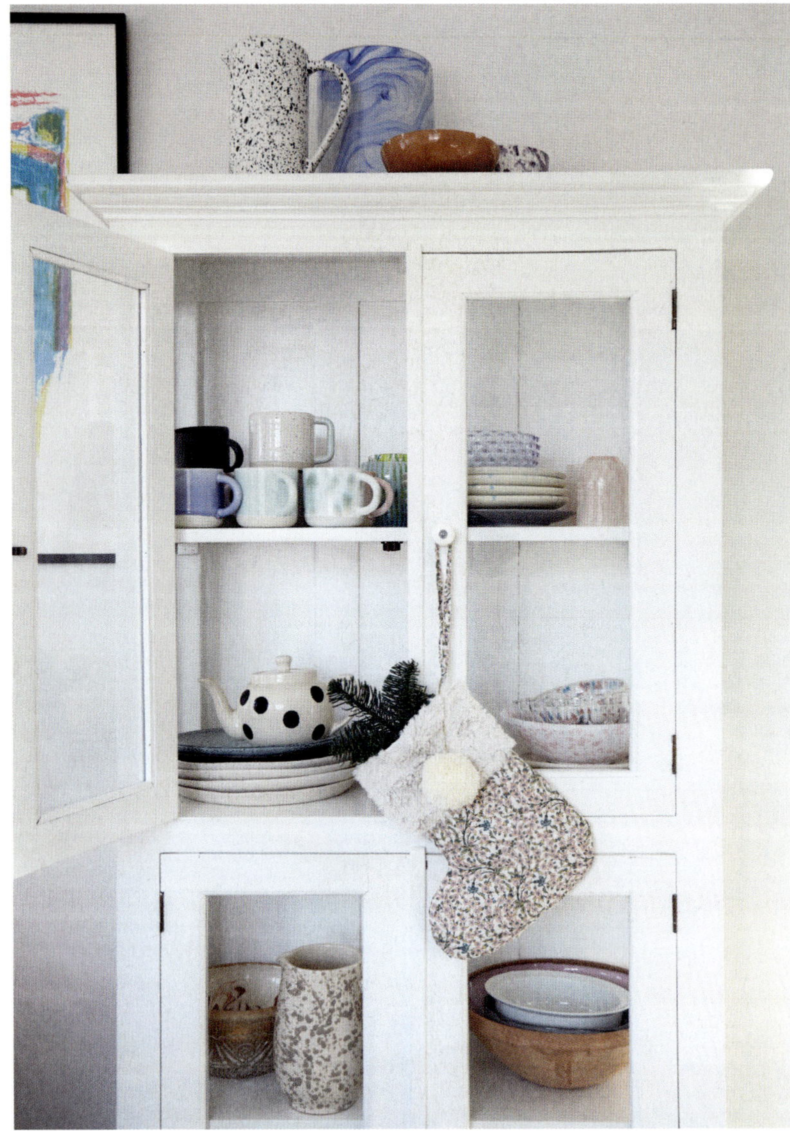

ANN-SOPHIE'S DESIGN TIP

Hang a coat rack at the children's height so they can help hang the outerwear in place. Children love when they can join in and feel part of the community.

TRADITIONS

Traditions hold great significance for the family, fostering a warm Christmas atmosphere and providing a sense of presence and comfort. "I love to come to church on Christmas Eve, this is where the Christmas peace and tranquility resides," Ann-Sophie shares, as she prepares to celebrate Christmas, embracing all the cherished traditions that accompany it."

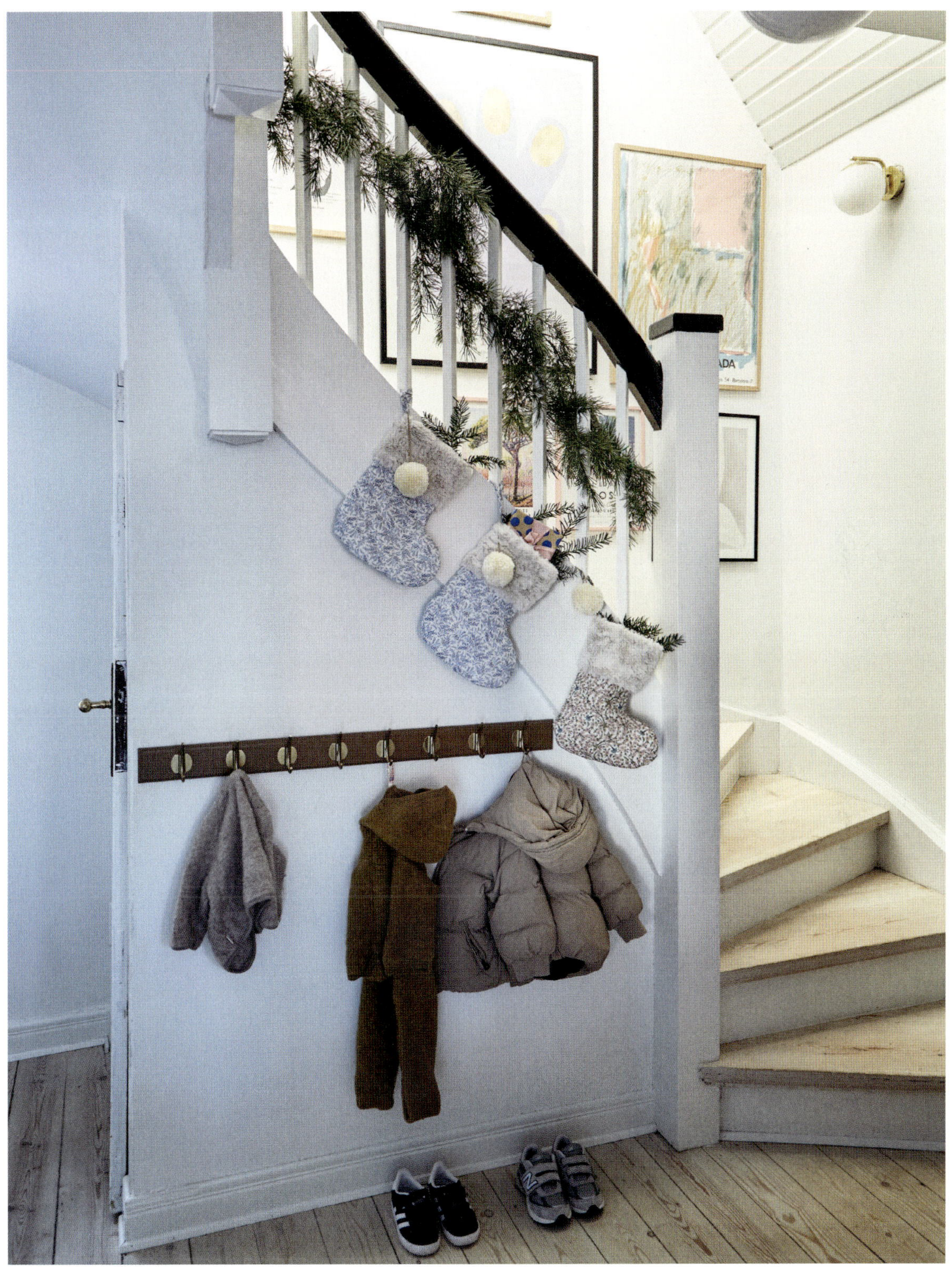

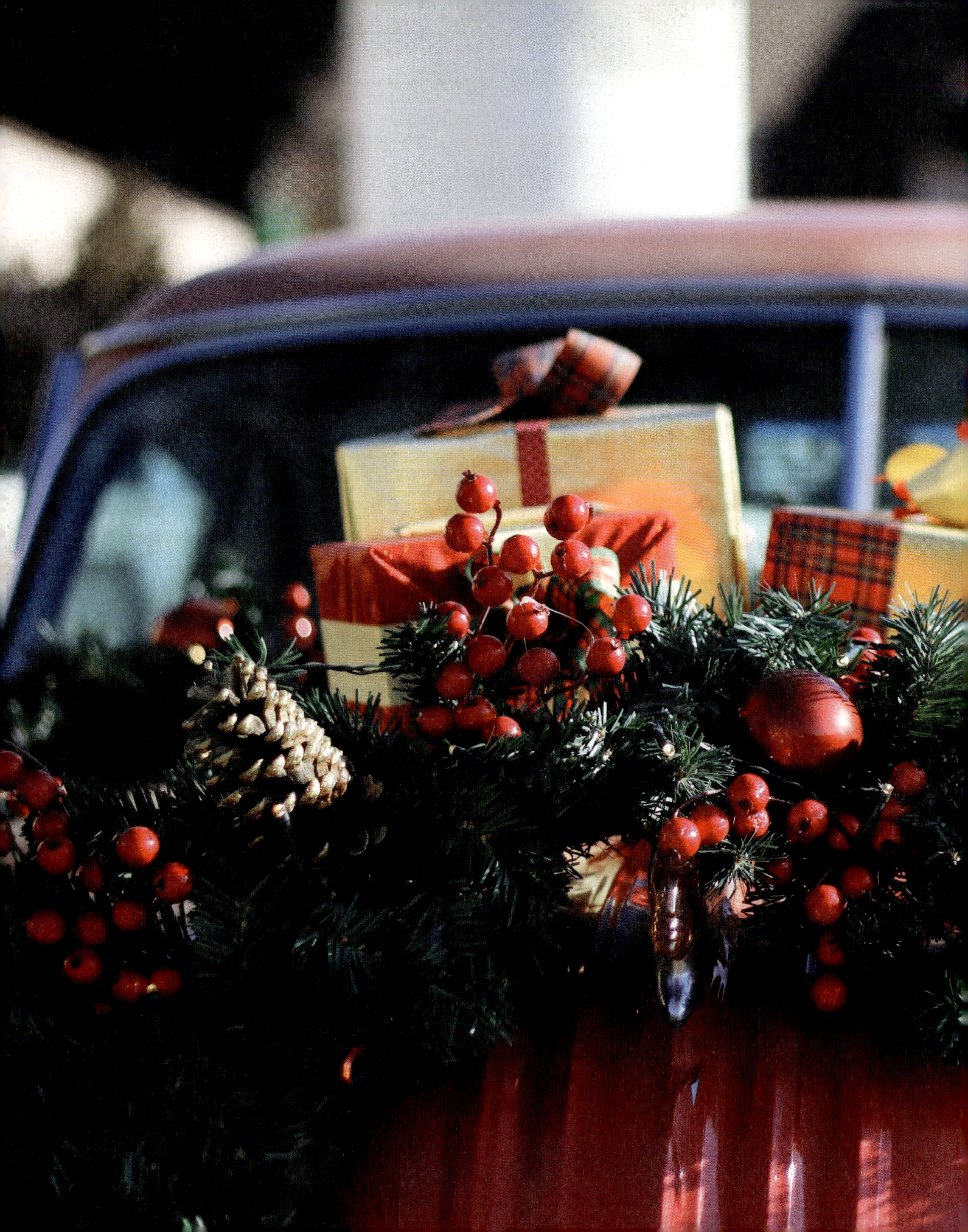

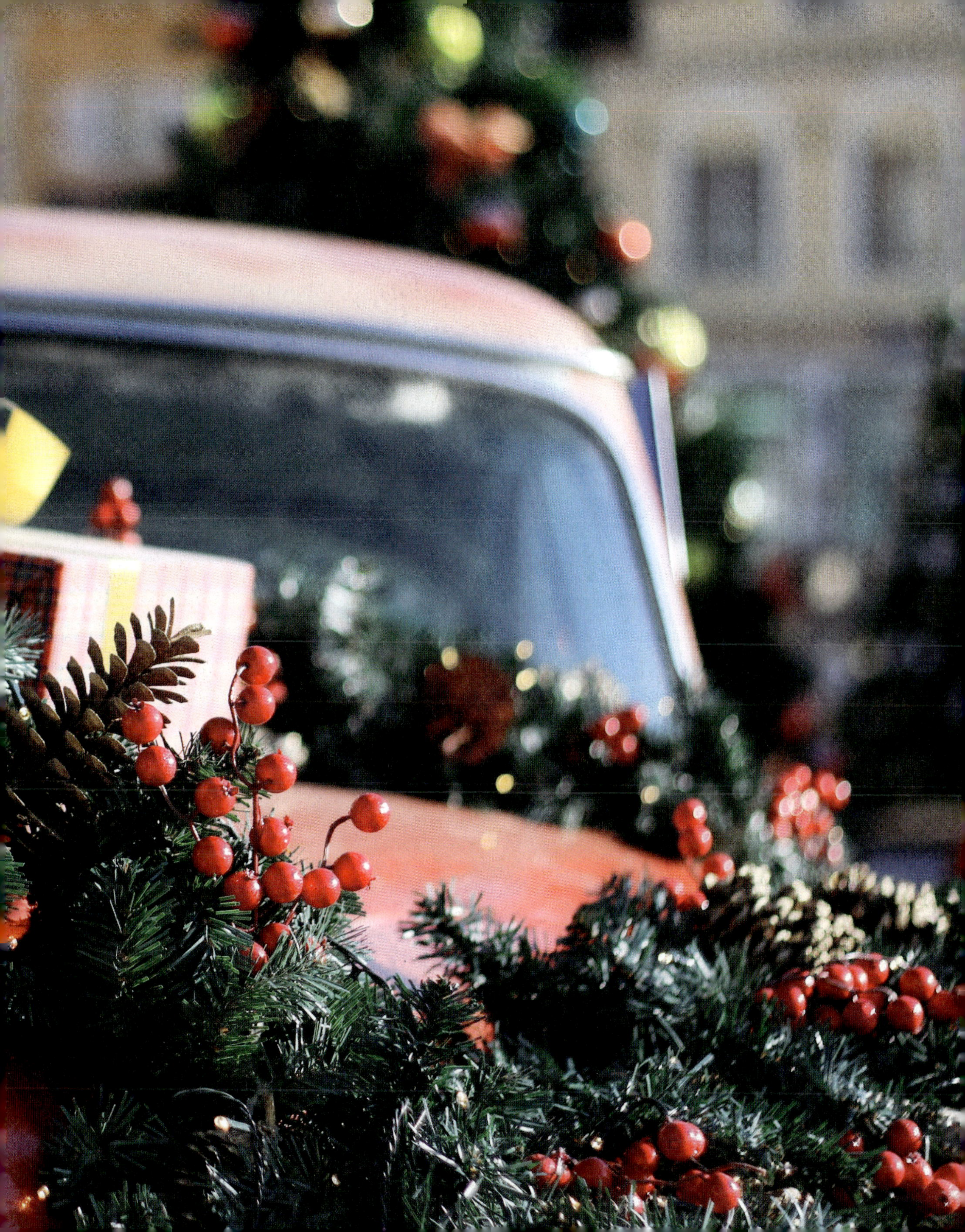

INDEX

FEATURES

PRODUCTS

INDEX

PRODUCTS | IMAGE CREDITS

Page 160: Hanging paper stars: Cecile and Boyd (www.cecileandboyds.co.za) | Cork bottle cooler: Wiid Design (wiiddesign.co.za)
Page 164: Plates with personalized sayings: The Blue Café (www.thebluecafe.co.za) | Christmas candy set: Yuppiechef (www.yuppiechef.com) | Ngwenya water glasses: Wiid Design
Page 167: Spekboom Christmas tree: Renu-Karoo (www.renu-karoo.co.za) | Linen cushion cover: Kooperasie Stories
Page 168: Terracotta mug: Wiid Design
Page 177: Art prints: FABREK and Galerie Maeght (maeght.com) | Mistletoe: Bungalow (bungalow.dk) | Side table: &Tradition (andtradition.com) | Candle holder: Mette Joensen and FABREK
Page 180 top left: Vase: FABREK | top right: "Globe" lamp: HAY (hay.com) | bottom right: Popcorn and croissant tree ornaments: Vondels (vondels.com)
Page 181: Sofa and coffee table: Eilersen (eilersen.eu) | Plaid: Silkeborg Uldspinderi (silkeborg-uld.com) | Posters: Hein Studio and LouLou Avenue via FABREK | Advent wreath: WildFlowers
Page 182: Cups on the shelf: Peter Shire
Page 183: Artwork: Galerie Maeght | Bench: Trævarefabrikernes Udsalg (traevarer.dk) | Christmas tree ornaments: Sissel Edelbo (sissel-edelbo.com) | Vase: FABREK
Pages 184/185: Tableware, vases, tablecloth, blue linen napkins: FABREK | Candlesticks: Hübsch Interior (hubsch-interior.com) | Brass Christmas tree: ferm LIVING (fermliving.com) | Dining table: ILVA (ilva.dk) | Chairs: Carl Hansen & Son (carlhansen.com) | Pendant lamp "Radiohus": Design by Vilhelm Lauritzen for Louis Poulsen (www.louispoulsen.com)
Pages 186/187: Christmas stocking: FABREK | Ceramic cups: FABREK | Dotted teapot: Søstrene Grene (sostrenegrene.com)

Cover: © Johan Sellén/Living Inside
Front and end papers: © Alla Mironenko/Shutterstock
Icons, Ornaments: Designed by Freepik

p. 2: © FollowTheFlow/AdobeStock; p. 5: © netrun78/AdobeStock; pp. 6/7: © Studioschastie/Shutterstock; pp. 8/9: Curated Lifestyle/Unsplash; pp. 10–21: © Ingrid Rasmussen / Frank Features / Living Inside; p. 23: © Archivist/AdobeStock; p. 24: SJ Objio/Unsplash; p. 25: © Paula Montenegro Stock/Shutterstock; p. 26: Jasmine Coro/Unsplash; p. 27: © Roxane Bay/AdobeStock; p. 28 (top): © Dirk/AdobeStock; (bottom): Pure Julia/Unsplash; p. 29: © Sergio Hayashi/Shutterstock; p. 30: Aaron Burden/Unsplash; p. 31 (top): Matthias/AdobeStock; (bottom): © emmi/AdobeStock; p. 32 (top left): © Mateo Londono Quijano/Shutterstock; (top right): © Jhon/AdobeStock; (bottom): © Luis Echeverri Urrea/Shutterstock; p. 33: © Cecilia Esguerra/Shutterstock; p. 34: © Kati Lenart/Shutterstock; p. 35 (top): Suna Valid/Unsplash; (bottom): © Alyona Raikher/Shutterstock; p. 36: © Nomad_Sould/Shutterstock; p. 37: © FamVeld/Shutterstock; pp. 38–51: © Alessandra Ianniello/Living Inside; pp. 52/53: Charlotte Cowell/Unsplash, starsforeurope.com; pp. 54–65: © Johan Sellén/Living Inside; p. 66: Anita Austvika/Unsplash; p. 68: Rob Wicks/Unsplash; p. 69: © Guajillo studio/Shutterstock; pp. 70/71: Patrycja Jadach/Unsplash; p. 72: Food Photographer Jennifer Pallian/Unsplash; p. 73: Curated Lifestyle/Unsplash; p. 74: Maryam Sicard/Unsplash; p. 75: Micheile Henderson/Unsplash; p. 76: Jed Owen/Unsplash; p. 77: Patrycja Jadach/Unsplash; pp. 78–87: © Jessie Prince/Living Inside; pp. 88/89: © Aerial-motion/Shutterstock; p. 90 (top): © Natalie Maro/Shutterstock; (bottom): © Cynthia A Jackson; p. 91: © Keitma/Shutterstock; p. 92: Roberto Nickson/Unsplash; pp. 94/95: © Stephane Debove/Shutterstock; p. 96: © Yulia/AdobeStock; p. 97: © Dolores M. Harvey/Shutterstock; p. 98: Philip Arambula/Unsplash; p. 99: © Meagan Marchant/Shutterstock; pp. 100/101: James Wheeler/Unsplash; p. 102: Getty Images/Unsplash; p. 103: Polina/Unsplash; p. 104 (left): © Dmitry Pistrov/Shutterstock; (right): © Lasse Johansson/Shutterstock; p. 105: © Juliya Shangarey/Shutterstock; p. 106: © Christian Weber/Shutterstock; p. 107: © Alexanderstock23/Shutterstock; p. 108: Cyril Gervais/Unsplash; p. 109: © Мария Балчугова/AdobeStock; pp. 110/111: Getty Images/Unsplash; p. 112: © Antônio José Girão de Souza/Shutterstock; p. 113: © bellemose/Shutterstock; p. 114: © Natah Visual/Shutterstock; p. 115: © tristan tan/Shutterstock; pp. 116/117: © Ranimiro Lotufo Neto/Shutterstock; pp. 118–133: © Claude Smekens / Living Inside; p. 134 (left & bottom): © Yulia/AdobeStock; (right): Andrej Lisakov/Unsplash; p. 135 (left): © anastasiyaand/AdobeStock; (right): Toa Heftiba/Unsplash; pp. 136–147: © Alessandra Ianniello/Living Inside; p. 148: Olivie Strauss/Unspalsh; p. 150: © Floral Deco/AdobeStock; p. 151: Jez Timms/Unsplash; p. 152: © Mint Images/Getty Images; p. 153: © Emrah/AdobeStock; p. 154 (left): Monika Borys/Unsplash; (right): Olivie Strauss/Unsplash; p. 155: Food Photographer Jennifer Pallian/Unsplash; pp. 156/157: © Yulia/AdobeStock; p. 158: © Juliia Kishun/Getty Images; p. 159: Daiga Ellaby/Unsplash; pp. 160–173: © Greg Cox/Frank Features/Living Inside; p. 174: Getty Images/Unsplash; p. 175 (left): © backiris/AdobeStock; (right): © b.Asia/Shutterstock; pp. 176–187: © Anitta Behrendt/Living Inside; pp. 188/189: Honey Fangs/Unsplash

Imprint

Editorial Coordination and Book Composition by
Nadine Weinhold
Production by Sandra Jansen-Dorn
Color Separation by Nele Funck, Robert Kuhlendahl
Prepress by Nele Funck, Robert Kuhlendahl
Proofreading by Kevin St. John

Published by gestalten, Berlin 2025
ISBN: 978-3-96171-700-2

1st printing, 2025

Printed in Slovakia by Neografia a.s.

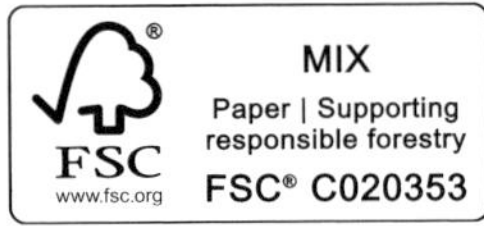

Bibliographic information published by the Deutsche Nationalbibliothek. The Deutsche Nationalbibliothek lists this publication in the Deutsche Nationalbibliografie; detailed bibliographic data is available online at www.dnb.de

For more information, and to order books, please visit www.teneues.com and www.gestalten.com

Die Gestalten Verlag GmbH & Co. KG
Mariannenstrasse 9–10
10999 Berlin, Germany
hello@gestalten.com

Düsseldorf Office
Waldenburger Straße 13
41564 Kaarst, Germany
verlag@teneues.com

teNeues Press Department
presse@gestalten.com

https://instagram.com/teneuespublishing

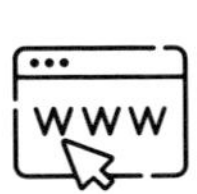

www.teneues.com

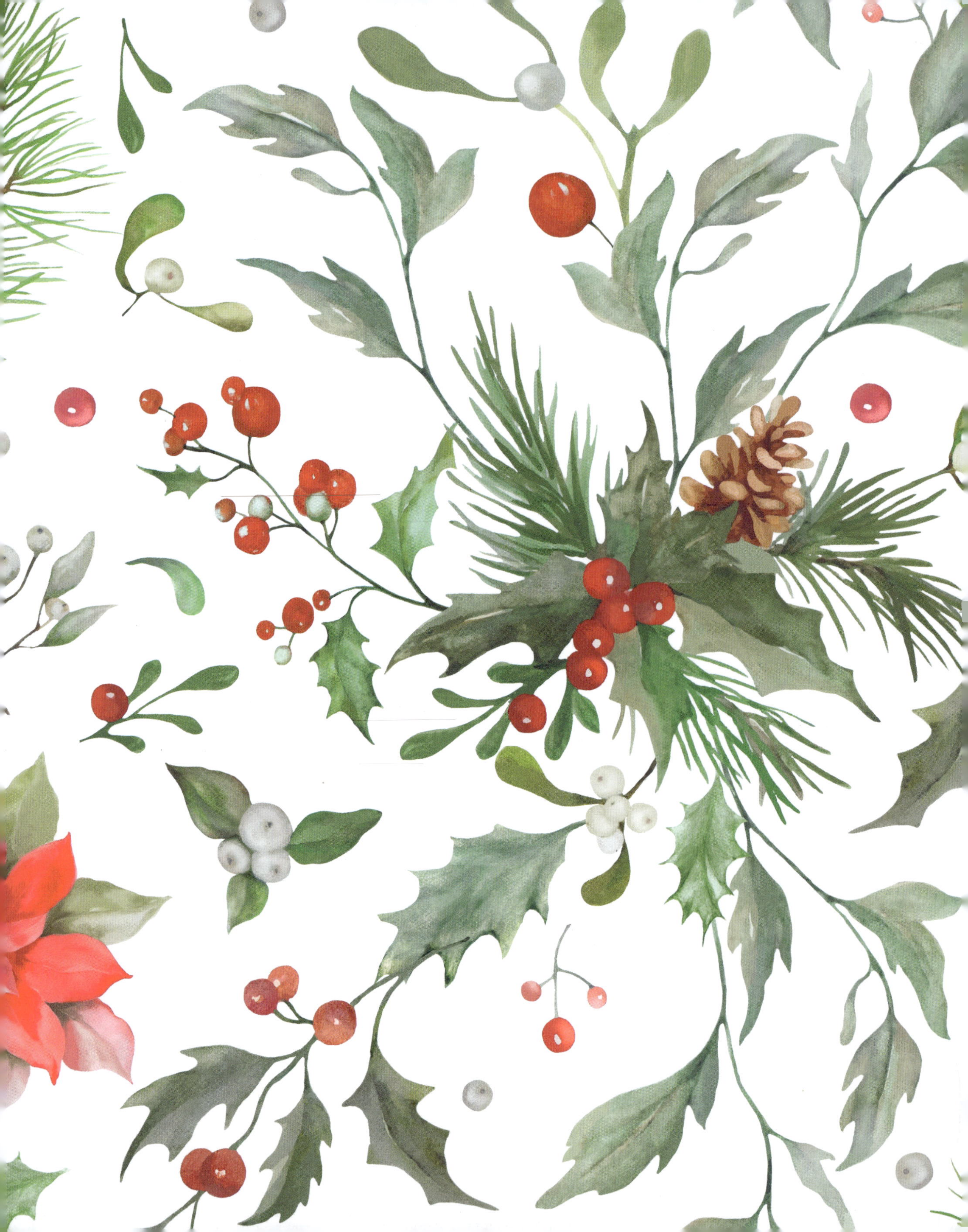